Chap 3 +4

Sport and British Politics
since 1960

To
D.H. and R.B.

without whom so little of this story
would have taken place

Sport and British Politics since 1960

John F. Coghlan

with

Ida M. Webb

 The Falmer Press

(A member of the Taylor & Francis Group)
London • New York • Philadelphia

UK   The Falmer Press, Rankine Road, Basingstoke, Hampshire, RG24 0PR

USA   The Falmer Press, Taylor & Francis Inc., 1900 Frost Road, Suite 101, Bristol, PA 19007

© J.F. Coghlan with I.M. Webb 1990

92818

306.483

First published 1990

British Library Cataloguing in Publication Data
Coghlan, John F.
  Sport and British politics since 1960.
  1. Sports. Political aspects
  I. Title
  306.483

  ISBN 1-85000-809-4
  ISBN 1-85000-810-8 pbk

Library of Congress Cataloging in Publication Data
Coghlan, John F.
  Sport and British politics since 1960/John F. Coghlan.
  Includes bibliographical references (p.).
  ISBN 1-85000-809-4. — ISBN 1-85000-810-8 (pbk.)
  1. Sports and state — Great Britain — History — 20th century.
I. Title.
GV706.35.C64 1990   90-32217
796'.0941 — dc20   CIP

Jacket design by Benedict Evans

Typeset in 10/12pt Times by
Graphicraft Typesetters Ltd, Hong Kong

Printed in Great Britain by Burgess Science Press, Basingstoke on paper which has a specified pH value on final paper manufacture of not less than 7.5 and is therefore 'acid free'.

Contents

List of Appendices

Acknowledgments

From the outset I was encouraged by my friends Peter McIntosh, Roger Bannister and senior colleagues at the Sports Council to set down the story of how sport has developed in Great Britain over the last thirty years and the part politics have played to assist or frustrate this development. I am grateful to them all for their encouragement and support particularly when the story became complex, more difficult to relate and 1990 seemed a long way away. I am indebted too to the talented ladies of the Information Centre at the Sports Council who never failed to lay their hands on information I knew existed but which I needed for confirmation and reference. To Dr Ida Webb, the former Principal of Anstey College of Physical Education, and until retirement in March 1989 the Assistant Director (Academic) at Brighton Polytechnic, I am particularly indebted for her close collaboration in this enterprise during the last nine months. Her critical appraisal of the text, her detailed assistance in referencing from her vast physical education background and her thirteen years service both on the Physical Education and Sport and Recreation Panel of the Council for National Academic Awards and as the Minister for Sport's nominee on the Greater London and South-East Councils for Sport and Recreation, have been crucial and of immeasurable assistance to me in giving the required slant that is needed to help those studying the history of the period.

I wish publicly to thank my wife Elizabeth for four years of reading my writing, typing drafts and then retyping them; not an easy task at any time but one made more difficult by the habit of her cat sitting alongside the typewriter as she worked. She has lived for very many years with sport and politics, she deserves a rest.

Finally I am mindful of the very many men and women, well-known and unknown, who week in and week out play, referee, organize and administer sport at every level in every city, town and village; they are the true spirit of British sport and have made the story I tell one of continuing hope for our country.

To my former colleagues on the staff of the Sports Council I shall be forever indebted for their inspiration, enthusiasm and idealism; it was an honour and a privilege to lead them in the many enterprises we shared and it is good to see so many of them today in positions of prestige and great responsibility.

John Coghlan
Wargrave
April 1990

Preface

Within weeks of my retirement from the Sports Council where I had been Deputy Director-General for eight years following my ten years as Regional Director for the West Midlands, a number of colleagues and friends in the Sports Council, higher education and the media variously suggested that I should record the developments of sport in Britain during the time I had sat at the centre or close to it. They suggested that so much had happened since 1960 and the task should be done before the memory faded, people moved on and original sources dried up.

I was also becoming aware that students working for degrees at under-graduate and postgraduate levels, particularly in sports science, sports studies, movement and physical education, were reporting a dearth of resource material in the study of contemporary developments in sport in Great Britain. The paucity of literature in this field was brought home to me in a personal way at the West London Institute of Higher Education where the Principal, Dr. John Kane, a long-standing friend from our days together at Loughborough College in 1947–48, had asked me to lecture on British and international sport as a Visiting Professor.

I therefore felt that I had an obligation to give an account of what had transpired from the Deputy Director-General's perspective at the Sports Council and to set this in the wider context of sport and British politics. I have attempted to weave the main strands in the development of sport in Britain during the last thirty years into the text, avoiding the temptation to sensationalize matters by personal anecdotes which might well have been interesting in themselves but would have added nothing to the history of the period. In the preparation of the manuscript the selection of material to omit has proved more difficult than the decision of what to include. In describing the principal events that have affected the development of sport in Britain since 1960 my aim was to display the momentous changes that have taken place as a result of statutory and non-statutory action that have given opportunity to so many more at every level of attainment. This progress has brought undoubted benefits to many who seek enjoyment and fulfilment through sport; it has also brought the evils of drug abuse, violence, commercial manipulation and greed that test the very basis of sporting values, and the traditional ethic of fair play. The selection of national teams today draws on a far broader base than was the case thirty years ago. Historically class and station in life played a major role in British sport. Today this is less so and the trend will continue. The coming of the Sports Council in its various forms added a new dynamic to progress. It has acted as a focus and a stimulus; it has also acted as a servant to the national governing bodies of sport, the bedrock of sport in Britain. The *Sport for All* movement, unheard of in 1960, took root in the seventies as part of the social fabric of society; the philosophy on which the movement is based is rarely questioned today, only the means by which it can have greater appeal. Provision for greater opportunity to participate in sport and physical recreation is, in the 1980s, accepted by municipal authorities and the general public as a social service; only in Whitehall is this principle still questioned but then those that question it have no need of the service.

The enlightened physical education programmes in our schools and the tradition of dedicated teacher involvement in the coaching of games has for many decades been responsible for the reservoir of talent and interest on which clubs and national sports bodies have drawn. The economic pressures and assaults upon the education service are a constant threat to this great tradition; the mean-spirited and 'little men' who are prepared to sacrifice a fine tradition for short-term gain must not succeed.

Two great threats hang over British sport — inadequate funding and the ever-increasing threat of governmental interference. The story must begin in the nineteenth century if one is to understand the influence British politics have had on sport during the last thirty years; it will end with a glance towards the 1990s and the prospects for the future. Sport cannot stand above and apart from the economic, social and cultural life of the society in which it flourishes; it is touched by all around it. Sport must be involved with politics if sport wishes to have a fair share of the national wealth to assist development, promote excellence and contribute to the mass sport movement; sport in Britain has come increasingly to realize this and benefit from involvement. Sport has also learned that 'he who pays the piper calls the tune' and sometimes the tune is not that which sport would choose. How then has sport acted since government came into sport in a major way? — this book tells the story.

The fight must always be to safeguard the integrity of the voluntary sports movement in Britain; notable casualties have already been reported in this struggle, but failure to battle on will see sport becoming increasingly under the control of the bureaucrat and apparatchik, not at club level but where the levels of power are manipulated often for reasons quite unconnected with sport, the central corridors of Westminster. Is this what the nation wants?

Section I
Introduction

Chapter 1

In the Beginning . . .

The origins and the nature of sport in Britain today can be traced back to the nineteenth century and need to be examined in the social context of those times (see Mandell, 1984, chapter 7, pp. 132–57, Scase, 1977). Whilst there is certainly a history of sport in Britain well before the last century, chronicled and recorded (see, for example, Brailsford; 1969; Brasch, 1972; Mangan, 1988; Strutt, 1801; Mason, 1989; Holt, 1989) it is only in the post-1800 period that any semblance of organized sport appeared (see, for example, McIntosh, 1952, McIntosh *et al*, 1957; Titley and McWhirter, 1970; Robertson and Kramer, 1974; Lovesey, 1979; Darwin *et al*, 1952; Marlar, 1979; Tyler, 1976).[1] The principal influence on the development of sport at this time was the public schools which grew rapidly in number as the Industrial Revolution developed, creating an ever increasing middle-class (see, for example Mangan, 1986; Bamford, 1967; Fisher, 1899; Boyd, 1948). It would appear that the playing of games in the boarding schools developed from informal activity to a more organized basis as games began increasingly to be seen as character-forming.[2] This view prevailed well into the modern era and even today there are those who will attribute to the playing of sport qualities that many believe to be exaggerated. The 'carry-over' aspects of playing games are forever a topic of argument and debate, and whilst most will agree that sport has social benefits (see, for example, Hargreaves 1982; Williams, 1967), the majority would not today claim for sport the character-moulding qualities that were historically the main reason for playing games.

Broadly speaking, the growth of sport in Britain in the public schools during the nineteenth century was confined to team games, although Swedish and German gymnastics played a wider role in the context of physical education.[3] The ancient Universities of Oxford and Cambridge not surprisingly followed the pattern of sport development in the public schools. The post-1945 era, when these two Universities were to be open to all who had the academic ability, was far off and therefore recruitment was almost totally from the old and the new public schools (see Appendix 15).

The latter part of the nineteenth century saw the emergence of what today are known as national governing bodies of sport. Sport by 1850 had extended beyond the public schools and the universities, teams were springing up around the country, and some central control for rules, laws and competition was needed. Illustrative of this was the formation of the Football Association in 1863, the Amateur Swimming Association in 1869, the Rugby Football Union in 1871, the Badminton Association of England, the Hockey Association and the All England Women's Hockey Association in 1895. Competition was well underway; Henley Royal Regatta started in 1839 but the Amateur Rowing Association was not formed until forty-three years later in 1882. The first 'Wimbledon' was in 1877, whilst the first 'varsity athletics meeting took place in 1864, before the formation of the Amateur Athletic Association in 1880. At the other end of the social spectrum church and working men's clubs provided the focal points for very many sports clubs from some of which famous football clubs developed, for example, Aston Villa Football Club.

By the turn of the century the pattern of British sport was set (see McIntosh, 1987). The development of voluntary organizations, banded together for common purpose, has been the pattern from the outset. Today 'new' sports emerge in much the same way as the 'old' sports, albeit often with financial assistance from public authorities. The British Olympic Association was set up in 1905 and from then onwards, until the Sports Council was established as an advisory body to HM Government in 1965, the development of British sport followed the established pattern. The numbers of sports grew, participants increased steadily as playing fields, swimming pools and sports clubs were created. Municipal authorities provided playing spaces, public golf courses, swimming pools and a few running tracks, whilst private clubs for tennis, cricket, hockey and rugby were established in every city and town throughout the land. The growth of drill in elementary schools, physical training in the state grammar schools, associated with games coaching often based on the public school system, introduced progressively a wider range of citizens to sport.

Industrialism by the 1920s had brought increased leisure and affluence for many. This was to continue into the 1930s despite the grave period of depression at the start of the decade. By 1938 Britain was a very wealthy nation with a vast overseas empire and a massive industrial power-base.

Factories, offices and churches between the two World Wars included sports sections in their social activities and thus the base from which national teams were selected was considerably widened as leagues, cup competitions, and a wide range of 'representational' opportunities at city, town and county levels emerged.

Some sports (such as lawn tennis, badminton, squash and rugby football) retained the social image of their origins, whilst others (such as soccer, boxing, swimming and cycling) developed a more working-class ethos. This pattern was to remain until late into the twentieth century and vestiges still exist today. Probably the greatest single factor responsible for the development of a broader base to most sports across the spectrum of society is the desire for international sporting success. This desire, allied to the general move in society for a more classless approach to matters based on ability, has, in itself, introduced new elements into sports administration in Britain and a comparison of the methods of selection and therefore the teams selected to play for their country today with those of the 1930s, and indeed the 1950s, will indicate clearly the ways in which many sports have developed during the last fifty years. The award winning film *Chariots of Fire* (1982) based on the Olympic Games of 1924 shows a team selection far removed from that of 1988.[4]

The development of sport during the nineteenth century and the first half of the twentieth century reflects the social development in Britain (see, for example, Harris, 1975). The many forces in society that interact upon each other produce the society of the times, and sport is merely one expression of this phenomenon. Sport in a Socialist society today reflects that society whilst sport in a Western democratic society mirrors the society from which it takes origin (see, for example, Holt, 1981; Ponomaryov, 1974; Riordan, 1978; Scase 1977). The political climate of a country affects the way in which sport is organized and developed. Sport has become a political football with international tensions and disputes having their repercussions, often profound, on international sport which is why the appeal 'to keep politics out of sport' is naive in the extreme (see Macfarlane, 1986, preface; and Chapters 8, 9 and 11 in this volume).

Sport is a part of the social order of society and politics is very much about 'social order'; the way in which we wish to live and organize our affairs. The question, therefore, is not whether or not politics should be involved in sport but rather 'how' politics should be involved. Until the 1960s central government played little or no part in sport; by the mid-eighties there were those who believed it played too large a part and that, in effect, sport had become an instrument of HM Government's foreign policy.

At home, by 1980, football and hooliganism had become a major political issue. The rioting by Liverpool fans at the European Cup Final in Belgium (29 May 1985) resulting in thirty-eight deaths, and the ninety-five deaths by crushing at the FA Cup semi-final at Hillsborough, Sheffield (15 April 1989), allied to the Government's determination at that time to impose an identity card scheme on spectators, brought sport into the centre of political controversy and action.

The concept of physical recreation in Great Britain was transformed in 1935 on the personal initiative of Miss Phyllis Colson,[5] when the Central Council of Recreative Physical Training (CCRPT) was established, grant-aided by the then Ministry of Education later to become the Department of Education and Science. The CCRPT was, in 1944, to become the Central Council of Physical Recreation (CCPR) which it has remained in a somewhat changed guise to this day. This was a first bold attempt to provide a national comprehensive stimulus for post-school sport and physical recreation

5

at a time when the nation's fitness for the coming Second World War was in question. It would be quite wrong to give the impression that this was the raison d'être for Phyllis Colson and her colleagues in the physical education profession; for them it was a mixture of health, the appalling unemployment of the time, and at last a dawning realization by the governing bodies of sport that some form of collective cooperation could assist hugely their separate and corporate aspirations.

The history of the rise and flowering of the CCPR is encapsulated by the later Acting General Secretary Justin Evans in his excellent book *Service to Sport* (1974). Suffice to say that from the outset this organization gathered around it many of the illustrious names in sport, not least its President HRH Prince Philip, Duke of Edinburgh; Sir Stanley Rous; Lord Wolfenden; Lord Porritt; Baroness Burton; Lord Noel Baker; AGK Brown; AD Munrow; 'Laddie' Lucas; Ernest Major; Arthur Gem; Lord Hunt; Lord Aberdare; Sir Robin Brook; the Marquess of Exeter; Sir Harry Llewellyn; Peter McIntosh; Lord Wakefield; and a host of others distinguished in sport, academic and public life. A summary of the influence of the CCPR over the years is reflected in the opening paragraph of the Foreword to Justin Evan's history by HRH Prince Philip when he writes:

> Long before the purposeful use of leisure became a general topic of discussion Miss Colson and her fellow workers on the Council set about creating recreation centres, training leaders and coaches, encouraging participation and developing new recreational activities.

With the ending of the Second World War sport took up where it had been left six years previously. The advent of the first post-War Olympic Games held in London in 1948 signalled an international return to normality although there was no place for a German team, nor significantly did the USSR compete. The Butler Education Act of 1944, though aimed directly at the way education was to be shaped for the future, indirectly contributed enormously to the development of sport in Britain. Section 53 of this Act placed a statutory responsibility on local education authorities to provide facilities for physical education and games. Hitherto this matter had been purely permissive. Standards of provision were set for playing fields and gymnasia and thus the framework was established for the post-War children to enter adulthood having had a thorough grounding in physical education and sport. The narrower concept of sport and games was rapidly expanded into the broad physical recreational field, and schools were soon to include in their programmes a wider range of activities including what became known as 'outdoor activities' such as sailing, climbing, pot-holing, canoeing, fell-walking, camping and expeditions.

Local education authorities, and indeed individual schools developed outdoor activity centres in the wilder and more rugged areas of the country and parties of school children used these in term and during the holidays, often mixing physical activity with field studies. As a greater degree of affluence percolated down in society overseas expeditions and skiing holidays became popular and large parties from schools of all types found their way to the ski slopes of Austria, Switzerland and Italy, not only during school holidays but also during term as part of the now widening physical education curriculum. On the more traditional front some governing bodies of sport which long had coaching and training schemes for young people attracted the attention of the Ministry of Education and in 1947 the Minister agreed to assist financially with the salaries of an approved level of national coaches for the Amateur Athletic Association. This was the forerunner for the later schemes for similar assistance to many governing bodies of sport which the Sports Council took over in 1972 when it became an executive body by Royal Charter. The scheme exists today with assistance to over sixty governing bodies of sport for employment of coaches.

The CCPR in the period from 1946 to 1972 established seven National Recreation Centres, later to be termed National Sports Centres. This was a most imaginative and courageous policy. Clearly the provision of anything like these centres by statutory authorities was not possible until some type of central funding was made available when the Sports Council was established as an advisory body to HM Government in 1965. Five of these Centres were located in England at Bisham (1946), Lilleshall (1951), Crystal Palace (1964), Cowes (1965) and Holme Pierrepont (1973); Plas Y Brenin (1955) and the National Sports Centre for Wales (1972) in Cardiff are to be found in the Principality. The development of these Centres is continuous as facilities are added and improved to meet the high standards required for competition, preparation-training and coaching by the national governing bodies of sport. Today six of these seven (Cowes closed in 1987) original centres plus Glenmore Lodge, Cambrae and Largs in Scotland and Plas Menai in Wales take a significant portion of the budgets of the Sports Councils.

During the sixties the coverage of international and national sports events increased dramatically in quantity and quality as media technology advanced and this continues today with satellite coverage of sport through new and existing channels. With television now in virtually every home, sports programmes and events were watched by an increasing number of people. The great spectaculars of the Olympic Games in Rome (1960), Tokyo (1964) and Mexico City (1968) assisted the debate of how sport should be organized in Britain. The fifties produced their own glamour in the first four-minute mile by Roger Bannister (1954), the floodlight duels at the White City and on the football pitch, and British sportsmen and women were still successful in the international arena. Voices were heard calling for a new look at the structure of British sport, many having seen and witnessed developments in other countries. The concept of physical recreation had

7

gained ground; the belief that sport had a larger role to play in society was debated, and underlying it all the thoughts that Government should be in some way more involved were entering the minds of sports administrators.

It was against this background that the CCPR in 1957 set up the Wolfenden[6] Committee on sport with the following terms of reference:

> To examine the factors affecting the development of games, sports and outdoor activities in the United Kingdom and to make recommendations to the Central Council of Physical Recreation as to any practical measures which should be taken by statutory or voluntary bodies in order that these activities may play their full part in promoting the general welfare of the community.

At the time this action aroused no particular concern other than general broad interest and yet the results flowing from the fifty-seven recommendations were to alter the face of British sport within the decade. HM Government for the first would have a high profile and local government a challenge to construct and provide for sport to an extent never before envisaged. For the national governing bodies of sport the results were to enhance their capability to develop, expand and compete with the new challenges now seen in the international arena. For the public at large there was to be, for the first time, a formal recognition that society had a responsibility to provide opportunities for the community to participate in sport and physical recreation.

It is not possible to look into the minds of men but it is interesting to speculate on how far those who joined Sir John Wolfenden on his Committee saw the changing face of sport that would follow their findings and recommendations some years later.

In 1960 the Wolfenden Committee reported and made fifty-seven recommendations concerned with organization, administration, finance, young people, international experience, facilities, amateurism, the media, relationship with Scotland, Wales and Northern Ireland and with a clear recommendation as to the future structure of sport in Britain. Amongst those many and varied recommendations three fundamental issues were laid bare:

1　There should be a National Sports Development Council with public finance to assist the development of governing bodies of sport and to provide facilities.
2　There should be statutory involvement in financing of sport.
3　A crusade for more facilities should be undertaken.

The debate now started in and out of Parliament. A way ahead had been indicated; was this the way forward the British people wanted? Did it reflect the ethos that surrounded sport in Britain? Did it affect the subtle relationship that existed between statutory and voluntary organizations?

Should we go down the 'Wolfenden road'? Would we continue to need the British Olympic Association and the CCPR, as surely these functions, ran the argument, would be assumed by the proposed Sports Development Council? Underlying the debate that was to ensue lay the fundamental issue of the role of Government in sport, a role later defined quite clearly by the Royal Charter (see Appendix 1 to this volume) establishing the executive Sports Council in 1972, but still argued today when sport plays an international role never envisaged by those who a century before met together to agree rules and regulations for their sports and competitions.

In 1960 sport in Britain stood at the crossroads. To go forward to a new era with new structures and increasing public finance, or stand off and continue to walk the same road of those who gave sport to the world, reflected in the true amateur ethos that forms the very basis of fairplay and enjoyment through activity — this was the essence of the question. Would it be possible to get the best of both worlds; to carry into the sixties the values of the old reshaped in the modern context? Did progress necessarily mean loss of all that was valued, or could it mean the dawning of a new age for sport, open to all within the true Olympic spirit? Once again sport was faced with the social context in which it was practised and it was on this basis that the next steps were taken.

Notes

1   See also *The Badminton Library Series*: Shearman, M. *et al* (1904) *Athletics*, Sherman, M. *et al*, *Football*, Steel, A.G. *et al*, *Cricket*.

2   '   the growth of organized games and the cult of athleticism at public schools quickly made character-training its raison d'être and showed how, for one section of society at least, sport could be used to accustom boys to common action and to stir up emulation and to promote national solidarity and patriotism' (McIntosh, 1987, p. 57); see, for example: Lambert Royston and others (1975) *The Chance of a Lifetime? A Study of Boys and Co-educational Boarding Schools in England and Wales*, Weidenfeld and Nicolson; Simon, B. and Bradley, I. (Eds) (1975) *The Victorian Public School: Studies in the Development of an Educational Institution*, Gill and Macmillan.

3   *Sweden*   Ling's gymnastics. See, for example, Chapman, M.J. (1856) *Ling's Educational and Curative Exercises* (2nd edn), Balliere.

   Germany   McIntosh, P. (1952) *Physical Education in England Since 1890*, Bell (see chapter 6, pp. 75–103 and pp. 121–3).

   McIntosh, P. *et al* (1981) *Landmarks in the History of Physical Education*, Routledge and Kegan Paul, chapters VI, VIII and IX.

   Gaulhofer and Streicher, *Outlines of Austrian Elementary Physical Education*, (1922, Rev. 1959) and *Natural Gymnastics* (5 vols) (1956; 1959).

   Strutt, B.E. (Ed.) (1970) *Reshaping Physical Education*, Manchester University Press.

   See also: Holmberg, O. (out of print) *Per Henrik Ling, His Life and Gymnastic Principles*.

Physical Education Association of Great Britain and Northern Ireland (1964) *Nine Pioneers in Physical Education*,
PEA.

May, J. (1969) *Madame Bergman Österberg*, Routledge and
Kegan Paul.

4 In 1924 those selected came from a socially and financially elite group based
largely on athletics from Oxford and Cambridge. The dividing line between the
amateur and professional was clear and rigid. The base from which selection was
made was narrow. By 1988 the Sports Aid Foundation (see chapter 9 in this
volume) had been in existence for twelve years to assist those who were capable
of challenging for international success but who needed money to support them
with diet, travel, equipment, rent and other daily necessities. The distinction
between amateur and professional in some sports, for example, tennis, had long
been abolished; trust funds for athletes allowing them to earn money in competition and advertising, to be drawn mainly after retirement, were the norm in some
sports, for example, athletics. The base from which selection was made in many
sports, not all, for example, equestrianism, yachting, was broad.

5 Miss Phyllis Colson, CBE, General Secretary of the CCPR (1935–63). See Evans
(1974) chapter 11.

6 Sir John (later Lord) Wolfenden, CBE, Life Peer (1974); formerly Headmaster
of Shrewsbury School; Vice-Chancellor of the University of Reading.

Chapter 2

Debate and Decision 1960–1965

The beginning of a decade is a time to look forward and a time to look back. It is, of course, no more than a convenient peg on which to hang hopes for the future and reflections and lessons from the past. It was a happy coincidence that 1960 was both an Olympic Year[1] and a year that signposted a new way ahead for British sport.

A successful Olympic Appeal for £50,000 had ensured that the British team would go to Rome at maximum strength. The Chairman of the British Olympic Association (BOA), the Marquess of Exeter,[2] commenting after the Olympic Games on the twenty medals won, thought the performance 'highly satisfactory' and the media echoed these sentiments. It was therefore against this somewhat euphoric background that the Wolfenden Committee reported in September 1960 only a few weeks after the closing ceremony of the Olympic Games. The Press received the recommendations contained in the Report with warmth and enthusiasm, but of even greater significance was the general view of the national governing bodies of sport. They welcomed the proposals, seeing in them elements that could herald a new era for British sport. Editorial comment was widespread and generally favourable, and was not confined solely to the newspapers. *The Economist* carried a lengthy article, as did other journals, which in all amounted to a considerable impact on the British public. A government response to an official enquiry resulting in a report would be regarded as normal but a government response to a private enquiry set up by a voluntary organization, albeit itself grant-aided by the government, was nevertheless unusual and heartwarming. With hindsight it can be seen that this was a report no government could ignore. Not only did it touch directly on aspects of life affecting many citizens, and in particular youth, but it was supported by powerful personalities in both the House of Commons and the House of Lords.[3]

The next four years were frustrating to many who wished to see immediate action; after all, Britain would be competing in another Olympic Games in four years time and there was much to do to match the impressive developments now being seen in both Eastern and Western Europe. There was no immediate action, rather a process of gradualism that step by step moved inexorably forward to late 1964 and the final decision taken by the newly-elected (October) Labour Government to establish the Advisory Sports Council in 1965.[4] Whilst the national governing bodies of sport welcomed the proposals in 'Wolfenden', and they formed the bulk of the membership of the CCPR, the Executive Committee of the CCPR was split right down the middle concerning the major proposal to establish a Sports Development Council. All sorts of alternatives were proposed in an attempt to fudge the central issue and the major proposal. To avoid a split being seen publicly no votes were taken. Even the staff, as a group, were discouraged from expressing a formal, corporate view. Matters, however, were now moving on and as the major political parties were increasingly committing themselves to policies in the field of sports organization and provision of greater opportunities for people to participate in sport and recreation so the responsibility for the final decision moved gradually from the CCPR over the years to Government departments, Ministers and Shadow Ministers. Although the facade of the CCPR to retain the right of decision was maintained, the Council was faced with a fait accompli in 1964 and again, even more dramatically in 1972.[5]

In April 1961 the Wolfenden Report was debated in the House of Commons[6] whilst the House of Lords had discussed the matter two months earlier.[7] Both debates were disappointing if one was looking for commitment and action, for although the Government Front Bench had pleasant things to say, in no way did it indicate acceptance of the main proposals. Nevertheless, intentions to make good some of the deficiencies highlighted were signalled, and additional sums of money were allocated to budgets at the then Ministry of Education to help capital and current expenditure — £100,000 to capital; £100,000 to administration and coaching schemes of governing bodies.[8]

However, a sign that the argument for a new deal for sport was being won was given when in December 1962 Lord Hailsham, a Cabinet Minister and Lord President of the Council and Minister for Science, was made additionally 'Minister with responsibility for Sport'. The announcement and public response was somewhat low-key but for those close to the seat of power it was a joyous moment for at last sport had a voice, not only in the Government, but also influential in the Cabinet; since then no other Minister for Sport has been a member of the Cabinet.

The pleasure of having a Minister for Sport was dampened by the clear expression of view by Lord Hailsham that, whilst he agreed with the substance of the Wolfenden Report, he did not agree with the establishment of a Sports Development Council (see Evans, 1974, pp. 157–60).

It certainly looked therefore, at this stage, that sport was to be served by an executive department within the machinery of Government; this was a view reinforced with the appointment of Sir Patrick Renison[9] in early 1963 as Principal Adviser on Sport. Sir Patrick, a former distinguished Governor of Kenya, knew his way around the 'corridors and offices' in Whitehall and clearly could influence affairs. What was worrying, however, was the thought that the 'control' of British sport was to be handled through a Department of State and not a body of men and women steeped and well versed in sport as proposed by Wolfenden. Although the Minister and his officers freely consulted with the major bodies for sport such as the British Olympic Association, the CCPR and the National Playing Fields Association (NPFA), they made it quite clear that it was the Government, and not any advisory group, which would decide priorities and agree action. Looking back now, nearly thirty years on with a totally different scenario which includes an executive Sports Council, there would appear to be in government some element of nostalgia for this period with the Government calling the tune to an increasing extent; or perhaps it is simply a question that certain styles of government cannot abide not having all power centralized within the machinery of government which provides the financial resources.

Despite certain qualms as to the direction sport was going increased financial support flowed from Government. Both development of private sports clubs with new and enhanced facilities, and assistance to national governing bodies of sport for coaching and headquarters administration, benefited by the injection of greater resources. In 1963 the grant-in-aid budget for facilities at the Ministry of Education rose from £153,793 for that year to £627,051 in 1965. To help the national sports bodies the budget of £332,331 for 1963 was raised to £403,801 in 1964, with a budget of £488,753 programmed for 1965.[10]

Despite this activity there was, especially in the governing bodies of sport, considerable disquiet that nothing was being done to help in the international field as the opportunities for vital international competition were increasing rapidly as air travel became cheaper and more abundant. Always on the horizon loomed the Tokyo Olympic Games of 1964 and the necessary preparation for these if Britain was to compete with good chances of success. It would be overstating the case to say that eventually Lord Hailsham gave way to pressure, but well on into 1963 in the late autumn, the Government let it be known that financial assistance would be available to help British teams compete internationally overseas.

It was Lord Hailsham's task to coordinate the input from the very many Ministers and government departments that had some aspect of sport and physical recreation within their control, whether it was buildings, water, finance, or now foreign affairs, and there is no doubt that not only was this done effectively and with understanding, but it became manifestly clear that it was not the intention of the Government to control, but rather to assist, sport. The policy of the Government was explained in March 1964 at a meeting at Shell House attended by nearly 300 delegates of sports bodies and international organizations which Lord Hailsham addressed.

This event was a milestone in the history of sports development in Britain, for not only did the Minister detail and explain the Government's policy on sport, but he also dealt with the many questions that his statement raised. For the first time in the history of the British sports movement a Minister had a responsibility for sport and saw fit to talk about this, and his policy, with those he was in office to serve. Hailsham said that he had been able to increase financial support for club facility developments, coaching and administration, and he also announced that £14.6m was earmarked at the Ministry of Housing and Local Government for local authority loan-sanction in 1964 for projects for sport; he contrasted this with the £6m available in 1961.

First steps were taken in cooperation with the national sports bodies to draw up a list of the large-scale facilities that were needed, whilst the Medical Research Council was invited to advise the Minister on all aspects of medical matters touching on sport.

Traditional sport continued to attract considerable attention but other recreational affairs were not standing still. The enormous growth of outdoor activities, whilst welcomed generally, brought its own special problems. Concern for danger and risk to so many more than hitherto pointed to the need for leadership training. In 1964 the British Mountaineering Council (BMC), acknowledging its responsibility in this matter, established the Mountain Leadership Certificate,[11] aimed at providing a prescribed course of rigorous training supplemented by an assessment of capability for those who had responsibility for groups of young people in the hills and mountains. Jack Longland,[12] an Everest climber, and later Vice-Chairman of the Sports Council, assumed the Chairmanship of the Mountain Leadership Board and gave it inspired guidance for the next decade.

With the pressures on the fragile countryside from farming, conservation and increasing recreational activity, HRH Prince Philip took a keen interest and chaired a first 'Countryside in 1970' Conference in November 1963 which was sponsored by the Nature Conservancy Council (NCC) and attended by some 100 interested organizations.[13]

This Conference highlighted the problems and devised ways in which conflicting interests could co-exist. A second conference on the same theme was arranged in 1965. It is safe to assume that these conferences inspired the 1968 Countryside Act and the establishment of the Countryside Commission[14] which was to play such a major part in promoting recreation, both formal and informal, in the countryside in the next decade.

Sir Patrick Renison had given way to Sir John Lang as Principal Adviser on Sport in January 1964. Under Sir John's leadership the Coordinating Committee of civil servants from the many Government departments concerned with sport prepared and issued a joint Ministry of Housing and Local Government and Ministry of Education Circular in August 1964 entitled *Provision of Facilities for Sport*. This will be discussed later as it was a prelude to the establishment of Regional Sports Councils in 1965.[15]

Politically the next General Election was looming as the autumn of 1964 arrived, which for sport was to prove of crucial importance. In October a

Labour Government was elected to power under Mr. Harold Wilson as Prime Minister. True to an election pledge (see Labour Party Manifesto, 1964) the Prime Minister appointed Mr. Denis Howell[16] Joint Under-Secretary of State for Education and Science, Minister with responsibility for Sport, and he further announced that the Government intended to honour its pre-election promise and establish a Sports Council.

The circle was now closed; the reforms that the Wolfenden Committee had urged had taken four years to bring about and the Government was now inextricably linked with sport. Lord Hailsham and his colleagues had achieved many good things and created the systems that now made it easier to operate in Whitehall. It is idle to speculate, but nevertheless of great interest to wonder, whether or not there would have been a Sports Council if the Conservative Government had been returned to power. There is no doubt that Lord Hailsham and Sir John Lang were opposed to such a move; would their successors have been equally so? Certainly by 1970 when a later Conservative Government took power it had very clear ideas[17] that it wanted an arms-length organization, a Sports Council with executive powers and with greater authority.

Notes

1 Summer Olympic Games — Rome; Winter Olympic Games — Squaw Valley, USA.
2 Marquess of Exeter (Lord Burghley) IOC Member (1933–81); Chairman, British Olympic Association (1936–66), President (1966–67); President, Amateur Athletic Association (1936–76); Olympic Games 1928 — Gold Medal, Hurdles; 1932–4th place, Hurdles; AAA Hurdles Championship 1926, 1927, 1928, 1930 and 1932.
3 Lord Aberdare and Lady Burton in the Lords: Mr. D. Howell in the Commons. Sir John Wolfenden addressed the Parliamentary Sports Committee in December 1960.
4 The Labour Party Manifesto pledged a Labour Government to create a Sports Council. On 3 February 1965 the Government announced in both Houses of Parliament that they had decided to honour the pre-election pledge and establish a Sports Council which would be advisory to the Government (Hansard, House of Commons 3 February 1965. Col. 1082). See Appendix 2 to this volume for membership.
5 The Sports Council was established by Royal Charter on 4 February 1972. This gave the Council executive powers and a large measure of independence. See Appendix 1 in this volume.
6 The House of Commons debated the Report on 28 April 1961. Complimentary speeches were made by Kenneth Thompson, MP, a Junior Minister in the Ministry of Education, and by Denis Howell, MP, for the Opposition. The Minister expressed reservations about a Sports Development Council saying the government wanted longer before recommending the kind of arrangements 'for achieving the end desired'.
7 Lord Aberdare initiated a debate on the Report in the House of Lords (15 February 1961) which gave the Bishop of Chester, a member of the Wolfenden

Committee, the opportunity for a maiden speech. The Lord Chancellor, Lord Kilmuir, responded saying that the Government was 'considering the Report in the light of the CCPR's comments'.

8   The Chancellor of the Exchequer, Selwyn Lloyd, MP, on 8 May 1962, following his Budget speech, announced £1m to be added to the capital investment programme in the current year and the Ministry of Education to be authorized to spend an additional £200,000 under the Physical Training and Recreation Act (1937).

9   Sir Patrick Renison (January 1963–January 1964). Principal Adviser on Sport to Lord Hailsham. Chairman of the Co-ordinating Committee of Officials of Government Departments concerned with sport.

10   *The Sports Council — A Report 1966*, p. 13. Figures quoted are for England and Wales under the jurisdiction of the Secretary of State for Education. Figures are also given in this Report for Scotland.

11   The Mountain Leadership Certificate was established in 1964 and administered by a Joint Board of the CCPR and the British Mountaineering Council. An initiative mainly by the CCPR's Outdoor Activities Advisory Committee, the MLC was concerned with training for leadership in mountain activities.

12   Sir Jack Longland, Kt, (1970); Director of Education Derbyshire (1949–70); Athletics 'Blue' at Oxford; Everest Expedition (1933); President, Alpine Club (1973–76); Wolfenden Committee (1957–60); CCPR Executive (1961–72); Sports Council (1966–74) (Vice-Chairman from 1971); Countryside Commission (1969–74); Royal Commission on Local Government (1966–69).

13   Nature Conservancy (Ed.) (1964) *The Countryside in 1970. Proceedings of the Study Conference*, Fishmongers Hall, London, 4–5 November 1963, HMSO.

> 'The idea was to get together the users and owners of country land; developers; recreational, amenity and scientific bodies, industry and government officials; and, of course the conservationists, to see what might be done. In the end a common policy for the future must be worked out, but before that can happen everybody concerned with the problem must first become aware of the problem as a whole and then be ready to co-operate and even compromise with others in trying to solve it.' (HRH Prince Philip, Foreword to the Report of the Proceedings).

Royal Society of Arts and the Nature Conservancy (1966) *The Countryside in 1970. Proceedings of the Second Conference*, November 1965.

14   The Commission replaced the National Parks Commission with wider powers and responsibilities including the establishment of country parks and picnic sites and the preservation of footpaths and rights of way. It became an independent agency in 1982, grant-aided by the Department of Environment. The Commission's role is advisory and promotional — not executive.

15   Joint Circular, Ministry of Housing and Local Government Circular No. 49/64 and Ministry of Education Circular No. 11/64, August 1964 (see Appendix 3 for text); See Chapter 3 in this volume, section entitled 'The Regional Sports Councils and the Development of Facilities'.

16   Denis Howell, PC, MP. Member for Birmingham, Small Heath (1961–   ); Privy Councillor (1976); Minister with responsibility for Sport (1964–70 and 1974–1979); Minister of State (1969–70 and 1974–79); Birmingham City Councillor (1946–56); Chairman of the Sports Council (1965–70); Chairman, CCPR (1973–74); Football League Referee (1956–70); President, Birmingham Olympic Council (1985–86); Silver Medal Olympic Order (1981). See Howell, D.

(1990) *Made in Birmingham*, part 2, for a politician's perspective on politics and sport 1964–90.

17 The Conservative Opposition established a small working group consisting of three persons, including Mr. P.B. (Laddie) Lucas and Mr. Jim Manning, the distinguished sports writer, to consider the future of the Sports Council and Regional Sports Councils in the event of a victory at the forthcoming election. There is no formal report on the record but their recommendations became the policy of the Government on being elected in June 1970 (see Chapter 4).

Section II

Years of Promise 1965–1970

Chapter 3

The Establishment of the Sports Council

On 3 February 1965 Her Majesty's Government announced in both Houses of Parliament the establishment of the Sports Council,[1] which was warmly welcomed by many but opposed by some who were fearful that this dramatic step would alter for ill the status quo in British sport.[2] There were those who feared for their positions in sport carrying, as such positions do, power and prestige that might now be in some way diminished. Others, less reactionary and more in tune with developments in Europe and elsewhere, saw this action as a giant step towards a new era, with the Government playing a strong supportive role but not wishing to be involved in day-to-day policy.

The Minister with responsibility for Sport, Mr. Denis Howell, MP, was to be the Chairman of the Sports Council, which would be an advisory and not an executive body. The terms of reference were simple, clear and all-embracing. The Sports Council would be responsible for advising the Government on all matters relating to the development of amateur sport and recreation. It would further have the responsibility for fostering cooperation among statutory authorities and voluntary bodies who were concerned in any way with sport and physical recreation (see Appendix 2 to this volume for precise wording).

The Minister for Sport (the abbreviated term by which he became known) was located in the Department of Education and Science as from the outset the Labour Government saw quite clearly the direct links the education services had with adult sport. This view changed later when the drive for more facilities was underway and the post of Minister for Sport was translated to the then Ministry of Housing and Local Government. Even at this early stage there were those who believed that the latter Ministry was more apt for this particular appointment (Chataway, 1966), but the general view, however, was that this was more of an educational appointment, and indeed the grant-aiding of sport that had taken place prior to 1965 had always been through the Department of Education and Science under the Physical Training and Recreation Act of 1937 (see Appendix 9 to this volume).

There was a feeling that although the Government had now agreed to implement one of the main recommendations of the Wolfenden Report '*Sport and the Community*' and establish a Sports Council, the advisory nature of the new body would prevent it from having teeth and a cutting edge. The official reason for this half-way step towards executive authority and budgetary control was that legislation would take too long, and action was needed urgently. This was of course factually so as the new Government had a programme of legislation it wished to embark upon and sport was not amongst its priorities. One suspects that this reason may well have been administratively convenient at the time because five years later, when steps were being taken to give executive powers to the Sports Council, Denis Howell opposed such a move arguing that there was greater strength in its being within the machinery of Government (Hansard, House of Commons, 15 July 1971 col. 820).

It was, however, quite clear from the beginning that the Sports Council, although advisory, was intended to be a dynamic and promotional body. It was to advise the Government but with the Government being largely represented by the Minister for Sport in the Chair, it was overwhelmingly likely that such advice would be accepted. After all where were the experts in Government to refute advice? As they were asking the new dog to bark they had no intention of barking themselves, although they reserved the right. Accordingly the Sports Council was asked to advise on matters concerning:

1   development of training and coaching;
2   priorities in sports development;
3   standards of provision for sports facilities for the community;
4   coordination of the use of existing and new community resources;
5   necessary capital expenditure;
6   research;
7   surveys of resources;
8   regional planning;
9   international competition involving British teams;
10   sport in foreign countries. (see Appendix 2 to this volume).

The announcement of the setting up of the Sports Council was accompanied by the news that Walter Winterbottom,[3] the former England soccer manager, and since 1963 General Secretary of the CCPR, was to be seconded to be the Director. Denis Molyneux, a brilliant academic from the Physical Education Department at the University of Birmingham was likewise seconded to become Deputy-Director.

With so much of the inspiration behind the original decision to set up Sir John Wolfenden's Committee of Enquiry coming from the Midlands it was not surprising that the Minister turned to his local University in Birmingham for the second of these appointments. As far back as 1956 a group of physical education academics at the University of Birmingham, under the leadership of their Director, David Munrow, later to join Sir John on his Committee, published '*Britain in the World of Sport*' which signposted the way ahead. In 1962 Denis Molyneux published a pamphlet which radically affected national thinking, *Central Government Aid to Sport and Physical Recreation in Countries of Western Europe.*[5] Munrow joined the Sports Council from the outset followed by Peter McIntosh,[6] another distinguished physical educationalist from the same University, who was to walk the stage nationally and internationally during the next twenty-five years to outstanding effect.

The Sports Council captured the imagination of many and therefore was able to draw into its membership in the early years distinguished and formidable personalities from the field of international sport and public life (Appendix 4). Roger Bannister (later to be Chairman when the Council became executive), Brian Close, John Disley, George Edwards, Peter Heatly, Cliff Jones, Kathleen Holt, Mary Glen-Haig, Elaine (Lady) Burton were all internationals, whilst the academic and professional brilliance of Sir John Lang, Bernard Donoughue, David Bacon, Michael Dower, Arthur Ling, David Munrow, Jack Longland, Laurie Liddell, Peter McIntosh, Bob Gibb, and Lord Porchester, was only equalled by the trades union experience of the highly talented Frank Leath. These and others served the Council well in the early task of deciding the way ahead and the priorities for action.

The Sports Council was physically located in Richmond Terrace, an outpost of the Department of Education and Science which had its main headquarters not too far away in Curzon Street. The Council was serviced by a small staff of civil servants. With the vast Whitehall experience of Sir John Lang, a former Secretary of the Admiralty, the Sports Council was well poised to make its mark in the 'corridors of power'; sport was lucky to have such a personality available as Deputy-Chairman to complement the adroit political acumen of Denis Howell.

From the outset Miss Sheila Hughes, who had been Walter Winterbottom's Secretary at the FA, continued to serve him in this capacity and later became Secretary to the Council, a post she continues to hold. An able and respected lady of considerable ability, she has served the Council loyally and with distinction.

Four fields of activity were quickly established, each to be serviced by a Committee of the Council. The International Committee was chaired by Lady Burton, whilst David Munrow took charge of the Committee for Sports Development and Coaching. The eminent neurologist and athlete Dr. Roger Bannister (later Sir Roger Bannister) was an ideal appointment to the Research and Statistics Committee, whilst Lord Porchester, with his considerable experience of local government, fitted admirably into the chair of the Facilities Planning Committee. Her Majesty's Government's professional interests were watched over by assessors from the Department of Education and Science and the Ministry of Housing and Local Government and thus the team and its structure was complete.[7]

The Sports Council turned immediately to the two main issues that it identified as being crucial to medium and long-term development; the need for more facilities and the need for a stronger injection of public funds into the administration and development of the national governing bodies of sport. Both of these issues had been debated five years earlier in 'Wolfenden' (pp. 2–39, 52–65, 108 and 109–10) and the Council quickly took advantage of both the thinking and the evidence displayed at that time. It was agreed that whilst the elite performer could be assisted immediately, the base of the pyramid to increase the number and quality of high-level performers depended on the provision of more and better facilities, and this would take some time to be achieved. Therefore the Council decided that a further level of administration and organization was required to speed on the campaign for more facilities. As the main providers would increasingly be the municipal authorities the Council agreed that a partnership between local authorities and sports people should be established regionally. In the early spring of 1965 Lord Porchester obtained the approval of the powerful local authorities' associations that Regional Sports Councils in England, and Councils for Wales and Scotland, should be established charged with the task of putting on the ground, and on the water, a new generation of facilities for sport in volume to a scale not previously envisaged. With the approval of the CCPR, the Welsh Advisory Committee, and the Scottish Council of Physical Recreation, the senior officer in each region and country would be required to be the executive officer of these new bodies, subject to approval by meetings of local authorities to be held later in the autumn of that year. The broad terms of reference for these Regional Sports Councils were to facilitate the regional coordination and provision of facilities and recreation.[8] This proposal was a master stroke and was later seen to be the 'jewel in the crown' of the Sports Council. Undoubtedly Denis Howell and Lord Porchester had a 'feel' for local government and timed this action to a nicety; their acceptance as respected individuals by the town hall leaders played a major part in bringing about the establishment of Regional Sports Councils.

There are many who believe that this development so changed the face of British sport in fifteen years (1965–1980) to make it such that this continues to be the major breakthrough in Britain to date. Local government has had a tradition, since the Baths and Washhouses Act (1846), the Public Health Act (1875), the Local Government Act (1894) and the Open Spaces Act (1906), of providing for public recreation, but the sheer scale and magnitude of the task now to be undertaken made everything that had gone before pale in comparison. In 1964 it is recalled that Britain had no more than three, possibly four, sports centres; sixteen years later England alone had in excess of 400.

Denis Howell will be remembered for many things in sport in Britain, but if everything else were forgotten, the decision to establish Regional Sports Councils will be recalled with gratitude and admiration.

The Regional Sports Councils and the Development of Facilities

The first welcome sign that Her Majesty's Government was concerning itself, in a formal sense, with sport came with the issue of what was to become generally known as the Joint Circular of August 1964. In reality this was a Circular (see Appendix 3 in this volume for the full text) issued by the Ministry of Housing and Local Government (49/64) and the Department of Education and Science (11/64) entitled *'Provision of Facilities for Sport'*. The Scottish Education Department had issued a similar Circular No. 550 in January of the same year entitled *Facilities for Sport and Recreation*.

This Joint Circular, published at the direction of the two Departmental Ministers and the Minister for Welsh Affairs, set out the concerns the Government had for the wider and more efficient provision of facilities for sport and for improved administration and organization. It referred to the voluntary administration of sport but pointed to the main burden of capital expenditure rightly falling on local authorities under various statutory provisions including the duties of local education authorities under the 1944 Education Act.[9] The Circular described its purpose as encouraging the further development of sport and suggested ways in which local authorities, in association with other bodies, might be able to make improvements and extend the range of facilities. It went on to detail increases in grant-aid under the Physical Training and Recreation Act of 1937 for capital projects by voluntary sports clubs, and for administration and coaching schemes of national governing bodies of sport. There is no doubt that this action by the Conservative Government in 1964, in advance of the establishment of the Sports Council five months later, laid down guidelines for the new Regional Sports Councils. Local authorities were urged in the Circular to carry out reviews of their areas and this was the first work to be undertaken by these new Councils of local authorities.[10]

With the agreement therefore of the local authorities' associations early in 1965 the Sports Council arranged regional meetings of local authorities with regional and county governing bodies of sport in the autumn of that year aimed at obtaining formal agreement to the setting up of the proposed Regional Sports Councils. The meetings were chaired by the Minister, supported by Lord Porchester, the Director and members of the Sports Council. The proposal to establish such Councils was warmly welcomed in all nine regions of England,[11] in Scotland and Wales. It should be noted that there already existed in the Northern region the Northern Advisory Council for Sport and Recreation; the constitution of this was ratified along with the others.[12]

It was agreed at these regional meetings that the senior officers of the CCPR in the nine English regions, in Scotland (SCPR) and in Wales, should head the secretariat needed for carrying out the administration and providing the technical input. In this way the CCPR regionally was inextricably linked with the Sports Council virtually from the outset, whilst it was not until 1968 that the headquarters staff of the CCPR took over the national administration of the Council.

Looking back it is remarkable to recall that in 1965 nobody knew the total number of facilities in Britain. Every local authority knew what it had by way of playing fields, swimming pools and the like but the overall picture was unknown. It was quite possible, and indeed had occurred, for a local authority to build a swimming pool a few hundred yards from what was planned in a neighbouring authority. Equally both were likely to be built with the same design faults as no system existed for pooling experience. It was decided that the task of assessing the level of playing-field provision was too great to start with, and in any case Britain had playing pitches, not enough it was agreed, but at least the pattern of provision was established. It was decided to concentrate mainly on built facilities to include indoor sports centres, swimming pools, stadia for athletics and cycling, and golf courses. Some regions extended their appraisals to water-based facilities and general recreation areas. The purpose of this exercise, whilst clearly to find out exactly what regions, and therefore the nation, possessed, had an even more important purpose.

By finding out what regions had deficiencies were highlighted, and therefore a programme of planned development and investment could begin.[13] Whilst the regional appraisals took upwards of two years to prepare, as a first planning exercise in sports provision, Regional Sports Councils embarked on a wide range of other initiatives. The extended use of existing school sports facilities was an early target and a greater level of dual-use was campaigned for vigorously.[14] Thirty years later this thorny problem still exists, but great inroads have been made.

A new policy of 'joint use'[15] was advocated whereby local authorities joined with education authorities to pay for and provide more and better facilities for sport to be available to schools during the day and the community in the evenings, at weekends and during school holidays. This policy meant that for the first time the Ministry of Housing and Local Government and the Department of Education and Science had to agree a system of coordinated funding so that loan-sanction from the former coincided with the programme of school building of the latter. With the considerable growth of new schools in the late sixties and seventies this policy was a great success and represented a sensible economic approach to value for money.[16] There were, and still are, problems inherent in the management agreements involved in these developments. The overwhelming success of this type of cooperation not only produced a wide range of facilities cheaply but, as later research was to show (See Cooper & Lybrand Associates, 1981), guaranteed a greater level of continuing participation in sport after pupils had left school at 16. Although some preliminary talking had taken place the event that finally turned the talking into policy was a conference of local authorities called by Sir Frank Price,[17] the Chairman of the West Midlands Sports Council in early January 1968 to crystallize the thinking and agree a way forward. As the appropriate government departments had to be represented at high level a policy and method of working had to be agreed by them beforehand and this was done. Accordingly the Director of the Sports Council was able to circulate to all Regional Sports Councils, a few weeks before the Conference, a letter entitled 'The Joint Planning of Sports Facilities' which formed the background for discussion and decision. This policy has been successful in Britain and its success has attracted Western European attention. Many years later the Sports Council was invited by the Committee for the Development of Sport of the Council of Europe to organize an International Conference on the topic of integrated facilities in November 1979,[18] whilst in 1984 reports were received that this policy was now being developed in Bahrain which no doubt will influence the Gulf area generally as these countries develop and expand both their educational and recreational programmes.

Regional Sports Councils further turned their attentions to the question of persuading local authorities to give more and wider rating relief to private sports clubs, to the acquisition of an ever increasing number of drill halls for sport as the Territorial Army was being run down, and to the need to obtain greater use of existing facilities owned and run by commerce and industry.

Water recreation also featured as a priority on many agendas for action[19] and a massive drive to bring waterways, lakes and reservoirs into greater use for sport and physical recreation met initially with in-built resistance from some of the water companies and from the Nature Conservancy Council but gradually good sense and co-operation prevailed. In 1965 the British Waterways Board (BWB) published '*The Facts about the Waterways*'[20] which shaped Government thinking. Consultations with Regional Sports Councils and other bodies, including the Sports Council and appropriate governing bodies of sport, heralded the Transport Act of 1968[21] which gave to the Board the positive duty to maintain 1100 miles of waterways, now designated 'cruising waterways', for angling, cruising and other recreational purposes. At the same time this Act gave powers to local authorities to assist financially in the maintenance of canals for recreation.

In 1966 a Joint Circular from the Ministry of Land and National Resources (3/66) and the Department of Education and Science (19/66) entitled, *Use of Reservoirs and Gathering Grounds for Recreation* referred to the increasing need for facilities for water sports and recreation and urged a review aimed at obtaining better access for potential users. By 1969 the Sports Council was able to report that some 120 water undertakers had opened reservoirs and gathering grounds for recreation with sailing on forty-five of these, canoeing on sixteen, water skiing on two, sub-aqua on nine and angling on seventy-four.[22]

From 1968 the argument for greater use of existing and new water was such that the British Waterworks Association was asking its members to give details of reservoirs where no recreation was considered possible, where it could be increased, and where new use could be accommodated. In but a few years progress had been quite spectacular. The vision and often courage of those in charge of water facilities deserved the greatest praise, with sport the richer for their actions. In many cases it was a simple question of old fashioned horse-trading in an effort to get a fair share of available water resources opened to sailing, canoeing, and the most difficult of all, water skiing; there were real technical obstacles to overcome with the purification of water, protection of valuable wild life sites, access and the existing rights of anglers.[23]

Twenty years on it would be inaccurate to believe that all the problems, encountered in the late sixties, no longer exist, they often do but the work started at that time has borne rich dividends both on inland and coastal waters to meet the great upsurge that took place then and in the seventies in water sports.

Regional Sports Councils involved the planning departments of local planning authorities from the outset in the facility appraisals and this activity meant that other planning matters were dealt with in a climate of greater understanding. The after-use of gravel workings for water recreation became a priority and the shining example of intelligent use of this policy was the creation of the National Water Sports Centre at Holme Pierrepont, Nottinghamshire in 1971,[24] officially opened by the Prime Minister, Mr. Heath, in 1973. The World Rowing Championships took place there in 1975 less than ten years after this policy was proposed. As a result of the focus of attention being turned on the need for multi-use of water many facilities were created. Three fine examples of new reservoirs encompassing water sports from the outset were Grafham Water in Rutland, Derwent Water in Northumberland and Draycott in Warwickshire all now under the control of regional water authorities.

Land used for playing fields is forever under threat from housing developments, motorways, by-passes and industrial estates if not secured by lease or by designation as private or public open space; even then it is never completely secure from compulsory purchase. With the lobby for sport increasing weekly in the sixties and with the case for more facilities being argued at many levels of public life and in the media, the need to retain what already existed became a virtual crusade. Planning authorities had to satisfy many demands and never satisfied all their customers but with the advent of Regional Sports Councils the case for sport was at last articulated with authority. Governing bodies of sport at regional and county level, together with staff who served the Councils, were increasingly seen at public planning enquiries when land used or needed for sport was under threat.[25]

On the organizational front sports associations at regional and county level recognized the value of banding together in some common forum; they were not only able to elect their representatives to serve on Regional Sports Councils but were able to speak and act authoritatively for sport. In this way the Regional Standing Conferences of Sport were established as democratic, voluntary sports bodies capable of wielding enormous influence by including many of the major 'names' in sport in Britain amongst their membership. At the purely local level local sports advisory councils sprang up in increasing numbers. These were councils of representatives of the local authority and the local sports clubs. Such local groups prospered in many areas and withered in others, often to reappear after an interval. They articulated the aspirations of the local communities by creating a lobby for facilities, running coaching courses, inter-town competitions, festivals of sport, sports personality of the year contests and generally attempting to do the work of the Sports Council and the Regional Sports Councils locally.

Although the Sports Council did not yet have its own financial resources to allocate, this had to wait until 1972 and the creation of the Sports Council as an independent body by Royal Charter (see Appendix 1 to this volume), its advisory powers allowed loan-sanction for major facilities for sport proposed by local authorities to be channelled to the right facilities. Likewise the grants that the Department of Education and Science made to voluntary sports clubs were allocated on the advice of the Sports Council. To facilitate this eminently sensible arrangement Regional Sports Councils, acting as agents for the Sports Council on behalf of the Ministry of Housing and Local Government and the Department of Education and Science, decided priorities from the increasing demand.[26]

Under the dynamic leadership of Denis Howell, the Minister with responsibility for Sport, and supported by a Sports Council of high esteem, integrity, ability and drive, the Department of Education and Science was persuaded to increase annually the sums of money made available to assist the development of private club facilities. In 1965/66, the first year of operation of the Sports Council, £739,695 was distributed to voluntary sports clubs in Britain for the provision of new facilities to augment their own resources; no grant was above 50 per cent of the total cost. By 1968/69 this sum had risen to £1,432,685. The picture on the loan-sanction side to assist local authorities to build pools, sports halls, stadia and new playing pitches was not so rosy. From a high of £16.41m in 1965/66 with a drop to £9.99m four years later is an indication that the Ministry of Housing and Local Government was not yet prepared to come fully to terms with needs.

Other agencies were now in the business of providing for recreation. The Countryside Act of 1968 gave powers to the Countryside Commission and local authorities to provide greater opportunity for outdoor recreation, generally of a more informal nature.[27] It was imperative that the Sports Council and the Commission should work closely together on those aspects of facility development where they had common interest. Conflict of use was, and still is, an issue but over the years it has been increasingly obvious to users of the countryside and water for sport and physical recreation that in a tiny island like Britain tolerance has to prevail if all are not to suffer. This is not to say that 'warfare' does not still break out, but happily it is rarer than in the sixties. From the outset the cooperation between the agencies was assisted by the simple fact that members of one organization often sat in committee on another. For example, Sir Frank Price, Chairman of the West Midlands Sports Council, was Chairman of the British Waterways Board; Jack Longland, a member of the Sports Council, served on the Countryside Commission; Lord Porchester, Chairman of the Facilities Planning Committee, was a member of the Forestry Commission for England. Happily this type of cross-representation continued to some extent for many years to come but in the early eighties began to fall away; by then, however, the Chairmen's Policy Group, consisting of the Chairmen of all the agencies concerned in any way with sport and recreation was well in its stride.

From the day the Sports Council was established in 1965 the need for standards of provision for sports facilities was a clear priority. As the Regional Sports Councils prepared to publish their appraisals of what existed it was clear that the need was acute. In West Germany the '*Memorandum on the Golden Plan for Health, Sport and Recreation*' had been published in 1960 by the National Olympic Committee,[28] and this set out very clear standards to make good deficiencies over a fifteen-year period. Eyes therefore were very much on this approach. It was to many a great disappointment that when the Sports Council published '*Planning for Sport*' in July 1968 it did not recommend specific scales of provision but rather laid down a complicated formula by which local authorities could assess their requirements.[29] This was of limited help in reality to Regional Sports Councils, although the publication stimulated a series of regional conferences which used the report and its conclusions as a basis for discussion.[30] To this day no specific standards have ever officially been set although unofficial standards have been declared as guidelines.

Global targets have been declared, as in '*Sport in the Seventies*'[31] and a decade later in '*Sport in the Community — The Next Ten Years*',[32] but many close to the issue are of the opinion that not to declare specific standards for communities, revised from time to time, has been, and still is a mistake.

Against all this activity, that set the pattern for the seventies, certain popular trends were seen although at that time little data was available. Outdoor sport grew considerably, while the demand for more indoor facilities for sport grew faster still, fuelled by the widening of the physical education syllabuses in schools as gymnasia and the new sports halls gave greater choice of activity. Spectator sports, such as football and cricket continued to decline in watching popularity; this decline taking its origin from the 1950s. Whether those who no longer watched had begun to play, or whether the changing social pattern of society took them into other activities, is not known as no records exist.[33] This was the market the new facilities were to tap, along with those who had had their appetites whetted by something other than the traditional sports in schools. Squash, badminton, basketball, volleyball, judo and dance were all to benefit from plans for facility development that were to emerge towards the end of the 1960s, as was swimming with the massive swimming pool building programme now envisaged. Sports requiring playing pitches were soon to be played on the first generation of artificial, so-called all-weather (a misnomer if ever there was) pitches. Skiers no longer would have to wait for snow, nor have to travel far to find it, as plastic artificial slopes were devised for example, at Crystal Palace National Sports Centre and at the new town of Telford on which to learn, practice and later compete.

Facilities provision for sport was to change dramatically as the work of the Planning and Technical Panels of the Regional Sports Councils delivered their programmes for local authorities and private clubs to digest. The planning was over for the time being; now was the time for action and the Sports Council, together with the governing bodies of sport at national, regional and county levels, in cooperation with the local authorities in Britain, were poised for take-off.

Taking Part in Sport — Participation

The fabric of sport in Britain is made up of many strands and sport is essentially a voluntary movement. There has always been, and there still is, a school of thought that seeks some supreme body vested with all the power and influence exercised by the main sports bodies which would be responsible for directing sport in Britain. As the sixties gave way to the seventies examples were often quoted of countries that had organized sport in this way to produce spectacular results at international level, and the USSR and the German Democratic Republic always headed the list of countries quoted. In 1960 the Wolfenden Report rejected this way forward, seeing the proposed Sports Development Council as a body of sufficient influence and vision capable of securing cohesion and co-operation with all sports bodies without loss of their autonomy. Governing bodies of sport had their own traditions and ethos, as did the umbrella organizations such as the BOA and the CCPR. The NPFA had traditionally done sterling work in arousing in many support for the need for more playing spaces for games and sport for all ages and particularly for the young. The regional network of the CCPR,[34] and the county structure of the County Playing Fields Associations, were themselves active lobbies around the country.

The question therefore of combining all the organizations into one supreme body was quickly dismissed by Wolfenden. During the years which followed, and deep into the eighties, the question of which organization did what and which was more important in British sport continued to dog development. Later the increasing role HM Government began to play will be discussed (see chapters 8 and 9 in this volume). In 1965, and indeed by 1970, it was not an issue other than seeing the Government as the enabling body capable of providing the national will, finance and appropriate legislation. From the outset HRH Prince Philip, Duke of Edinburgh, the President of the CCPR, has constantly returned to the theme of which organization is responsible for what and has repeatedly warned against the increasing encroachment by HM Government and the Sports Council in those areas of sports development rightfully belonging to the national federations.

When the Sports Council was established as an advisory body in 1965 the will to assist the voluntary sports movement was a prime objective. The sports structure existed, therefore it was logical that whatever the Sports Council could do to strengthen and support this structure would be good for British sport.

With participation in sport as the raison d'être of the Sports Council it saw its task initially as doing what it could to assist élite sport at international level and, at the same time, beginning the slow task of strengthening the administration and coaching structure of the national governing bodies of sport; building the base and strengthening the edifice.

International Development

An International Committee was charged with developing ways and means to assist internationally whilst a Sport Development and Coaching Committee began to grapple with coaching, administration and organization (see Appendix 2 to this volume). The International Committee had the twin responsibilities of advising on international sport at home and overseas and quickly announced it was ready to receive applications from governing bodies of sport for assistance under both these headings. The greatest need was for travel costs for teams, coaches and officials, and associated accommodation charges. It was decided that major multi sports events such as the Commonwealth Games, Olympic Games, World Student Games, and what became known colloquially as the Paraplegics Olympics, would be dealt with separately, but under the same broad principles. It was further realized that if Britain was to stage major national events, as befitted our standing in international sport, financial help had to be provided, and the principal costs here would be for accommodation for foreign teams and for the general organizational arrangements necessary for these occasions.

It is interesting to look back and recognize the wisdom of those who developed these procedures and this policy; they exist today only marginally modified in the light of experience. A particularly far-sighted decision was to agree a programme for funding attendance of approved delegates to conferences overseas to include coaches, technical officials, academics and other experts in the broad field of sport, sports studies, sports science and physical education. This has been a fruitful investment.[35] Whilst it was regarded as important that financial assistance be made available to permit more teams to travel more often to compete internationally, it was thought equally important to provide resources to increase the calibre of these teams. Accordingly a programme to finance preparation-training for national teams and squads on a four year-cycle, to match the Olympic cycle, was recommended to the Government, using the experience of the scheme that had been financed during the year preceding the 1964 Olympic Games in Tokyo. Such training was not necessarily confined to Britain when it could be shown that training overseas would be beneficial to the development of an athlete, for example, warm weather training in winter. In this way it became possible to finance training at high altitude in the French Pyrennees prior to the Mexico Olympics (1968) which were to be held at 7,000 feet.

In the Rome Olympic Games of 1960 British athletes gained two gold, six silver and twelve bronze medals; they were supported by a successful Olympic Appeal for £50,000 and there was no financial support from the Government. The Winter Games at Squaw Valley, USA only attracted a token representation from Britain; the Winter Games had yet to make a major mark on the wider Olympic movement. Twenty eight years later in 1988 the BOA called for £2m for participation in the Winter and Summer Games; a testimony not only to inflation but to the numbers taking part.[36]

In 1964 the Government, having very tentatively begun to flirt with an appointment of a Minister of the Crown who had some responsibility for sports matters, gave £30,000 to the Olympic Appeal. This 'appeal' to the public, and to business, is traditionally for the transportation of the Olympic team to the Olympic Games, for accommodation, and for fitting-out with team uniforms and clothing. If any surplus remains this is used to assist during the next Olympiad (the four-year cycle leading up to the Olympic Games) with the preparation-training of national squads and for the administration of the British Olympic Association itself. By 1968 the Sports Council had recommended the government that it should support the BOA in a different manner by underwriting, to some considerable extent, the Olympic Appeal for the Winter Games in Grenoble and the Summer Games in Mexico. Accordingly half the cost of travel, freight and accommodation for the selected team and officials, together with a daily pocket-money allowance for competitors, was underwritten to the value of £50,000. In the eventuality the Olympic Appeal raised sufficient funds and therefore the grant-aid from the government was a mere £5,025, although an additional £3,612 was awarded to assist the attendance of British delegates to meetings of the International Federations in Mexico.[37]

For the first time a safety net had been provided which would have been used had the Olympic Appeal not been so successful; this allowed for an orderly preparation of teams for the Olympic Games, confident that final selection did not totally depend on the generosity of the public, the man in the street or in the pub, or the ability of the individual athlete to contribute.

In the same manner the Government assisted British participation in the Commonwealth Games of 1962 in Perth (Australia), 1966 in Jamaica and 1970 in Edinburgh. The sums were respectively £4,093, £8,960 and, for the latter, a capital sum of £750,000 towards the cost of providing facilities to the correct scale and standard. Between the inception of the Sports Council and the end of 1970 sixteen events of an international nature had been financially supported in Britain.[38] In respect of preparation-training for the 1968 Olympic Games athletes from fourteen of the twenty-one Summer Olympic sports were assisted for training in this country and overseas, in all to a sum totalling £11,000.[39]

The pattern was thus set for the future, the guidelines were drawn, the governing bodies of sport had learned quickly how to plan ahead and now could raise their financial horizons. The cardinal principle that guided the Government in all instances, acting on the advice of the Sports Council, was that the national governing bodies of sport should still provide 50 per cent of the money needed for their international commitments; this principle has remained until today, although the percentage available from public funds has increased as years have passed. The philosophy behind this policy was enshrined in the independence of the voluntary organizations to order their affairs and enter into competition of their choice, knowing that a sizeable proportion of the cost had to be met from their own resources. In this way government assisted, but did not control, international competition; a policy that later was to be questioned in connection with the sporting contacts with South Africa, Rhodesia, Taiwan, the Moscow Olympics of 1980 (see Chapter 13 in this volume) and Argentina in 1982.

National Development

While the International Committee was dealing with the existing international problems of the governing bodies of sport, the Sports Development and Coaching Committee began to look to the medium and long-term future. They clearly saw that the base of the pyramid should be broadened, and through implementing policies of regional development of facilities implicitly accepted this responsibility. The fact that the Minister for Sport was a Minister in the Department of Education and Science, that the CCPR regionally from the outset and nationally from 1968 was responsible for the administration of the Sports Council and the Regional Sports Councils respectively and that the whole ethos of the new body was educationally based, made certain that society as a whole was within the Council's remit. Indeed the very title of the Wolfenden Report *Sport and the Community*, the genus of what was to happen from 1965 onwards, presumed this responsibility. However, it was not until 1972, under the chairmanship of the then

Dr. Roger Bannister, a member of the Sports Council from the outset, that Britain was to be exposed to the Western European Movement *Sport for All*. Many will say that this, when it came, was simply an articulation of a movement that had been underway in Britain for some time.

The terms of reference for the Sports Development and Coaching Committee made it clear that it was concerned with the general development of sport and participation across the board. The Government therefore sought the Committee's advice on three main areas requiring financial input:

(i)   current grants to national governing bodies of sport and other national sports organizations for improved administration, coaching and development services;

(ii) capital grants to local clubs, and any other similar organizations, to construct new and improved facilities;

(iii) capital grants for national scale facilities.

It was crucial from the outset for the Sports Council to gain the confidence of the national governing bodies of sport because many viewed with alarm the creation of a body that had within its power some part of their destiny.

The choice was really quite simple but it was not always seen this way. If the Government provided an increasing volume of financial resources to sport this could be administered by a Government department utterly unfamiliar with sport, or by a body at arms length from the Government acting on its behalf but made up of men and women well known and respected in the field of sport. There was, of course, a third choice, not to accept any money at all and therefore there would be, it was thought, no need for either a government department or a Sports Council.

Supporters of this latter option saw a Sports Council purely as a grant recommending body, whereas in practice it was far more and would become deeply involved in programmes for increasing participation, providing community facilities and research.

If a new era for governing body development had dawned then the administration of sport had to be strengthened. Honorary officers and officials have long been an invaluable part of the structure of sport in Britain, and still are, but professional well-trained full-time staff were considered essential if sport was to be run in a more business-like fashion. Likewise, if coaching schemes were to develop and more national coaches were to be appointed throughout sport, a sound headquarters organization was essential to back up the work in the field. From the base position of £565,000 allocated for coaching and administration in 1965/66 this financial support had grown to £740,000 by 1969 and by 1970 it amounted to £876,608.[40]

The appointment of development officers was seen as crucial for many governing bodies. Whilst the administrators, general secretaries and coaches were all involved in general and specific development, it was argued, growth in participation could only be achieved through the appointment of officers whose sole task was to promote, develop and expand such participation. This view was broadly accepted and the appointment of development officers marked a significant move forward particularly as these appointments were grant-aided from public funds. The number of these appointments has grown considerably expanding outwards in many cases to the appointment of regional development officers in many sports for example, tennis, rugby football and volleyball.

Early on the Sports Council had to clarify and restate its role to assist amateur sport, and in all cases of assistance the criteria that had to be applied always had 'need' at the top of the list. In the case of Olympic sports the definitions of amateurism and professionalism were quite clear, but in some non-Olympic sports the distinction between the two was becoming blurred and often irrelevant. The Sports Council, in the latter case, wisely judged matters on their merits and as long as the majority of club members played purely for recreation included these sports within its field of reference. The whole question of amateurism and professionalism entered the debating arena; it was to flare up from time to time during the next twenty-five years. By the early seventies the issues raised were fairly simple and capable of resolution; by 1990 it was hardly an issue.

Club Facilities

From an organizational point of view it always appeared strange that the Sports Development and Coaching Committee, dealing as it did mainly with affairs concerning the national governing bodies of sport, should have the responsibility for encouraging the development of voluntary clubs which appeared logically within the terms of reference of the Facilities Planning Committee (see Appendix 2 to this volume). However this practice was almost certainly because grants for all the work of the 'Development' Committee came from the Department of Education and Science whilst the 'Facilities' committee drew largely on loan sanction from the Ministry of Housing and Local Government. As time passed the lines of demarcation became increasingly blurred and the question largely academic; the Regional Sports Councils pursued the club development policy with relentless enthusiasm as the volume of money by way of grant aid from the Department of Education and Science increased annually.

National Facilities

The question of facilities suitable for international competition was left to the Sports Development and Coaching committee as it was appreciated that in the many discussions and dealings with governing bodies the subject of facilities for international, and indeed national, competition was bound to crop up. The CCPR had National Sports Centres at Crystal Palace, Lilleshall Hall, Bisham Abbey, Cowes and Plas-y-Brenin which were used largely for training and coaching and in the case of Crystal Palace for competition. These together with the stadia at Wembley for football, Twickenham, Cardiff Arms Park and Murrayfield for rugby football, and the various cricket, football and club rugby grounds were all the nation had capable of staging any prestigious event. For Britain there was no rich inheritance of a range of sophisticated facilities after an Olympic Games had been staged as in Rome, Tokyo and Mexico. The 1948 London Olympics had been run on a tiny budget with no new facilities; the 1970 Commonwealth Games in Edinburgh were a year or two away. Virtually therefore from scratch the programme for national facilities had to be established and funding had to be sought. The years that followed produced some fine national-scale facilities but, as will be discussed in detail later, in twenty-five years progress has been slow. It would not be over-stating the issue to say that for a variety of reasons, some of them the responsibility of the Sports Council and some of HM Government, the development of national facilities in Britain has been largely disappointing. One example at this stage must suffice to make this point. As a nation ranking among the top six in athletics in the world Britain in 1989 has only two indoor tracks, one tucked away in a large Royal Air Force hangar in Shropshire available since 1965, and a new track at the Kelvin Hall, Glasgow. As a nation Britain does not have a facility capable of staging for example the European Indoor Athletics Championship.

However slow and painful the process of providing for international competition has proved, nevertheless, there was progress.[41] In anticipation of the 1968 Olympic Games in Mexico the Sports Council persuaded the government to provide the first synthetic running track in Britain at Crystal Palace, and as Mexico was to have a 'Tartan' track so Crystal Palace had one too, and what an inspired investment this has proved. The National Equestrian Centre at Stoneleigh, Warwickshire, was built in this period with the help of public resources, and for the disabled the indefatigable Sir Ludwig Guttman was awarded some £30,000 for the development of the stadium, pool and sports hall for international paraplegic events at Stoke Mandeville. The building of the National Sports Centre for Wales in Sophia Gardens, Cardiff, started in 1969 and early discussions for the development of the National Rowing and Canoeing Centre at Holme Pierrepont proved so encouraging that an early start to this major project in the gravel workings outside Nottingham was sought.

These were exciting years as plans were laid and development took place; years of promise and early fulfilment under the leadership of Denis Howell supported by an enthusiastic and gifted Council.

The CCPR had taken over the administration of the Sports Council in early 1968 and this date marked the end of the formal secondment of the

General Secretary of the CCPR Walter Winterbottom. The administrative net was now tightening around British sport, and the Sports Council and the CCPR became more inextricably linked. From now onwards it needed only one administrative act to merge the work of the Council and the CCPR but this was not to be until 1972 following the change of Government, a Royal Charter and considerable acrimony (see Chapter 5 and Appendix 1 in this volume)

Notes

1 Hansard, House of Commons, 3 February 1965, col. 1082. See Appendix 2 to this volume for membership and terms of reference of the Sports Council and its committees.

2 For example, the National Playing Fields Association, established in 1925, had a clear and well-defined role on the facilities side and had in 1935 established a demarcation between their functions and those of the newly-created Central Council of Recreative Physical Training (CCRPT, later the CCPR). Amalgamation had been considered but rejected in favour of a Joint Advisory Committee under the Chairmanship of the Earl of Athlone. Henceforth the two bodies worked together, sometimes uneasily. In 1964 Quintin Hogg (Lord Hailsham had renounced his peerage by then) consulted the NPFA, the CCPR and the British Olympic Association concerning the Wolfenden proposal to establish a Sports Development Council. In replying to a debate on 23 June 1964 in the House of Commons, introduced by J.P.W. Mallalieu MP, Hogg said,

> In order to carry out the work ... one must have access to the composite bodies, the CCPR, the NPFA, the SCPR and the British Olympic Association. Either a Sports Development Council is the same as these bodies, in which case it is superfluous, or it is different ... in which case it is objectionable.

In November 1965 the NPFA and the CCPR jointly published the first technical Report on sports halls entitled '*Community Sports Halls*' — the result of work carried out by G.A. Perrin, ARIBA, Research Fellow at the London Polytechnic. This Fellowship had been established by the NPFA.

3 Walter Winterbottom, CBE, Kt (1978); England Soccer Manager (1946–62); General Secretary, CCPR (1963–72); Director of the Sports Council (1965–78).

4 Physical Education Department, University of Birmingham (1956) *Britain in the World of Sport*, Physical Education Association of GB and NI. Revised in *Physical Recreation* with editorial comment 1956. Debated at CCPR Staff Conference January 1957 and resolved that the Executive Committee of the CCPR be invited to respond to the challenge posed by the University pamphlet which pointed to the problems faced by amateur sportsmen and sportswomen in preparing for international competition. It gave a comprehensive review of the many factors affecting sport in Britain.

5 Molyneux, D.D. (1962) *Central Government Aid to Sport and Physical Recreation in Countries of Western Europe*, Birmingham, Physical Education Department, University of Birmingham. This pamphlet is a 'contribution to the debate

following the publication of the Wolfenden Report — *Sport and the Community'*.

6   P. Mc. Intosh, M.A. (Oxon); Deputy-Director of Physical Education, University of Birmingham (1946–59); Senior Inspector of PE, Inner London Education Authority (ILEA) (1959–74); Director of the School of PE, University of Otago, New Zealand (1974–78); Visiting Professor, Canada; Member, Sports Council (1966–74); Chairman, Facilities Committee; Committee Chairman, International Council for Sports Science and Physical Education (1971–83). Published: (1952) *Physical Education in England since 1800* (revised 1968), London, Bell (1957) *Landmarks in the History of Physical Education* (1957, revised 1981) with Dixon, Munrow and Willets, London, Routledge & Kegan Paul; (1979) *'Fair Play: Ethics in Sport and Education*, London, Heinemann; (1985) *The Impact of Sport for All Policy 1966–84* with Charlton, London, Sports Council; (1987) *Sport in Society*, West London Press.

7   See note 1 of this chapter (Appendix 2).

8   See Sports Council Report (1966) *Regional Sports Councils* p. 16, paragraphs 39–42; for terms of reference and structure.

9   See in particular sections 41 and 53 of the Act for precise wording. In summary these sections place a duty on education authorities to provide facilities for cultural and recreative activities for primary, secondary and full and part-time further education students. Permissive powers are given to establish, manage and maintain camps, holiday classes, playing fields, play centres, gymnasia, swimming baths etc. The authority can organize games and expeditions and can pay for them.

10   For example: (a) *West Midlands: Regional Recreation*, a first study on the major needs and deficiencies in the West Midlands, February 1967, *Dual Use of Existing and New Facilities for Sport and Recreation*, December 1967; *A Report: Proposals for the After-use of Sand and Gravel Workings for Sport and Recreational Purposes*, October 1968; (b) *East Midlands: The Drill-Hall as a Community Sports Centre*, March 1968; *Recreation in the East Midlands — An Initial Appraisal of Major Facilities*, September 1967.

11   Northern; North-West; Yorkshire and Humberside; East Midlands; West Midlands; Eastern; Greater London and South-East; Southern; and South-West. These regions very closely followed the boundaries of the recently-established Economic Planning Regions.

12   The constitution of Regional Sports Councils was not rigid and it was left to regions to modify the suggested pattern at the outset or in the passage of time. Basically and fundamentally a Regional Sports Council consisted of representatives of the County Councils, County Boroughs, Municipal Boroughs, Urban District Councils, Rural District Councils, Parish Councils and the regional and county sport bodies. The Minister for Sport made up to six personal nominations and the relevant Government Ministries (usually Housing and Education) provided assessors. Local authorities had about 80 per cent of the membership as it was the basic premise that they would be the main providers of facilities.

13   For example, the West Midlands Sports Council decided that a programme to make good the deficiencies in swimming pools should be announced listing geographic areas of need based on a standard of one 25 metre pool (at least) to be provided within half a mile for every citizen in urban areas and within six miles for rural areas.

14   Dual use was defined by the Dual-Use Committee of the West Midlands Sports Council in 1966 as: 'Use of local education authority-controlled physical recreation facilities by school and community throughout the year, including school holidays.' Later the definition was widened to include facilities belonging to the services and to industry.

15 See Joint Circular of August 1964 (Appendix 3) paragraph 2; ' "Joint Planning" means the planning and provision of facilities for sport and recreation by two or more authorities, or by two or more Committees within a single authority. In most cases this policy involves the Education Committee of a County Council and a District Council within the County, or the Education Committee and other committees within a County Borough.' (Report of a Conference of local authorities 'Joint Planning of Facilities for Sport and Recreation', West Midlands Sports Council 1968).

16 There are very many excellent examples throughout Britain, for example, Bingham, Nottinghamshire and Sidney Stringer School, Coventry; see *Towards a Wider Use* — a report of an inter-Association Working Party — District, County and Metropolitan — March 1976.

17 Frank Price, Kt (1966); Lord Mayor of Birmingham (1964–65); Chairman, West Midlands Sports Council (1965–69); Chairman, British Waterways Board (1968–84); Chairman, Telford Development Corporation (1968–71).

18 Council of Europe CDDS Priority Theme IV, *Integrated Facilities*, Report of a Seminar London 29 October–1 November 1979, London, Sports Council.

19 See for example East Midlands Sports Council (1967) *Recreational Use of the Wash, Canals and Waterways of the East Midlands*, Yorkshire and Humberside Sports Council (1967) *A Study of Inland Waterways and Recreation*; Eastern Sports Council (1968) *The Use of Inland Waters for Recreation*.

20 This report sets down physical and financial facts which very rapidly formed the basis of the Government's thinking on waterways policy, outlined for the first time in the White Paper on Transport Policy (1966) (Cmnd, 3057), London, HMSO.

21 The Transport Act, (1968): (a) placed on the BWB a new and positive duty to maintain 1100 miles of cruising waterways in a state suitable for cruising, fishing and other recreational activities; (b) established the Inland Waterways Amenity Advisory Council which was empowered to advise the Minister and Board on any proposal concerning amenity or recreational use; and (c) gave permissive powers to local authorities to give financial or other aid to maintain the inland waterways for recreation.

22 The Sports Council *A Review 1966–69*, published by the CCPR for the Sports Council.

23 For example: Blithfield Reservoir and Chasewater, Staffordshire; see (1972) *A Guide to Water Recreation* West Midlands Sports Council; for a comprehensive review of the position with water recreational facilities in the West Midlands post the Wolfenden Report (1960), and pre-Regional Sports Councils (1965), see (1964) *Inland Waters and Recreation*, a survey carried out for the CCPR by the Physical Education Department at University of Birmingham.

24 Official approval for development was given in 1969 by cooperation between the Nottinghamshire CC and the Department of the Environment acting on a recommendation from the Sports Council. A Director (Stan Dibley) was appointed in 1971. The Centre was transferred from the CCPR to the Sports Council in 1972 along with the other CCPR National Sports Centres when the Sports Council became independent by Royal Charter.

25 See Ministry of Housing and Local Government Circular 33/70 *Sports Facilities and the Planning Acts*; a classic example was in 1968 at Stratford-upon Avon. The Borough Council wished to build a swimming pool by the river. This was supported by the Regional Sports Council and the Midland District Amateur Swimming Association but opposed by the Shakespeare Trust which did not wish to see 'the meadows where Shakespeare trod' used in this way. Distinguished QCs represented both sides at a public enquiry lasting several days. The pool was built and adorns the site next to a major hotel that came later.

26 By 1969 the number and value of applications for grant had increased at such a pace that this outstripped resources available. A priority system was introduced and operated by Regional Sports Councils based on regional needs.

27 Provision of picnic sites and country parks, access to open country, lakes, rivers and canals for informal recreation.

28 'Planning began in the Federal Republic of Germany in 1955 and was completed by 1959. The Report was an appeal to the nation, on the basis of the surveys completed, to make good over a period of 15 years deficiencies in facilities for all types of sport and physical recreation.' (Molyneux)

29 See *Planning for Sport*: pp. 24–33 for pitches, courts, bowling greens, non-turf areas; pp. 34–37 for athletics and golf courses; pp. 45–50 for swimming pools; p. 57, paragraph 144, for sports halls (an admission that an assessment is not possible); pp. 66–76 for dual use and joint planning.

30 West Midlands Sports Council *Joint Planning of Facilities for Sport and Physical Recreation*, Report of a Conference of local authorities and government departments together with policy statements.

31 (1972) *Sport in the Seventies — Making Good the Deficiencies — The Need for a Planned Programme of Capital Investment on Sports Facilities*, London, HMSO. This was a simple, cheap, printed pamphlet with a pull-out map showing by sub-divisions of Standard Regions 'major requirements and potential deficit' for 'major sports facilities'. It was printed in great volume and circulated very widely throughout England and Wales as a very effective propaganda statement.

Summary of Capital Investment Needs (at 1972 prices)

Assessed Demand	£m	
Indoor swimming pools	58	447 pools
Indoor sports centres	160	1 per 90,000+
		1 for every 50,000
Golf courses	29	350 municipal courses
Regional specialist facilities	18–25 — estimate	
Sports grounds	12–15 — estimate	
Minor facilities	25–30 — estimate	

32 Published by the Sports Council in 1982. A comprehensive statement of need for the decade supported by well-researched statistics. See chapter 5 of the report, 'Planning, providing and managing facilities'.

33 *ibid*, chapter 2, paragraph 1, 'The 1960s and the growth in outdoor sport and recreation'.

34 *Regions of the CCPR in 1970 — boundaries*: North East; Yorkshire; North Midlands; East; London and South East; South; South West; West Midlands; North West; Northern Ireland; Wales.
    Regional Sports Councils in 1970 — boundaries: Northern; Yorkshire and Humberside; East Midlands; Eastern; Greater London and South East; Southern; South Western; West Midlands; North Western.

35 For example a strong British 'team' of delegates was funded (75 per cent of travel) to the Olympic Sports Science Congress in Eugene (USA) in 1984 and Cheonan (South Korea) in 1988.

36 Winter Olympics (Calgary) fifty-seven competitors; Summer Olympics (Seoul): 382 competitors.

37 Traditionally the majority of International Sports Federations take the opportunity to hold General Assemblies and Committee meetings at the time and Venue of the Olympic Games when most, if not all, of their members are present. International Sports Science and Physical Education organizations too

use this opportunity, many having attended the pre-Olympic Sports Science Congress.

38 *The Sports Council — A Review 1966–69*, Appendix B for costs and grant paid.
39 *ibid*
40 *The Sports Council — A Review 1966–69*, Appendix C; *The Sports Council Annual Report 1972/73*, Appendix III.
41 By 1973 the Sports Council's annual report was able only to report developments at the National Sports Centres under its control (transferred from the CCPR when the Sports Council was established by Royal Charter); see chapter 6 for examples of progress 1972–79.

Chapter 4

Sport in the Sixties

Historians will note that for Britain the sixties were years of considerable change for sport, not only in terms of organization and structure but in terms of philosophy.[1] Whilst it is true that no philosophical change takes place overnight, it is equally true that the mid-sixties saw a new school of thought triumph and the old school of thought begin a steady decline. The British approach to sport had, for over a century, inspired the world to take up sports the British invented and develop these to such a stage so as to allow many countries to compete on even terms, and subsequently in many sports to be supreme. This is how it should be; the pupil taking over from the master and achieving greater things; there should be pride in this process not agony. That the British were no longer the best in every sport they originated was not the disaster some would have us believe; it is an indication that sport is now a world-wide phenomenon, an international force, a force that can, and often does bring people together in friendly rivalry irrespective of colour, ideology or religion. The international perspectives will be discussed later in the context of the seventies and the eighties (See Chapter 13). By the mid-sixties sport in Britain was entering a new era as for the first time the Government became heavily involved directly in supporting sport both at international and local levels.

In the sixties the concept of the 'amateur' came into question as tennis, soccer and cricket abolished the distinction between the amateur and the professional. The influence which the public schools and the ancient universities of Oxford and Cambridge had on British sport from early days was diluted as sport became an activity for a wider range of people. (See Figures 12 and 13 in *Sport and the Community — The Next Ten Years* and Chapter 6 in this volume.)[2] The provision of opportunity to participate by the community purely for fun became increasingly to be seen as a social service,[3] and the basis of British international teams became in most instances wider. On the darker side the ethic of 'fair play' came into question, not directly but by the need to win. The drug-abuse question (see Chapters 7 and 11 in this volume) came to the fore, and increasingly the influence of the media and commercialism (see Chapter 11 in this volume) began to be seen not always as influences for the good of sport. Sadly violence became associated with watching some sports.

This was the era when sport in Britain came to be 'professionalized' as public authority finance was increasingly made available to pay the wages and salaries of more full and part-time administrators and coaches to support the large army of unpaid officials, secretaries, treasurers, coaches and committee men and women at every level throughout the country. The mood of the sixties crystallized the political thinking of the early seventies and governments, both Labour and Conservative, reacted accordingly to put shape and substance to this sentiment. Reports, White Papers and Government Circulars concerned with sport and physical recreation emerged regularly from Whitehall to support the view that public authorities were concerned with this aspect of leisure-time and were prepared to do something about it.[4]

The traditions of the long-established national governing bodies of sport were in no way directly threatened by the considerable activity that now surrounded sport, although some thought they were and resisted change. The total acceptance of the rights of the duly constituted national federations of sport were endorsed and strengthened by the Sports Council with whom a dialogue was opened in the new situation that the post 1965 period provided.[5] Prestigious bodies such as the BOA, at first somewhat fearful that the establishment of the Sports Council might undermine its authority with the Olympic sports, quickly came to see that no threat existed. The Olympic Charter of the International Olympic Committee (IOC) was always a safeguard against any takeover by government, or a government appointed body,[6] but at times of change there were those who believed any change could affect materially the status quo. Indeed, the Olympic movement in Britain was now to be further enhanced as public funds were channelled to it for competition and administration.[7] The integrity of the BOA was never at any time threatened by the developments now occurring. The Association enjoyed a fruitful period of expansion under successive distinguished Chairmen[8] for many years until the 1980 'USSR-Afghanistan affaire' burst upon it to test its independence as never before; a test it survived under the Chairmanship of Sir Denis Follows[9] to emerge stronger than before.

There was a new excitement about sport in Britain, a feeling of creativity and enterprise despite the national economic situation which was not good. During the 1960s the British people enjoyed sporting success by teams and individuals. For example the winning of the World Cup at soccer by England in 1966, the first time this competition was played in Britain, gave the whole nation a fillip. On the day of the final, city, town and village streets were deserted as families sat glued to their television sets. At Wimbledon, Angela Mortimer in 1961 gave Britain its first Ladies' singles title since the legendary Dorothy Round in 1937. Eight years later in 1969 Ann Jones did likewise.

This decade saw the beginning of what was virtually a new field of research and documentation in sport. Prior to 1965, apart from some bald facts, there was little to draw on in the field of sport sociology and sports science in Britain. If a case were to be made for a greater public investment in sport then, ran the argument, more information must be available to sustain that case. Dr. Roger Bannister, later to be the first Chairman of the Sports Council under the Royal Charter and later still to be knighted for his services to sport, chaired the Research and Statistics Committee of the Council (see Appendix 2). This was an inspired nomination as Bannister, the first man to run the mile in under four minutes in May 1954, and therefore a man who was 'a legend in his lifetime', was in his professional life a consultant neurologist of considerable eminence. The former qualification gave him credibility with the public at large, the latter gave him credibility with his peers as he set about the task of developing both a sociological and medical base in sports research and documentation. The support of the Deputy-Director of the Sports Council, Denis Molyneux (see Chapter 3), was critical to the success of the programme and happily these two formidable minds complemented each other. Studies were put in hand concerned with the demand and supply of facilities for sport, and these included investigations into attitudes, aspirations and motivation.[10] On the medical front studies relating to competition at altitude were particularly apt at this time. Supported by a grant from the Government on the advice of the Sports Council, the BOA was able to mount a research operation in Mexico prior to the Olympic Games in 1968, 'Altitude and Temperature Acclimatization' by Dr. L.G.C. Pugh.[11]

One very specific topic, drug abuse in sport, had begun to worry sports administrators both on ethical and moral grounds. The use of anabolic steroids to develop muscular strength for increased performance in power events such as shot-putting, discus throwing, weightlifting and swimming began to give concern. Medical men were pointing to their inability to detect such use clinically and therefore in 1969 the Sports Council offered a grant of £6,154 to the Department of Chemical Pathology at St. Thomas's Hospital Medical School for a three-year research project starting in 1970. Three years later Professor Brooks, who headed up this work, was able to announce that by screening it was now possible to detect the use of anabolic steroids; the method of screening used was by urine sampling. Encouraged by this breakthrough the Sports Council, now under the Chairmanship of Roger Bannister an implacable opponent of drug abusers, extended the research project for a further two years. This far-seeing initiative was, later in the seventies, to develop into a drug-control and testing centre of great sophistication and international repute at Chelsea College, University of London, under the direction of Professor Arnold Beckett. The scientific fight against this unacceptable side of high-level sport as more sinister substances manifested themselves as the years went by, is described in some detail later as governments were drawn into the issue (see Chapter 7 in this volume).

The encouragement of scientific work in universities and other institutions of higher education in the fields of applied and experimental psychology and physiology, in so far as these disciplines touched on sport, heralded the start of a programme that was to lead to cooperation with many bodies and agencies.[12] Cooperation with the Social Science Research Council, the establishment in 1978 of a permanent physiological testing centre at Loughborough University and the creation in 1983 of the National Coaching Foundation (NCF) (see Chapter 11 in this volume) were to come much later, but each of these later developments takes its origin from early basic beginnings.

A National Documentation Centre for Sport was established in June 1969 with Sports Council finance where good work was already being done in this field at Queen's University, Belfast. The purpose of this Centre was to support the work of specialists by way of an abstraction service, drawing as necessary on similar centres in other parts of the world. The field of activity of this National Documentation Centre widened considerably over the years.[13] It moved to the University of Birmingham[14] in the mid-seventies where it exists to this day as a Centre housed in the main library of the University, available to sports coaches, academics and specialists in sport and physical recreation.

With the impetus given to coaches and coaching generally it was logical that the British Association of National Coaches (BANC) should be formed in 1966 which gave status and authority to those who served the national governing bodies of sport. There has always been in British sport a somewhat schizophrenic attitude to coaching and coaches and nothing rouses the sporting passions more quickly than the topic of coaching. Perhaps it is a throw-back in the psyche to those halcyon days when athletes just took off their coats and ran, or perhaps it is a revulsion against the pressurized training systems of today which are for some the negation of sport. Britain learned the lesson that coaches are necessary the hard way and suffered set-backs in the fifties with the loss of pioneers in the field like Geoff Dyson[15] who did so much for so many athletes and yet was ousted by those in authority at that time. In was the new wave of coaches in the sixties such as Ray Williams in rugby, Geoff Gleeson in judo and Bert Kinnear in swimming that set the foundation laid by earlier pioneers. The emergence of the BANC, not without misapprehension in some national governing bodies, set the seal on the early work and produced a responsible professional organization of talent and integrity. Some sports, having within them various interests and voices, organized themselves in such a way that they could respond to the Sports Council for dialogue and grant-aid, and this process has continued ever since. For example in cricket the ruling body was the MCC, which is a Club, a very prestigious Club indeed, but not a governing body. Steps were taken by the cricket authorities to create in 1968 the MCC Council, later the Cricket Council, as a governing body for the sport. The angling confraternity made up of many different interests such as sea-angling, salmon and trout, and coarse fishing, took an initiative and created in 1966 the National Anglers' Council (NAC) in which all angling interests play a part. In 1977 the Martial Arts Commission (MAC) was set up to bring all disciplines within one body in the fashion of the anglers. To date the golfers have not seen fit to rationalize their structure relying on the Royal and Ancient, a Club, to continue to be the ruling voice for the sport despite the plethora of male and female golf unions that exist in addition to the Golf Foundation established in 1952 and the now defunct Golf Development Council.

When in 1965 for the first time the Sports Council began to take stock of the facilities that existed for sport in Britain they quickly identified a service that was needed which would ensure that local authorities planning to build sports centres, swimming pools, tracks or pitches, had the best technical advice available to them. Although traditionally Building Bulletins were published by the Ministry of Housing and Local Government and the Department of Education and Science on a variety of topics,[16] building for sport was neither a priority for them nor a specialism. It was agreed that a Technical Unit for Sport (TUS) be established jointly supported by these two Ministries mainly concerned with sport.[17] This Unit, as its name suggested, would specialize in research and design for sports buildings. Additionally the Unit's brief included the responsibility to carry out development projects in the design and construction of facilities to demonstrate good value for money. This was a major breakthrough for sport as from now onwards all that was best in design, materials and playing surfaces from around the world would increasingly be made available to those whose task it was to provide facilities for sport whether they were in the public or private sectors. The economy that has been effected over the years by this advisory service has been considerable. The increasing volume of advice and service, in addition to knowledge derived from design projects, ensured that no promoter of facilities had to start from the beginning and could rest assured that his plans and proposals would be rigorously subjected to detailed examination to ensure technical viability and value for money.[18]

In the autumn of 1969 Denis Howell, now at the Ministry of Housing and Local Government, was promoted to the rank of Minister of State. This was a great fillip for sport as now sport had a minister of considerable seniority and political power. It was also a recognition by the Prime Minister of the fine work done by Howell and of his general acceptability by those he sought to serve.

On the legislation front the Local Government Acts of 1958 and 1966, which introduced general rate support grant for local authorities, withdrew from central government the powers to make direct grant-in-aid to statutory authorities to help them provide sports facilities. The effect of this legislation was to transfer to local authorities more power and responsibility for their own expenditure and public borrowing. The choice therefore of whether or not a local authority should build a sports centre or swimming pool rested increasingly at the local level, although HM Government retained the overall responsibility for total public expenditure under various headings, and controlled the volume and availability of loan sanction. As it happened these moves fell neatly into place to assist sport. Through the work of the Regional Sports Councils, well into their stride by the end of the decade and with facility development plans worked through and approved, the drive to build and the willingness to do so was also gaining momentum within the municipal authorities. The skilful work of the Principal Regional Officers (later to be designated Regional Directors) of the CCPR and their staffs serving the Regional Sports Councils was critical to the success of the facility programme, for if it had faltered at this stage it would have taken a decade to start it again. By this time Peter McIntosh had taken over from Lord Porchester as Chairman of the Facilities Planning Committee (see Chapter 3) of the Sports Council and under his wise and steady leadership the drive forward was maintained with gathering momentum.

With hindsight it is clear that the deft touch of the Minister for Sport, his Vice-Chairman Sir John Lang, Lord Porchester, Peter McIntosh and the Director Walter Winterbottom, steered the Regional Sports Councils into positions of considerable influence by exploiting the arrangements that successive governments had carried through. The appeal for facilities was mainly to local authorities as they were in a position to respond, if they so wished, and so the full weight of the argument and the case for sport was directed at this target.

The largest cloud on the horizon was the economic state of the country which undoubtedly retarded development. As the sixties gave way to the seventies and then to the eighties, it became clear that every government elected embarked upon a period of retrenchment in the face of economic setbacks, and yet the growth of capital made available to sport and recreation by local authorities during the period rose in real terms at an encouraging rate.[19] The fact that expenditure for sport is but a fraction of the total public expenditure is almost certainly one major factor by way of explanation. Another, probably the most important of all, was that at last Government at both central and local levels had arrived at the firm conclusion that the State had a decisive role to play in providing more and better opportunities for its citizens to enjoy sport and recreation. The tacit acceptance that leisure was a facet of life which should be welcomed rather than decried was growing. In 1970 the Government in the House of Commons said,

It is the policy of the Government to foster the development of sport and physical recreation in the widest sense and to provide greater opportunities for members of the community to enjoy these in forms in which they are interested. (Hansard, House of Commons, 5 May)

As the decade came to a close with a General Election in the offing midway through 1970 it was time to reflect on the ten years that had elapsed since Wolfenden had reported with such high hopes. Sir John Wolfenden wrote thus expressing his thoughts:

I personally remain convinced that an Executive Sports Council, of the kind which the 1960 Report proposed, is the proper and logical instrument for progress and development of the kind which we all want to see. But this personal opinion in no way diminishes my admiration for what the Sports Council has done since its establishment five years ago or my recognition of the growing help which successive governments have given to amateur sport over the past ten years. In a great many areas, from assistance to British sportsmen in international competitions to the strengthening of the voluntary organizations, much has been done; and unreserved tribute should be paid to Ministers, the Sports Council and the CCPR for these advances. When the economic skies lighten we can reasonably hope for further progress over the next ten years, remembering always that the keynote of the 1960 Report was the general welfare of the community. (CCPR Annual Report 1969/70, page 1)

Sir John's commitment to the need for an executive Sports Council, as opposed to the advisory body that now existed, was not shared by all. The Minister for Sport, Denis Howell, was planning a high-level consultative meeting for the spring of 1970 with Chairmen of Regional Sports Councils and their Secretaries aimed at obtaining an endorsement for the status quo. At the same time the small private group set up by the Conservative Party (see Chapter 2 in this volume) to consider how an executive body could be brought into existence following the anticipated victory at the forthcoming election was coming to its conclusions. This group included Mr. P.B. 'Laddie' Lucas,[20] the distinguished and highly decorated Battle of Britain pilot and Mr. Jim Manning, Sports Editor of the *Daily Mail*. Although they had no public locus, considerable determination was applied to know their thinking. Privately it became clear via political off-the-record sources that it would be advising that the Sports Council be established as an independent executive body. The thinking was that the 'new' Sports Council would retain all the advisory functions the present Council now had but it would have additionally the responsibility for carrying out the grant-aiding function to voluntary organizations at present carried out by the Ministry of Housing and Local Government and formerly by the Department of Education and Science. This group also thought that the Sports Council should have an independent Chairman and should become an organization very similar to the Arts Council.[21] It felt that the present Sports Council was too closely attached to the Government which meant that it did not have absolute freedom of action and speech.

The Conservative Party had yet to win the 1970 election and the Royal Chapter was two years off, but it was now known by a few that the future Government was already thinking of establishing an independent body, an 'arms length' organization. Paradoxically twelve years on a later Conservative Government, through the Minister for Sport Mr. Neil Macfarlane, was to tighten its tentacles around the Sports Council which an earlier administration had created as an executive body and seek to use it as an instrument of government policy.[22]

The lines were then drawn clearly as 1970 arrived; on the one hand the Labour Government wished to see the present position maintained with the Minister of Sport as the Chairman of the Sports Council, whilst the Conservative Opposition saw the Sports Council taking the next step forward and having executive powers under an independent chairman. The broad feeling in the national governing bodies of sport was mixed tending to favour the status quo; in the CCPR there were those who favoured change, the Wolfenden recommendation, and those who favoured leaving things as they were. At this point in history argument was still academic as the General Election was six months away. It was soon to be seen, however, that the 'Wolfenden' view would again, as in 1965, confront sport with yet a further major challenge and opportunity.

Notes

1 'The sixties were the years of "never had it so good" (Harold Macmillan, Prime Minister.) economically. The people had put behind the austerity of the early 1950s ... More time, money and mobility and the development and promotion of consumer leisure products led to the desire to see new places and do new things. Hundreds of thousands of people flooded into the countryside at weekends and holidays ... they went to picnic, sightsee, ramble and play sport.' (Sports Council, 1982, Chapter 2).

2 The very considerable growth in higher education allowed many more young people to enjoy sport during their undergraduate years.

3 By 1971 the Government claimed to recognize a 'recreational explosion' throughout the country. This was welcomed as 'a positive good'. 'The British people are reaching out in their millions for a higher quality of life. They want to escape from the pre-package society into a world of physical contest.' (Hansard, House of Commons, 15 February 1971.)

4 Appendix 5 to this volume offers a range of examples. This is certainly not all.

5 Between 1966 and 1969 the Sports Council met 174 national governing bodies of sport in Britain to learn of their problems and to discuss development. By the latter date most had submitted five (or four) year programmes but some had not. See *The Sports Council — A Review 1966–69*, appendix A for those met.

6 See Olympic Charter (1982) National Olympic Committees, paragraph C, Autonomy. 'NOC's must be autonomous and must resist all pressures of any kind whatsoever, whether of a political, religious or economic nature.'

7 Grant-aid to Olympic sports for administration, coaching and preparation training started in 1965/66 and has continued since. Some ad hoc grant-aid took place

before this date on a limited scale. Between 1965–1972 the BOA received £12,326 in grant-aid, and between 1972–75 £10,113.

8 Marquess of Exeter (Lord Burghley) (1936–66); Lord Rupert Nevill (1966–77); Sir Denis Follows (1977–83).

9 Denis Follows, CBE (1967); Kt (1978); Chairman, BOA (1977–83); Secretary, FA (1962–73); Hon. Treasurer, CCPR (1977–83); Silver Medal Olympic Order.

10 *Enquiries*: Indoor Sports Centres; Golf Courses; Swimming Pools. *Regional Studies* — factors influencing demand and location. *Studies of Selected Sports* — horse-riding; rugby football; water-based recreation. *Development of research techniques*. (See *The Sports Council — A Review 1966–69* for fuller details pp. 24–5).

11 This study produced a range of practical advice to athletes taking part in the 1968 Olympic Games. For example, evidence was provided showing that a minimum of one month of acclimatization was essential before competition.

12 For example: (a) Royal College of Physicians; Department of Health and Social Security; Health Education Council; (b) Publications: '*Trends in Leisure Participation and Problems of Forecasting*, SSRC-Sports Council; *Trends in Leisure 1919–1939*, SSRC-Sports Council; *Leisure and the Role of Clubs and Voluntary Organizations*,' SSRC-Sports Council; (c) Conference 'Exercise, Health and Medicine' — co-sponsors Medical Research Council, Health Education Council, Sports Council (1983).

13 The Centre serves the needs of teachers and researchers. It assembles references from national and international sources; obtains copies of articles from overseas and arranges translations.

14 Bill Slater, Director of Physical Education at the University of Birmingham, a member of the Sports Council, initiated the discussion on the transfer with the University Librarian. John Coghlan, Deputy Director-General of the Sports Council, handled the brief for the Sports Council

15 See, for example, Dyson (1964).

16 For example, Department of Education and Science (1966) *Building Bulletin 'Playing Fields and Hard Surface Areas'*, 28.

17 The TUS was established in 1968 and located initially in the Buildings Branch of the Department of Education and Science. In 1972 after the Sports Council became independent and executive the Unit transferred to the Council. It was, and still is, composed of architects, quantity surveyors and heating and mechanical engineers.

 The Unit first concentrated on the planning, standards of construction, engineering services and running costs of medium-sized swimming pools. To date the TUS has had two Heads — Mr. Geoffrey Hughes and Mr. Geraint John which has assisted in maintaining continuity.

18 The TUS has published many technical publications usually recorded annually in the Annual Report of the Sports Council. A listing of these is available from the Sports Council's Information Centre. Examples: *TUS Handbook of Sports and Recreational Building Design*, 4 volumes; Data Sheets, for example, Table Tennis No. 42; Badminton No. 56; Energy Data Sheets, for example, Boilers No. 9; Solar Energy No. 12; Lighting No. 15. *Ozone Plant for Swimming Pool Water Treatment; An Approach to Low-cost Sports Halls; Facilities for Squash Rackets*.

19 Some examples taken from McIntosh and Charlton (1985) p. 36, table 2.

Capital and current expenditure	£m	Inflation Rate %
1969	87	5.4
1970	101	6.4
1971	123	9.4
1974	252	16.0
1975	352	24.2
1980	722	11.9

(*Sources*: Sports Council Annual Report; Blue Books on National Income and Expenditure; W.H. Martin and S.J. Mason *Trends in Participation and Spending on Sport*)

20 P.B. 'Laddie' Lucas, CBE (1981); DSO (1943) & Bar; DFC (1942); Croix de Guerre (1945); Golf: Walker Cup (1936), (1947) and (1949); Sports Council (1971–83); MP (1950–59).
21 The Arts Council was established by Parliament, incorporated by Royal Charter (1946) and funded by the Government to foster the practice, understanding and enjoyment of the Arts in Great Britain. There is a Scottish Arts Council and a Welsh Arts Council whose Chairmen are members of the Council. It works through advisory panels, boards and committees who advise the Council.
22 Hansard, House of Commons, 9 July 1984, col. 744. Debate 'Sport and Recreation'. The Minister for Sport (Neil Macfarlane)

> The Government have the Sports Council as their agency to fulfil many objectives ... As my Department's agency I ask the Council to undertake tasks or policies. For example, my initiatives to seek more community use ... are being carried out by the Sports Council. At my request it carried out an investigation into the losses of recreational grounds.

Later:

> I asked the Sports Council to look at the organization of athletics.

The Times (April 1985)

> I believe there should be an enquiry into the terms of reference of the Sports Council's Charter and the present involvement of the Department of Environment and its Minister for Sport (Macfarlane). All the indications suggest that it is the Government's intention politically to manipulate sport ... (David Miller, Chief Sports Correspondent).

Later (May 1985):
On the appointment of John Smith as Chairman of the Sports Council.

> Having been appointed by Neil Macfarlane, the Minister for Sport, how likely is it that the new Council Chairman will resist some of the redirection being imposed ... There must be a suspicion ... that the nature of the appointment is specifically to make it less likely that this is possible; that the role of the Minister and the DOE in the Council's affairs will increase rather than diminish. (David Miller, Chief Sports Correspondent)

Section III

Years of Decision 1970–1980

Chapter 5

Implementing the Manifesto

In the run-up to the June 1970 General Election firm positions concerning the status and role of the Sports Council were adopted by the interested parties and the vested interests. It was quite clear to those close to matters that the role and status of the Sports Council, and indeed the role of the Minister of Sport, rested on the outcome of the General Election. The Labour Party's view was status quo whilst the Conservative Party was committed to 'make the Sports Council an independent body and make it responsible for the grant-aiding functions at present exercised by the Government.'[1] It is interesting to recall that those who proposed this latter view saw its implementation by statute for as yet no public mention had been made of bringing this about by Royal Charter.

The ambiguous role of Walter Winterbottom, both the Director of the Sports Council and General Secretary of the CCPR, was highlighted as never before, but this he handled adroitly serving both masters with commendable zeal and at the same time nudging matters towards the logical end that would result in an executive Sports Council being formed in lieu of the existent advisory body. In the autumn of 1969 Winterbottom had prepared and circulated a paper to the Sports Council, the Chairmen and Secretaries of the Regional Sports Councils and the Executive Committee of the CCPR, entitled *The Sports Council and its Future*.[2] In this constructive and far-sighted paper a fair balance was struck, but it was nevertheless clear which way the author was thinking. Comments and observations were sought from all to whom it was addressed. The CCPR Executive Committee endorsed the not surprising opinion of its General Purposes and Finance Committee which favoured the current arrangements, albeit with a proposal aimed at strengthening the somewhat tenuous links at national level which the CCPR had with the Sports Council. It should be emphasized that this was not a unanimous view, as there were those who continued to support the 'Wolfenden line' favouring an executive Sports Council which would absorb the current functions of the CCPR.

In March 1970 Denis Howell, the Minister for Sport, convened a high level meeting at Lilleshall National Sports Centre to which he invited Members of the Sports Council, Chairmen, Vice-Chairmen, and Secretaries of Regional Sports Councils and members of the Sports Councils for Scotland and Wales, to consider the way forward.[3] Obviously, and quite understandably, the Minister was consulting as to the future on the assumption that the forthcoming General Election would result in a further Labour Government. This was typical of Denis Howell, discussing and consulting with those in the field, confident that he had the respect and confidence of those he consulted; a master politician and a minister of great integrity and vision. This two-day meeting was a no-holds barred affair and views as to the consensus opinion that emerged have differed over the years. There certainly was unanimity of view that the arrangements and organizations of the preceding five years had been excellent, and it was agreed much progress had been made. From the point of view of the Regional Sports Councils the existing set-up needed little if any change, but nationally the argument of 'advisory' versus 'executive' waxed loud and long. Howell's view that an advisory national Sports Council was best because it was enmeshed into the machinery of government was persuasive. He saw the CCPR as being responsible for servicing both the Sports Council and Regional Sports Councils as now, assisting the governing bodies of sport nationally and locally, and generally coordinating the views of sport at national level through some type of 'Sports Parliament'.[4]

A strong argument mounted by some who saw the way forward through an executive Sports Council at 'arm's length' from the Government rested on the position of the Minister for Sport. It was agreed by this side of the debate that with Denis Howell as the Minister the present set-up would almost certainly be all right, but Howell would not always be the Minister and therefore the Sports Council should be apart from the Government to pre-empt any problems that might arise if a weak Minister were to be appointed, or one who knew little about sport. Others believed that irrespective of who was Minister for Sport the Sports Council should be an independent executive body funded by the Government through Parliament. On balance the majority at the meeting favoured the status quo although no vote was taken, and indeed a vote would have been inappropriate as this was purely a part of the consultative process. With hindsight it is too simplistic and quite unjust to condemn the 'status quo' approach of the CCPR as reactionary and lacking in vision. Many of those who did not wish to see the establishment of an executive Sports Council were the same visionaries who had helped create and develop the CCPR, but they were now fearful of governmental involvement in what was essentially a voluntary sports movement in Britain. Those who favoured the 'Wolfenden' changes believed that the right role for government could be found in any new structure and in any case they wished to see a positive, supportive governmental involvement. It is ironic looking back to see that whilst the appropriate role for the Government was established by the 1972 Royal

Charter, which worked admirably under the successive Chairmanship of Sir Roger Bannister (1972–1974), Sir Robin Brook[5] (1974–1978), and initially under Dick Jeeps[6] (1978–1985) the Charter began to be compromised. From around 1981 onwards the independence of the Sports Council, following the sacking of Hector Monro,[7] an admirable Minister for Sport, was in jeopardy and remains so today. At that point party politics began to surface under a Minister Neil Macfarlane,[8] who increasingly wished to control sports affairs, either directly or through the Sports Council where weak leadership failed to stand up to the pressure and ceded power and influence point by point. His view was made quite clear after he had left office: 'The truth is', said Macfarlane in the preface to his book *Sport and Politics, a World Divided* published in 1986, 'that sport has become a political football with international tensions and disputes having their repercussions on international sport'.

With a Conservative victory in the General Election of June 1970 sport lost its first true Minister for Sport, Denis Howell, and Eldon Griffiths,[9] somewhat surprisingly, was appointed to take on this role in his position as a Joint Parliamentary Under-Secretary of State at the then Ministry of Housing and Local Government. Charles Morrison[10] had for some years 'shadowed' Denis Howell and had gained wide respect for his knowledge and interest.[11] It had been assumed that with a Conservative victory he would succeed but this was not to be the case either then or in the future.

Sport said goodbye to Denis Howell with great feelings of affection. He had served in his post from October 1964 and the continuity by someone versed and steeped in sport had ensured that dramatic progress had been made in virtually every field of endeavour. Politics, in the party sense, had not affected decisions or policies and he was genuinely liked and respected by those who carried other political labels.

No account of party politics had been taken in membership of the Sports Council nor in appointments of Chairmen of Regional Sports Councils. Those invited to serve were prepared to do so for their love of sport and their belief in the aims and objectives that were being set. This state of affairs continued largely under Griffiths and Monro in a bi-partisan approach to sporting issues. However, by way of contrast during the time Macfarlane was Minister for Sport matters descended from the pinnacle of idealism and service to sport that had set the tone in those early years. Now the political caucus ruled as those with little knowledge of sport, its ethos and ideals, schemed to emasculate the Sports Council and bring it increasingly to be a tool and instrument of government.

If public funds are used to finance sporting activities, isn't it proper that politicians should make political decisions affecting these

Footnote: See Howell, D. *Made in Birmingham*, Part 2, for his perspective on sport and politics.

funds? After all they are accountable. (Macfarlane, 1986, preface, lines 29–31)

No thoughts of this kind were in the mind of Eldon Griffiths when he chaired his first meeting of the still advisory Sports Council on the eve of the Commonwealth Games in Edinburgh. Here on 15 July 1970, in his introductory address to the Council, he made it quite clear that this was

> not the proper time to speculate on what form the relationship between the CCPR and the Sports Council might in the future take. We are not going to hurry. We are not going to make changes for the sake of making changes — or simply to create an impression of activity. Whatever decision we reach will be taken against a background of the fullest consultation with all interested parties. (Evans, 1974, p. 217)

With this statement to ponder upon and with the knowledge that everything pointed to an executive, independent Sports Council, the members of the Council, having welcomed the Minister as their new Chairman, adjourned to enjoy the superbly organized Commonwealth Games taking place for the first time in Scotland.[12]

During the autumn and winter of 1970 and early 1971 Eldon Griffiths made it his business to get to know the sport scene in Britain, not having had the advantage of 'shadowing' sport in opposition. He visited every Regional Sports Council and assiduously continued to chair meetings of the Sports Council whilst consulting as promised with bodies and individuals both publicly and privately.[13] Sir Stanley Rous,[14] the distinguished Chairman of the CCPR and President of FIFA, conducted negotiations on and off the record on behalf of the CCPR and its staff with great diplomacy and vision. Whilst the final outcome was not in question, as the new administration was committed to an independent Council, the means of achieving this status were very much open to debate. Some members of the CCPR Executive were concerned that if the CCPR accepted a total merger with the Sports Council the position of the forum of national governing bodies of sport and recreation would be unclear. The sports bodies made it known that they would seek some form of advisory or consultative status with any Sports Council that absorbed the CCPR, otherwise they could see that their power and influence would be diminished. (Evans, 1974)

In March 1971 a meeting of national governing bodies of sport, presided over by Robin Struthers of the Hockey Association, agreed that the Sports Council should become a statutory organization but continue to be advisory; an ambiguous declaration indeed, particularly as the meeting thought the CCPR should have closer links with this 'executive-advisory' Sports Council by direct representation on the Council and through the services of its staff. This opinion echoed almost word for word the view of the Executive Committee of the CCPR who, in a letter to the Minister on 1 April 1971, offered the same suggestion coupled with two alternatives; should the Government decide to go ahead and establish an executive Sports Council the CCPR's current functions could be integrated with such a Council, or the CCPR could continue to service both the new Sports Council and the Regional Sports Councils whilst retaining its broad service-to-sport role (CCPR records). Whilst it is not formally on the record what must have been clear to Eldon Griffiths was that sport, not for the first time, was divided as to the way forward and therefore in such a circumstance consensus was a forlorn hope. Accordingly on 10 June 1971 the Minister for Sport, in a written Parliamentary answer to a question in the House of Commons, announced the Government's decision on the future structure of sport in Britain (Hansard, vol. 818, cols. 365–7). Whilst not stopping the debate this statement resolved the position that had been under discussion since the Conservative Government was elected. For the Wolfenden supporters this was final victory; it had taken eleven years to achieve it, but now it was at hand. The Parliamentary answer that brought this about was as follows:

The Government has decided to seek from Her Majesty the Queen a Royal Charter for the establishment of an Independent Sports Council with executive powers. Her Majesty will also be asked to approve the grant of Royal Charters to new Independent Sports Councils for Scotland and Wales which will replace the existing advisory bodies. This decision has been taken after careful consideration of all the factors and representations made,

It is the Government's intention to foster the development of sport in all its aspects, to stimulate the provision of more and better facilities, and to ensure that these, and those which already exist, shall be used to their fullest capacity. The Sports Council has a leading part to play in this; but it is not enough for the Sports Council merely to advise. Accordingly the government has decided to enhance the Council's status, give it independence and extend its role, so that it may be enabled to take positive action to further this policy.

The members of the Sports Council, which will include Scottish and Welsh representatives, will be appointed by my Rt. Hon. Friend the Secretary of State in consultation with the Secretaries of State for Scotland and Wales. I am pleased to be able to announce that Dr. Roger Bannister has accepted my Rt. Hon. Friend's invitation to become Chairman on a part-time basis.

Exchequer aid will be given to the new Sports Council to carry out its tasks and help to meet the growing needs of sport. Parliament will be asked to provide additional funds for this purpose. The new Council's functions will include the provision of appropriate grants for sporting organizations, activities and projects; assistance to British representative teams competing in international sports activities and the handling of links with international and foreign sporting bodies; the provision and management of national sports centres; and the forging of closer sporting links with and among local authorities, the armed services, private enterprise and the large spectator sports.

The new Scottish and Welsh Sports Councils, whose members will be appointed by the respective Secretaries of State, will be responsible for sports matters in Scotland and Wales, including the administration of grant aid.

The new Sports Councils will have discretionary powers to make grants to local authority sports projects of a specialist nature or of wider than local significance.

Direct grant aid from Government sources for the capital provision of purely local club facilities will in general be discontinued, but the funds now used for this purpose will continue to be available to Sports Councils, who will have discretion to make such local grants in special circumstances.

It is intended to retain the nine regional Sports Councils in England with certain extensions of their functions. The new structure will also include arrangements for governing bodies and other national sports and recreational organizations, as a group to advise the Sports Council and to be represented on its membership.

Detailed arrangements will take some time to complete, but I hope that the new Sports Councils will become operative before the end of the year.

I should like to pay tribute to the valuable work the present Sports Council has done in the six years of its existence. On behalf of my Rt. Hon. Friends the Secretaries of State for Scotland and Wales, I would like also to pay tribute to the work of the existing Advisory Sports Councils for these countries.

I shall be inviting the CCPR, which has done such good work for many years, to join in setting up a working party to consider its place, and the role of its staff, in the new arrangements.

At the same time Eldon Griffiths sent a personal letter to each of the Chairmen of the nine Regional Sports Councils in England telling them what he proposed to do and expressing the hope that these Councils would assume wider responsibilities (see Appendix 7). No mention was made of Northern Ireland in the Minister's statement. It was to be early 1974 before the Northern Ireland Sports Council was established under the Chairmanship of Donald Shearer.

The die was cast; what remained to be completed was the agreement on how to bring this about. Although the CCPR was a grant-aided body it was a voluntary organization and therefore not subject to Ministerial decision.

The Minister now had to persuade the CCPR to wind up its affairs and merge its staff and assets, which included the National Sports Centres, with the Sports Council, at this stage a shell. The Sports Council needed the staff of the CCPR to carry out its work and in any case the staff were currently running the Regional Sports Councils. Conversely, although never stated in tones louder than a whisper, it was clear the Government would not fund its new Sports Council and continue to fund the CCPR with which it sought a merger. It was left therefore for the CCPR to accept the offer of the Minister, amalgamate with the Sports Council and agree to transfer staff and assets. Of real concern, however, was the fact that in winding-up the CCPR the consultative forum of national governing bodies would be lost. Such a position gave great concern to the CCPR and the national federations of sport; both argued in the months ahead that some consideration should be given to the retention of a national forum in the new arrangements.

On 9 July 1971 the CCPR, through its Executive Committee, agreed to go into voluntary liquidation but argued that an independent body should be established representative of the national governing bodies (see CCPR Executive Committee meeting minute). Earlier at a meeting of sports bodies Eldon Griffiths had suggested that some type of standing conference of governing bodies could be established to stand alongside the Sports Council, very much like the Regional Standing Conferences that had been set up alongside the Regional Sports Councils. Clearly drawing on this experience the Minister suggested that such a national forum would be independent, would elect its own officers and generally be responsible for its own affairs as a voluntary organization. Additionally it would have the right to nominate members for consideration by the Minister for places on the Sports Council.

Matters were proceeding smoothly until, at the Annual General Meeting of the CCPR in November 1971, the President, HRH Prince Philip, dropped a bombshell by declaring that he personally did not like the proposal that the CCPR should be wound up but he agreed to accept the decision of the AGM. This was the first formal statement by Prince Philip showing himself opposed in principle to involvement by the Government in sport in the way proposed, and it is a theme he has returned to many times over the years.[15] There is no doubt that this powerful intervention ruffled a few feathers in Whitehall and elsewhere but as it rallied support due regard had to be taken. Accordingly the draft of the proposed Royal Charter was scrutinized with great care by Ministry officials to see that the clause establishing a 'consultative body' was sufficiently clear to satisfy, to some extent, the Royal objections. There is no shadow of doubt that the decision to retain the name CCPR for the 'consultative body' established by the Royal Charter owes its origin to Prince Philip's intervention, and proved once again that his Presidency was not purely titular. The interest and support given to sport over the years by HRH is real and substantial and he leaves no-one in any doubt as to where he stands. His views may be popular or unpopular, modern or old-fashioned depending on one's own stand-point but clear they are and based on considerable practical experience at both national and international levels.[16]

With Prince Philip again in the chair the Extraordinary General Meeting of the CCPR in April 1972 approved the transfer of the assets of the CCPR to the Sports Council subject to satisfactory arrangements being agreed for the staff and the continuance and development of the primary work of the CCPR.

In this way HM Government achieved its object of staffing the Sports Council with skilful and experienced staff and Prince Philip and his supporters retained a 'CCPR' albeit with redefined objects to take account of its new status and its relationship with the Sports Council.

The objects as agreed in 1972 were:

1   To constitute a standing forum where all national governing and representative bodies of sport and physical recreation may be represented and may collectively and through special groups where appropriate formulate and promote measures to improve and develop sport and physical recreation.
2   To support the work of the specialist bodies and to bring them together with the other interested organizations.
3   To act as a consultative body to the Sports Council. (Evans, 1974, p. 226)

It is of considerable importance to note these objects for in the forthcoming years the CCPR was to take unto itself fields of endeavour not envisaged at the outset, which as a voluntary organization it was perfectly within its rights to do but which were to create problems and accusations of overlapping of functions with those of the Sports Council.

In December 1972 Prince Philip was re-elected President of the CCPR and Robin Brook (later Sir Robin Brook and Chairman of the Sports Council) was elected Honorary Treasurer. In April 1973 Denis Howell, the former Minister for Sport, was elected Chairman, having been invited by Prince Philip to serve. For many this was a controversial election as Denis was known to be opposed to the establishment of the executive Sports Council. Seeds of dissension had been sown and a period of confrontation began; this soon brought the new CCPR into conflict with the Sports Council which has continued to a greater or lesser extent to the present day. Underlying all is the argument on the role of a State-sponsored body as opposed to a voluntary sports body.

Whilst all these administrative and organizational matters were being resolved the draft of the Royal Charter, constituting a Body Corporate under the name of 'The Sports Council', was approved by Her Majesty the Queen at Buckingham Palace on 22 December 1971, 'with the advice of Her Privy Council'.[17] The Sports Council was formally constituted by Royal

Charter on 4 February 1972 and all now became reality — Wolfenden was fulfilled.

The Royal Charter clearly established four things:

1 The independence of the Sports Council.
2 The work of the Sports Council building on that of the CCPR.
3 A body representative of the national organizations of sport.
4 The regard that has to be taken of Government policy. (See Appendix 1.)

Dr. Roger Bannister since his appointment had been announced in Parliament had wasted no time and quickly galvanized his new Sports Council into action with Sir Jack Longland as Vice-Chairman. The Council reflected the broad interests of sport and physical recreation and included a number of sportsmen and women currently involved actively in international sport and physical education such as Peter Heatly, Doug Insole, Bob Wilson, David Munrow, Peter McIntosh, Lord Rupert Nevill and Sir William Ramsay (see Appendix 8).

Whilst the national politics of sports organization were being resolved the facility development programmes in the regions were gaining momentum guided by the deficiencies pinpointed by regional appraisals (see Chapter 3 in this volume). By 1970 some 250 joint-planning schemes had been completed or were underway aided by a very considerable new school building programme. The Department of Education and Science had at last steeled itself to grasp the nettle of joint provision. There were many ideological hurdles that had to be cleared before the publication of DES Circular 2/70 *The Chance to Share* could see the light of day but when it did it made a considerable impact. Clearly and with precision this Circular spelled out the advantages and disadvantages of joint-provision but set out forthrightly the possibilities that existed to provide good facilities economically.[18]

In the interim period between the arrival of Eldon Griffiths as Minister for Sport and Chairman of the advisory Sports Council, and the assumption of office by Roger Bannister as Chairman of the executive body, work on the national statement of need for facilities was concluded under the draft title *Capital Investment 1971–1981 on Facilities for Sport and Recreation*.[19] The paper was considered at a meeting of the Sports Council on 12 October 1970, when the Minister stated that

> In the present period of stringency, with the declared intention of the government to cut public expenditure, he, being Minister with special responsibility for sport, could not, as Chairman of the Sports Council, put his name to such a document. (Sports Council minutes)

This situation highlighted for many the dilemma there would always have been with the Minister as Chairman of the Sports Council — the

Council wishing to develop one course of action involving public expenditure, and the Minister not able to support the Council of which he is the Chairman because Government policy is otherwise inclined.

This was a dilemma from the outset in 1965 but almost without exception matters were resolved amicably in the times of Howell and Griffiths. In the 'reign' of Macfarlane, despite the fact that he was not the Chairman, he attempted to control the Sports Council in a way not envisaged, nor permitted by the Royal Charter, and he did this either through directions to the Chairman, through civil servants who made the Minister's views known very specifically at meetings, or by place-men serving on the Council itself.

The Governmental influence pervaded virtually every financial and social policy decision during Macfarlane's period in office and whilst this was resisted on some occasions, overall the Sports Council acquiesced. In reality the Minister for Sport has little or no locus with policy, except in the rare instances that might be invoked under paragraph 3 of the Royal Charter where the 'Council in the exercise of its functions shall have regard to any general statements on the policy of our government' (see Appendix 1 for full text); this seemed to be a detail that could be conveniently overlooked as was made quite clear when Macfarlane stated:

> ... there are no terms of reference for a minister with responsibility for sport, and, indeed there are no legislative guidelines. (Macfarlane, 1986, pp. 64–5)

At a special meeting of the advisory Sports Council on 25 November 1970, a mere six weeks after the meeting when the Minister spoke of his problem in supporting a considerable financial demand, Peter McIntosh pointed out that at the previous meeting the Chairman (Griffiths) had prevented free discussion on the 'Capital Investment' draft report and went on to say that this would be less likely under an independent Chairman. This point the Minister agreed with wholeheartedly emphasizing that this underlined the need to have the Sports Council at arms length from government. By 16 December the Minister was of the opinion that this report, now entitled 'Provision for Sport' was good and useful and he saw no reason why it should not be published and indeed was prepared to write a suitable Foreword.[20]

May 1972 saw the first factual assessment of need for indoor swimming pools, indoor sports centres and golf courses ever made in Britain. The 'shopping list' for the nation had been drawn up and required a ten-year programme of development. It represented the sum of the regional appraisals of facilities and, most importantly, it put a price to the list of needs. Inflation was soon to make a nonsense of stated costs, but the scale of national public investment was clear in every way. The Sports Council asked for the following for England and Wales:

1 *Swimming pools* — 447 at a total cost of £71.940m.[21]
   i.e. (a)   25m by 8.5m – 136
         (b)   25m by 12.5m – 166
         (c)   25m by 12.5m + learner pool – 122
         (d)   33⅓m by 12.5m – 16
         (e)   33⅓m by 12.5 + learner pool – 7
2 *Indoor sports centres* — 815 at a total cost of £148.410m.[22]
3 *Golf courses* — 485 18-hole courses, exclusive of land cost, £43.650m.[23]

In an effort to publicize this demand a simple but hugely effective pamphlet entitled *Sport in the Seventies — Making Good the Deficiencies*[24] was widely circulated. Despite cynicism in some quarters and incredulity in others the media generally gave a wide airing to this campaign. It was clear that the stated need and the arguments for additional provision won enormous sympathy and political support at municipal level where involvement in Regional Sports Councils and facility appraisals had already indicated growing support.[25]

A year later in 1973 volume II of *Provision for Sport* dealing with the need for specialist facilities to encourage high-level performance was published by the Sports Council. This publication provided a helpful guideline but it was not so well conceived as volume I and did not make anywhere near the same impact. It lacked a clear rationale and scientific base and understandably did not appeal to local authorities in the same way as did the demand for swimming pools and sports centres. Nevertheless, over the years it enabled much to be provided in association with community recreational facilities.[26]

On 4 February 1972, the Sports Council was formally established and constituted by its Royal Charter and a new era for British sport dawned under the distinguished leadership of Roger Bannister. At the same time separate Sports Councils for Scotland and Wales were set up likewise by Royal Charters on 21 January 1972, and 4 February 1972, respectively. The Sports Council was given overall responsibility for British affairs, hence the membership by the Chairmen and vice-Chairmen of the Welsh and Scottish bodies, whilst the Sports Councils for Wales and Scotland were responsible for their own national domestic matters. The role of Northern Ireland had at this stage still to be resolved but they were brought into the 'family' as observers from the outset.[27]

Athletes, administrators, the sporting public and the media were now looking to the summer of 1972 and the Olympic Games at Munich, some with the Berlin Games of 1936, the Nazi propaganda Games, still in mind. None envisaged in their wildest nightmares the horror and tragedy that was to strike in Munich that plunged the Olympic Games into the centre of world politics, protest and terrorism (see Killanin, 1983, Chapter IX).

The Executive Sports Council

Sport in Britain in 1972 was on the threshold of a further leap forward with organizational issues that had been debated for so long finally resolved. Sport had the best of both worlds; it remained free of state control but had the benefits of increased state financial involvement assured through an independent Sports Council. The peculiar status of a body established by Royal Charter is such that only by Statute, other than the Privy Council, can it be removed. Therefore constitutionally it is not a prey to political mood and fashion except for the all-important annual vote of financial resources from Parliament which, in theory, can starve it of money. Any change to the Royal Charter has to be agreed by the Sports Council which then has to petition the Privy Council.

Basically, therefore, the Sports Council is virtually impregnable so long as the Chairman, members and senior officers fight to withstand assaults on its independence and its right to make all decisions, large and small subject only to the clause to 'have regard to any general statements on the policy of our Government (see Appendix 1, paragraph 3). The Council does not have to agree with the Government of the day, it does not have to pursue its policies but it does have to take notice of them. It is on this rock that the independence of sport in Britain is constitutionally assured so long as those who defend the rock believe in the cause and are strong enough to withstand the considerable pressures from Government and Whitehall.

Although the 1972 Summer Olympic Games in Munich were upon Britain, the effective policies that had gone before were sufficient to ensure that those who were worthy of selection to represent their country had adequate financial backing to take part. The British Olympic Association organized a very successful national appeal which ensured they did not have to fall back on the Sports Council's agreement to underwrite two-thirds of the travel cost of competitors. However, a grant of £6,738 was made to assist the travelling expenses of British technical officials and provide a modest pocket-money allowance for competitors.

The Olympic Games were superbly staged, as was the pre-Olympic Sports Science Congress under the patronage of the International Council for Sport and Physical Education (ICSPE). The story of the tragedy of Munich, with the assassination for political ends of Israeli athletes and officials, marred forever the glorious festival of the Olympic Games, and singled out this major sports event as a venue for political protest in the future with the various and somewhat bizarre boycotts at Montreal (1976), Moscow (1980) and Los Angeles (1984), although, sad as these were, mercifully they did not involve loss of life.[28]

It is not the purpose of this narrative at this stage to relate in detail the events of Munich, Montreal, Moscow and Los Angeles, but rather to point to the sober fact that each event reflected the growing part international politics were beginning to play in sports affairs.

The part that Scotland and Wales played in the development of sport in Britain after 1970, where this is not under the British role of the Sports Council, will be explained subsequently as this was, and is, crucial in the context of national development. (see Chapter 10 in this volume). With Royal Charters granted to Scotland and Wales, and with legislation promised for Northern Ireland, it was important for all constituted elements in the United Kingdom to work together constructively.

The aims of the Sports Council and the Sports Councils for Scotland and Wales are largely identical and enshrined in the main object 'to develop and improve the knowledge and practice of sport and physical recreation in the interests of social welfare and the enjoyment of leisure among the public at large and to encourage the attainment of high standards' (see Appendix 1, paragraph 2[a]). However, from the outset in 1972, it was considered sensible to define more accurately and specifically aims and objectives which all would work towards. Accordingly the three Sports Councils made known their agreed statement of aims which were henceforth to guide their policies, actions and inter-Sports Council deliberations. These were, and still are:

1   To promote general understanding of the importance of sport and physical recreation in society.
2   To increase the provision of new sports facilities to serve the needs of the community.
3   To encourage wider participation in sport and physical recreation.
4   To raise standards of performance in sport and physical recreation. (Sports Council Annual Report 1972/73, page 5, paragraph 1.17)

The philosophy behind these clearly-defined aims is that sport and physical activity are contributors to the well-being of people; that they are enjoyable activities; that they are fun and pleasurable. No claim is made for specific health benefits at this stage. This basic philosophy was maintained for some years until research and evidence from a wide variety of sources began to link sport and physical recreation additionally with direct health benefits, often to be associated with attitudes to life-style, eating habits and smoking.

Funding

Inflation during the seventies and eighties has in many respects made figures virtually meaningless except in comparative adjusted scales. For its first year of operation the Sports Council was allocated £3.6m to begin its task and this low-base figure has been an albatross round its neck during the years that have followed. Apart from some windfall allocations the grant-in-aid of the Council has only marginally increased over the years, and every effort to break out of the strait-jacket of public expenditure budgeting has been largely nullified.

In percentage terms the figures look reasonably impressive, but in terms of volume annual allocations were woefully short of what was needed. At no time has the government of the day since the inception of the executive Sports Council made any serious or meaningful effort to meet the budgetary demands made upon it by the Council.

The following Table indicates the grant-in-aid for the period 1973-80 together with the inflation rate for each year:

Table 1: Grant-in-aid 1973–80

Financial year ending	Grant £m	Percentage	Inflation rate %
1973	3.6		9
1974	5.0	38.9	16
1975	6.6	32.00	24.2
1976	8.3	25.8	16.5
1977	10.2	22.9	15.9
1978	11.5	12.7	8.3
1979	15.2	32.2	13.4
1980	15.6	2.5	18.00

Source: Sports Council (1983) *The Financing of Sport in the UK*, Information Series no. 8, London, Sports Council, p. 11, table 5.1.

While these figures did represent some increase, and it would be churlish not to acknowledge the value to sport of what was made available, the lift-off that had been hoped for nationally never materialized although the ground-swell in the country for greater investment in sport and recreation was responded to by the municipal authorities in far greater measure. Starting from a larger base the expenditure by local authorities on sport and recreation in the period 1973–1980 (Table 2) was impressive and made real impact on provision of facilities and the public rate of participation:

Table 2: Local authority expenditure on sport and recreation 1973–80

Financial year ending	£m expenditure	Percentage increase
1973	191	
1974	252	31.9
1975	336	39.7
1976	365	9.4
1977	376	2.9
1978	409	16.7
1979	546	22.7
1980	682	27.3

Source: *ibid*

Although in percentage terms the growth of the local authority figures year on year was not so large as those of the Sports Council the sheer volume of expenditure, even set against inflation, was such that real progress was made despite years of cut-back, recession and retrenchment imposed by central government in the continuing effort to cut public expenditure. Provision for sport and recreation was beginning to get a larger percentage slice of local public rate-fund expenditure. From 2.35 per cent in 1971/72 the volume rose to 4.07 per cent in 1975/76 falling to 3.7 per cent in 1977/78, never to fall again below this figure, and rising to marginally over 6 per cent by the end of the decade.

Sport for All

Calling for a three-fold increase in Government grant-in-aid to meet the programmes for sport development Roger Bannister, with the full backing of the Council, decided immediately to launch a *Sport for All* crusade in Britain calling on the experience already to hand in Western Europe.[29] The broad purpose of the campaign, which was ongoing, was to develop a new awareness in public authorities of the value of sport to the mass of the people of every age, colour and ability in every community throughout the land. This was to be a massive effort to change the thinking of those in positions of power and influence, and by the anticipated response from the public impose a new pressure on those who had the capability to provide. The Sports Council saw itself as the focal point for governing bodies of sport, for those statutory and private authorities and organizations already willing to provide, and for the general public. With the facility programme well underway in regions, and with the national statement of need *Provision for Sport* widely circulated and canvassed, the seeds were already sown for a vibrant *Sport for All* campaign. Accordingly in the early autumn of 1972, with the warm glow of national success in the Munich Olympic Games fresh in the mind, the campaign was launched in Britain which was to trigger off a response in the years ahead in so many ways, some of them foreseen some of them unforeseen (see McIntosh and Charlton, 1985, for a critique of progress.) This dynamic sports movement, already alive in Western Europe, was to spread rapidly around the world as it touched upon the hopes and aspirations of people everywhere; the British experience of the next few years was to play a significant and constructive part in this process.

The launching of a *Sport for All* campaign by The Sports Council in association with the Sports Councils for Scotland and for Wales in 1972 began to change the aim of official policy from satisfying wants to influencing the climate of opinion about the value of sport in society, increasing participation in sport and physical recreation and promoting sport as a desirable social concept. (*ibid*, paragraph 1:16, p. 14. See also Sports Council Annual Report 1976/77)

Notes

1 The recommendation of the Lucas/Manning Group (see Chapter 2 in this volume).

2 This was a confidential memorandum with restricted circulation. Although a personal view, it encapsulated the views of a considerable number of Sports Council members. 'The Sports Council, a Review 1966–69' in the opening chapter 'General Review' hints at the way Winterbottom was thinking. In paragraphs 20–3 the benefits of being linked with the machinery of government are described but the final sentence talks of 'further consideration of this important issue'.

3 Evans (1974) is firmly of the view that the 'majority supported the retention of the status quo', and he was present throughout. The author of this book, John Coghlan, was also present but does not believe the issue was as clear-cut as that. The Minister certainly held this view and was in the chair; he took the uncommitted with him but there was a sizeable number, probably a minority but only just, that wanted the 'Wolfenden' recommendation independence from the Government.

4 This was a term often used by Denis Howell when describing the role of the CCPR. This persisted in the slogan *The View of British Sport* used frequently by the later 'new' CCPR and is in current use today. At this meeting Howell described four main functions of the CCPR (and SCPR) if the present arrangements prevailed:

(i) to service the Sports Council and Regional Sports Councils;
(ii) to administer the National Sports Centres;
(iii) to assist the governing bodies of sport in coaching and development work;
(iv) to bring together the forum of sports bodies at national level to provide a 'voice for sport'.

5 Robin Brook, CMG, OBE, Kt (1974); Legion of Merit; Legion of Honour; Croix de Guerre; Order of Leopold; Director, Bank of England (1946–49); HM Government Director, BP, (1970–73); Sports Council (1971–78 — Chairman from 1975); Honorary Treasurer, CCPR, (1961–77); Sports Aid Foundation (1975–); Olympic Games (1936 and 1948); British Sabre Champion (1936). See also appendix 6 to this volume.

6 R.E. (Dick) Jeeps, CBE; Chairman, Sports Council (1978–85): Rugby caps — England 24; British Lions 13 (SA, 1955 and 1962; NZ, 1959); President, Rugby Football Union (1976–77). See also appendix 6 to this volume.

7 Hector Monro, MP (1964–), Kt (1981); Minister for Sport (1979–81); Scottish RFU (1958–77 — President 1976–77). See also appendix 6 to this volume.

8 Neil Macfarlane, MP (1974–), Kt (1988); Parliamentary Under-Secretary of State, Department of Education and Science (1979–81); Minister for Sport (1981–85), Department of the Environment. See also appendix 6 to this volume.

9 Eldon Griffiths, MP (1964–), Kt (1985); Minister for Sport (1970–74); Chairman, Special Olympics (UK). See also Appendix 6 in this volume.

10 Charles Morrison, MP (1964–), Kt (1988); Wiltshire County Councillor (1958–65); Chairman, South-West Regional Sports Council (1966–68).

11 As a Chairman of a Regional Sports Council he was at the heart of affairs. As 'shadow' Minister he visited regions and toured developments. Despite being a Conservative MP he was appointed to be Chairman of the SW Regional Sports Council; a not unique situation in those days before party politics began to mar the scene.

12 Edinburgh staged the Commonwealth Games for a second time in July 1986. Thirty-two Commonwealth countries boycotted the Games on account of the refusal of the British Prime Minister (Mrs. Margaret Thatcher, MP) to impose economic sanctions on South Africa on the issue of apartheid. See also chapter 13 in this volume.

13 He spoke at the AGM of the CCPR in November 1970; he met the staff a month later. He attended a meeting of forty-seven governing bodies of sport on 17 February 1971 under the Chairmanship of Robin Struthers of the Hockey Association. He met the Executive Committee of the CCPR on a number of occasions.

14 Stanley Rous, CBE, Kt (1949); Secretary, Football Association (1934–61); President, FIFA (1961–74); Chairman, CCPR (1945–73).

15 For Prince Philip's statement at AGM of CCPR November 1971 see minutes of meeting and Annual Report.

16 Prince Philip was for many years president of the International Equestrian Federation — an Olympic sport. See CCPR Annual Reports for his views on sport.

17 'At the Court of Buckingham Palace. The 22nd day of December 1971. Present, the Queen's Most Excellent Majesty in Council.
Whereas there was this day read at the Board the Draft of a Charter for constituting a Body Corporate under the name of "The Sports Council": Her Majesty, having taken the said Draft into consideration, was pleased, by and with the advice of Her Privy Council, to approve therefore, and to order, as it is hereby ordered, that the Right Honourable Reginald Maudling, one of Her Majesty's Principal Secretaries of State, do cause a Warrant to be prepared for Her Majesty's Royal Signature, for passing under the Great Seal a Charter in conformity with the said Draft, which is herewith annexed.'

W.E. Agnew

18 This Circular was intended to accelerate development not only in provision for sport but also for music, craft and drama. This gave clear notice of intention to cater on a broad front for leisure needs within the framework of cooperation between two or more authorities or between Committees in single authorities.

19 A paper proposed by the Facilities Committee of the Sports Council under the Chairmanship of Peter McIntosh.

20 Sports Council (1972) 'Provision for Sport — Indoor Swimming Pools: Indoor Sports Centres; Golf Courses', HMSO.

21 *ibid*, see table 3, p. 4.

22 *ibid*, see paragraph 4.16, p. 3.

23 *ibid*, paragraph 5.15, p. 10.

24 The pamphlet was circulated in large numbers to local authorities, sports bodies, Regional Sports Councils and the media. The national requirements for swimming pools, indoor sports centres, golf courses, national and special regional facilities, sports grounds, minor projects, countryside and water facilities were stated. Commercial and industrial provision featured as did joint provision schemes.

25 The Planning Officers of the Counties and County Boroughs constituted the Technical Panels of the Regional Sports Councils and it was they who quantified

the need and proposed the regional strategies for development of new facilities. This involvement tied in the local authorities.

26 The case was argued and demonstrated for specialist provision. Ice and roller-skating rinks, diving pools, indoor athletic tracks, gliding and parachuting centres, regional sailing and riding centres were some of the facilities described and quantified at a price of £22.229m at 1970 prices.

27 The 'troubles' in Northern Ireland delayed legislation although by a draft Order-in-Council the intention to set up an Executive Sports Council in Northern Ireland was declared. In the meantime J.C. Lapsley, Vice-Chairman of the Youth and Sports Council for Northern Ireland and Chairman of its Committee for Sport, attended Sports Council meetings as an observer.

28 See: Killanin (1983); chapter 13 in this volume, section on The Olympic Games — Moscow (1980) and Los Angeles (1984), boycotts — *Montreal* — the 'black' boycott because of a rugby tour by New Zealand to South Africa; *Moscow* — by many 'Western' countries led by USA ostensibly because of the invasion of Afghanistan in December 1979 by the USSR; *Los Angeles* — by many 'Socialist' countries ostensibly because of security, but by common consent as tit for tat for 1980.

29 See Council of Europe Resolution (76) 41 of the Committee of Ministers, 'Principles for a policy for Sport for All' defined by the Conference of European Ministers for Sport, Brussels (1975) published by the Council of Europe in 1977. In particular see p. 3, 'Background and comments' paragraph I. 'Sport for All was adopted in 1966 as the major long-term objective for the sports programme of the Council of Europe'.

In 1968 an international planning group was set up 'to define the content of the idea of sport for all'. The Council of Europe 'European Sport for All Charter' was adopted in 1976.

Chapter 6

The Growth of Leisure Time and Facilities for Sport and Recreation

To understand why there was an 'explosion' in the growth of leisure time and facilities for sport and recreation in the 1970s it is important to have some knowledge of the fundamental nature and historical growth of leisure time in this country.[1] The part sport as a leisure time activity has played in occupying for many the increasing time at their disposal is the story, in many respects, of the growth of sport in British society since the Industrial Revolution.

For the Puritan in days past leisure time was sinful and even today references are made to such phrases as 'the Protestant work ethic', or 'the Devil finds work for idle hands to do'. A common private view in the nineteenth century which has carried over to some extent into the twentieth century, was that if the toiling masses toiled then they would have little time for banding together when, in addition to taking part in recreational activities, they might get round to discussing their lot in life which could prove detrimental to the status quo, not to say the enormous wealth such toil was producing for the few. Against this background therefore participation in formal sport at the turn of the century was generally low although some sports such as football, rugby, swimming, rowing and lawn tennis had already organized themselves into national governing bodies for these activities (see Chapter 1 in this volume). Facilities for sport of an organized nature were scarce and people worked hard physically six days a week which meant when Sunday arrived it was in every respect required as a true day of rest. Between the two World Wars of 1914–18 and 1939–45 efforts by the Trade Union movement resulted in a general standard five-and-a half day week,[2] with the dream of a five day, forty hour week as a goal; a goal not achieved until post-1945.

Class played a major part in the structure and evolution of sport in Britain, and many sports developed as activities for what were known as the 'leisured classes'. Lawn tennis, squash, skiing, badminton and rowing were very much class-orientated in the first part of the twentieth century, as was rugby in England, but not in Wales, and golf in England but not in Scotland. Many sports were upper-class or middle-class orientated because they not only took their origins from the public schools and the ancient universities of Oxford and Cambridge, but also because these classes represented strata of society with more leisure time at their disposal and more money to spend on such activities.

By 1900 a growing desire to make provision for purposeful use of increased leisure time had emerged and was reflected in the social pattern characteristic of the early twentieth century. Concern for health, which for some was linked to morality, was a spur and a range of public facilities including public swimming baths and parks began to proliferate. Swimming baths were also associated with provision for washing and bathing as many houses lacked such facilities, whilst parks provided urban amenities for walking, for viewing ornamental flower-beds and for concerts in bandstands but certainly not for the playing of team games.

The records show that by 1938 the average hours worked per week were forty-six-and-a-half compared with fifty-four hours in 1900.[3] In 1925 one-and-a-half million workers enjoyed annual holidays with pay, but this had risen to over five million by 1938.[4] Immediately prior to the Second World War in 1939 the holidays with pay issue was gathering momentum due very considerably to trades union pressure based on European experience especially that of France.

Marginally before the First World War and considerably between the wars, the emergence of the middle-class and a better paid working-class with more disposable income available helped to create an increasing leisure climate. The growth of public dance-halls, the cinema with the coming of the 'talkies', and increased spectator attendances at football and cricket matches were all symptoms of this growing affluence and increased time in which to spend some of the fruits of such affluence.[5] The inter-war years witnessed a move by a large section of the urban population to use the countryside for recreation in their new-found leisure time, and this was assisted by cheap and frequent public transport. The technical development of the motor car rapidly brought car ownership to a wider section of society, with the arrival in the late thirties of the £100 Ford saloon. Large sections of the population were therefore mobile and many were either hiking, rambling or cycling; relevant associations and clubs experienced great upsurges in interest. By 1938 the Cycling Touring Club (CTC) together with the National Cycling Union (NCU) boasted a 60,000 membership spread over 3500 clubs.[6] The Youth Hostel Association (YHA), still strong today, started in 1929 and within three years had recruited 50,000 members who enjoyed the facilities of 130 hostels.[7]

The outdoor activities boom of the thirties, to be repeated in the fifties and sixties, had some bizarre overtones. On the one hand some critics saw in this echoes of the *Strength Through Joy* campaign in Nazi Germany post 1933, whilst others manifested the movement in the cult of nudism.[8]

Figures for participation rates in sport are virtually non-existent until the 1960s, which makes historical comparisons notoriously unreliable. However there are broad indicators available by looking at cricket, tennis, golf and football clubs that started up in the twenties and thirties using facilities of their own or the increasing number of pitches, tennis courts and bowling greens being made available by municipal authorities in recreation grounds and public parks.[9] The increase in family holidays to the seaside witnessed the growth of popular resorts such as Blackpool, Margate, Weston-Super-mare, Bournemouth and Scarborough, and whilst the sea and sand were the first priorities outdoor swimming pools, often known as lidos, boating lakes, public tennis courts, often with holiday tournaments, bowling greens both flat and crown, and putting greens, were prime attractions for the visitor.[10] For the upper and middle classes, and the wealthy, Wimbledon, Henley and Cowes formed part of the season, bastions of privilege with social overtones reflecting the current social structure of tennis, rowing and yachting, none of which were as yet available to any considerable extent to the artisan or the working class.[11] Whilst the working class, particularly in Scotland and the North of England, continued to produce the great footballers of the era such as Tommy Lawton and Alex James, it needed the son of a Labour MP, Fred Perry, to shake the foundations of lawn tennis by winning the Wimbledon Singles Championship three times in succession in the thirties to show that this was a game that had universal appeal.[12] Throughout sport the strict demarcation lines of amateurism and professionalism were drawn and membership of certain sports clubs was only open to those who came from particular professions and backgrounds (see Chapter 7)[13]

Paradoxically the thirties saw the two extremes, on the one hand mass unemployment for the working class giving unwanted leisure to many, and on the other hand the rise of consumerism, car ownership, house-building and increased personal wealth to the majority of the middle and upper classes for them to enjoy the increased leisure time and facilities for recreation, including sport, that this provided. Throughout the massive social upheaval that had taken place since the latter part of the nineteenth century, culminating in the affluent years of the late thirties bringing hitherto unimagined leisure time to so many people, central government did virtually nothing by way of policy or guidance, leaving it to local government to provide a range of public recreational facilities and the voluntary sports movement to act for itself as it thought fit. The National Fitness Campaign, started by the Government in 1937,[14] was largely disastrous and cut sharply across the early work of the Central Council of Recreative Physical Training, the forerunner of the CCPR, established in 1935.

The Physical Training and Recreation Act of 1937 acknowledged the need to improve the opportunities for ordinary people to take part in sport and was enlightened action by Parliament which has stood the test of time to this day (see Appendix 9 for a summary of the main points in the Act). These were meagre offerings to the leisure boom that was underway, all brought abruptly to a halt on September 3, 1939 with the outbreak of the Second World War.

There was very little leisure time available to people in Britain during the 1939–45 war as the country struggled for survival as it stood alone, and then for victory in association with its allies. The remainder of the forties, and to some considerable extent the fifties, is largely uncharted and unrecorded in terms of leisure and participation in sport, although the national and international events, successes and failures, are well documented. The arrival of the five-day working week with its forty hours of work brought the 'week-end' phenomenon and consequently greatly enhanced opportunity for leisure activities. Immediately post-war, in austerity Britain, articles and comment relating to the reconstruction of Britain occupied much space and time in the press and on radio together with the reporting of the traditional popular sports soccer and cricket.

A great boom in pre-war activities such as the cinema, countryside recreation, ballroom dancing and soccer spectating took place as people picked up where they left off in 1939.[15] Records of club membership, club affiliations and governing bodies of sport are scant and not very accurate and it is difficult to quantify to any extent the scale and volume of the popular playing of games, including attendance at swimming pools. The evidence that is available is largely hearsay, anecdotal and by reminiscence but points to considerable participation as sports clubs, sports organizations and governing bodies began to throw off the restrictions and the deprivations imposed by the war.

It was not until the early sixties that the sociologists, researchers and academics began to study seriously the leisure phenomenon that had gained momentum throughout the century and began to expose data concerning the way people were beginning to use both their increased leisure time and the disposable income arising from virtually full employment.[16] These were the years described by Prime Minister Harold Macmillan as those in which the British public had 'never had it so good', as incomes increased considerably and hours worked decreased. More women were working than ever before and car ownership was rising rapidly. In 1962 33 per cent of households in Britain had the use of a car compared with 58 per cent by 1980, but associated with this dramatic increase was the decrease in local transport, both rail and bus.[17] Longer train journeys and a developing network of competitive coach services, cheaper weekend journeys and a greater range of travel options, allied to more casual short holidays, added a new dimension to leisure opportunities away from the home and place of work. By the early eighties four weeks annual holiday was the norm plus increased office and factory closing over the Christmas and New Year period which for those in work presented even more leisure options. The statistics from the Henley Centre for Forecasting record that whilst the money spent on holidays, drinking and gambling was so large that the spending on sport appeared to be very modest, nevertheless figures did show that the spending on sport was projected to grow more rapidly than every other area of leisure spending save that for television, stereos, video recorders and suchlike: It was anticipated some £700m would be spent in 1985 on sport by consumers.[18]

It was Michael Dower, in a survey undertaken for the Civic Trust, published in the *Architects Journal* on 20 January 1965, who described the social change brought about by the leisure boom as the *Fourth Wave — The Challenge of Leisure*.[19] Dower, at one time a member of the Sports Council (1971–1972), wrote:

> Three great waves have broken across the face of Britain since 1800. First the sudden growth of dark industrial towns. Second the thrusting movement along far-flung railways. Third the sprawl of car-based suburbs. Now we see under the guise of a modest word, the surge of a fourth wave which could be more powerful than all the others. The modest word is leisure.

This publication had a profound effect on sport and recreation policy-makers and providers, and stimulated both action and research.[20] Whilst the oil crisis of the early seventies, and the consequent recession in the Western world, has distorted some of its projections, the underlying verities and the main thrust of Dower's fundamental argument is as true today as it was twenty-five years ago. The demand by Dower for land, water, better housing, a better deal for young people, more creative use of city parks, the establishment of permanent leisure sites and attractions, regional parks, and more imaginative plans to cater for sport and long holidays was virtually a blue-print from which those involved could derive inspiration and work to achieve. The new concept of the indoor sports centre, as exemplified by Billingham Sports Forum (opened in 1967) and Harlow Sports Centre (opened in May 1964), was described in detail for, at that time, apart from the Crystal Palace National Sports Centre (opened in May 1964), these two and one or two others were the forerunners of a brave new world that was to give indoor sport a future as yet undreamed of.

With some degree of certainty it is possible to show statistically how some sports activities developed in the sixties, although it was not until 1966 that accurate participation figures were given in sport surveys. Many national governing bodies of sport only began to assemble and formalize their membership statistics during the sixties as such data was usually required when they talked to the Sports Council about financial support to help development programmes. Likewise, until the Regional Sports Councils had carried out their regional appraisals of major facilities in the latter half of that decade, data on usage of facilities for sport were nationally unknown. Historically many sports such as golf, rugby union, hockey and squash provided the majority of their new facilities through voluntary sports clubs.

Other sports were either totally, such as swimming, or largely, such as athletics, or mainly, such as football, cricket and to some extent tennis, dependent on publicly provided facilities, although tennis and cricket also had a significant number of private clubs. Badminton relied heavily on school gymnasia and church halls, whilst ice-skating, roller skating, tenpin bowling and ballroom dancing relied almost entirely on commercial provision. The growth of television and car ownership contributed to a massive decline in spectators at football and cricket grounds as choice of activity was now wider and more families took their recreation together.

The broad trends, started in the sixties, continued through the seventies and into the eighties to a remarkably consistent degree allowing for variations as new sports such as sail-boarding gained in popularity and an old established sport such as squash rackets suddenly found itself with tens of thousands of new participants using the very many new squash courts provided at public sports centres, private clubs and by commercial operators. Basketball, volleyball and badminton experienced very considerable growth in the twenty-year period 1964–1984, both in numbers and participants, and in the standards of high-level performance due to the provision of over 800 sports centres and many school sports halls from virtually a nil sports hall position. Hitherto, these sports sought their facilities in school gymnasia, which were usually far too small, YMCA halls and any other halls that could give them length, width and height.

These makeshift facilities are still used extensively today but the considerable provision of sports halls, designed to take account of the needs of these sports and others, with the right level of lighting, good floor surfaces and good equipment has given as enormous boost to sports requiring large indoor, well-lit spaces. The development of synthetic outdoor playing surfaces in the late 1970s has genuinely provided what are in effect all weather facilities which have superseded the hard shale-type porous surfaces of the late fifties and sixties. The technology in the area of artificial surfaces has developed rapidly in a fiercely competitive commercial market and the impact out of doors on sports such as hockey has been profound. Question marks still remain as to the efficiency of plastic surfaces for competitive football at the highest level.[21] The capability of taking upwards of twenty matches per week at local club level on such surfaces has ensured play in inclement weather and has made the maximum use of expensive land in inner city areas. The financial windfall that the Sports Council had late in 1982 and early 1983 (£3.75m), along with local authorities, saw an impressive range of artificial synthetic playing pitches constructed in the winter of that year which gave much needed leisure opportunity in many socially and recreationally deprived areas of Britain. Tenpin bowling had a spectacular rise in popularity in the sixties but in the early seventies the sport was attracting a mere 20 per cent of the numbers at its peak of popularity. Skateboarding had a meteoric rise in popularity in the mid-seventies only to fall away to a keen hardcore of enthusiasts within the space of three years. Women's sport expanded; hockey, netball, lacrosse, all grew in popularity.[22]

Reviewing the field of participation in sport as a leisure pursuit from the evidence available from 1945 until 1980 it is possible to conclude with a fair degree of accuracy that bowls membership rose from about 28,000 to a little over 100,000, whilst the Football Association reports that in the same period the number of football clubs rose from around 12,000 to 40,000, but the number of teams in each club is unknown. The Rugby Football Union believes the number of clubs playing their code of football doubled in this period of thirty-five years from 10,000 to 20,000 clubs but again the number of teams per club is not always known; considerable anecdotal and hearsay evidence does show that the growth in teams per club was very considerable indeed and involved youth and colts teams to take account of the growth of rugby in schools.

The boom in outdoor activities, started before the 1939–45 was (see Chapter 2), has continued to show an increase ever since. Whilst the trend towards growth was already endemic in society the widening of physical education syllabuses in schools in the fifties and sixties to include outdoor activities and expeditions, together with an increase in field and nature studies, and the willingness by local education authorities to purchase, equip and run mountain and field activity centres gave outdoor countryside activities an enormous boost.[23]

An exception to this record of growth is cycling, the boom activity of the thirties, for with greater car ownership the dangers on the roads were increased and the number of cyclists declined, Happily as the eighties arrived the popularity of cycling began to rise again assisted to some extent by an increasing provision of cycling pistes, the cross country sport of cyclo-cross, the health awareness propaganda and the deterrent effect of the price of petrol for motor cars.

In the 1970s the Chairmen of the principal leisure-orientated agencies came together in common purpose to act with some degree of coordination in the main thrusts that they deemed necessary in the leisure policy field. The Chairmen's Policy Group was composed of the Chairmen of the Tourist Boards, the Countryside Commissions, the Sports Councils of the UK, the Nature Conservancy Council, the Forestry Commission, the British Waterways Board and the Waterspace Amenity Commission. The three local authority associations, the Association of District Councils (ADC), the Association of Metropolitan Authorities (AMA), and the Association of County Councils (ACC) were also members. This membership comprised a formidable forum of opinion and expertise.

A discussion paper prepared by this policy group in 1983 *Leisure Policy for the Future*, published by the Sports Council, defined leisure as 'that time which is not committed to paid work, homework, sleeping and personal maintenance'. This paper pointed out that, in the view of the Chairmen of the principal agencies that had a stake in the broad recreation spectrum, there were four main factors that caused the rapid growth of leisure time:

(i)   the reduction in time spent at work due to more and longer holidays, and a continuing move towards a shorter working week;

(ii) longer periods of retirement due to a national movement towards earlier retirement associated with improving pension arrangements, and the fact people are today living longer than hitherto;

(iii) the advent of greater automation in the home which results in less time needed to be spent on household chores;

(iv) the sad state of affairs whereby over three million working people were unemployed giving them unwanted leisure time.

This view was not seriously challenged, coming as it did from an impeccable source and it summarized the events that had taken place in the 1970s that had led to a greater growth of leisure time.

Perhaps the most important conclusion arising from the high level conference of leisure policy-makers arranged by the Chairmen's Policy Group in 1983 was that the assumptions of the mid-sixties that leisure demand would continue to grow rapidly until the year 2000 had changed since 1973. Demand depends on the state of the British economy and the balance between activities is influenced by social change and technical developments. The growth of leisure in Britain was ever thus, and during the last century has reflected the social and economic advances made in society. An affluent society, even one perhaps not so affluent in relative terms as hitherto, will decide for itself how it uses its resources. There is a body of opinion that believes that once workers have achieved the standard of living they seek, with sufficient disposable income to do and buy what they need, some tend to opt for greater leisure time in preference to even greater income; the quality of life is becoming for many more important in industrialized societies than hitherto and more people are asking the question as to why they work. It therefore follows that once they believe they have enough to meet their needs then extra work is to be avoided. Such reasoning has no merit whatsoever for the ambitious, the workaholic, the highly motivated and the deeply absorbed, but for the mass of workers the realization has dawned that life has more to it than work.

The increasing involvement by central Government in leisure-related issues either directly or through the specialized agencies represented on the Policy Group has ensured that the needs for people's leisure are today largely understood. The Sports Council's admirable strategy for the eighties *Sport in the Community — The Next Ten Years* (1982), the product largely of Professor Alan Patmore, who so admirably chaired the Sports Council's Policy Planning Group, and the Council's Principal Research Officer, the very able Michael Collins, painted the picture for sport as it was seen in

1982 and backed its argument with logic and statistics. The decade of the seventies was summed up thus: —

> For sport in Britain the 1970s were years of remarkable achievement; achievement in facility provision, in the growth of playing sport indoors, and in challenging for world supremacy in several sports. (*ibid*, Foreword, p. 7)

and it wisely advised that:

> Sport must be understood and planned for against wider changes in society. (*ibid*, Summary, p. 2)

The leisure industry in Britain is today huge and growing and involves in excess of 8 per cent of the actual work force. The increasing demand is being met by public authorities, voluntary organizations, commercial enterprise and by people themselves. Leisure provision has become accepted as a major element of social policy and is talked and written about in the press, radio and on television. It features in the financial sections of the newspapers as leisure is business and many public and private companies are in that business. The emphasis is now very much on identifying and meeting the needs of people as defined by them and not simply supplying more of what was provided before.

Sport and physical recreation have made a significant contribution to the needs of society, across a fairly broad spectrum, with the *Sport for All* campaign and the many different emphases presented through this strategy. However *Sport for All* is still for many merely a slogan.

The British contribution to the Council of Europe's evaluation study of 1984 (McIntosh and Charlton, 1985) pointed very clearly to the unpalatable fact that, whilst more sports were being played and being played more often, certain groups of potential players that were non-participants when the campaign started in 1972 were still largely non-participants in 1980 (*ibid*, chapter 11). The national governing bodies of sport can only do so much and in any case their main role is the organization of competition. The leisure and recreation departments within local authorities, a feature that has developed significantly since the reorganization of local government in 1974, have a continuing major role to play in what is essentially a social service.[24] Local government in the main accepts this responsibility but national governments have been slow to act in any dynamic way other than to establish agencies at arms length such as the Sports Council and the Countryside Commission. Such agencies are, by statute or charter, charged with working in this field, but successive governments have continued to starve them of the necessary resources.

The Sports Council is of the opinion that the evidence of the 1970–80 decade points very clearly to the fact that many people of all ages and abilities wish to play sport; to play for fun, for the sheer enjoyment of taking part and because they feel better if they do so.[25] For many this is their declared need for the increasing leisure time at their disposal. For a nation to invest a greater slice of the available resources in physical health-giving activities makes not only social sense but even to the sceptic and the cynic it makes very good economic sense when they contemplate the annual bill for the national health service.

It was against the backcloth of this broad philosophy, largely proven in the early eighties but still only a strong feeling in the seventies, that the Sports Council in 1972 embarked on the campaign for the range of facilities necessary to meet the demand that was manifesting itself in Britain as the leisure age dawned. The late sixties had seen the groundwork laid, the shopping lists prepared and a sound start made to the programme. Now as Roger Bannister and his Sports Council contemplated the scene they knew where they were going and proceeded with a commendable sense of urgency. It would have been easy to fall into the trap of taking the blunderbuss approach and attempting to hit every target in sight at the same time; this did not happen and the Council concentrated initially on the voluntary sports clubs and the public authorities, confident that they could build rapidly on what the advisory Sports Council had started. With these two programmes well underway an assault was launched on the social problems in the inner cities some few years later.[26]

Regional Sports Councils were crucial to the scale of progress as it was at this level that the local argument was won or lost. It was here too that policies relating to water facilities and access to hills, mountains and the countryside generally were pursued for in the final analysis success often lay within the gift of planning authorities. National policies were created but individual schemes had to be picked off one by one out on the ground. The relations between the regions and the centre were excellent and national policies reflected regional experience.[27]

Meeting the Demand for Facilities for Sport and Recreation

Voluntary Sports Clubs

With the advent of executive powers for the Sports Council the authority for grant-aiding private sports clubs passed from Whitehall to the Council. Additionally the Sports Council now had the power to assist statutory bodies financially with their projects although the facility for loan-sanction rested with the appropriate Ministry, the Ministry of Housing and Local Government, shortly to be the Department of the Environment. Earlier in 1971, within the Government's overall strategy of devolving to local authorities the responsibility for local decisions, the Minister for Sport had announced that the policy of grant-aiding voluntary sports clubs from central sources for purely local projects should cease forthwith with local authorities assuming this role under the existing powers of the 1937 Physical Training and Re- creation Act (see Appendix 9). This created something of a bombshell and an effective lobby was mounted for the Sports Council to be able to con- tinue to offer grants to local club schemes when these were larger than local, or of such an exceptional nature that it was not reasonable for a local authority to assume the financial burden. There are reasons to believe that the initial statement, which caused some dismay, was the result of a too tight interpretation of policy in Whitehall. John Coghlan was then the Regional Director for the Sports Council in the West Midlands and in a discussion he had with Mr. Peter Walker, the Secretary of State for the Environment and a local MP, it became clear it was not the intention of ministers to be so drastic. In the event a phasing-out period was agreed, and whilst these broad regulations existed until the Labour Government was returned to office in 1974, there is considerable evidence to show that they were inter- preted loosely.

A sizeable minority of local authorities accepted the challenge of assist- ing in the manner laid down by the Government although as time went by this response dwindled and assistance from local authorities became more frequent through the granting of rate-relief to clubs that owned their own property or who had leases on such facilities; the history of this too shows a patchy and uneven pattern.

In 1972, during the first year of operating independently, the Sports Council spent £1m on grant-aiding new and improved facilities for private clubs, and by the following year this had risen to £1,158m. In 1974 this was reduced to £880,000 to keep faith with the Government's wish that local authorities should carry more of the burden.[28]

By 1977 grant aid to voluntary clubs was at £1.1m, virtually the same as five years before but in effect it was less owing to inflation. This was disappointing but not surprising in view of the fact that the Sports Council had begun to assist to an increasing extent facilities within the social field from a budget that only kept pace with inflation (see Chapter 5 for inflation figures).

In the five-year period 1972–76 £4.7m was spent by the Sports Council supporting club projects representative of thirty-six different sports: golf, squash, rugby union, sailing and tennis all had over £300,000 each, whilst sports such as netball, orienteering, weightlifting and caving each had less than £2000.[29]

Public Facilities

Whilst the impact of grant-aid to sports projects was crucial to voluntary sports clubs and represented great value for money, for no grant was in excess of 50 per cent of the capital required and many were much lower, the major breakthrough was the ability the Sports Council now had to grant-aid statutory authorities to provide what was needed in specific locations. Over the years there have been many debates as to whether this form of grant-aid, modest as it inevitably has to be, has been money well spent. What value, the critics have always said, is a mere £50,000 to a project developed by a large town or city costing say £1.5m? Very little it has always been conceded in monetary terms but of major importance in terms of prestige and the seal of approval that goes with a Sports Council grant. Additionally such modest sums have often proved crucial in paying for a higher specification, or the addition of an ancillary facility that raises the standard of the project such as a glass back-wall for squash, or a weight-training room. In many respects the ability of the Sports Council to support projects financially gave a solid validity to the demands made in regional appraisals and in *Provision for Sport Volume I* (see Chapter 5). The targets set for swimming pools, indoor sports centres and golf courses were considered feasible and were based on broad standards. For instance a standard of one indoor sports centre for 50,000 people plus additional centres for every extra 40,000 was well below prevailing standards in West Germany with their 'Golden Plan' (see Chapter 3), and in Holland and Denmark who all had sterner targets. The ability of the Sports Council to stimulate development by pump-priming with some financial assistance was crucial and welcomed by local authorities.

It was a coincidence, but for sport a very happy coincidence, that the call for greater public investment in sports facilities came as preparations for local government reorganization were in hand (see Local Government Act 1974). Many of the smaller local authorities decided that if amalgamation was inevitable it would be better if balances carefully hoarded and preserved over the years were spent on local amenities that would benefit local communities for years to come. The period between 1973 and 1977 saw facilities for indoor sport virtually trebled and the growth of indoor swimming facilities increased by some 70 per cent. In the period 1972–1980 significant inroads were made on the targets set by the Sports Council for pools and sports centres (Table 3).

Table 3

	Existing provision 1971	'Provision for Sport' target for 1981	Provided by 1981
Indoor sports centres	12	815 new	449 new
Swimming pools	440	447 new	524 new

Source: Sports Council Annual Reports.

These figures for 'new' provision, although recorded in good faith, should only be regarded as indicative as precise definitions of what is and is not a sports centre have never really been agreed and swimming pools can be either single pools or complexes of pools. Nevertheless, even allowing for inevitable minor discrepancies in the collection of data, the figures are impressive and include the extraordinary year of 1974/75 when 137 sports centres and 190 new swimming pools were opened; a vintage year owing something, if not everything, to local government reorganization. In the case of golf courses some interesting statistics emerge. In the period 1960–1979 over 300 golf courses were constructed compared with less than twenty between 1940 and 1959. Quixotically the best period for golf development in Britain was between 1890 and 1919 when during this thirty-year period well over 300 golf courses were established, whilst the period between the two world wars, 1918–1939, produced only half of this number.

With increasing public and private expenditure it became urgent that the best advice available was required if errors in design and construction were not to be perpetuated. The Technical Unit of Sport had the prime responsibility in this area. Not only did it accept responsibility for vetting projects but the staff also embarked on a number of development projects to demonstrate advanced design and value for money on the basis that if successful future building would be influenced. Such work also provided a test-bed for new materials and equipment. The swimming-pool complex at Ashton-under-Lyme and the low-cost sports hall project at Rochford in Essex were early examples of this policy. An important addition to this design-work was the publication of an ever-increasing range of bulletins, leaflets and pamphlets as design guides. Some early examples were *Approach to Low Cost Sports Halls, Air-supported Structures, Facilities for Squash Rackets, Film and Broadcasting Requirements in Sports Facilities*, all published in 1975.

Ten years later, following energetic efforts by the staff of the TUS, the degree of sophistication of technical advice had risen considerably with major advances being made in data available on energy conservation and playing surfaces. The major contribution of the TUS to architects and designers was the *Handbook of Sports and Recreational Building Design* which sold at £100 per set when published in 1980; this is constantly under review and revision.[30]

To assist capital development of facilities by statutory authorities the Sports Council provided pump-priming finance in 1972 to the extent of £150,000. This had by 1977 risen to a shade over £1m and a year later this had moved upwards to £1.334m.[31]

The Inner Cities

For some time the Sports Council had been showing concern that in furtherance of the *Sport for All* policy specific programmes would need to be mounted aimed at specific target groups. Sport was now entering the social field with a vengeance and was to remain there henceforth.

By 1976 it had become very clear that the development of facilities in Britain, whilst moving forward apace, was often missing the inner cities and other areas of social deprivation. The cause of this was not difficult to see. The local authorities which were predominantly less involved in the ravages of decay and dereliction were able to advance programmes of development that enriched their localities whilst those that included these blighted areas had the financial consequences arising from such conditions to face. Whilst successive governments acknowledged these special problems, and urban-aid programmes were organized and financed, the problems were daunting and enough money was never made available. Special arrangements were made by the Sports Council to assist these areas of special need which were clearly defined as 'those local areas within towns and cities where living conditions are particularly poor by national standards and pressure on social services is severe'.[32] This was a far cry from the élitism of high-level performance, of the international arena and the Commonwealth and Olympic Games. This was carrying the *Sport for All* philosophy into the mean cities and deprived environments and was in direct fulfilment of the Royal Charter that laid upon the Sports Council the responsibility

> to develop and improve the knowledge and practice of sport and physical recreation in the interests of social welfare and the enjoyment of leisure among the public at large in Britain. (see Appendix 1, paragraph 2[a])

In conjunction with the Government, the Council used four clear indicators to guide the implementation of policy to bring increased opportunity to deprived local communities. High unemployment, population density, a high proportion of young people, and low socioeconomic groupings were the principal indicators selected to identify areas of inner cities that should be singled out for special care and attention.[33] A crash programme of low-cost local facilities was begun offering up to 90 per cent grants for low-cost schemes, kick-about areas and modest conversions of redundant buildings.[34] In 1976, the first year of the operation of this scheme, £730,000 was made available to assist 120 projects which included some fifty-eight hard-surfaced kick-about areas. The decision by the Sports Council to concern itself with areas of special need and urban deprivation was endorsed in June 1977 by the Government's White Paper *Policy for the Inner Cities* which suggested that sport and recreation for young people might help to improve the quality of life for many, some of whom might otherwise be attracted to delinquency and vandalism (see Appendix 5).

It was acknowledged from the beginning that good leadership was needed in this situation as the provision of a range of local facilities would not necessarily bring every young person from the street corner to the place of sports activity. A number of experimental leadership schemes were embarked upon, partly funded by the Sports Council but with a financial input and encouragement of the appropriate local authority, aimed at learning quickly how best to marshal resources and develop schemes. Courses for teachers and leaders were arranged as were coaching sessions for football, boxing, weightlifting, athletics, cricket and table tennis. From these rudimentary almost crude beginnings the seeds for more ambitious programmes were sown as lessons were learned, culminating in 1982 in the *Action Sport* pilot programmes in London and the West Midlands at a cost of £3m over three years.[35]

The entire spectrum of social deprivation, decay and dereliction in the crumbling inner cities is a social problem sharpened by a century of neglect and indifference. For politicians it is a daunting problem faced as they are with the financial verities of the day. Broadly speaking the situation facing the country in the seventies had been brought about by the failure of successive governments to recognize long-term shifts in jobs and job opportunity, a less than dramatic sustained programme of slum clearance, all exacerbated by insensitive application of physical, social and economic planning policies. The drive and determination to create ring-roads and throughways through the cities, to provide ever taller blocks of flats, had often created concrete deserts, urban wildernesses devoid of feeling, humanity and warmth. This was certainly not done in the knowledge of what would follow, rather the reverse, but the results were often socially disastrous. It was Desmond Morris the anthropologist who said, in *The Naked Ape* that man could not live by central heating alone, and this is a lesson learned from the massive post-war reconstruction that provided quality of housing, sanitation and health which was good, but failed to provide the vital human ingredients needed to bring about a rising standard in the quality of life which was bad.[36] Additionally large areas of British cities had been laid waste by the bulldozer to await the arrival of finance that very often was not forthcoming. Where these traumatic events have not taken place housing in the public sector has been allowed often to deteriorate and multi-occupancy to flourish bringing different social problems. Sport and physical recreation cannot solve these grave problems by themselves, but they can and do provide an essential ingredient to the package of improvements and betterment that are financed by central and local government programmes.[37]

Thus it was that the Sports Council in 1976, under the Chairmanship of a patrician and merchant banker, Sir Robin Brook (see Chapter 5 in this volume), grasped the nettle and began to inject additional finance for facilities into areas of physical and social deprivation. It was, therefore, possible for successive governments to see that money spent in this way did indeed make a significant contribution to enhance the quality of life. Later this view was to be dramatically highlighted in 1981 with the riots in Brixton and Toxteth and the Government's policy decision to provide additional resources for sport and physical recreation to help alleviate social problems.

This decision arose from the day when the Secretary of State for the Environment, Mr. Michael Heseltine, given the task by the Prime Minister to 'do something' at Toxteth walked the 'road to Damascus' and saw vividly and emotionally the plight of the socially deprived; from that day further resources began to flow in greater volume and his appreciation of the part sport could and did play was generous and warming.[38]

Football and the Community

In the spring of 1978 Denis Howell, now a Minister of State, convened a meeting at which the Secretary of the Football League, Alan Hardaker, Alan Everiss the Secretary of West Bromwich Albion FC in his capacity as Chairman of the League Clubs Secretaries Association and John Coghlan the Acting-Director of the Sports Council were present. At this meeting the Minister unfolded his plan to inject money into development schemes at football league clubs to provide community recreation facilities aimed at involving young spectators more with their clubs in an effort to cut down on the escalating violence at football matches. This money was to be directed to the Football League. Coghlan urged the Minister to use the Sports Council for the development of this programme and this view was endorsed by Hardaker, himself a member of the Council. The Minister agreed and accordingly in June 1978 Denis Howell announced a £1m grant to assist league football clubs with the development of their grounds for use by the community. This imaginative scheme had the full support of the Football Association, the Football League and the Professional Footballers Association and some fifty-seven of the ninety-two football league clubs expressed an initial interest. Finally twenty-nine football clubs and eight rugby league clubs were selected for financial assistance in the first year's programme and the Football and Community Development Programme was underway.[39]

The principal criteria employed in the selection of clubs to benefit from public grant aid were:

1 The desire of the clubs to be community-minded.
2 Clubs with problems of hooliganism and violence sited in urban areas.

The range of initial schemes was impressive and included the provision of synthetic-surfaced play areas, floodlighting of existing playing spaces, and conversions of existing facilities for use by the local community. Sheffield United FC provided an indoor sports hall from a conversion of the Yorkshire Cricket Club's old indoor cricket school, whilst in London West Ham United FC adapted its existing indoor training facility to make it suitable for community use.

The promotion by the Minister for Sport and the Government of this policy, using the Sports Council for its execution, attracted a response from the Football Grounds Improvement Trust which made £250,000 available in 1978 so that more clubs could participate.[40]

Whilst no claims were ever made that this scheme would eliminate violence and hooliganism associated with football spectators it was an imaginative way of harnessing clubs to the communities they purported to represent and at the same time added to the supply of much needed local facilities in densely populated urban locations.

By 1978 facility development in the inner cities via special programmes was well underway and attracting grant-in-aid from the Sports Council as a result of sharp policy thrusts. Projects falling within areas of special need and urban deprivation, prototype projects that demonstrated new ideas and thinking and football and the community schemes were assisted to the tune of £2.352m in that year.[41]

National Facilities

At the other end of the scale the need for facilities capable of national and international competition was known and appreciated. It was policy from the beginning of the Sports Council in 1965 to work towards providing access to facilities of the right scale and standard for all competitive sports so that major competitions, including full international events, could be staged.

Hand in hand with this policy was the determination to provide centres where national teams and squads, at every stage of development, could train and prepare in the best possible conditions. It would be a mistake to believe nothing hitherto existed capable of staging international competition; many sports had facilities available to them which were capable of providing venues for international competition but expectations were rising year by year. In some cases, for example, Bisley for shooting, facilities needed considerable refurbishment and updating. Priority therefore was given to those sports that did not have a facility capable of international use, with a further priority given to those facilities that needed, not only a face-lift, but often radical modifications to modernize to the required international specifications and standard.[42]

The agreed plan was to advance this policy from three angles:

(i)   by assisting financially schemes put forward by local or other statutory authorities;
(ii) by assisting financially governing bodies of sport to develop projects of their own;
(iii) by development of the National Sports Centres wholly owned and administered by the Sports Council for the use by governing bodies of sport including Crystal Palace, owned by the Greater London Council but run by the Sports Council.[43]

There was nothing wrong with this plan as a plan in 1972, nor is there anything wrong with it in 1990. It was admirable in every way except for one crucial factor that was not taken into account originally — the unwillingness of the Government and local government to commit themselves to provide the necessary finance. This is equally true today and is understood on all sides; at no time to this day has government given a meaningful significant sum of money to the Sports Council on the understanding that such a sum will be used to finance a major national project costing many millions of pounds; it has always been that any money spent in this way has to be gouged from existing budgets.

There was no reason to believe in 1972, when the Conservative administration established the Sports Council as an independent executive body by Royal Charter, that it and its successors would starve the Council of the financial resources necessary to carry out its allotted task, nor that local government, in the form of the major cities, would rarely have the money to build and manage the prestigious facilities required under the label 'national'. Most of the Western European countries were finding themselves able to provide to this scale and therefore it was reasonable to believe that Britain could and would do likewise. How wrong this thinking has been is shown by the list of major facilities that do not exist in Britain today.[44]

The inability, under Treasury regulations, for the Sports Council even from its limited resources to save, scrape and salt away capital sums so that from time to time meaningful contributions could be made to entice likely developers to build, has been a crucial factor in the slow progress made in this area of activity. Hidebound financial regulations by the Treasury, no doubt sensible and proper in most areas of public expenditure, have militated against the best use of public resources made available to the Sports Council and have inhibited progress. Some Ministers for Sport have fought to have these arrangements modified and have failed honourably, others fearful no doubt for their political futures have not even tried. The failure to acquire the ability to create a sinking-fund for major facilities lies with Whitehall and government and their unwillingness to provide sufficient resources to finance a meaningful national development programme.

Success, at a price, has followed the declared aim to develop the National Sports Centres administered by the Sports Council for competition and high level training and coaching. The price that continues to be paid is the annual deficit on the running of the National Sports Centres and the cost of the investment programme; money that could be used so profitably and to such advantage in other areas of activity if freed from this burden.[45]

By 1973 England and Wales had seven National Sports Centres and Scotland two, all owned or partly owned and run by the three Sports Councils. These were:

1   Crystal Palace — jointly financed with the Greater London Council — multi-sports and high level competition.

2   Bisham Abbey, Marlow — multi-sports.
3   Lilleshall Hall, Shropshire — multi-sports.
4   Plas-y-Brenin, North Wales — outdoor activities centre.
5   Cowes, Isle of Wight — sailing centre.
6   Holme Pierrepont — jointly financed with the Nottinghamshire County Council — National Water Sports Centre.
7   Cardiff, Wales — National Sports Centre for Wales.
8   Glenmore Lodge, Cairngorms, Scotland — outdoor activities centre.
9   Inverclyde, Largs, Scotland — multi-sports.

The major stadia for football, rugby and cricket provided suitable venues for these sports, and athletics and swimming were establishing themselves at Crystal Palace. Indoor sports had to make do with halls not built for their purposes and presented the greatest challenge.

In 1972 the Sports Council spent £600,000 on capital expenditure on national facilities, almost entirely at its own National Sports Centres. By 1978 the Council was spending £1.836m with £261,000 spent on National Centres provided by governing bodies or local municipal authorities for caving, shooting, cycling, equestrianism, skiing and fencing.[46]

Whilst possible local authority developers were from time to time coming forward with ambitious plans and hopes rose, very little materialized within the national context. All too often the inability of the Sports Council to offer large attractive capital grants contributed to the shelving or abandonment of major schemes with the inevitable frustration that followed; the system of assisting local authority major developments was not right, and this state of affairs persists to this day.

Many other countries, for example, the Federal Republic of Germany, Holland, Eire, Denmark and Italy, fund major developments from national lotteries or the income from football pool betting; two concepts from which all British governments have turned their faces adamantly.

Although the planned take-off for large scale national facilities has never really taken place, largely because the system negates action in the public sector, good planning and judicious use of finance, nevertheless, permitted the Sports Council to embark on a useful range of schemes that provided sorely needed facilities for élite training and competition.

During the period 1972–78 the following major facilities were provided:

(a)   The National Water Sports Centre at Holme Pierrepont jointly with the Nottinghamshire County Council.
(b)   A 25 metre training pool at Crystal Palace.
(c)   Extensions to the National Equestrian Centre at Stoneleigh, Warwickshire.
(d)   Large Sports Workshop, 68 metres × 37 metres in size, at Bisham

Abbey for indoor games; later to become in 1981 the National Tennis Centre.

(e) A National Training Centre for weightlifting at Bisham Abbey.

(f) A modern 50 bedroom hostel block at Bisham Abbey.

(g) Provision of a national diving boat for the British Sub-Aqua Club.

(h) A National Championship squash court at Wembley for the Squash Rackets Association.

(i) A 5,000 seat stand at the track at Crystal Palace.

(j) The purchase, jointly with the North Yorkshire County Council, of Whernside Manor as the National Caving Centre.

(k) An international wooden-surfaced cycling track at Leicester.

(l) Improvements to the Bisley ranges for the National Small-bore Rifle Association.

(m) An artificial grass pitch at Lilleshall Hall.

(n) A National Gymnastics Training Centre at Lilleshall Hall.[47]

To these must be added developments in floodlighting, upgrading of existing pitches, new surfacing for worn training areas, provision of squash courts, upgrading of changing accommodation and many other minor works at the National Sports Centres.

The ability of the Sports Council to meet requests of governing bodies and programme, from meagre resources, sufficient finance to provide this wide range of facilities was a tribute to the financial acumen of the then Chairman and senior officers of the Sports Council, in particular those who had any responsibility for ensuring the cash-flow that permitted such development. Considerable public and private discussions centred on the need for a large purpose-built National Indoor Arena capable of staging international events including athletics, and these were to continue in a variety of forms well into the eighties. It was not until 1987 that it became clear that advanced planning in Birmingham, London and Sheffield might well give us one or more National Indoor Arenas in the early nineties.

After the great success of John Curry in the skating events at the Winter Olympics of 1976 in Innsbruck, when he took the gold medal in the individual skating competition, popular feeling throughout the country was for a greater investment in indoor skating facilities and the need for a National Skating Centre was underlined. Despite valiant efforts by the Sports Council and the National Skating Association to persuade a major local authority to build a National Centre all came to nothing. For several years Manchester City Council not only expressed their willingness to build but actually went ahead to detailed planning stage supported by the offer of grant-in-aid from the Sports Council; hopes were high only to be dashed when plans were abandoned as costs escalated. Today Britain still has no National Skating Centre despite the great Olympic successes of John Curry and Robin Cousins in 1980, and Christopher Dean and Jayne Torvill in 1984.

There are many who reflect with great sadness on what might have been if the Sports Council had had the financial capability of providing Manchester with half the capital sum required, instead of less than 20 per cent, or if the Government had had the interest and the will to step in with such a modest sum. In these hypothetical circumstances there is no doubt that the larger local authorities in Britain would be lining up to provide much needed national facilities that would add lustre to their municipal images and at the same time provide superb facilities for their citizens at a modest local cost; the nation would have been well served at the élite level and so would the community within the context of sport for all.

Despite the somewhat slow and disappointing progress in providing modern, well-equipped national scale facilities for Britain many world championships were staged between 1972 and 1980 supported by public funds, commercial sponsorships and often income from television coverage. The World Rowing Championships at Holme Pierrepont, the World Orienteering Championships in Scotland and the World Cycling Championships at Leicester were three events that attracted wide interest but many other events at world level such as squash, waterskiing and women's hockey in 1975 and table-tennis in 1977 were staged. Such events, widely televised, created an increased demand from the public. For example, the popular appeal of gymnastics, usually women's gymnastics, following the superb television coverage of the sport at the 1972 Munich Olympics which put the elfin-like Olga Korbut into every sitting room in the nation, created a renewed pressure on the need for more facilities and coaches at every level and encouraged the international gymnastics spectaculars arranged by the British Amateur Gymnastic Association at Wembley Arena. Sport attracted television, television attracted commercial sponsorship, and nationwide viewing led to greater participation which in turn led to the need for more facilities.

Water Recreation and the Countryside

Throughout the sixties increased leisure time and greater car ownership imposed increased pressure on natural resources in Britain, helped by the development of outdoor pursuits in schools as part of the expanding physical education syllabus. It was becoming evident that resources for water sports and countryside activities had to be provided in greater volume and those that existed had to be brought into greater use where this was not the case.

In the sixties the Sports Council had developed good working relationships with other agencies which had responsibility for natural resources. The Countryside Commission, established as a consequence of the 1968 Countryside Act, the British Waterways Board under the distinguished chairmanship of Sir Frank Price (see Chapter 3), and the Nature Conservancy, were the principal agencies involved together with the Tourist Boards and the Forestry Commission.

Soon after taking office the Conservative Government announced that the water resources of the country were to be reorganized and declared their intention to establish an interest in water recreation through the creation of the Water Space Amenity Commission. With the Water Bill safely through Parliament regional water authorities were established, each with a statutory requirement to provide for water recreation (see Appendix 5, paragraph 3). The water recreation committees that had long been established by Regional Sports Councils quickly developed sound working relationships with regional water authorities and their appropriate committees; indeed the membership of both overlapped widely which contributed to effective and constructive work.[48]

From these early arrangements for cooperation and joint work, assisted by Sports Council grant aid, many reservoirs hitherto unavailable for recreation were brought into use as were rivers, canals and lakes. Coastal areas had their own problems but the surge of interest in sailing witnessed the growth of marinas. Such an explosion of increased usage did not occur without problems and heartache. The greater use by canoeists of rivers caused friction with anglers, whilst water skiers continued to find it difficult to obtain facilities on account of noise and pollution problems.

In the countryside, access was the major obstacle and still is today, but the Countryside Commission has continued to do excellent work in this field and many problems have been resolved or eased with imaginative schemes and access agreements. The Nature Conservancy Council, mindful of its statutory responsibilities, had to tread very warily indeed in conceding use of water and land sites for other purposes but tact and diplomacy in an atmosphere of give and take eased many of the potential areas for conflict. The development for sailing of Blithfield reservoir, South Staffordshire, a prime conservancy site, was a classic example; there were many more.

The early seventies were years of considerable progress in opening up water and countryside areas not previously available. New reservoirs were designed with recreation very much in mind. Two classic examples of sound planning and design, with cooperation and an input from all appropriate agencies, were at Draycott, near Rugby, and Empingham, Rutland. These examples are given because they were huge and costly but many smaller successes were recorded.

The after-use of gravel workings for water recreation, and sometimes land-based recreation, took on a different dimension as planning officers began to build into planning consents after-use requirements. Thorpe Park, Surrey, adjacent to the M3 motorway, is a prime example of good after-use of gravel extraction. It stands with the National Water Sports Centre as one of two sound examples of fulfilling a need for both national scale facilities and facilities for community recreation. The development of the Cotswold Water Park, a medium to long-term project, provided much needed water recreation opportunity in a part of the country short of water facilities generally. The volume of work in the Trent Valley to develop gravel-workings for recreation was accelerated by a study carried out jointly by the East and West Midlands Sports Councils in cooperation with the Regional Water Authorities, the governing bodies of water sports and the local planning authorities.[49]

By 1978 the problems concerning the extended use of existing water were largely overcome except for conflict of use where some degree of incompatability existed owing to the huge and increasing demand on finite resources. Access to the countryside for the millions who wished to take their recreation therein remained a problem despite notable successes, and this was to feature later in 1982 in the Sports Council's strategy for the eighties *Sport in the Community — the Next Ten Years* as a problem that had to be tackled radically.[50]

In some mining areas of Britain the National Coal Board's Opencast Executive responded to the environmental lobby by restoring the scarred land after open-cast use to recreation for playing fields and golf courses. In the same way the National Coal Board accelerated the landscaping of many slag-heaps to produce pleasant green areas which often were capable of use for organized sport. The appalling disaster at Aberfan in the sixties dramatically and tragically highlighted the need to give high priority to this work and today a green and pleasant landscape has often taken the place of so many eyesores surrounding pit towns and villages, the inheritance of the Industrial Revolution and its aftermath.

Water, pleasant countryside, derelict land reclamation and after-use of gravel extraction have contributed greatly to providing a beautiful landscape where this did not exist previously and such developments have added to the stock of both formal and informal recreational facilities. The governments of the day, both Labour and Conservative, contributed by sound legislation and some financial assistance to local authorities mainly through Derelict Land Grants from the Department of the Environment. The will of the period was to attempt to deal valiantly with a recreation explosion, all that was lacking in the final analysis was sufficient finance to tackle the problem root and branch and not piecemeal. Nevertheless, much was achieved with relatively little as the national will existed despite the financial problems that the country was facing due to the oil crisis and mounting inflation.

Summary of Progress

The seventies certainly saw considerable progress in providing for the sport and physical recreation needs of the nation: there was a growing feeling and awareness that public authorities had a responsibility in this area of social activity. The inertia of the fifties and early sixties was a thing of the past;

there was now a new and exciting mood in the air that at last Britain was once again on the move in sport as users flooded to take advantage of the new facilities that appeared in their neighbourhoods. Local signs indicating the whereabouts of the 'Sports Centre' and the 'Swimming Pool' were commonplace as a new generation of local authority elected members and officers moved into positions of authority and influence conditioned by the planning and propaganda of the sixties. The 'battle of the mind' at local level was largely won by the end of the decade despite there still being pockets of resistance and traditional thinking conditioned by the pre-war and immediate post-war situation. The availability of finance to support ambitious plans was the major stumbling block as it is today. The Town Hall has always given higher priority than Whitehall to the needs of local communities because it is more in touch with local sentiment and aspirations, and probably in the final analysis is more democratic in its decision-making.

The Sports Council and Regional Sports Councils elicited considerable support from municipal authorities but failed to get the same response from Whitehall. Ministers for Sports, Eldon Griffiths and then Denis Howell, again following the 1974 General Election, strove manfully for the sports cause in Parliament and in government and achieved a certain level of success when set against the in-built conservatism of the Whitehall system. Denis Howell as a Minister of State, and a considerable power within the Labour party, was able and willing to flex his political muscles and increase the money available to sport in percentage terms; he never flinched from taking the system head on and scored a number of successes. Sport, unlike the arts, was not fashionable and although it had an articulate élite within the Establishment, they were never mobilized to write, argue and lobby for the cause with some notable exceptions such as Lord Cobham, Lord Byers, Baroness Burton and Lord Wolfenden.

The era of Sir Roger Bannister, knighted for his services to sport in 1975, and Sir Robin Brook (see Appendix 6), was marked by considerable impressive progress in the provision of facilities despite formidable obstacles and setbacks. The response by the local authorities to the challenge to build and provide was considerable, and the willingness of successive governments to provide enabling arrangements was commendable. What was lacking was a higher level of public investment at national level; this would have called for radical rethinking in the corridors of power and this sadly was not forthcoming.

The Cobham Select Committee Reports of 1973,[51] the White Paper 'Sport and Recreation' of 1975 (for a summary of these and other papers see Appendix 5), and sundry Departmental Circulars all assisted, some considerably, but the great breakthrough did not happen; progress was therefore inevitably slower than had been hoped for but the country was on target to a considerable extent to achieve the task set by Bannister and the Sports Council in 1972 for the provision of new swimming pools and indoor sports centres.

Notes

1 For those wishing to pursue the subject in depth reference can be made to the following standard works: Gratton and Taylor (1957); Patmore (1983); Clarke and Crichter (1985); Walvin (1978); Glyptis (1989); Haywood, Bramham and Kew (1989).

2 See Sports Council — SSRC Review *Trends in Leisure 1919–1939.*

3 *ibid*, p. 9.

4 *ibid*, pp. 9. and 10.

5 *ibid*, pp. 34–40.

6 *ibid*, pp. 46–7.

7 *ibid*, pp. 50–1. Initial support came from religious and philanthropic bodies. Basic accommodation was one shilling (today 5p) at locations often remote. In 1933 the YHA organized walking tours for the unemployed; this paternalism attracted very few. The leaders of the movement saw it as promoting international understanding. Some anecdotal evidence indicates that those who used continental hostels developed a deep suspicion of Fascism which was a rising force in Europe in the 1930s. Some believed the movement was an effort to divert the energies of a potentially troublesome working class. See also Coburn, (1950).

8 *ibid*, p. 53.

9 Sports Council — SSRC Review (1979) *Leisure and the Role of Clubs and Voluntary Groups.*

10 Sports Council SSRC Review (1980) *Trends in Leisure* 1919–39, pp. 10 and 11.

11 For the history of these events see Burnell (1989), Heckstall-Smith (1955) and Barrett (1986)

12 Fred J. Perry (born May 1909); Singles Champion: Wimbledon, 1934, 1935 and 1936; USA, 1933, 1934 and 1936; France 1935; Australia, 1934; Davis Cup — 20 ties; 52 matches; victories: singles 34, doubles 11, defeats 7.

13 Golf and tennis clubs were particularly prone to selective membership by profession and social background. Usually this was by practice rather than by regulation in the constitution of the club.

14 See Evans (1974) chapter 3. In January 1937 the Government issued a White Paper *Physical Training and Recreation* outlining its plans for physical fitness mainly in the development and expansion of existing facilities and organizations. School provision was to be raised but arrangements were planned 'for those whose daily environment of the office or the workshop makes the provision for physical improvement particularly desirable'.

A National Advisory Council was to be established 'to survey the field and methods'.

A National College of Physical Training was to be installed 'to train teachers and do research work ... with the physiology of PT'.

Lord Aberdare was Chairman of a Fitness Council which included Philip Noel-Baker, MP, Lord Burghley (later Marquess of Exeter), Stanley Rous, Wavel Wakefield, MP, Prunella Stack; all 'big' names in sport pre and post the 1939–45 war.

The PT and R Act (1937), which established the National Fitness Council, became law in July 1937. Twenty-two area committees were set up, staffed by salaried staff; the bureaucracy attracted great criticism.

The National Fitness Council died at the outbreak of the Second World War.

15 Sports Council *Sport in the Community — the Next Ten Years*, see chapter 2,

figures 10 and 11. See also press of the time for match attendances and governing body records.

16 See bibliographies in, for example: Sports Council-SSRC Reviews: *Trends in Leisure 1919–1939* (1979), *Trends in Leisure Participation* (1980), *Leisure and the role of Clubs and Voluntary Groups* (1979); and Sillitoe (1969).

17 Henley Centre for Forecasting; Government household surveys.

18 Henley Centre Report *Leisure Futures — Fact Pack*; Leisure Management, January 1985, p. 13; *Leisure Policy for the Future* — published by the Sports Council for the Chairmen's Policy Group 1983.

19 A Civic Trust Survey reprinted from The Architects Journal of 20 January, 1965.

20 The conclusion on p. 189 formed a blueprint for some of the early work of the Research Committee of the Sports Council of which Dower was a member.

21 In 1989 the Football League banned the use of synthetic surfaces for First and Second Division clubs as from the start of the 1991/92 season. Queens Park Rangers was the first First Division club to lay a synthetic surface in 1981; it was abandoned at the end of the 1987/88 season. Luton Town have continued to use their synthetic pitch and will only obey the League with great reluctance. Another club with a synthetic pitch is Oldham Athletic.

22 See Sports Council *A Digest of Sports Statistics for the UK*; Information series No. 7; and Sports Council (1982) *Sport in the Community — The Next Ten Years*.

23 For example Birmingham Education Authority and Walsall Education Authority both had outdoor activity and field study centres in Wales. There were many more. Later in the eighties financial pressure on local authorities caused the closure of many outdoor activity centres.

24 House of Lords — 2nd Report of the Select Committee 'Sport and Leisure', July 1973, paragraph 358.

25 Sports Council Annual Reports 1973–4 et seq.

26 1975 saw the Sports Council launch its first initiative into what were called Areas of Special Need — reflecting the House of Lords Select Committee's recommendation concerning Recreation Priority Areas — (paragraph 179).

   The 1975 White Paper *Sport and Recreation* (see appendix 5 to this volume) coined the phrase Areas of Special Need (paragraph 56).

   From this date the Sports Council embraced a 'deprivation' policy; see Chapter 12 'Sports Council Policies and Grant-aiding Programmes'.

27 The Director of the Sports Council met Regional Directors as a group about every two months. Facility trends and needs were aired and on this consensus national policies were framed. Regional views were shaped through dialogue with public authorities and regional or county governing bodies of sport; in this way priorities for expenditure were established.

28 Sports Council Annual Reports 1973–4 and 1974–5; Facilities.

29 Sports Council Annual Reports. Appendices 'Current Grants to Sports.'

30 The four volumes boxed are only available from the Architectural Press, 9 Queen Anne's Gate, London SW1.

31 See Sports Council Annual Reports for these years — Financial Appendices.

32 Sports Council definition — 1976, Annual Report 1976–7, p. 11.

33 Sports Council Annual Report 1976–7, p. 11.

34 For example: (a) Ault Hucknell, Derbyshire — a former social area was converted into a gymnasium and the car park to a hard porous floodlit area; (b) The Customs House in Middlesborough was converted into an indoor recreation centre; (c) Birmingham — redundant slipper baths converted to a weightlifting and fitness training area.

35 Consult GL and SE Region and West Midlands Region of the Sports Council for

detail but for broad description see Sports Leadership in *Inner Cities*; Sports Council Annual Report 1982–83, p. 12.

36 See Second Report from the Select Committee of the House of Lords *Sport and Leisure* paragraphs 92–97 and paragraphs 179–82. Also appendix 5 (5) Synopsis of this Report.

37 See Department of Environment's Circular 17/83 *Urban Programme Circular 24* — paragraph 1.

38 In December 1982 the Sports Council was allocated an additional £2.5m by the Secretary of State (Heseltine) to be allocated for facilities in the inner cities and other deprived areas. A month later in January 1983 a further £1.75m was given.

39 The clubs selected covered a wide geographical area. Financial details of grants are held by the Facilities Unit at the Sports Council.

40 Sports Council Annual Report 1978–79 — Football and the Community, pp. 4–5.

41 *ibid*, Schedule VI, p. 22.

42 For example: extensions to the National Equestrian Centre at Stoneleigh; a podium for the British Amateur Gymnastics Association; national championships court for squash; upgrading at Bisley.

43 This Centre comprises in the main a major sports hall with spectator accommodation, 50 metre pool, 25 metre training pool, squash courts, international athletics track with spectator accommodation, residential block. For detail see Evans (1974) pp. 116–21.

44 Britain does not yet have, for example: (a) a National Indoor Arena (one is being built in Birmingham); (b) an international swimming pool to current specification; (c) an ice-rink to international competition specifications.

45 For example — total running costs less income for six national sports centres administered by the Sports Council:

1972–73	£155,259
1974–75	£494,248
1978 79	£1,097m
1982–83	£2.16m
1986–87	£2.934m
1987–88	£2.79m — centres reduced to five after sale of Cowes

Note: Capital Expenditure is not included. All financial data obtainable from analysis of Sports Council Annual Reports.

46 Sports Council Annual Report — Financial Appendices.

47 A compilation of data from the Sports Council's Annual Reports.

48 For example Sir William Dugdale, Chairman of the West Midlands Sports Council's Water Recreation Committee was appointed Chairman of the Severn Trent Regional Water Authority.

49 'Recreation in the Trent Valley' — Report of a Working Party convened by East and West Midlands Sports Councils 1974.

50 See page 38: 'One way of arranging access is through management agreements between local authorities and the landowner under the Countryside Act 1968'.

51 First Report from the Select Committee of the House of Lords *Sport and Leisure* — 29 March 1983; Second Report 25 July 1973.

Chapter 7

Development of High Performance and Mass Participation in Sport and Recreation

The earlier work of the advisory Sports Council, and before that the experience of the Government in assisting some national governing bodies of sport with modest financial assistance for salaries of coaches and international travel costs to major sports events, was sufficient for the newly-structured executive Sports Council to work on when it considered the development of elitism in sport.[1] At the other end of the spectrum the work of the CCPR regions, over many years, was equally a good basis on which to construct policies aimed at widening the participation opportunities for the community at large. The growth of facilities in the late sixties and early seventies, allied to the confident predictions in the short and medium terms for continued and expanding growth, represented an encouraging backcloth against which developmental and financial planning could constructively take place. The Royal Charter had made it quite clear that the Sports Council had very precise powers in the field of participation (see Appendix 1, paragraph 2[a]).

The governing bodies of sport and 'the man in the street' were now both waiting to see how they were to be assisted, on the one hand to achieve greater things for Britain in the major sports arenas of the world and on the other hand to be able to play a local game of football, cricket, squash or badminton.

The *Sport for All* campaign, shortly to be launched, by its very definition, encompassed the total spectrum of participation; those, however, who were within the formal structure of governing body sport and aspiring to higher levels of achievement needed a different approach to those lower down the ladder and those who were not yet involved in sport.[2]

For the élite it was therefore largely but not wholly a case of trying to do more of what had already been started, whilst for the development of mass sport it was necessary to start many new things, not least of which was to devise ways to bring back to sport and physical recreation the countless millions who had abandoned it either on leaving school or in their early twenties.[3]

The Development of High Performance in Sport

It was tacitly accepted that the majority of governing bodies of sport were not capable of generating sufficient finance from their membership to allow them to compete with distinction in international competition at the various levels that were being increasingly established by international federations. Exceptions were sports such as football, rugby union and cricket which had the capacity to attract large audiences which financed their affairs, but even here there were areas of endeavour that sometimes required public finance. The Sports Council decided that rapid results could be achieved if they acted quickly with the organized sports bodies and accordingly went into a round of meetings in 1972 aimed at reaching fundamental agreement on programmes which would be funded on an ongoing basis so that forward planning could take place. It quickly became clear that the most effective way to assist the national governing bodies of sport was by offering finance to:

    (i)   improve administration;
    (ii) increase coaching and development schemes;
    (iii) increase membership;
    (iv) raise standards of performance;
    (v) increase and improve international competition.[4]

Good professional administration was considered to be the cornerstone of development supported by the many voluntary officials that historically provided the strength in British sport. The employment of more and better coaches charged with the raising of individual standards, and the further training of regional, county and club coaches was thought to be fundamental to the whole issue of widening the base of performance and increasing the level of competition. Hand in hand with administration and coaching the need for promotion of sport through the establishment of new clubs aimed at increasing membership and subscription revenue was agreed and this called for the appointment of more sport development officers. These officers did not confine themselves solely to aspects of work concerned with people but were further charged with the task of encouraging and stimulating the provision of facilities both in the private and public sectors.

On the international scene not only was increased financial assistance needed to send teams overseas more often but it was also needed to ensure that when they did travel they were well prepared. As an act of faith the Sports Council doubled the 1973 overseas travel grants by the end of 1974.[5]

In the years that followed improvements in the range and level of assistance were made relating to accommodation allowance for competition overseas and to the size of parties eligible for grant-aid which expanded to include coaches, doctors and technical officials. Expeditions and dance festivals were brought into the general arrangements and benefited organizations such as the British Mountaineering Council and Dance and Movement.[6] In 1974 the international travel grants to governing bodies of sport were raised to 75 per cent of the total cost and this level has been maintained to 1990.

In addition to the national governing bodies of sport other national sports organizations were assisted to an increasing extent between 1972 and 1980. These were generally corporate bodies such as the National Playing Fields Association, the Physical Education Association of Great Britain and Northern Ireland, the British Sports Association for the Disabled, the Sports Turf Research Institute, the British Colleges Sports Association, the Women's Inter-University Athletics Board and the British Olympic Association. This list is certainly not exhaustive, and every organization did not get grant-aid every year, but it is indicative of the breadth of interests which were assisted in their development as the years went by.[7]

When in 1973 the Sports Council moved into more spacious accommodation at 70 Brompton Road, London, the opportunity to house in a seemly fashion a goodly number of governing bodies of sport was seized. The dream of having a *National House of Sport* has always been splendid to contemplate but the concept has never been capable of total realization for a variety of reasons, not least of which is the wish of some governing bodies to be separate from any other and the hard financial fact that sufficient finance has never been available to put such a proposition on offer. Brompton Road was a very successful halfway house and provided services and back-up to many governing bodies who were happy to be under one roof because they either simply liked it that way or because it made financial sense. When in 1981 the Council moved somewhat downmarket to Upper Woburn Place the opportunity was not only lost again but in fact less accommodation was on offer to realize the House of Sport concept. The reality of the situation was such that the CCPR, a tenant of the Sports Council at Brompton Road, moved into their own premises in Victoria in early 1981 and took some sports bodies with them. Happily in 1983 the Sports Aid Foundation was able to move back as tenants of the Sports Council again which facilitated many arrangements.

In the period under review from the setting-up of the executive Sports Council in 1972 until 1980, during which the Council had direct control over its financial resources, the level of support to governing bodies and other national sports organizations for current expenditure rose considerably, apart from 1978, even allowing for inflation. (see Table 4.)

The decline in financial support in 1978 is accounted for by the very considerable build-up of centres of excellence at regional level, drug testing and associated research, and the development of participation within the *Sport for All* context in the urban deprivation programme. By 1979 the allocations were again on their way upwards (in excess of £4m), matters

Table 4: Sports organizations — Current grant-aid

Year	£m
1972–3	£ .607
1973–4	£ .939
1974–5	£1.289
1975–6	£1.987
1976–7	£2.463
1977–8	£3.779
1978–9	£3.587
1979–80	£4.064
1980–81	£5.000

Source: Sports Council Financial Statistics

having been adjusted. Alongside the considerable expansion in the volume of public money that national sports bodies and organizations enjoyed, allowing them to expand their activities and compete more equally internationally, a range of other initiatives saw the light of day in the seventies that directly affected high-level sport.

Centres of Excellence

In the 1975 White Paper *Sport and Recreation* there were many references to the development of excellence and the need to be more imaginative in tapping the nation's athletic resources at every level of society (see paragraphs 62 and 63 and Appendix 5 in this volume). Minister for Sport, Denis Howell, gathered around him a small but knowledgeable working group that considered excellence and its development in depth. It was agreed that a way forward would be to create a network of centres of sporting excellence throughout Britain in as wide a range of sports as possible. Such centres it was thought should be located so as to give easy and cheap access to young people; they should be well staffed, should have medical back-up services at hand and should be such that they fitted into the overall development pattern of the national sports bodies. It was acknowledged that not every centre of excellence would be alike, would not necessarily offer the same range of activities and would not be administered and financed in the same fashion. What was agreed, however, was that a network would create greater opportunity for a larger number to enjoy first-class coaching, close personal attention and therefore the base of team selection at every point would be widened.

As with all new concepts there were those who disliked the whole idea from the start seeing the autonomy of the sports bodies in some way threatened. There were others who pointed to the fact that centres of sporting excellence already existed for many sports, which was true but they were not enough in number, and in any case the new proposals complemented and supplemented what already existed and in no way threatened them. The Sports Council gave moral and financial backing to this initiative and in January 1977 the first centre of excellence arising from the Government's proposals in the White Paper opened in Leeds as a partnership between the Leeds City Council, Carnegie College of Physical Education, now a constituent body within Leeds Polytechnic, the University, Leeds Athletic Institute and St. James's Hospital. The complexity of this initial scheme typified the whole approach to centres of excellence relying as it did on the goodwill of institutions, people and services to work together to achieve a common goal. The Leeds Centre offered high-level coaching and support in a wide range of activities embracing basketball, badminton, gymnastics, judo, swimming, table tennis, and volleyball for 150 aspiring talented young people.

By the end of 1977 other centres had developed in Manchester and Birmingham and by 1978 the Sports Council was able to report proudly that centres of excellence of infinite variety existed in each of its nine regions covering some twenty-two sports in all, not all of which were Olympic activities. Each centre of excellence took advantage of local conditions and opportunities for cooperation but all subscribed to the same basic formula and met the general criteria laid down at the outset. Each centre by definition had to be an integral factor in the national plan for each governing body whose sport was included; the sports bodies themselves playing a critical role in the selection of those nominated to attend and in monitoring performance.

The National Sports Centre at Crystal Palace and the Headquarters of REME at Arborfield in Berkshire both became involved in the work of centres of excellence, the latter due to the involvement of the Olympic Gold Medallist Captain Jim Fox who saw to it that the Modern Pentathlon Centre was based there in association with local sports centres. Centres of Excellence as per the White Paper were concerned not only with individual sports but included team sports such as hockey, volleyball, basketball and lacrosse which featured in a number of locations. The critics of this evolving scheme were often fearful that sport was to some extent moving out of the control of the governing bodies which was proved subsequently not to be the case. Others, pointing to the already existing system of clubs of high standard in a variety of sports with good coaches available to them, were concerned that a centrally backed system would destroy the existing local structure. It was to be many years before the critics were largely silenced, but it would be untrue to say that mistakes were not made in the development of this scheme. The majority of mistakes which occurred were unfortunately the result of lack of thorough consultation with the voluntary sports bodies which understandably aroused suspicion, but these were largely sins of omission and not of commission due to the enthusiasm of those involved to get on with the task in hand.

Drugs in Sport

The spectre of drug abuse in sport began to be an issue in the late sixties. Artificial aids to high-level performance were not a new phenomenon although happily until the 1970s the problem was somewhat isolated and had not unduly worried the international sports federations. Since 1970 Professor Brooks and a research team at St. Thomas's Hospital Medical School in London had been working hard on developing an effective and foolproof method of detecting the use by athletes of anabolic steroids. It was generally accepted 'locker-room' knowledge that some of the 'heavy men' in international track and field were probably taking these steroids to build muscle and bulk. With the Chairman of the Sports Council himself a medical doctor it was clear that a close interest would be taken in this field of activity. The problem was two-fold, first medical in that medical experts were pointing very clearly to real physiological damage occurring in those who resorted to drug abuse, and secondly ethical and moral in that to gain an unfair advantage over an opponent via the laboratory in this way was tantamount to cheating, counter to the fair play ethic, and contrary to everything that sport stood for.

By 1973 Professor Brooks was able to report success in that he and his colleagues had developed a method of screening to detect the use of anabolic steroids by athletes. This breakthrough was generally welcomed, apart from within the darker recesses of sport, and the International Olympic Committee (IOC) took a firm decision to accept the test officially. War was now declared internationally on athletes, coaches and indeed doctors, who in the interests of attaining Olympic and World Championships were prepared to cheat and run the appalling risk of permanent damage to health. Stories began circulating that this country or that country was ambivalent towards drug abuse of this sort, condoned the use of drugs, or in some cases actually prescribed them. Athletes with enormous bulk appeared on tracks around the world or on television screens but failed to turn up at events when testing was to take place being reported injured or 'suffering from a virus'. This behaviour gave credence to the whispering campaign. Girl swimmers from some countries developed musculature of frightening proportions with performances in the swimming pool to match, only to lose this body development on retirement. The swimming events of the 1976 Olympic Games in some cases demonstrated the alliance of body bulk and high-level attainment and fuelled the gossip that abounded. From time to time the testing system reported a positive test on an athlete, swimmer or weightlifter and the international federation acted, sometimes drastically, sometimes leniently, but those close to the scene were firmly of the opinion that the merest tip of a very nasty iceberg was all that was being seen.

By 1977 Professor Brooks had been joined in his work by Professor Arnold Beckett of Chelsea College, University of London, who was to carry on the work of establishing a drug-testing laboratory in his College, thus giving Britain a unique joint testing centre. At this stage the United Kingdom was leading the world in this field and the Sports Council, while continuing to assist with funding, was beginning to increase the opportunity given to national governing bodies of sport to use these facilities on an ongoing basis in an effort to keep their sports 'clean'.

This pioneering work by these eminent medical scientists was increasingly recognized overseas and testing for anabolic steroids became to be the norm rather than the exception at major international events. By the end of 1978 the Drug Testing Centre was operating firmly at Chelsea College under Arnold Beckett to such an extent that in the autumn of that year he considered it sensible to convene a seminar of governing bodies most likely to be affected by the creeping contagion of drug-abuse. This seminar aimed at alerting sports organizations to the very real and grave dangers that now existed in their sports and Beckett called for vigorous action nationally and internationally.[8]

The Chelsea Centre rapidly created a name for itself in the international sports world and Professor Beckett and his colleagues were in great demand. Over the years that followed Beckett was to be the principal adviser on drug abuse to the IOC and was to play a major role in future Olympic Games, World Championships and other major events as the use of even more sinister drugs for example, stimulants to the nervous system (cocaine, corticosteroids, human chorionic gonadotrophin [HCG]), began to be apparent.

Royal Commission on Gambling

In February 1976 the Labour Government set up a Royal Commission on Gambling. Normally sport would not be concerned with such a happening but in this cases the Commission was asked to enquire into how money raised from gambling could be used to support good causes including sport. The current taxation arrangements of the 1970s, still in force in 1990, were such that tax paid by football, horse and dog racing went into the general Treasury coffers and it was not expected that there would be any reversal of this arrangement. The idea of a national lottery, very prevalent in Europe, had often come up for discussion and it was confidently expected that this concept would be examined and recommended in some form so that sport would benefit. Mr. John Disley, Vice-Chairman of the Sports Council and a member steeped in knowledge about sport in addition to being an Olympic bronze medallist, was appointed a Commissioner as was Mr. David Coleman the 'top' BBC sports commentator who likewise had considerable expertise in this field.

Although the Sports Council prepared a detailed statement of evidence, drawing very much on overseas experience and practice, it presented its views with certain misgivings. Fundamental to the whole issue was the clear and firmly held view that no matter what resources might be made available from other sources to assist the development of sport the major responsibility for expenditure fundamentally lay with central and local government, in other words with the State. Faced, however, with successive annual grants from government far lower than what was required, the Sports Council on behalf of the British sports movement generally, and with some uneasiness, argued a case for a share of any financial hand-out that might follow the setting up of a National Lottery on the basis that any such resources would be used for major facility development where little progress was being made in Britain.[9]

Hopes were high when the Royal Commission reported in July 1978 as sport was listed as a 'good cause' that should be assisted if the recommended National Lottery were established. Although a national opinion poll carried out in 1975 showed that some 72 per cent of the population was in favour of a National Lottery the case was lost and the whole matter shelved when the Conservative Government was returned to power under Mrs. Margaret Thatcher in 1979.

Perhaps the whole issue was too much to accept, or perhaps both the Labour and Conservative parties feared to grasp the nettle as the former merely talked about the recommendations and the latter ignored them. For sport it was a further chance lost to do something radical and dynamic, to bring a fresh approach to the chronic problem of lack of financial resources. In the years that followed no further initiatives presented themselves which, if taken, would have altered the future direction for the provision of major facilities: it continued to be a case of a little more of what had been hitherto, often ground out of a reluctant Department of the Environment which itself, vast as it was, was often left starved of resources. Meanwhile in Western Europe sport continued to thrive on the proceeds of national lotteries and football pools which supplemented the resources made available from central and local government. The only bonus that accrued to sport from the Royal Commission was the legalizing of small lotteries and in the aftermath many local authorities and clubs ran lotteries for the benefit of sport.

Coaching, Research, Information and Documentation

In 1975 the idea of a National Research Centre was canvassed openly as the volume of research and investigative work in universities, polytechnics and colleges in the field of sport, recreation and leisure grew rapidly. The cost of such provision and the organizational problems presented by such a concept, it was realized, were formidable. Whilst the idea of a physical centre gradually faded the need to build up a sophisticated information and documentation service was acknowledged and ways to achieve this within overall budgets could be envisaged.

In a simple form an Information Centre had been established by the

National Playing Fields Association in 1969 to support the technical work being done jointly with London Polytechnic. In 1972 it seemed sensible to transfer this embryonic work to the new executive Sports Council with the object of widening its base to form a true focal point for the collection and dissemination of data primarily in the domestic field but increasingly, as permitted by the Royal Charter, in the international sector. Such a move provided an opportunity to coordinate the work of the Information Centre as it grew and developed with that of the National Documentation Centre, established likewise in 1969, at Queen's University, Belfast.[10] Whilst the Information Centre dealt with information on sport generally, and responded to an increasing volume of enquiries as its database and reputation grew, the National Documentation Centre provided a bibliographic service mainly for teachers and researchers in the field of sport and physical recreation, and drew extensively from the outset on international sources. In 1975 the National Documentation Centre moved to a more central location at the University of Birmingham under the general auspices of the University librarian.

With its extended terms of reference the Information Centre, located at the headquarters of the Sports Council, widened and developed its services and linked itself firmly with the Clearing House for sports information sponsored by the Council of Europe's Committee for the Development of Sport which was located in Brussels (Galerie Ravenstein, 4–27). By 1976 the advent of new technology in data retrieval permitted the Information Centre, under the very professional and expert management of Mrs. Joan Gordon, to join in the early work of the Viewdata system sponsored by the Post Office in Britain which grew and flowered into the sophisticated Prestel service of today; a service providing sports information of every kind at the press of a button and with the use of a telephone.

Whilst a National Research Centre as such was never a feasible proposition when the idea was promoted in 1975, the alternative services now being provided and made available to researchers, academics, teachers, coaches, administrators, journalists and the general public expanded quickly to give a unique and efficient system at a fraction of the cost envisaged originally for a research centre.[11]

With the knowledge of developments in Western European countries, such as the Federal Republic of Germany and France, and in Eastern Socialist Countries, such as the German Democratic Republic and the USSR, the agreement in principle to establish a National Coaching Unit or Centre was not surprising when it was forthcoming in 1975.[12] If, ran the argument, Britain is to raise the level of performance and the number of participants in sport, as mandated very specifically by the Royal Charter, then more and better coaches for all sports at every level are needed. Much good work in the sports sciences was being accomplished in universities, polytechnics and colleges and institutes of higher education. Coordination, however, was long overdue, as were the means of ensuring that results, obtained from good research, were made available to those who could use them profitably. Not for the first time in the history of sport development in Britain were ideas thwarted by lack of money. It was not until 1982 that a firm decision was taken to proceed with the proposal to establish the National Coaching Foundation (NCF) and only then because the haphazard growth throughout the country of courses in the sports sciences for coaches threatened to engulf the Sports Council.[13] The Deputy Director-General of the Sports Council was then charged with the setting-up of the NCF at an institution of higher learning, and this was done in the spring of 1983 based in Leeds Polytechnic. The appointment of Dr. Nick Whitehead, the former Olympic sprinter and a Principal Lecturer at Carnegie College, as the first Director quickly followed. The events leading up to the selection of the institution at which to base the Foundation and a description of the way the Foundation works, will be described later in Chapter 11 in some detail. At this stage it is worth recording that from agreement in principle to inauguration the process took eight years, mainly on account of cost, but also on account of the many problems faced in 1975 in getting acceptance of a physical location for the project by many of the academics working in the field who not unnaturally saw the logical location for such a Foundation in their university, polytechnic or college.

Major International Sports Events 1970–1980

The Winter Olympic Games of 1972 took place in Sapporo, Japan whilst the Summer Games were celebrated in Munich which forever will be recalled as the place where Palestinian terrorists struck at the Israeli team in the early hours of 5 September and murdered twelve of their fine athletes. Dobson and Payne in their book on terrorism *The Carlos Complex* refer to an interview with a Palestinian spokesman in connection with this terrible event and quote his views on the whole episode:

> We recognize that sport is the modern religion of the Western world . . . so we decided to use the Olympics, the most sacred ceremony of this religion to make the world pay attention to us. (Killanin, 1983, p. 98)

The political consequences of this foul deed were enormous and the Olympic Games remain forever besmirched by this wholesale act of barbarism. Overall Britain won four gold, five silver and nine bronze medals in the 1972 Olympiad which was superbly organized both in Japan and in the Federal Republic of Germany.[14]

Four years later in Montreal politics again played a major part although happily with no loss of life on this occasion. Competitors from Taiwan were initially refused entry visas by the Canadian Government despite earlier assurances to Lord Killanin,[15] President of the IOC, that the Olympic Charter would be upheld and visas would be issued to athletes from all countries that wished to participate. This whole affair was complex in the extreme involving the People's Republic of China who were not then in the Olympic Movement but with whom Canada had recently resumed diplomatic relations. The Canadian Government, led by Prime Minister Pierre Trudeau, was under pressure from the Government of mainland China who, at that stage, had made it known that the price for returning to the Olympics was that China should control Taiwan. Under some pressure from Lord Killanin the Prime Minister agreed to grant visas to Taiwanese athletes if they agreed not to use the name 'Republic of China' at the Olympic Games. Taiwan refused this condition despite being authorized to continue to use their flag and anthem, and they therefore returned home (see Killanin, 1984, pp. 133–4). Almost immediately Mr. Abraham Ordia, President of the Supreme Council for Sport in Africa, but now representing the majority of the African National Olympic Committees, demanded that New Zealand be banned from the Olympic Games as their national rugby team, the All Blacks, had recently played a series against South Africa in South Africa. This request was rejected out of hand and therefore twenty-four hours before the Olympic Games opened the sad sight of tearful Africans dominated the scene as they made their way to the airport and so home. The age of the boycott had begun in the Olympic Games (*ibid*, pp. 134–5).

Once again the Games were marred by controversy and dissension as political muscle was exercised. Away from the politics the athletes ran, jumped, threw, swam, rowed, boxed and lifted as hitherto. It was a sad Games for Britain with an overall tally of three gold, five silver and five bronze medals to show for their endeavours at Montreal in the summer to add to the one gold medal by John Curry at Innsbruck the winter before.

On a much happier note the Commonwealth Games were held at Christchurch, New Zealand in 1974 and at Edmonton, Canada in 1978. These were truly once again the 'Friendly Games' and assisted in removing to some extent the bitter taste of Munich and Montreal. Pitched at a lower level of performance, and in an atmosphere of festival, the Commonwealth Games in this decade shone out as a beacon in the darkness and underlined the true values of sport, competition, friendly rivalry and the right level of nationalism. Sadly even the 'Friendly Games' were to succumb to political boycott in 1986 in Edinburgh over the British Government's refusal to apply economic sanctions to South Africa.[16]

The Olympic Games of Munich and Montreal were glorious festivals of sport but they were forerunners of the bizarre events of 1980 and 1984. Lord Killanin and the IOC laboured valiantly to limit the damage done and strove hard to overcome the political aberrations of the times motivated by those who, for ulterior motives, were prepared to destroy all that sport stood for.

The Olympic Games in Moscow in 1980 and Los Angeles in 1984 proved to be exercises in super-power machismo, achieving nothing but heartache for athletes who had striven hard for years to represent their countries at the Olympic Games only to have their hopes dashed by men and women who cared little for sport, for young people or indeed for international friendship and understanding made on the tracks, in the swimming pools and in the arenas of international competition.[17]

By 1978 Britain had staged an impressive programme of world championships with the peak year being 1975 when seven such championships were held including the World Rowing Championships at the newly-opened prestigious National Water Sports Centre at Holme Pierrepont, Nottingham. In 1977 the World Table Tennis Championships were held at the National Exhibition Centre near Birmingham which gave a great uplift to this already popular sport.

For many the most exciting British performer of the seventies was the incomparable ice-skater John Curry who crowned a glowing career in 1976 by winning the European, World and Olympic titles in the space of a few months. In so doing Curry demonstrated a brand of excellence in sport that inspired the great successes in skating that were to follow; he thrilled the nation with his art and grace as Britain followed his great performances on television.

Amateurism and Professionalism

The problems of defining amateurism have been with British sport from the nineteenth century when the Rugby League was established separate from the Rugby Football Union on the issue of broken time in 1895. Cricket and tennis had in the 1960s resolved their problems with amateurism and professionalism by abolishing the distinction altogether and simply labelling their participants as 'Players'. The gentlemen and players division in cricket disappeared in 1963 whilst Wimbledon was declared an 'open' tournament with prize-money at stake in 1968; the rest of the cricket and tennis world followed suit. In soccer the principal casualties in taking this step in 1974 were the disappearance of the Amateur Cup in the domestic field and participation in the soccer tournament at the Olympic Games. Professional tennis and soccer players were re-admitted to the 1988 Olympic Games on condition they were not paid and in the case of soccer under additional stringent regulations.[18]

The sports scholarship schemes in North America, and the state-employed athletes in the Socialist countries, were, and still are, nothing more than camouflage for certain types of professionalism. With standards in international competition rising annually it was becoming more difficult in many sports for aspiring internationals to work a five-day week and devote sufficient time to training to ensure peak performance in addition to the time required to travel to the increasing number of international events now featuring in the international calendar. The officers of sports bodies not in the Olympic Games, such as badminton, have been able to cope with these social changes in an ordered manner and have introduced financial arrangements more in keeping with the times. They have only had to consider their own sport in these matters. In the case of the Olympic Games, with very many different winter and summer sports to contend with, ten and twenty-six respectively in 1988, the movement towards greater flexibility has been more difficult. Early in the seventies the IOC was floating the idea that its rules should be amended to permit amateurs to receive financial help towards the cost of training and the necessity to be away from work for greater periods of time. In 1973 the Sports Council in Britain was indicating that it was receptive to these more flexible proposals, in that if sufficient finance could be made available disparities between athletes the world over would be reduced. With this concept in mind a discussion paper was circulated by the Council to national and international organizations canvassing reactions to the tentative proposal that perhaps it would be wiser for all sports to go 'open', although the paper conceded that considerable finance would need to be raised to support athletes if such a major step were taken. This paper was not generally well received.[19]

By the end of 1975 the Sports Aid Foundation (SAF) had been established in Britain in anticipation of the increased volume of financial support that would be required when and if the IOC amended its rules in this connection; a step that confidently anticipated change and prudently demonstrated a commendable state of preparedness.[20]

At the IOC's session during the Montreal Olympic Games in 1976 the Byelaws to Rule 26 on 'Eligibility' were amended, as had been foreshadowed, to permit preparation-training of any duration, subject to the principle that an athlete's health must not suffer. The amendments further stated that an athlete must not be placed at a social or material disadvantage, and in the final schedule to the Byelaw to Rule 26 the conditions which would bar participation were itemized (see Appendix 10 in this volume).

Encouraged by these changes in the Byelaws concerned with eligibility, and having discussed preparation-training plans for the 1980 Olympic Games with national governing bodies, the Sports Council, supported by the Sports Councils for Wales, Scotland and Northern Ireland, dropped a bombshell when, in a press release, it quite unequivocally declared itself in favour of 'open' competition in a public declaration. This created a controversy of considerable proportions and the Sports Council was openly accused of interfering in matters which rightfully belonged to the Olympic sports, the international federations and the IOC. However, despite the controversy the statement did present a welcome opportunity for many to look hard and long at the abuses and unfairness of the current system where 'shamateurism' had long existed making a mockery of fair play and equal competition.

With the SAF coming on stream Britain was well organized to use the new flexibility in the amateur regulations for Olympic sports providing only that sufficient private money could be raised by the Foundation to meet the increasing volume of demand that was now being made by national sports bodies.[21]

The amateurism and professionalism issue will never disappear from sport until 'open' competition is the accepted rule, and whether that is a desirable aim raises an entirely different question and debate. In the meantime, the narrower confines of amateurism had been extended considerably by the decision of the IOC in 1976. Western European athletes were now able to compete more fairly with North American and Socialist competitors. For the developing countries in the Third World, striving to get a first step on the achievement ladder with little finance to support them the price of competing had been raised dramatically and it was to continue to escalate year after year from now onwards.

The Sports Aid Foundation

It was a Tuesday afternoon in the late spring of 1975 when the Director of the Sports Council, Walter Winterbottom, asked John Coghlan his Deputy Director, very recently promoted from running the West Midlands region for the Sport Council, to call on him.

'Get over to Frankfurt and see how the Deutsche Sporthilfe scheme works in West Germany and start something similar here' said Winterbottom. On such briefings, laconic in the extreme, Sports Council policy was usually enacted in those days and it sufficed; a far cry from today with the over-burdened bureaucracy of papers, drafts of papers, financial appraisals, sub-committees and the endless round of meetings. However on this occasion, somewhat perplexed, the Deputy Director asked for a little more detail before booking the flight and making arrangements to meet friends in the Deutscher Sportbund (DSB) (the German Sports Federation, established in 1950) who would no doubt be able to help. It transpired that in 1967 the DSB and the German Olympic Committee had established the Sporthilfe to raise funds to assist sportsmen and women preparing for high-level competition. Such financial aid was designed to assist the development of peak performance by relieving athletes of any financial hardships that might occur. This was the West German response to the college sports scholarship scheme of North America, and the heavily state subsidized full-time athletes of the Socialist countries who were often nominally employed in some state occupation that permitted them all the time needed for training and competition and provided a wage or salary at the same time.

For some months Walter Winterbottom, seized with the idea of emulating the West Germans and thereby creating a mechanism for injecting finance into élite performance, had privately discussed with Lord Rupert Nevill, the Chairman of the British Olympic Association, whether the BOA would care to develop this idea for Britain. Whilst technically and administratively the Sports Council could well have allotted grant-aid from public sources for this purpose such use, it was thought, would be politically sensitive when so many other social programmes were unfulfilled, and in any case here was an opportunity to tap other sources imaginatively as élite level performance had a high sponsorship profile. Lord Rupert, who additionally was a member of the Sports Council, believed this was not a task for the BOA but pledged full support for the Council if they went ahead and established a body similar to that in West Germany.

The Minister for Sport, Denis Howell, was kept fully informed and enthusiastically supported the plan to establish a 'sports aid' body charged exclusively with the responsibility to raise funds from fresh sources to support, in a material way with finance, those athletes from all sports who needed help to realize their full potential. The Minister went so far as to include reference to this concept in his White Paper *Sport and Recreation* in August 1975 (see paragraph 62 and Appendix 5 in this volume).

The maximum co-operation and assistance was given by the Deutsche Sporthilfe through its distinguished Chairman Herr Josef Neckermann, the former Olympic Gold medallist, and its Director Herr Gunter Pelshenke. Based on the West German experience the SAF was established in Britain in the autumn of 1975 with a view to getting to work immediately to raise funds to assist potential medal-winners for the forthcoming 1976 Summer Olympic Games in Montreal.

Mr. Peter Cadbury, a very successful businessman, was invited to be Chairman whilst the Sports Council agreed to provide the initial resources to accommodate and run the Foundation. The Deputy Director was given the responsibility to develop the operation, establish the structure, draft the guidelines and set up the necessary machinery to raise funds and proceed to recommend grants as soon as possible. He was further charged with paving the way to the appointment of a Director that would signal the independence of the new organization. Within two months Peter Cadbury decided that his way forward was not in sympathy with some of his colleagues on the Foundation and withdrew. Such a start could well have been the death-knell to a new fledgling organization that in any case was being looked at with suspicion by some governing bodies of sport who thought they might lose their sponsorships, but 'cometh the hour cometh the man' and from the shadows Paul Zetter,[22] the Chairman of Zetter Pools Ltd, emerged to take on the task. Early in 1976 Alan Weeks, well-known as a television sports commentator, was appointed to be Director. The partnership of Zetter and Weeks was to prove over the years ahead a team of great flair, ability and integrity and their contribution to British sport has been considerable. Alan retired in 1983 whilst Paul announced his retirement as Chairman a year later at the Annual General Meeting in September 1984, but agreed to remain on the Board of Governors. Noel Nagle[23] succeeded Alan Weeks.

From the outset the SAF gathered into its fold as governors successful businessmen who not only could give time, and were prepared to do so, but also had connections in the city, in commerce, industry and show business.

Whilst the constitution of the Foundation gave ex-officio places as governors to the Chairman of the Sports Council, the Chairman of the BOA and the Chairman of the CCPR which ensured cohesion of effort, Paul Zetter had as his two principal lieutenants in fund-raising Tony Stratton-Smith and David Nations. The former was a sports journalist by profession but was by then Chairman of a major company in the 'pop' world, whilst the latter was a wealthy businessman and a dynamic water-skiing coach, restless and urgent in all he did. Shortly these were joined by Eddie Kulukundis,[24] the theatrical impresario and David Coleman, the BBC sports commentator. These few have achieved prodigious things for élite sport through their association with the SAF and have given unstintingly of their time. Sadly David Nations died in 1981 and Tony Stratton-Smith in 1986. Their untimely deaths robbed the Foundation of gifted, generous and tireless workers.

A significant feature of the Board of Governors is that membership has attracted many wealthy and successful men from business, the professions and public life, most of whom, passionately interested in sport, have made major contributions to the work of the Foundation. In 1983 Mr. Denis Thatcher, the husband of the Prime Minister, became a governor, shortly to be joined by Mr. Cecil Parkinson, MP, a distinguished athlete in his younger days, a Cabinet Minister, and Secretary of State for Transport (1989).

From the start Winterbottom and Coghlan saw that the only way to ensure financial control over individual expenditure by nominated athletes was by channelling grants through the governing bodies of sport. To do otherwise would have been to place amateur status in jeopardy and weaken the control the governing bodies rightly had in the preparation-training of their high-level performers. Tacitly it was accepted that the governors of the Foundation did not wish to sieve and select from the many applications that would be forthcoming, and indeed did not feel themselves competent to do so. Accordingly from the outset a Committee of Advisers was established made up of distinguished 'wise men' of sport, all of whom were in touch with sport at national and international levels, whose integrity and reputations were beyond reproach and who commanded universal respect. This Committee over the years has had the responsibility for deciding the criteria for grants, for reviewing applications made by governing bodies of sport on behalf of individual sportsmen and women, and for recommending individual financial support to the Board of Governors. For many years this Committee of Advisers has been chaired by Bill Slater,[25] a former international soccer player and Captain of England.

Between late 1975 and early 1984 over £2m was raised by the SAF. It took six years to raise the first £1m and the next three to raise the second million which was indicative of the growing support business and industry was giving to help Britain achieve its sporting potential in international competition. A unique dimension that the Foundation brought to the sponsorship of British sport was through the linking of sport with show business. New imaginative ideas for fund-raising have been a feature of the Foundation from the beginning: the earliest link with the 'pop' world came through the generous donation of receipts from concerts in the United Kingdom by Elton John,[26] whilst schemes with major concerns such as Tesco's supermarkets, British Car Auctions, Diner's Club and Birds Eye have reaped rich dividends for sport. The early involvement of Sir Jack Cohen and Sir Leslie Porter of Tesco's led to the creation of the 'Sir Jack Cohen Memorial Fund' which ensures that one athlete annually is awarded a grant of sufficient magnitude that allows him or her to train and prepare without regard to any parental or family contribution to training costs.

Sir Leslie Porter[27] succeeded Paul Zetter in April 1985 and he in turn handed over to Eddie Kulukundis three years later.

The establishment of regional arms of the SAF towards the end of the seventies has had only qualified success to date but, nevertheless, has provided much needed help to aspiring top-level performers at county and regional levels when they would not otherwise have qualified for national Foundation grants.[28] The years ahead should see the regional arms develop significantly, particularly as the national economy picks up as they rely very considerably on business and commerce more directly linked to local communities.

The success of the SAF from the start is one of the happiest British sports stories to record, and just as Britain was helped by West Germany to develop its 'Sporthilfe' so Britain has helped other countries to do the same based on the British experience. An enjoyable by-product of the enterprise of the Foundation is the Annual British Sports Ball which takes place in the spring with the support of the CCPR and the BOA. Whilst this is not intended to be a fund-raising event, but simply a glamorous occasion for those who are involved in sport in Britain to meet and enjoy themselves, it does make a useful contribution to the funds due to the enormous support given by many commercial and business firms.

The Development of Mass Participation in Sport

The Sport for All Campaign

Long before the slogan *Sport for All* was invented President John F. Kennedy in an address to the American nation in 1961 said:

The strength of our democracy is no greater than the collective well-being of our people,

and he went on to urge 'an increase in our facilities and the time devoted to physical activity'.

In the same speech he recognized the real problems that all who have attempted to put action to these words have found when he said,

I urge that in all communities there be more coordination between the schools and the community, parents and educators and civic-minded citizens in carrying forward a vigorous programme for physical fitness — a programme that will stir the imagination of our youth, calling on their toughest abilities enlisting their greatest enthusiasms.

Although President Kennedy was speaking in the aftermath of the Korean War, when the physical qualities of so many young American servicemen had been found wanting, he was, without knowing it, describing the *Sport for All* movement that took shape and substance in the Council of Europe in 1966 (see Chapter 11 in this volume).

Although 1966 was not the first time that governments had adopted policies and programmes promoting physical activity amongst citizens it was the first time a political grouping of nations had embraced an overall policy of this sort. Ten years later, in September 1976, the Council of Europe published the European *Sport for All* Charter.[29] This Charter recommended member states of the Council to base their national policies on the principles contained within it, and although the Charter had no mandatory authority, its impact was considerable in Western Europe and indeed far beyond.[30]

The general acceptance of *Sport for All*, and what it implied by the Council of Europe was due quite clearly to the fact that Western Europe, through those who represented member states in Strasbourg, sought to bring back to the word 'sport' some of its earlier broader meaning and universal appeal. Thus *Sport for All* was defined as something 'quite different from the original concept of sport, embracing not only sport proper but also, and perhaps above all, various forms of physical activity from spontaneous unorganized games to the minimum of physical exercise regularly performed'.

With Walter Winterbottom, the Director of the Sports Council, playing a crucial role in the Council of Europe on behalf of the British Government, and therefore a party to what other countries were doing in developing sports policies, the start of the 1972 campaign was well planned, researched and programmed in line with Western European thinking and the *Sport for All* Charter that was then at the earliest stage of drafting.

The Sports Council's *Sport for All* Manifesto[31] was published to coincide with the start of the British campaign and 500,000 copies were distributed. This Manifesto set out the agreed aims of the Sports Council, the Scottish Sports Council and the Sports Council for Wales and represented a clear demand for more facilities to meet the increased growth in participation. Promotional aids such as car stickers, posters, button-badges and banners were widely distributed whilst the media responded with considerable enthusiasm to the campaign. The charisma of the name 'Roger Bannister' was a significant factor and attracted its own publicity, but the cause was good and appealed to the public imagination.

The campaign from the earliest beginnings has been concerned with the role of sport in British society.[32] *Sport for All* in Britain attempts to extend to every section of society the beneficial effects of sport on social, educational, cultural and more latterly, health development. The campaign has always placed its main emphasis on attempting to provide the best possible opportunities for the greatest number of people, although latterly it has attempted a greater degree of selectivity with specific target groups. In Britain the campaign has never divorced elitism from the broad mass of participants as in some countries, for example, West Germany which talks of 'elite sport' and 'mass sport' as two separate, distinct and unrelated entities. In Britain the campaign has always aimed at stimulating participation at all levels. An examination of the successes and failures of the *Sport for All* campaign to date will follow later, suffice to say that at no time in the early years was there any policy direction that sought deliberately to exclude any section of society, rather the reverse (see Chapter 12 in this volume) It was only when the evidence began to emerge later pointing to lack of success with certain sections of the community that policies were agreed which positively discriminated in favour of the deprived.

The very wide range and variety of activities covered by the word 'sport' in the *Sport for All* slogan breaks down into four clear groups:

    (i)   competitive games and sports such as football, hockey, tennis and athletics;

    (ii)   outdoor activities such as climbing, walking, sailing and canoeing;

   (iii)   movement and dance which includes keep fit, Medau, ballroom dancing, skating and aerobics;

    (iv)   conditioning activities such as jogging, cycling to work or daily exercises.

Some activities fall into more than one category but broadly they are separated by the competition element as opposed to general physical recreation.

Since the beginning of the *Sport for All* campaign the Sports Council has refined and added to its aims and objectives. in the promotion and development of the campaign, but the aims established early on have survived throughout. These aims, described in detail by McIntosh and Charlton in their report for the Sports Council *The Impact of Sport for All Policy 1966–1984: A Way Forward*, fit broadly into six areas:

    (i)   to increase the rate of participation of the public at large;

    (ii)   to improve the performance of all sportsmen and women at every stage;

   (iii)   to establish the principle that the provision of opportunity to participate in sport and physical recreation is a social service not unlike education, health and housing;

(iv) to bring the social benefits of participation to a wider population. In this aim concepts of maintenance of moral standards, social welfare, unification of society and the general fitness and vitality of the nation are encompassed;
 (v) to create wider opportunities for the greater enjoyment by the community of their leisure time through physical activity;
(vi) to improve the quality of life.

Later in 1977 by acknowledging that participation in sport has real beneficial health aspects a further aim was accepted:

(vii) to promote the concept of better health through regular physical activity.

The Sports Council's objectives in attempting to achieve these aims are many and various. Special emphasis has been placed on particular objectives over the years with specific campaigns aimed at particular target groups such as the disabled, the family or the over-50 age group. It is interesting to observe that all but two or three objectives were defined in the seventies, most in the early part of the decade, which points to the sombre fact that probably not as much thinking, nor drive, was applied in the late seventies and early eighties until the strategy for the eighties, *Sport in the Community — The Next Ten Years*, was published in 1982. It is not possible to compile a definitive list of objectives of the *Sport for All* campaign as some are vague, some overlap and some repeat earlier statements in more up-to-date terms. However, it is possible from a close study of reports and papers to clarify principal objectives and McIntosh and Charlton have completed this task with their research. Few would disagree with them that the following re- present the main objectives, although no claim is made for this list being completely exhaustive:

Objective 1: Promotion of sport within target groups of non-participants with special reference to:
(a) School leavers
(b) Youth sport
(c) The disabled
(d) Over 50 age group
(e) Retired people
(f) The family
(g) Mothers with young children
(h) The unemployed

Objective 2: Promotion of excellence
(a) Development of regional centres of excellence
(b) Provision for young gifted performers

Objective 3:   Social benefits
(a)   Development of the 'areas of special need' concept, mainly in inner cities
(b)   Development of a greater understanding of the need of ethnic minorities
(c)   Combating social unrest in inner cities

Objective 4:   Cooperation with commercial and business interests
The development of:
(a)   Commercial investment in sports facilities
(b)   Sponsorship for the élite, talented young people and the mass sport performer.

Objective 5:   Medical-health
The reduction of coronary heart disease.

Objective 6: Facilities
(a)   The development of more and better facilities at national, regional and local levels associated with the need for greater capital investment.
(b)   The greater use of existing facilities both in public and private ownership.
(c)   The opening up of natural resources such as reservoirs, gathering grounds, rivers, lakes, coastal areas and the countryside to sport and physical recreation.

The Sports Council made it clear from the outset that the *Sport for All* campaign was a campaign for sport as a whole and anyone who subscribed to its aims was welcome aboard. The governing bodies of sport have been encouraged throughout to promote *Sport for All* and to form new structures and clubs to meet the increasing volume of participants. The grant-aid policies of the Sports Council have been constructed to enable sports organizations help themselves in these matters and some, but certainly not all, have responded to the challenge and the opportunity to develop their own activities.

Research has been directed at *Sport for All* in an effort to give a sounder rationale to policies and schemes, and this has not been confined to work in Britain alone. Professor Brian Rodgers, a member of the Sports Council and Chairman of its Research Committee, undertook in 1976 a research project of considerable complexity and importance of the Council of Europe. This study entitled *Rationalizing Sports Policies*[33] was published in Strasbourg in January 1977 and is an effort to put sport in Western Europe into its social context by making international comparisons. This excellent study profoundly affected the thinking in Britain, and the Technical Supplement published a year later is compulsory reading for all sports administrators, policy-makers and students concerned with the growth and development of the phenomenon of *Sport for All*.[34]

This report by Rodgers formed the substance to the *Sport for All* debate at the Second Conference of European Ministers responsible for Sport held at Lancaster House, London April 4–7 1978.[35] In his introductory speech the British Minister for Sport, Denis Howell, back now for a second term in office, opened the proceedings and stated:

> May I say to begin with, what we have done at Brussels[36] and in the whole sphere of the *Sport for All* movement has been to promote the right of citizens to the enjoyment of sport and leisure ...

Not one of the ministers present at the Conference demurred from his view that governments had a major role to play in developing opportunities for their citizens to take part in sport.

The development of a British *Sport for All* campaign made it of crucial importance for the Sports Council to involve itself to a far greater degree than hitherto in international collaboration with other national and international organizations. The experience of others was now brought to bear increasingly on British developments and policies and British experience was likewise exported. This matter will be expanded later when international affairs are discussed in some detail (see Chapter 13). The story of the development of *Sport for All* in Britain would be incomplete without acknowledging the very real contributions made to our national programmes by other Western European experience and research.

In the period up to 1980 the slogan *Sport for All* gradually worked its way into the nation's vocabulary and increasingly began to be used in magazines and the press, and on radio and television. Large banners bearing the slogan were to be seen at Wembley Stadium, Lords, Wimbledon, and at major national and international sporting events throughout the country. More and more organizations began to use the slogan for their own ends. The year 1975–76 was designated as *Sport for All the Family Year* with a special focus on family recreation. The Silver Jubilee year of 1977 was used to highlight *Sport for All* by way of a two-day event in Hyde Park London in honour of HM the Queen's Jubilee which attracted intensive press, radio and television coverage nationwide. This most ambitious and successful national event was supported by a wide range of regional events including inter-sports centre competitions, displays, festivals of sport and schools of sport sponsored by well-known public companies such as Guinness, Tarmac, Vaux and the *Evening Standard*.

Preparations for the 1979 campaign were guided by the Sports Council's Medical Advisory Group under the distinguished chairmanship of Professor Jerry Morris, the eminent cardiologist. In support of this campaign Professor Fentem of the University of Nottingham Medical School was commissioned to identify from existing literature and sources the evidence of the relationship between exercise and health. Peter Fentem's report was later published under the title *The Case for Exercise* and its findings fundamentally altered the thinking and policies of the Sports Council (see Fentem and Bassey, 1977). At this stage a fundamental policy shift for the Council took place as it sought increasingly to justify the demand for additional expenditure on providing sport and physical recreation opportunities for a wider range of people on health grounds. In 1977 a joint conference of the BBC, the Health Education Council and the Sports Council had been convened resulting in an agreement that all three bodies would cooperate in 1979 in a joint campaign under the title *Feeling Great*.[37] Sadly, in 1978, the Health Education Council launched its own independent campaign with the slogan *Look after Yourself* with virtually the same aims as those agreed for the projected joint campaign. This unilateral action was a shock and a disappointment and represented a great national opportunity lost. The Sports Council, faced with this situation, decided to lower its sights and link the year 1979 to positive health through sport in the *Sport for All — Come Alive* campaign.[38]

There were many factors that contributed to more people taking part in sport in the seventies such as increased car ownership, longer holidays, the shorter working week, greater affluence and the growth of more and better facilities. *Sport for All* caught the mood of the times and gave a focus to the considerable social changes that were taking place in society. Figures concerning participation can be notoriously unreliable but there can be no doubt that the number of people taking part in sport and physical recreation in Britain during the seventies increased considerably.

The number of squash clubs registered with the Squash Rackets Association rose from 1,057 in 1970 to around 4,480 by 1980 whilst the membership of badminton clubs rose from about 45,000 to 1.1 million during the same period. The Football Association recorded the formation of a further 5,000 clubs during the decade whilst the English Bowling Association reported an increase from 70,000 members in 1970 to upwards of 110,000 by 1980. Women's hockey clubs remained approximately the same in number but the number of girls' clubs in schools rose sharply. Rugby union showed a rise in the number of clubs whereas tennis showed a decline. Whilst these examples represent clear trends the statistics can confuse as well as inform. Illustrative of this point is the fact that in the seventies a large number of tennis clubs merged to form bigger clubs and the record does not show whether this type of development led to a greater or lesser number of participants. Likewise existing rugby clubs often formed more teams to take account of demand and this development will not be shown in the bare 'growth of clubs' statistics.

The growth of outdoor participation in physical activities was considerable and followed from the general increased interest shown in schools in the sixties.

The provision of more swimming pools, more sports centres and a wealth of small facilities, often associated with specific activity clubs such as pistol and small-bore shooting ranges, scrambling hills, indoor bowls rinks, gave increased local opportunity to those seeking a venue for their preferred activity.

Whilst increasingly there was considerable objective evidence available pointing to greater participation, it was not until 1984 that an overall review of the success or otherwise of *Sport for All* policies took place. With hindsight it can be seen that despite an increase in the numbers taking part in sport, in some cases a considerable increase, the pattern of non-participation remained virtually the same from the first campaign in 1972 by certain groups in the community that could be clearly identified. This having been said the *Sport for All* campaign in the seventies was largely successful taking into account the pitifully small sums of money available to publicize and promote it. Those receptive and waiting for the call responded well but many neither heard the call nor responded to it if they did; this was a major problem that faced the policy-makers as the seventies gave way to the eighties.

Notes

1 Grant-aid by the Government to national voluntary sports organizations in Great Britain for the five years preceding the establishment of the Sports Council was

1960/61	£195,922	1963/64	£381,127
1961/62	£254,769	1964/65	£467,167
1962/63	£304,522		

Source: *The Sports Council — A Report*, November 1966, p. 13.

2 'Sport promotes physical fitness for all ages ... it can be therapeutic to the mentally ill and handicapped. It is also a valuable outlet as an antidote to work; quiet relaxation from noisy work or strenuous exercise after desk-bound hours ... for all of these reasons it is necessary to see that opportunities for sport reach all in society.' Sports Council Annual Report, 1974–75, p. 4.

3 See *Sport and the Community* (1960) (The Wolfenden Report), chapter 3.

4 Sports Council Annual Report 1972–73, paragraph 3.6.

5 1972–73 £188,842; 1973–74: £420,120 (Sports Council Financial Statistics).

6 1972–75: Mountaineering — £65,599; Dance and Movement — £108,499 (Sports Council Financial Statistics).

7 Sports Council Annual Report lists specific grants to organizations in financial appendices.

8 The seminar was held on 18 October 1978 and was attended by representatives of nineteen governing bodies of sport. There was no formal report. By 1978 only six governing bodies were testing.

9 A submission of evidence was made by the Sports Council to the Royal Commission. On 1 October 1973 Roger Bannister gave a quote to John Morgan of the Daily Express in which he said '... if the Government is not prepared to

allocate enough money to meet sport's essential needs in future, then there may be a case for an overall levy on gambling that would benefit all sports'.

10   The Sports Council financed the establishment and operation of the Centre. Queen's University was selected because of the earlier work in this field by Mr. A. McDonald who was on the staff of the University.

11   The first mention of the proposed Central Institute for Research is in the Sports Council's Annual Report for 1975–76 (p. 5) '... there is a compelling need to establish a central institute for research in recreation within a University complex to support the work that can be contracted with other units and the commercial market. This centre would provide a stable work situation for a mixture of sociologists, economic planners, geographers, management and operational research workers.'

12   A 'National Coaching Unit' was first mentioned in the 1975–76 Annual Report of the Sports Council (p. 10) but it was recognized that 'it is not possible within present resources to provide the grant to embark on this desirable development'.

13   The Council for National Academic Awards (CNAA) had for some years been validating first degree courses in sports studies, sports sciences, movement studies etc. Regions of the Sports Council had begun to tap into the expertise available in universities, polytechnics and colleges and at the request of county and regional sports bodies had begun to put together courses to improve coach education.

14   Official reports of each Olympic Games are prepared and published by the British Olympic Association.

15   Michael, Killanin, 3rd Baron; IOC, Member (1952–80); President (1972–80); President, Olympic Council of Ireland (1950–73).

16   A report is prepared by the English Commonwealth Games Council after each Games but it is not published. These reports are available to researchers at the offices of the British Olympic Association.

17   See Chapter 13 for further details of the political machinations concerning the Olympic Games of 1980 and 1984.

18   In the 1988 Olympic Games no soccer player could take part who had played in the World Cup Competition. In 1992 the soccer competition will be open to all but players must be under 23 years of age.

19   The British Olympic Association reacted against the views expressed and the Sports Council was asked not to interfere with Olympic affairs. Reference to the initiative is made in the Sports Council's Annual Report 1973–74, p. 7.

20   A first official mention of an 'SAF' is in the Sports Council's Annual Report 1974–75, p. 6. See later in this chapter and Chapter 11 for further details of SAF.

21   Subventions to individual athletes by the SAF through the governing bodies of sport opened the way for some sports, traditionally all amateur such as athletics, to develop trust funds for 'top' sportsmen and women allowing them to earn money by advertising and by competing. This money they draw upon for current training needs. Upon retirement the trust fund is at their disposal.

22   Paul Zetter, CBE (1981); Chairman, Sports Aid Foundation (1976–85); Chairman, Southern Council for Sport and Recreation (1985–87); Sports Council, Member (1985–87).

23   Noel Nagle retired from the Army as a Brigadier to become Director of the SAF.

24   Eddie Kulukundis OBE (1988); Chairman, SAF (1988–   ); Chairman, Knightsbridge Theatrical Productions (1970–   ); Member, Lloyds & Baltic Exchanges; Governor, Royal Shakespeare Company.

25   W.J. Slater OBE (1982); Director of Physical Education, University of Liver-

pool (1964–70); University of Birmingham (1970–83); Sports Council (1974–83); Director of Development Services (1984–89); Chairman, Lilleshall National Sports Centre (1979–83); Wolverhampton Wanderers FC (1951–62); English International; Footballer of the Year (1960).

26 Elton John, musician; composer; superstar in 'pop' world; Chairman, Watford FC (1976–89) Member, SAF.

27 Leslie Porter, Kt (1983); Chairman, Tesco PLC (1976–85); Chairman, SAF (1985–88).

28 The nine English regions of the SAF together with Scotland and Wales made grants of £71,030 in 1982–83; by 1988–89 this had risen to £208,402.

29 Council of Europe European Sport for All Charter. Resolution (76) 41 of the Committee of Ministers; September 1976. On the Principles for a Policy of Sport for All.

30 See: *Sport and International Understanding*, Proceedings of the Congress, Helsinki, 7–10 July 1982; edited by Maaret Ilmarion, printed Germany; Springer-Verlag, (1984) in particular p. 236 et seq 'The Extent, Context and Organization of International Co-operation in the Past, Present and Future in Respect of Sport for All', UNESCO (1978) 'International Charter of Physical Education and Sport'.

31 Can be seen at the Information Centre at the Sports Council in London. It encouraged 'governing bodies of sport to get people to take part in sport at all levels'. In particular it spoke of 'those missing out on sport' and sought 'to fill the gap for them'.

32 See McIntosh and Charlton (1985) for the most comprehensive review and critique to date.

33 Published by the Council of Europe's Committee on Sport (CCC/DC (77) 11–E) under the title *Rationalizing Sports Policies. Sport in its Social Context-International Comparisons.*

34 This Supplement: (a) gives fuller technical detail; (b) describes the statistical treatment of these materials; (c) undertakes speculative statistical exercises on the data-sets; (d) draws together tentative data-sets on sports finance; (e) evaluates the diverse 'and very unsatisfactory statistical evidence'; (f) recommends possible approaches to a major international participation survey, a motivation enquiry, an international facilities inventory, and preliminary studies of sports finance.

35 See Council of Europe Report *2nd Conference of European Ministers responsible for Sport*, London, 4–7 April, 1978, ref. CMS (78) 11–E.

36 Brussels was the 1975 venue for the 1st Conference of European Sports Ministers. The texts adopted are included in 'Texts Adopted at Meetings of European Ministers responsible for Sport 1975–86', Council of Europe MSL-6 (88) BI-E.

37 This joint campaign aimed to market active participation. The idea stemmed from the Canadian 'Participaction' campaign which started by getting people out of their chairs, leaving their cars to walk 'around the block', to play with the family and to sense the feeling of well-being that follows such activity. For the first time the Sports Council's Annual Report 1976–77 speaks of 'plenty of evidence from abroad that sport benefits from exercise campaigns'.

38 The campaign was launched in September 1978. A circulation of 500,000 posters and 110,000 information packs was made to clubs, sports associations and public authorities. A telephone advisory service was established at the Sports Council. Medical guidelines and details of national jogging, walking, cycling and swimming schemes were distributed. Regional Sports Councils and local authorities latched on to the campaign that involved both old and young and the disabled. Roger Pontefract, a talented Sports Council Officer, directed the campaign.

Chapter 8

Sport and Politics

Sport is linked with Government and with politics and it is naive to believe or wish it to be otherwise. Sport reflects the society in which we live and politics are concerned above all with society, its standards, its ethos, its culture and its economics.

> Sport is part of the social superstructure and therefore strongly influenced by the prevailing socioeconomic system — not something in itself and not divorced from politics. (Ponomaryov, 1981)

Although the appointment by successive governments of a Minister for Sport, and the establishment of the Sports Council by Royal Charter in 1972, had underlined the linkage of sport with politics in Britain, it did not follow that the Government actually controlled sport nor did it follow then that it wished to do so. The increase in public finance at national and local levels for facilities for sport, for the wages and salaries of those charged to administer and develop activities and programmes, and for many of the actual programmes, involved political will and decision both in Parliament and in the town halls throughout the land. The partnership built up between the statutory authorities and voluntary sports organizations prospered in the seventies, within the overall financial restraints that then prevailed, to the general benefit of sport in Britain.

During the period 1970–1980 the Conservative and Labour parties formed Governments and each administration was responsible for a range of public statements, papers and reports concerned specifically, or in some cases indirectly, with sport, physical recreation and the broad area of leisure. The principal statements, including the very important 1975 White Paper *Sport and Recreation* have been summarized in Appendix 5 to this volume.

Debates on sport in the House of Commons are rare but that of 15 July 1971, which took place after the new Conservative Government had announced its plans for an independent Sports Council, but before these plans had come into effect, is worth recording as it was sharp, to the point and stormy. Students of the period will read the Official Report in Hansard (cols. 811–66) but the timing was significant as it was the last public attack made by former Minister Howell on his successor before the publication of the Royal Charter, and as such set the scene for the years to come for both parties in or out of power. In attacking the Government for the steps it was to take the Opposition motion read as follows:

> That this House deplores the cancellation of local sports club grants and the reduction of grants to British international sports teams . . .

and it went on to condemn the suspension of the scheme for grant-aiding local youth club projects and the rejection of the report *Youth and Community Work in the Seventies* (*ibid*, col. 811).

This Opposition motion was defeated by 191 votes to 161 whilst a Government amendment in the following terms was approved by the same margin:

> That this House welcomes Her Majesty's Government's decision to fulfil its election promises by establishing an independent sports council with enhanced status, wider powers and larger funds at its disposal; believes the sports council should have wide discretion in the allocation of those funds for local and regional purposes . . .'

and went on to note with approval continued support for the Youth Service (*ibid*, cols. 871–2).

The debate ranged over the whole field of government intentions for an executive, independent Sports Council and the steps that needed to be taken to ensure a better future for sport in Britain. It is interesting to recall that two future Prime Ministers, Mrs. Margaret Thatcher and Mr. James Callaghan, supported the Minister with responsibility for Sport and the Shadow Minister respectively in the division lobby.

Between 1970 and 1980 Britain had three Ministers for Sport (see Appendix 6 in this volume), Denis Howell, Eldon Griffiths and Hector Monro. They were completely unalike in the way they interpreted their role. Howell, knowledgeable, gregarious, personable, interventionist and opposed to an arms-length body; Griffiths, charming, non-interventionist, more concerned with other ministerial duties apart from sport but determined to carry out his party's policy to establish an independent body. Howell understood the local government scene and carried political 'clout' in the Labour Party; Griffiths, a forceful speaker had little knowledge of local government but did have the ear of the Prime Minister. He, having set matters on the road, largely withdrew whereas Howell maintained a high profile both in and out of office. Monro was quiet, knowledgeable and effective; constructive in all he did.

During the same period the Sports Council had five Chairmen, Howell and Griffiths while the Council was still advisory, and then Roger Bannister, Robin Brook and Dick Jeeps (see Appendix 6 in this volume) following the granting of the Charter. It would be difficult to choose three more different personalities. Bannister, an eminent neurologist with a unique niche in sporting history as the first sub four-minute miler, the amateur par excellence, highly motivated with an almost frightening sense of purpose, brought a formidable intellect, style and a sense of direction that set the standard against which successors would be measured for some time to come. Brook, a wealthy merchant banker, a man of the City, somewhat austere and shy, an Olympic fencer, wartime member of Special Operations Executive (SOE), friend of Cabinet ministers, poor public speaker but brilliant committee man, loyal to those who served him but contemptuous of party political manoeuvring, dealt only with the 'top' in Whitehall i.e. ministers and permanent secretaries, and brought the Sports Council to a pinnacle of prestige and effectiveness in the field. Jeeps was not a university man like his immediate predecessors but was a fruit farmer when appointed. He relied on 'gut' reaction rather than intellect or persuasive argument and although he knew what he wanted to achieve he often could not see the way to accomplish this and thereby suffered in his dealings with Whitehall. He lacked style and the Council accordingly moved down-market. Outstanding with the media he enjoyed a high profile particularly with the press, but his inability to see the greater design caused him to meddle 'down the line' in the professional work of the staff which created management problems. His 'feel' was right and he felt strongly about the under-privileged in sport. His great personal record as a rugby international for England and the British Lions over many years greatly helped his public image in the field of public relations but the Council lost credibility as it was seen to abandon more and more its independent line of action. There was a sigh of relief all round when he resigned in 1985 to be replaced by John Smith.[1]

Over at the British Olympic Association Lord Rupert Nevill (Chairman, 1966–67) served with distinction for eleven years before handing over to Denis (later Sir) Follows in 1977 (see Chapter 4 in this volume). Again the contrast between these two first-rate Chairmen was quite stark. Lord Rupert, aristocrat, equerry to HRH Prince Philip, member of the Sports Council, Chairman of the Greater London and South-East Sports Council, had style, elegance, charm and devotion to service; good to be with and always enjoyable company. Follows, former Secretary of the Football Association and before that a trade union leader, had his own brand of style and how effective that was! Passionate about sport, almost to a fault, he won worldwide acclaim for his stand against Mrs. Thatcher's Government over the 1980 Olympic issue in defence of the freedom of sport. In many respects he was a giant and in others a tyrant as he revelled in ferocious argument for any cause he embraced. Scars are still carried by those who fought with him in his capacity as Honorary Treasurer of the 'new' CCPR, for their annual grant; formidable in argument and presence, but never vindictive, he stood his corner and like the good trade union leader he was he knew the moment to compromise and settle — a likeable and respected man.

The Central Council of Physical Recreation, established as the consultative forum of governing bodies of sport to the Sports Council as prescribed by the Royal Charter, had three Chairmen between 1970 and 1980; Sir Stanley Rous (1945–72); Mr. Denis Howell (1973–74) and Mrs. Mary Glen Haig (1974–80).

Sir Stanley was the grand old man of British sport having been a schoolteacher, football referee, Secretary of the Football Association, President of the Fédération Internationale de Football Association (FIFA) and linked with sport nationally and internationally for a lifetime (see Chapter 5 in this volume).

Denis Howell, out of office in June 1970, accepted the invitation of Prince Philip to stand as Chairman for the 'new' post-Royal Charter CCPR, Sir Stanley having decided that it was time to withdraw after nearly thirty years in the chair. Called back to office in 1974 Howell handed over to Mrs. Mary Glen Haig,[2] the former Olympic fencer. She had for many years played a major role in sports administration, one of the few women in Britain at that date to do so, and in 1982, following the death of the Marquess of Exeter, she was invited to become a member of the IOC.

The relationship and interplay of these principals, their strengths, weaknesses, foibles, friendships, partnerships and rivalries is the background to much that took place in sports administration during this period. From the beginning Howell had made his position quite clear in not wanting an executive Sports Council and when he returned to power in 1974 the relationship between him and Bannister, exacerbated by Howell's spell at the CCPR, was uneasy always and often tense. Bannister was determined that the role of the CCPR should be confined to that described in the Charter and he called the tune; Howell had in many respects to follow while he was at the CCPR. An example of this was the refusal of the Sports Council to fund the presence of the Chairman of the CCPR in Christchurch, New Zealand for the Commonwealth Games of 1974. With Howell back as the Minister Bannister's position was difficult as the Minister wanted and supported an increased role for the CCPR against the wishes of the Sports Council. It is to the great credit of both Bannister and Howell that they rarely allowed their differences to spill over from the committee room. Sir Robin Brook was invited by Denis Howell to be Chairman of the Sports Council when Sir Roger retired at the end of 1974 and they got on well and worked together. The 'Stacey Affair'[3] in 1977 concerning the successor to Walter Winterbottom, described in detail later, soured the relationship and the last six months of his Chairmanship were affected by this incident. There was a rumour that Brook would have liked to be invited to stay on but no evidence exists for this assumption and it is doubtful in view of the clash that occurred publicly over the Director's appointment. The dual role that he played as Chairman of the Sports Council and Honorary Treasurer of the CCPR created tension as the Council decided the level of grant to be made annually to the CCPR; with hindsight it would have been wiser to relinquish the Treasurership.

Jeeps was appointed by Howell largely on the press reports of his successes during his recent year in office as President of the Rugby Football Union. Within a year Labour was out of office and Hector Monro was appointed Minister for Sport in 1979. Howell and Jeeps worked well together but later, while Neil Macfarlane was Minister, Howell in opposition bitterly attacked the supine attitude adopted by Jeeps in connection with the departure of the Vice-Chairmen, Disley and Atha, and the Director-General and his Deputy, Jones and Coghlan.

Denis Howell hankered for the days between 1965–1970 when he was both Minister and Chairman of the advisory body, not for any purposes of self-aggrandisement but simply because he genuinely thought this to be the best way to promote and develop sport in Britain. Strenuous efforts were made by him when back in office to see if the Royal Charter could be revoked or amended to bring the Sports Council into the public posture he supported but to no avail and the Charter stood firm. Eldon Griffiths as Minister for Sport played a stand-off role in sport, interested and ready to do all he could to support Roger Bannister in Parliament and the country whilst Denis Howell when Minister played a more interventionist role and wished to be more involved at the scene of action. With Robin Brook as Chairman of the Sports Council the view of Denis Howell did not alter, but by then he was reconciled to the system established by his predecessor and loyally and constructively worked within it for the benefit of sport. Whilst Ministers were always willing to make their views known, and do everything they could to impress these upon the Sports Council, there were no instances on record, apart from the appointment of a successor to Winterbottom, when force majeure was applied in an effort to bend the Council to ministerial will, unlike the situation which prevailed later in the early eighties when Neil Macfarlane was the Minister (see Chapter 4 in this volume).[4]

Sir Walter Winterbottom (see Chapter 3)

During the periods of office of Eldon Griffiths and Denis Howell, Roger Bannister and Robin Brook the significant figure of Walter Winterbottom, the Director of the Sports Council, loomed large. A former England football team manager and Director of Coaching from 1946 until being appointed General-Secretary of the CCPR in 1963, it was he who played such a considerable role in the merging of the CCPR into the Sports Council. He was bitterly opposed to the emergence of a 'new' CCPR and in its early days, after its formal establishment in 1973, did much to curtail its power and influence. A giant in many ways, Winterbottom was a man of vision, authority and dedication who achieved fine things for sport in Britain for which he was rightly honoured and for which he is remembered. A mixture of gentleness, kindness, understanding and single-mindedness marked the man who had the ear and respect of ministers and Chairmen alike. There are some who believed he coveted the 'crown' itself and saw himself as a possible Chairman when the Sports Council was established by Royal Charter in 1972; if so, this was never shown. There is hearsay evidence to indicate that there were those who feared his authority and expertise and would have liked to have seen him sidelined in 1972 in favour of a senior Civil-Servant appointment. This particular threat to Winterbottom's power and authority came to a head while he was in Rome on official business. The theatrical comparison with Julius Caesar on the steps of the Forum while the conspirators prepared to strike is maybe stretching literary license too far, but the private intervention by some senior staff, who made it quite clear that a Civil Service appointment was unacceptable, caused the matter to be quietly dropped; Winterbottom returned from Rome unaware of the threat that had been posed in his absence. He was the man the staff of the Sports Council wanted as their leader, and he was the man they had until his retirement at the end of March 1978. From 1972 he served Bannister and Brook with great loyalty, skill and devotion and he did likewise to Griffiths and Howell. He straddled the sports scene in Britain with wisdom and panache. He disappointed some close to the scene when, with the approach of retirement in the spring of 1978 on reaching the age of 65, he manoeuvred behind the scenes to stay on, no doubt in the belief that he was irreplaceable, a not uncommon trait in those who have held power for so long. When this was seen not to be possible he washed his hands of the succession problem as the Sports Council plunged into controversy, acrimony, unwanted publicity and ministerial intervention. This opting out, regrettable as it was, does not diminish in the final analysis the massive contribution made to British sport by Sir Walter Winterbottom. The great tragedy was that he was never invited after his retirement to play any further major strategic role in sport in Britain;[5] a great loss to the country in knowledge, experience and wisdom but some of his actions latterly had not endeared him to some of his senior colleagues who were loath to involve him further.

The 'New' CCPR

The emergence of the 'new' CCPR with a revised Memorandum and Articles of Association on 9 April 1973 to take the place of the former organization as 'the body representing national organizations of sport and physical recreation ...' (see Appendix 1 paragraph 6[3]) owed its existence very considerably to its President HRH Prince Philip, Duke of Edinburgh (see Chapter 5). The appointment of Denis Howell as Chairman in the period during the Conservative administration of Mr. Edward Heath was inspired in many ways but was also provocative. Peter Lawson, a fairly junior member of staff of the Sports Council's Yorkshire and Humberside region, was seconded as General Secretary and immediately seized the opportunity to prove his worth by tackling his appointment with enthusiasm and style. With Lawson's secondment terminated by his permanent appointment in 1974 the CCPR set about establishing itself as the voluntary voice of sport in Britain. The Scots and Welsh opposed this label as they had their own umbrella organizations for sports bodies, in the case of Wales the Games and Sports Committee of the Sports Council for Wales and in Scotland the Standing Conference of Sport.

With hindsight the English set-up can be seen to have had all the problems that have developed between the CCPR and the Sports Council over the years built-in at the outset, underlining the conflict of view as to whether an appointed body like the Sports Council, or an elected body like the CCPR, should be the premier voice and authority for sport in Britain. The overlapping of functions, the duplication of effort and the clash of personalities, have all contributed to friction between the two bodies and yet members of both organizations have often been dismayed at what has been said and done in their name and have distanced themselves from it feeling powerless to influence affairs differently.

The CCPR had the right to nominate seven of its members to the Sports Council via a rubber-stamping operation by the Minister for Sport.[6] The 1975 White Paper laid down improved liaison conditions and successive Ministers for Sport have through joint consultative arrangements brought about better relationships and understanding (see paragraphs 20–2). Despite these valiant and time-consuming efforts fresh controversies have flared up from time to time giving fuel to the media and dismaying the vast majority of the British sports movement. A constant theme in the Presidential addresses by Prince Philip during the seventies, and into the eighties, has been the disharmony between the two organizations. Basically from the outset the different sport ideologies of the two bodies, overlaid with personality clashes, produced a situation that has harmed the image of British sports administration at home and overseas and has led to some confusion.[7]

The British Olympic Association remained wisely aloof and apart, enjoying productive arrangements with both the CCPR and the Sports Council and concentrating on their role and function in British sport under the wise leadership of Lord Rupert Nevill and Sir Denis Follows. Sir Denis was ably supported from 1977 by the very effective General Secretary Dick Palmer who took over, after a brief period of interregnum, from the experienced Sandy Duncan who had retired in 1975.

The national sports bodies, whilst often deploring the frequent clashes between the Sports Council and the CCPR which usually won undue press coverage, continued to work positively with both bodies and sensibly rarely entered into the debate. For them the power struggle in the administration of British sport, whilst certainly not irrelevant, was not of prime consideration as they pursued their own business, increased their allocations of public resources to help them do so and continued to prepare teams for the many national and international events established by themselves or their international federations. By 1980 the majority of governing bodies of sport, where need had been proved, were receiving grant aid for administration, coaching, preparation-training and international travel from the Sports Council and this very considerable injection of financial resources permitted forward planning on a scale not hitherto possible.[8]

Parliamentary Interest in Sport

Political influence in matters affecting sport is crucial if policies requiring public finance are to be pursued with any chance of success. It was considered important therefore that, in addition to developing good working relationships with ministers and shadow ministers, effective liaison arrangements needed to be established with the many Members of Parliament who had a keen interest in sport. Accordingly from 1972 onwards the Sports Council entered into an ongoing dialogue with the All-Party Parliamentary Committee on Sport which drew membership from both the House of Commons and the House of Lords. The provision of briefing data, and a regular programme of meetings, both informed and encouraged support from Parliamentarians for the sports policies that were being pursued and acted additionally as a means by which MPs could obtain advice and assistance on problems in their constituencies concerning sports facilities, clubs, under-use of school facilities, loss of recreational land and many other related issues. This dialogue was both useful and productive but from 1978 onwards, for inexplicable reasons, it waned, apart from spasmodic meetings and personal contacts. The Parliamentary Committee continues to operate to this day, either as an all-party arrangement or on some occasions on a single party basis. What it lacks, and this is certainly no fault of the Members of Parliament who serve on it, is a sharpness of focus and bite which can only be provided by the major sports organizations singly or collectively. Occasionally some burning issue is brought to its attention but generally the opportunities have not been taken to inform Members which results in the sports lobby being carried in both Houses by a handful of individuals rather than a solid cohort. It would be true to say that sport has still to come to terms with the power of politics to assist, too often seeing politics as being detrimental to the cause.

Planning and Land-Use

The loss of recreational land has been a grave problem for sport for many years with the expansion of housing in towns and cities, the development of motorways, industrial estates and services connected with modern living. The threat to playing fields and sports clubs in inner cities and on the periphery of towns and conurbations by development was real in the sixties and seventies and continues unabated today joined now by the increasing threat to school facilities as falling rolls make schools redundant. Adequate legal protection has never been made for recreational land although the formal designation of land as private or public open-space on approved official town maps has helped. The high prices paid for land for development, in particular housing development, has continued to prove tempting to sports clubs who with planning consent have been able to realize large sums of money for redevelopment. Whilst this has denuded the urban areas of many local facilities it has certainly permitted new clubs, often larger and better equipped, to be created elsewhere. However, when clubs have had short leases, or no lease at all, the financial temptation by land-owners to give notice of closure to quit and then sell, has usually proved too great and the casualty list of club losses has been considerable. With sport more collectively organized, the power of Regional Councils for Sport and Recreation[9] greater, the dialogue with MPs and ministers more meaningful, the Sports Council having direct access to the Minister for Sport in the Department of the Environment which deals with land-use and planning matters, and the planning process giving greater acknowledgement to the need for recreational facilities within communities, the loss has slowed down to some extent. Despite this progress prevailing legislation in the seventies did little to prevent continual haemorrhage, a state of affairs that continues to this day.

Despite the gloomy record of continual loss on the debit side many new, bright and modern facilities were assisted with purchase of land, or long leases, that ensured use for sport in the future, and municipal authorities showed themselves increasingly sympathetic to the granting of the necessary long leases on publicly-owned land. Legislation introduced in 1968 established a revised planning machinery for local planning authorities which consisted of a strategic overview supplemented by local plans, both of which contained procedures for taking account of recreational needs for land and buildings.[10] The Officers and Planning Panels of the Regional Sports Councils (after 1976 the Regional Councils for Sport and Recreation) played an active role from the beginning in the formulation of structure and local plans. By contributing to this planning process requirements were built in which gave some measure of protection to land used for sport and recreation and for future requirements for both buildings and land. Whilst this 'built-in' process was certainly no guarantee that land designated for sport would remain inviolate, it did mean that any change of use required ministerial approval and this process allowed time for appeals and lobbies to be mounted. The appearance of representatives of national and regional governing bodies of sport with Sports Council officers at local planning enquiries became commonplace, and inspectors conducting public enquiries were increasingly aware of the cause and arguments mounted and the evidence on which these were based. In the seventies sport, and the needs of sport, was an issue that could not lightly be brushed aside in the political context as more and more it became linked with the very fabric of society.

Sport and Trade

The Sports Council inherited from the CCPR in 1972 a Sport Trade Advisory Panel that had been chaired by J. Eaton-Griffiths since 1954. 'Laddie' Lucas (see Chapter 4), a member of the Sports Council, took over responsibility for this Panel. The Panel was a joint body comprised of representatives of the sports trade in all its aspects, both those representing particular organizations such as the Sports Goods Distributors and the British Manufacturers of Sports and Games, and individuals with knowledge of this business together with interested Sports Council members. Through an interchange of views and ideas the sports trade became aware of Sports Council and general sports policy in Britain, and could react commercially to it, whilst the Sports Council learned of the problems faced by the commercial interests in sport at home and abroad which allowed it in turn the opportunity to assist in Whitehall and with ministers. Overseas trade enquiries come from many sources and increasingly through the commercial attachés at British embassies around the world. The Panel concerned itself with the timing of the notification of these enquiries to the sports trade, dissatisfied that so often they came too late to British business and consultants resulting in lost contracts. Work with the Department of Trade and Industry, the Foreign and Commonwealth Office, the British Consultants Bureau and the British Council produced a more streamlined procedure, but concern continued to grow that the British Government did not fully realize the potential trade and political spin-off in the world of sport both in the oil-rich countries of the Gulf and the developing countries generally.

Towards the end of the decade the persistent overtures from the Panel brought about a welcome governmental initiative. In late 1978, following his retirement, Sir Walter Winterbottom was appointed by the Minister for Sport as a consultant 'to advise the Government on ways in which British interests overseas could be promoted through sport and ways in which British manufacturers of sports equipment may be better able to compete with foreign firms'.[11] This appointment came about through discussions the Minister for Sport had with the Sports Council, the Chairman of the Sports Trade Advisory Panel, and subsequently with ministerial colleagues in interested Departments of State. By now it was increasingly noted that the British Government, either directly or through agencies, offered only minimal support for the provision of coaches, administrators and teachers of sport overseas compared with other European countries as a consequence of which export business suffered. In 1979 Sir Walter reported to the Minister who was now Hector Monro, a General Election having taken place and the Conservative administration of Mrs. Margaret Thatcher having been returned to power.[12] His report showed that a mere £17,000 was allocated to sports programmes overseas from money made available to the British Council through the Foreign and Commonwealth Office. This compared with France which had a budget of FF 10.6m, in addition to the cost of the salaries of 400 teachers of physical education serving overseas, all provided by the Government to the tune of FF 100,000 per teacher. In the Federal Republic of Germany in the same year DM 11.2m were provided to support their overseas sport aid programme. Winterbottom's concise and clear report made specific recommendations which the Sports Council largely endorsed in a short statement to the Government suggesting a way ahead based on the evidence displayed (see Appendix 11 to this volume).

Sir Walter's report, with suggestions for making progress by the Sports Council, was circulated by officers in the Sports Section of the Department of the Environment to other government departments. The response was discouraging; in some cases the issue was misunderstood, perhaps deliberately so, and the whole matter was dropped never to be seriously raised again officially by the Government. The problems that existed in the seventies exist to a considerable extent in 1990: nothing really has changed and opportunities to increase business by the provision of sports buildings and consultancies continue to be left largely to individual private companies assisted as best they can by British Embassies overseas.

The British Council's resources to commit coaches, teachers and administrators of sport continue to be pitifully small, faced as they are with cutbacks, but their interest, concern and best endeavours continue to make much of very little. A pathetic attempt by Neil Macfarlane, the Minister for Sport, in 1982 in a visit to the Gulf to create an initiative failed before it really started due to inadequate preparation, lack of briefing and the will to follow up possibilities afterwards. In all a sad and sorry story by comparison with Common Market partners and the Socialist countries of the Eastern bloc whose political influence and share of the market advances yearly in the developing world.[13]

The Succession

There now occurred in British sport as 1977 came to a close one of the more bizarre and quite extraordinary happenings of recent times. At the time of a meeting of the Sports Council in Glasgow in October of that year, it was common knowledge that the Director, Walter Winterbottom, would reach the maximum retirement age of 65 the following March; a formal announcement by the Chairman, Sir Robin Brook, of this fact was therefore expected. The meeting ran its course without any such announcement to the amazement of members and senior officers present until with 'any other business' called the matter was raised by a member. There then followed a lengthy and somewhat acrimonious debate as to the ways in which the succession was to be arranged, for clearly it had not been the intention of either Winterbottom or Brook to make any statement. It can only be surmised that the Chairman would have proceeded on his own as time was pressing and the Council did not meet again until early December, thereby denying formal consultations with the Council on this matter.

Pressed therefore to take action and advertize publicly the post of Director of the Sports Council, and instructed to keep members informed, Robin Brook put matters in train. Interviews were held in December with a short-list drawn up by the Chairman, the two Vice-Chairmen and the current Director. Two internal candidates were interviewed; John Coghlan the Deputy Director of the Sports Council and George Glasgow the very able Director of the Sports Council for Northern Ireland. Six external candidates were invited to complete the short list. Although some, including the media, thought that Winterbottom's Deputy would succeed him as he had for two-and-a-half years carried much of the heat and burden of the day at the top of the organization whilst the Director concentrated on the European connection emerging rapidly in the Council of Europe, this was certainly not a foregone conclusion. Throughout Winterbottom played an odd and somewhat ambiguous role and eventually appeared to wash his hands of the whole affair. Did he expect to be invited to stay on or did he have views on the succession at odds with his Chairman? Certainly a number on the Appointment Board made their preferences well known before the formal interviews which fuelled gossip and rumour.

In the event Nicholas Stacey, an external candidate, was the nomination of the selection panel to succeed Winterbottom. As the appointment of the Director and his Deputy have to be agreed by the Secretary of State for the Environment, as laid down in the Royal Charter, permission to make this appointment was requested after it had been approved by a majority of the Sports Council at a meeting on Monday 19 December. The Minister for Sport, Denis Howell, acting for the Secretary of State, refused to confirm the appointment when formally approached two days later. In a letter to Howell, Neil Macfarlane, MP, who had some share in the Opposition 'shadow' for sport, supported the Minister's action criticizing the selection procedure as totally the 'wrong way' to have arranged matters. Hector Monro, the 'Shadow' Minister for Sport also supported Denis Howell. Both Monro and Macfarlane were later to be appointed Ministers for Sport in the Thatcher administration.

Sir Robin Brook was now faced with three choices: should the Sports Council recommend Stacey again, should they accept the ministerial ruling and offer a further nomination from the short list, or should they scrap the whole business and start again by re-advertising? The volume of media coverage for this affair was quite extraordinary and embarrassing for the candidates whose merits and supporters were listed and commented upon from day to day.[14] Throughout Nick Stacey behaved with dignity, never once entering the fray with anything but the comment that he would like to serve. On Tuesday 10 January, a special meeting of the Sports Council was convened to consider the way ahead. The meeting authorized the Chairman and the two Vice-Chairmen, John Disley and Bernard Atha,[15] to go again to Westminster to seek a change of mind by Howell, not before some very disparate views had been expressed at the meeting at which only one officer, the retiring Walter Winterbottom, was present. John Coghlan, about whom there had been some considerable speculation as to his chances of being appointed, took himself off to Canada a few days beforehand at the invitation of the Canadian Sports Federation to speak at their Annual Conference in Regina, Saskatchewan. There he met the Federal Minister for Sport, Mrs. Iona Campagnolo, to advise on the delicate steps that were needed to be taken with the Canadian national federations of sport if the Federal Government was to play an increasing role in sport; a scenario not unfamiliar to him in the United Kingdom context.

The Minister for Sport, for the second time, refused to accept the nomination of Stacey and the position of Director was promptly re-advertized which once again occasioned considerable media coverage as the virtues and defects of possible candidates were discussed in public.[16] On 13 January, in a written reply in the House of Commons to Mr. Nigel Spearing, MP, the Minister gave the only formal clue to his reasons for acting as he did, and was empowered to do, when he said,

> The Sports Minister must be satisfied that the Director of the Sports Council was competent to be accounting officer for the Council's public expenditure.

and he continued by saying that he had to be sure that the Director was qualified in matters of sport and physical recreation and could be expected to hold the confidence of the Council and those with whom it worked in the promotion of sport. He went on to state

> After careful consideration I was unable to endorse the recommendation of the selection board.[17]

He concluded by telling the House that he had given the Chairman of the Sports Council a full explanation of his decision. Since that date no further reasons or statements have been made and Sir Robin Brook has never divulged the full contents of the letter from the Minister.

Walter Winterbottom retired on 31 March 1978 full of honour for his great services to sport but knowing that his conduct during the business of appointing his successor had been less than enthusiastically approved in certain quarters.

The Deputy-Director was appointed Acting-Director of the Sports

Council for the period 1 April–31 May 1978, and received great encouragement and support from the staff and the many members of the Council who had supported his candidature. In the meantime a fresh short-list was drawn up including Emlyn Jones[18] the Director of the Crystal Palace Sports Centre and John Wheatley[19] the Regional Director for the South West: both senior Sports Council officers who had not been short-listed for interview the previous December. With the retirement of Sir Robin Brook imminent on 31 May the Chairman-Elect, R.E.G. Jeeps (see Chapter 5 in this volume), was an important member of the interviewing panel. On 3 May Emlyn Jones was appointed and the appointment received the required approval from the Minister.

George Glasgow withdrew his candidature and Professor Brian Rodgers, Chairman of the Research Committee, withdrew from the interviewing board; both for reasons unstated. From the outset to the conclusion politics thus played a vital role in the succession. The Sports Council took time to recover from this catalogue of events in the following years and remained flawed by them. The power of the Minister for Sport had been exercised dramatically and reputations had been damaged at the Sports Council.

There are those who believe that the new Chairman of the Sports Council could have been someone different if the events of December 1977 and January 1978 had not taken place. This is purely speculation but shrewd observers are of the opinion that John Disley, the senior of the two Vice-Chairmen, might well have been invited to serve if the press had not identified him so closely with the original choice of Stacey giving the appearance of opposition to Denis Howell, which was not so. As it was early in 1978 Denis Howell, via a number of sources, was canvassing and taking soundings concerning a successor as Chairman to Robin Brook. At that time the Chairman was expected to give two days per week to the work of the Sports Council and was paid pro-rata on the basis of the salary paid to an Under-Secretary in the Civil Service. Men and women able and willing to take on these arrangements were not many, attractive as the job was, as it necessitated private means or a job that permitted time away without loss of career prospects. By 1984 the Chairmanship was deemed to require four days a week which put another complexion on matters as this entitled the holder to a not inconsiderable salary, but this was certainly not the case in 1978.

Many of the senior officers let it be known that 'Laddie' Lucas would be their choice. Here we had a dynamic, charismatic personality, an international golfer, a former Conservative MP, a semi-retired successful business man, a former Beaverbrook journalist and a man of great charm and integrity. The name of Lieutenant General Sir James Wilson was also talked about as was that of Michael Steele-Bodger, the former President of the Rugby Football Union and a veterinary surgeon. All three were members of the Sports Council and had been, or were, involved in sports administration at the highest levels. In the event the Minister invited Dick Jeeps, a recent

President of the Rugby Football Union and a Cambridgeshire fruit farmer to take on the Chairmanship and the invitation was accepted. The new Chairman had plenty of drive and determination, but there were question marks over his international experience in sport and nationally his experience was largely limited to rugby football. He had not been a member of the Sports Council but had, for a short period, been Vice-Chairman of the Eastern Regional Sports Council. Privately many reservations were voiced about this appointment, often tinged with surprise. No one denied that Dick Jeeps' sporting record was a considerable asset but several wondered how he would cope with the mandarins in the Civil Service, and by association the Rugby Union's attitude to sporting links with South Africa, they thought, could prove a handicap.

Before the 'replay' of the Director interviews Jeeps let it be known that he did not want an 'egg-head or university type' in charge, which as events transpired over the years was precisely what he did need to complement the considerable flair in public relations and 'gut reaction' to issues which he had. He needed clever staffwork to keep the governmental predators at bay, to provide the convincing argument, to match the 'egg-heads and university types' in Whitehall who held little brief for him and his cause, but he opted not to have this support and virtually from the start was up against the forces of reaction within the Government.

When on 1 June 1978 the new Director of the Sports Council, Emlyn Jones, joined the Chairman Dick Jeeps at Brompton Road the Council had a team that had only marginally been involved in the mainstream of recent development work; Jones had been at Crystal Palace National Sports Centre since 1962 and Jeeps was new to the Council. This background was both a strength and a weakness; a strength in that new ideas and policies could be looked for unencumbered by what had gone before; a weakness in that the political subtleties of life at the centre of British sport were largely unknown. The next few years were to prove whether or not this blend was capable of carrying forward the momentum developed by Bannister, Brook and Winterbottom, to put sport even more firmly on the map in Britain.

The 'Stacey affair' and the traumatic events of late 1977 and the first quarter of 1978 left their mark on British sports administration and diminished the status of the Sports Council in the eyes of many who were dismayed at the squalid manoeuvering that had taken place. For the national governing bodies of sport it was merely a cause célèbre that brought sport unwanted publicity but they were not touched by it; they and the Commonwealth Games Councils of England, Wales, Scotland and Northern Ireland were far more concerned with the forthcoming Commonwealth Games in Edmonton, Canada, scheduled for the summer of 1978. These Games were most enjoyable for competitor and spectator alike; contested fiercely and with determination but overriding everything the spirit of the 'friendly games' prevailed. Edmonton, both the municipal authority and the people of the city, were most generous and hospitable hosts, and superb organization made the whole event memorable for all who were privileged to be present.

Immediately prior to the Commonwealth Games Minister for Sport Howell despatched Coghlan to Moscow to conclude the work on an Anglo-USSR Memorandum of Understanding on Cooperation in the Field of Sport and Physical Recreation. Peter Lawson, the General-Secretary of the CCPR, was deputed to accompany him. This Memorandum was to be the first of such agreements between Britain and other countries and was broadly as a consequence of a long-standing Cultural Agreement Britain had, and continues to have, with the USSR and other foreign governments. Having arrived in Moscow they were whisked off that night for a two-day cultural visit to Leningrad which included the Kirov Ballet. Back in Moscow the work on the final drafting of the Memorandum was followed by a lunch given by the British Ambassador in honour of the Chairman and Vice-Chairman of the USSR Committee for Physical Culture and Sport, Sergei Pavlov and Victor Ivonin. After many toasts of friendship all was set for the official and formal signing of the Protocol next day by the British Ambassador and John Coghlan. Later that afternoon a telephone call from the Embassy to the Metropol Hotel where the two Britons were staying summoned them back. After suitable security arrangements had been made they were told that the Soviets had that afternoon concluded the trial of the well-known so-called dissident Mr. Yuri Orlov and had imprisoned him. The Ambassador had gone to make a formal protest to Mr. Gromyko, the Soviet Foreign Minister, and the British Foreign Secretary, Dr. David Owen, was to make a statement in the House of Commons that afternoon which came through on the telex while they were at the Embassy. In due course the Ambassador returned and confirmed that as a mark of grave displeasure the signing of the Protocol was cancelled by the British Government forthwith. Coghlan returned to his hotel and attempted to telephone his wife to let her know he was returning earlier than planned; in this he was thwarted as he could not now make any telephone connection outside Moscow, as all lines sounded as though out of order. Their hosts, the USSR Committee for Physical Culture and Sport, continued to treat them with impeccable hospitality and friendliness for all had known each other for some time; they went to a football match that evening, enjoyed a good dinner together and completed a second revision of the text of the Memorandum next morning with Victor Ivonin, not Sergei Pavlov, in the Chair. That afternoon the Ambassador, Lawson and Coghlan returned to England; this Memorandum was signed with no publicity later in the year. Orlov remained in prison for many years before he was released and allowed to emigrate to the USA.

The signing of such sports agreements is commonplace throughout the world, particularly where governments have an executive role in sport, but the signing of such agreements by a British Government places an onus on the national sports bodies and the Sports Council who have to finance such arrangements, which means in effect that their resources are to some extent committed by government action. Nevertheless, Britain cannot forever remain out of step with the rest of the sports world without damaging the international programme presently enjoyed; consultation and agreement by government, sports bodies and the Sports Council is essential if this way forward is to be smooth and without rancour. In a somewhat similar vein the so-called 'Gleneagles Agreement' of June 1977,[20] entered into by the British Government for the very good reason of preventing boycott problems at the Commonwealth Games in Edmonton in 1978, was ratified without prior consultation with the national sports bodies. Whilst most would entirely applaud the sentiments of 'Gleneagles', aimed at preventing sports contacts with countries practising apartheid in sport, the fact that the sports bodies were presented with a fait accompli has been resented ever since despite the fact that many international federations of sport and the IOC exclude South Africa from international competition.

Sport and politics will continue to mix, the debate must always be not 'whether' but 'how' they should mix in Great Britain so that the interests of sport and the government of the day coincide and do not conflict.

Notes

1 John Smith, CBE (1982) Kt (1990); Chairman, Liverpool F.C. (1973–); Member, Sports Council (1980–89), Chairman (1985–89); Member, Football Trust (1980–); Member, Football Association (1981–); Director, Football League (1981–); Chairman, Committee of Enquiry into Lawn Tennis (1980).
2 Mary Glen-Haig, C.B.E. (1971); Sports Council (1966–82); Chairman, CCPR (1974–80); Vice-President (1982–); Vice-President, SAF (1987–); Member, IOC (1982–); Olympic Games (1948, 1952 and 1956); Commonwealth Games Gold Medals Fencing (1950 and 1954).
3 (Rev.); N.I. Stacey; Deputy Director, Oxfam (1968–70); Director, Social Services, Ealing (1971–74), Kent (1974–85); former Olympic sprinter (1952); President, Oxford University AC (1951); nominated for post of Director of the Sports Council in 1977, appointment vetoed by Minister for Sport (see later in this chapter 'The Succession').
4 For example, Macfarlane reversed a decision by the Sports Council to rebuild, together with the GLC, the track at Crystal Palace in time for the European Cup Final in 1983. He only 'authorized' a much cheaper refurbishing job. This was gross interference with day-to-day Council business and was quite unprecedented. Sadly the Chairman did not fight this order as he was fully entitled to do under the Royal Charter.
5 See 'Sport and Trade' section later in this chapter. In 1983 Winterbottom chaired an advisory group on sports surfaces and in particular surfaces for soccer. The report *Artificial Surfaces for Association Football* was published by the Sports Council in 1985.
6 This prevailed until mid-1988 when Colin Moynihan, Minister for Sport, drastically reduced the Sports Council from thirty in all to fourteen plus a Chairman and a Vice-Chairman. The CCPR's 'right' was abandoned although their Chairman, Ron Emes, was invited to serve as a member.
7 The CCPR has an annual conference of sports administrators in the autumn at

Bournemouth. This attracts 'top' speakers from a broad range of backgrounds, for example, media, business, marketing and politics.

8   Financial appendices to Sports Council Annual Reports give details sport by sport. By way of illustration in 1973–74 sports bodies were receiving £765,631 (sixty bodies) in grant-aid; by 1980–81 this was £4.63m (sixty-four bodies).

9   Regional Sports Councils became Regional Councils for Sport and Recreation following an announcement in Parliament on 14 April 1976 (see Hansard, Vol. 909 Cols. 566–567). The Minister of Sport's statement is printed as Annex A to the Department of the Environment Circular 47/76 *Regional Councils for Sport and Recreation*. These Councils embraced sport as hitherto but also all other forms of outdoor recreation, including conservation. Secretarial support was to be provided jointly by the Sports Council and the Countryside Commission — this never came about due to Sports Council opposition.

10 Structure plans; available for inspection by the public at the offices of local planning authorities.

11 See Sports Council Annual Report 1977–78, p. 10. 'The Sports Trade Advisory Panel'.

12 This was not a public report although it was referred to the Chairman of the Sports Council for comment.

13 'Sports aid' to developing countries has never been seen as figuring on the priority list of successive British Governments unlike, for example, Finland, Sweden, the Federal Republic of Germany, France, USSR, the German Democratic Republic, Poland and China. Aid, by way of financial and human resources, is made available by many countries to maintain or develop political spheres of influence, to encourage trade and business, and for altruistic humanitarian reasons. The International Sports Federations, IOC and UNESCO all have aid programmes in place. The European Sports Conference in Athens (1987) made recommendations, following a report of their Working Group, urging a greater level of bilateral arrangements between developed and developing countries. This documentation is available at the Information Centre of the Sports Council in London.

14 The story ran and ran for several weeks. The *Times, Guardian, Daily Telegraph, Daily Mail, Daily Express* and the *Daily Mirror* all carried the details and engaged in speculation. For example: 'Nick Stacey has I understand been nominated by the Sports Council to succeed Walter Winterbottom as Director. He has the support of several senior members of the Sports Council but Howell is known to favour John Coghlan ... widely regarded as Winterbottom's deputy and successor. Among others ... were Bill Slater former Wolves and England half-back.... Emlyn Jones, Director of Crystal Palace and Chris Field, Director of recreation at Greenwich' (*Daily Mail*, 21 December 1977).

'Field emerges in major row' (*The Guardian*, 20 December 1977).

'Stacey veto angers Sports Council' (*The Guardian* 23 December 1977).

'Howell turns down Stacey' (*Daily Mirror*, 23 December 1977).

15 Bernard Atha; Principal Lecturer, Huddersfield Technical College; Leeds City Councillor; Chairman, Yorkshire and Humberside Sports Council (1966–76); Vice-Chairman, Sports Council (1976–80).

16 Press reports on 11 January 1979: 'Sports job back on market' (*The Guardian*), 'Stacey still denied' (*The Guardian*), 'Veto kills sports post for Stacey' (*Daily Telegraph*), 'Sports Council's choice rejected again' (*The Times*).

17 Hansard, House of Commons 13 January 1978, Vol. 941, Cols. 840–42.

18 Emlyn Jones, MBE; Staff member, CCPR (1947–72); Sports Council staff (1972–83); Director, Crystal Palace National Sports Centre (1962–78), Director-General (1978–83).

19 John D. Wheatley; Staff member, CCPR (1985–72); Sports Council staff (1972–88), Director-General (1983–88).
20 Commonwealth Statement on Apartheid in Sport. June 1977. Known colloquially as 'The Gleneagles Agreement'. See Appendix 12 in this volume for full text and Chapter 13.

Section IV
Years of Concern 1980–1990

Chapter 9

Changes at the Top, First Decisions and Consequences

At the Sports Council by 1980 the new team of Jeeps and Jones was bright and lively and early on sought to raise the profile and image of the Council. Dick Jeeps' experience in sport was largely confined to rugby football whilst Emlyn Jones at Crystal Palace had been out of touch with the mainstream of the Sports Council but nevertheless had great experience and knowledge of national governing bodies of sport from his sixteen years working with them at the National Centre. This lack of previous recent involvement was not necessarily a handicap as fresh eyes looked at old problems and some new answers emerged. The approachability of both was in sharp contrast to the rather retiring Sir Robin Brook and the authoritarian Sir Walter Winterbottom. Both Jeeps and Jones had a feeling and instinct for public relations which was of considerable help to the work of the Sports Council in the first few years but later the lack of any real depth in the direction the Council was going, associated with greater Government interference which Jones fought but which Jeeps more and more acquiesced to, weakened the overall position. Emlyn Jones had a warm and compassionate feeling for the social programmes with which the Sports Council was involved and initiated some imaginative projects such as *Action Sport*;[1] he fought hard for more resources for sport and has a deep instinctive feeling for the aspirations of the national sports bodies. Dick Jeeps relied on him greatly in the early years of their partnership and brought to it his own brand of instant instinctive reaction and feel, but as the years went on observers detected a growing impatience with the high profile Jones enjoyed, and believing he no longer needed the considerable wisdom and experience of his Director-General, Jeeps began to distance himself and listened more and more to those in and around Government who resented and disapproved politically of many of Emlyn Jones's statements and actions.[2]

In 1981 the politically astute Bernard Atha (see Chapter 8 in this volume) was not reappointed as a joint Vice-Chairman of the Council and was replaced by Ian Mc.Callum[3] whose background in sport was minimal and who was quite unknown to the sports confraternity. A year later John Disley (see Appendix 4 in this volume), the other Vice-Chairman was not reappointed and here the Sports Council lost its most knowledgeable member who had served for the most part from 1965. These were grievous losses for sport and pointed to an underlying unease at political involvement.

Matters came to a head in the autumn of 1982 when suddenly and quite unexpectedly Emlyn Jones, at the age of 62, announced his early retirement as from the end of January 1983. From that day Jones has maintained a dignified silence about the whole affair. Within a few weeks Dick Jeeps was offered a further five years as Chairman by Neil Macfarlane, the Minister for Sport, and this he accepted. In the middle of 1983 the Deputy Director-General too announced early retirement in the autumn of that year at the age of 60, likewise without making any public statement. In the space of one year the Sports Council had lost its two most senior and experienced officers and the Shadow Minister for Sport, Denis Howell, repeatedly, both in the House of Commons and in the country, asked for explanations, accusing the Minister of political interference. No official explanations or personal statements have been made to date and there the matter rests. Sport went about its business, surmising but not completely knowing what caused the political upheaval of 1983, but seeing more and more the long arm of government meddling in the sports affairs of voluntary sports bodies and eroding the independence of the Sports Council enshrined in the Royal Charter.

Emlyn Jones was succeeded as Director-General by John Wheatley, the former Regional Director of the Sports Council in the South West and latterly Director of Administration at Headquarters. With this appointment it became clear that the Minister and the Chairman wanted a Director-General who would not seek a high personal profile, would conform to government wishes; one who would not 'go out on a limb' or 'rock the boat'; in other words an administrator, a managing director, and this they now had. In 1988 Wheatley resigned to be replaced by David Pickup,[4] a former senior civil servant and latterly Deputy-Secretary to the Association of District Councils.

Throughout this period British sport had four Ministers for Sport (see Appendix 6 in this volume) Hector Monro, whom the Prime Minister, Mrs. Thatcher, appointed on assuming office in 1979; Neil Macfarlane, who took over when Hector Monro was quite astonishingly 'sacked' in 1981; Dick Tracey[5] who served briefly, and latterly Colin Moynihan[6]: Monro was a quiet and effective Minister who believed in the independent sports movement coming as he did from great experience with the Scottish Rugby Union. A great supporter of the Sports Council, his period in office was constructive, imaginative and forward looking; he was missed enormously when he was removed from office. He and Denis Howell had a great rapport over many years as ministers and shadows to the benefit of sport in Britain, as neither attempted to make party political capital when in office, but rather acted in a bipartisan way to the considerable benefit of the sports policies they pursued or supported. Neil Macfarlane was a friendly likeable personality, with a great facility for public speaking assisted by a keen personal interest and involvement in sport. Although the departure of Sir Hector had been regretted, as this represented a considerable loss for sport in Parliament and in the country, the arrival of Macfarlane as a lively young politician with former ministerial experience in the Department of Education and Science was greeted with goodwill.

After an initial bright start the whole issue of violence in football engulfed Macfarlane and one sensed that the Prime Minister was constantly at him in this connection. The question of whether this is a matter for the Minister of Sport is doubtful as it would appear to be more within the responsibility of the Home Office and the law and order question.

During my four years as Minister of Sport the greatest problem I encountered was the behaviour and control of English fans (soccer) in this country and abroad. (Macfarlane, 1986, p. 10)

He did well nationally and internationally on this issue but failed to make any real impact on the national sporting scene other than meddling in the affairs of the Sports Council where he had little or no locus. His unwillingness to listen to the many wise men and women in sport, and to those involved in the Regional Councils for Sport and Recreation, allied to his clear, if repeatedly denied, aim to be more involved with executive action in British sport, ensured that he was not greatly missed when the time came for ministerial change in 1985. This was a pity, for in Opposition he worked constructively and listened to the CCPR, the BOA, the Sports Council and the national federations of sport. He failed to do this in office and as a consequence in mid-1984 the press began to raise the whole question of whether there was a need for a Minister of Sport in the working relationship between central Government and sport.[7]

Of major significance to sport in Britain was the death of Sir Denis Follows, the Chairman of the British Olympic Association, in 1983. It was he who led the opposition to the governmental assault on the Olympic movement in 1980 when the Prime Minister was urging boycott of the Moscow Olympics (see Chapter 13 in this volume). Those who agreed with this stance admired the tenacity and strength of spirit that stood firm against the strongest possible political pressure when he argued that political disapproval must not be borne only by Olympic athletes whilst business and commerce continued untouched by the furore created by the Soviet invasion of Afghanistan in December 1979. During the short time British sport enjoyed his leadership of the national Olympic movement he made a major impact on the international scene and in particular with the IOC and the Association of National Olympic Committees (ANOC) that had come into being a few years previously. Charles Palmer,[8] the then Secretary-General of the General Assembly of International Sports Federations (GAISF) and

President of the British Judo Association (BJA) in his capacity as Vice-Chairman of the BOA, succeeded Sir Denis in the run-up to the Sarajevo and Los Angeles Olympic Games in the winter and summer of 1984. A formidable figure, both in appearance and international stature, Palmer brought his own style of leadership and flair to the BOA, quite different from that of Denis Follows, but equally emphatic. Never one to suffer fools gladly, and ever ready to speak his mind and not dissemble, Charles Palmer did not suit everyone in his period of inter regnum. At the election for Chairman in the autumn of 1984, in the aftermath of a successful Olympic Games for Britain, he was opposed by the very able and knowledgeable Sir Arthur Gold,[9] Chairman of the Commonwealth Council for England and at that time President of the European Athletic Union, and Mrs. Mary Glen-Haig (see Chapter 8 in this volume). In the eventuality Charles Palmer was re-elected with Arthur Gold a close runner-up; both were equally rich in experience, very well-known on the international circuit and very adroit in negotiation. Britain was again well served by two such distinguished men leading the National Olympic Committee. Change followed the 1988 Summer Olympic Games in Seoul when in a closely contested ballot Gold defeated Palmer for the Chair of the BOA, thus reversing the election of 1984.

HRH Princess Anne (the Princess Royal from June 1987) took over the Presidency of the BOA on the death of Lord Rupert Nevill (see Chapter 8 in this volume) and being a recent competitor herself at Montreal in 1976 she brought youth and a new vigour to this office. Since her acceptance of the Presidency she has worked tirelessly and assiduously for the Association. She was present at the Winter Olympic Games at Sarajevo (1984) and Calgary (1988) and in the summer at Los Angeles (1984) and Seoul (1988). Like her father, the President of the CCPR, she is no cypher but has firm and clear views and is prepared to work hard for the cause.

With the death of the Marquess of Exeter in 1982 a vacancy on the IOC had occurred, although Lord Luke[10] was still a long-standing member. Whilst there is no right for Britain to have two nationals on the IOC, historically it has been so and speculation arose as to the successor to the Marquess of Exeter (see Chapter 2 in this volume) Lord Burghley of Olympic fame in the twenties. Although it was known that the President of the IOC wished to extend the female membership, the front names, with those who purported to know, were Sir Roger Bannister, Sir Arthur Gold, Charles Palmer and Denis Howell; all admirable candidates of quite different dispositions, strengths and weaknesses. In the event none of these was invited but rather Mrs. Mary Glen-Haig, the former international fencer and successor Chairman to Denis Howell of the new CCPR. A member of the Sports Council for many years, both when it was advisory and executive, prominent in national sports affairs and in every respect a suitable candidate for the IOC it was nevertheless a surprise when Juan Samaranch,[11] the IOC President, invited her to join Lord Luke as the second British representative. In 1988 Lord Luke decided to stand down from the IOC and HRH the Princess Royal was invited to take his place. This was a popular choice as she had not only represented Great Britain in the Olympic Games but had recently taken over from HRH Prince Philip as President of the International Equestrian Federation. Britain now had two lady members on this prestigious body.

At the CCPR Keith Mitchell, a physical educationist at the University of Leeds, and a major force in national and international basketball took over from Mrs. Glen-Haig as Chairman in 1981 and brought a different style of leadership which was quiet and effective. Peter Lawson, the talented, highly motivated but somewhat abrasive General Secretary, continued to reflect a confrontational posture to the Sports Council which those with the best interests of British sport at heart had hoped would disappear when Dick Jeeps became Chairman and Emlyn Jones Director-General as neither had in any way been involved in the earlier causes of friction between the two bodies.

The suggestions concerning consultation in the 1975 White Paper, coupled with the cross-representation on committees of both organizations, helped in the short-term to alleviate the tension but sniping and sometimes guerilla warfare erupted whenever a 'who was responsible for what' situation occurred. As Macfarlane said in his book *Sport and Politics — A World Divided*:

> The CCPR and the Sports Council should be the country's most respected organizations in sport and recreation. The CCPR reflects the collective views of governing bodies and the Sports Council being the vehicle for putting public money in the form of government grants into sport ... Every Sports Minister since 1974 has found himself caught up in the petty feuding and personal rivalries. It has been debilitating for sport in England. (p. 83)

In 1987 Ron Emes, with a lifetime of involvement in canoeing behind him, took over as Chairman of the CCPR from Mitchell and in due course was invited to become a member of the Sports Council.

The CCPR provides services such as insurance and advantageous travel to its members, runs an excellent annual conference which attracts speakers of note to talk on topics of relevance in sport, and stimulates debate on burning issues of the day. The development of the Community Leaders Award in the early eighties, strongly supported by Prince Philip, was an imaginative initiative, filling a clearly identified need. With 1985 designated as the International Year of Youth it was expected that the progress already achieved in this area of endeavour would rapidly expand in association with the newly-established Sports Council's Community Sports Leadership Advisory Panel. In the eventuality the Leadership Award continued to develop, and although in 1987 the Sports Council was talking of giving community leadership 'high priority' discussion was still confined to 'framework and structure', relying on regional action to experiment and carry out projects.

As 1984 drew to a close another and most serious wrangle emerged between the CCPR and the Sports Council concerned with the very basis of the 1972 agreement between the two bodies. Contentiously the Sports Council attempted to reopen the issue of its obligation to meet the administrative costs of running the CCPR to a level which is generally accepted as reasonable. This delicate issue had largely been settled in the late seventies by goodwill on both sides and a fair degree of compromise all round; now, due to Sports Council insensitivity, it burst out again with threats from the CCPR to take the issue to legal arbitration. In early January 1985 the Sports Council climbed down and conceded not only this issue but much else.

These squabbles have acted against the best interests of sport since 1972. Hopefully, an end to this state of affairs is in view with the new Director-General of the Sports Council, David Pickup, looking at things afresh. Time will tell whether or not this view is too optimistic. The system is clearly wrong and has not been helped by the personalities that have stalked the stage despite the brave efforts by many over the years to staunch the wounds inflicted on British sport and arrive at an agreed modus vivendi broadly acceptable to both organizations.

It was against this background, of many changes being made at the top in many areas of British sports administration, that the Sports Council published in 1982 its strategy for the development of sport at élite and mass sport levels. This strategy entitled *Sport in the Community — The Next Ten Years*, was certainly the most profound, researched and coherent case for sport made in Britain since *Sport in the Seventies* had astounded Britain with its challenge to build and construct what appeared then to be a formidable volume and range of facilities. The strategy for the eighties is a concise document of research and statement, statistics and challenge, set against a backcloth of the changing face of Britain. It points to the successes in raising the level of participation in sport during the previous decade and to the considerable building programmes undertaken to make good the deficiencies defined in the sixties. Without any apology it points equally to failures and sectors of society untouched largely by the progress to date. The cost for the programmes the strategy espoused was entered as a £40m p.a. charge for the first five years. Whereas *Sport in the Seventies* a decade before spoke only of buildings, this strategy for the eighties speaks equally of people whether they be active or latent participants, coaches or administrators. Boldly the Sports Council declared its aim to get four million more people taking part in outdoor sport and three million more in indoor sport before the end of the decade. Identifying a younger and an older age group for special attention the Council specified the 13–24 and the 45–59 age groups as being especially worthy of attention as the former covered the school-leaving sector and the latter covered the middle-aged in the period before retirement.

By stimulating new thinking and by setting bold new targets the Sports Council committed itself to a crusade that called for the maximum cooperation of national governing bodies of sport, municipal authorities and central government. Significantly it pointed out that in terms of public facilities the Sports Council's grants over the years preceding had stimulated between six and nine times as much investment, whilst in the voluntary sector, mostly private sports clubs, between three and four times as much money had been forthcoming in response to grant aid.

For the first time in a formal sense, other than in the *Come Alive* campaign of the late seventies, the Sports Council argued a case that participation in sport and physical recreation 'is part of self-administered preventive medicine' and pointed to the volume of evidence that demonstrated that sport and physical activity are helpful in preventing a range of diseases, including heart disease, and other mental and physical ailments.

This brave statement of aim and purpose was well received by the media and was widely reported and commented upon. It had a lively response from local government through the Regional Councils for Sport and Recreation who had published, or were about to publish, their own strategies called for way back in 1975 by the Labour Government's White Paper *Sport and Recreation*.[12] The response from the governing bodies of sport was virtually nil as was that from the CCPR; not that this demonstrated a lack of interest but rather the sober fact that there is still today, after many years of progress and development, a lack of understanding as to the part sport plays in the social field, or even if that is not true in some cases there still exists a belief that this is not really their concern. A response from HM Government was even more emphatically not forthcoming other than a broad general welcome which meant all or nothing. One had to assume sadly the latter as the next annual grant-in-aid made by the Government to the Sports Council took no account of the strategy and represented a mere fraction more in real terms than had been provided the year before; a poor response to the call for £40m. The well-known Whitehall tactic of requiring more information, more financial appraisal, and more cost benefit was the only positive, or negative, depending on the point of view, response. As the end of 1984 approached the staff of the Sports Council were involved in the preparation of what was described as a 'corporate plan' at the behest of the civil servants serving the Minister for Sport, taking them away from urgent developmental field work for some wordy exercise of no real value to the job in hand. If ever there was a plan for sport for the eighties *Sport in the Community — The Next Ten Years* was just that. If sport in Britain was to advance work developing all that the strategy proposed should have been the priority and not some fruitless Whitehall inspired exercise ordained by those who knew little about sport as they shuttled from one section to another in the Department of the Environment in the development of their careers.

In 1988 the Sports Council published a review of the strategy formulated for the eighties *Sport in the Community — Into the Nineties* (appendix 4 to the report lists regional strategies for sport and recreation in full). A consultation paper *Which Ways Forward* had been previously circulated to 1200 organizations of which 345 replied. This consultation exercise asked sixty questions about trends in sport and society and the roles providers could or should play in the future. An analysis of the responses showed 'a clear consolidation of planning and management in local authorities and in many . . . voluntary organizations'.

This review showed that virtually all the indicators of demand for sport, such as sales of goods, use of facilities, readership of sports magazines and the results of polls, showed continued growth in the early eighties which mirrored similar findings in other developed economies. The changes in society since *Sport in the Community — The Next Ten Years* was published were detailed together with an analysis of the way sport in Britain was moving. Very courageously, and with precision, an assessment of success or failure to date was recorded and fresh targets for the remainder of the decade were set. From a wealth of figures and statistics it is clear that the General Household Survey figures show a 'quite significant increase in participation rates between 1980 and 1983'; accordingly the target figures have been revised upwards. Of particular interest is a table showing trends in frequency of participation in individual activities (appendix 3 in the report, figure A 3.3, p. 86). Overall the figures show a clear increase in participation and when looked at for the decade 1976–86 they are impressive, being nearly 50 per cent up for outdoor activities and around 30 per cent for indoor activities.

This was an exciting document that demanded attention from government and governing bodies of sport; sadly once again it did not get it. The Government was much too wary and cagey to get itself embroiled in the intellectual argument this detailed and scholarly report displayed; it was easier to ignore it and pass by on the other side. The media too do not take easily to this type of analysis, preferring in the main the more sensational news story, and yet within such reports lie the data and material that could alter the face of British sport if given full media attention and emphasis. Somehow there is a feeling that sport is only about action and not about arguing cases unless the case is glaring and newsworthy such as drug abuse in sport.

With Neil Macfarlane as Minister for Sport in the early eighties, during the time Dick Jeeps was Chairman of the Sports Council, the grip of government tightened round the Council. Often during this period the question was raised as to where the Royal Charter and its imperatives had been filed. It appeared to have been lost, or at best mislaid, as Macfarlane tightened his hold on the levers of power and increasingly bent the Council to his will.

In May 1985 Jeeps retired midway through his second period of office clearly at odds with the Minister. A few months later Macfarlane resigned hours ahead of a Government reshuffle by the Prime Minister. In four years two Ministers, one Chairman, two Vice-Chairmen, the Director-General and the Deputy Director-General had all moved out in one way or another; quite a clear-out at the top and indicative of grave unease that was felt in many quarters over excessive governmental interference in sports matters. John Smith (see Chapter 8 in this volume), who had been a member of the Sports Council for some time, was appointed Chairman. Here was a man of wisdom and experience and someone capable of restoring to the Sports Council at least some of its former independence; not a man to be pushed around. Richard Tracey, MP, was a surprise choice as Minister for Sport as he was largely unknown in the sports world. He played a quiet supportive role to the governing bodies of sport and the CCPR, BOA and Sports Council. He did not attempt to dictate or impose his will and in the short time he was given did a useful job for sport in and out of Parliament.

In 1987 Colin Moynihan, MP, succeeded Tracey. Now Britain had a young, dynamic Minister for Sport with the charisma of a silver Olympic medal and a knowledge of what it was like at the top of his sport. He struck up a sound personal friendship with Sebastian Coe, since July a Vice-Chairman of the Sports Council. Together they did some good things for sport[13] as each had a high media profile, and in the case of the Sports Council John Smith wisely used this to good advantage. Sadly, and somewhat inevitably, Moynihan became bogged down with the football hooligan issue and clearly under instructions from the Prime Minister gave notice that a Football Spectators Bill was to be introduced into Parliament making entrance to Football League grounds only possible through identity cards. From the outset this created a furore with football clubs, the police, spectator interests and Parliament. It was to be late January 1990 before the Government abandoned this move following publication of Lord Justice Taylor's report *The Hillsborough Stadium Disaster; 15 April 1989* when ninety-five spectators at an F.A. Cup semi-final match died, Taylor expressed himself against an idenity card scheme (see Chapter 14 in this volume and Appendix 16) and the Home Secretary accepted this view.

Not content with this battle the Minister decided to cut the Sports Council membership from thirty to fourteen and he did this by not reappointing two vacancies that became available and by calling on others to resign. Senior and well-respected sports administrators such as 'Larry' Lamb (Rugby Football and Badminton), and John Humphries (Chairman of the Southern Council for Sport and Recreation), objected to this off-hand action which also called for the resignation of Richard Sharp (Chairman of the South-West Council for Sport and Recreation) and his colleague Jim Cochrane, Chairman in the North-West and a former President of the Lawn Tennis Association. Five of the CCPR members of the Council were also removed leaving only their Chairman, Ron Emes. All of this was totally unnecessary and to date has achieved nothing but ill-will and a resentment despite Moynihan's plea that this streamlined Council would cut out bureaucracy and make decision-making quicker. Whilst the jury is still out on Colin Moynihan rumours from the jury-room are that he has become more of a liability to sport than a benefit; a great pity, he promised so much. He may yet achieve something positive, but the indicators are not optimistic.

The political pressures on him from high-up can only be imagined as there must be some logical explanation for his actions that could not have been foreseen when he took office.[14]

In the spring of 1989 John Smith's term of office came to an end and Peter Yarranton,[15] the Chairman of the Greater London Council for Sport and Recreation, took over with Professor Alan Patmore staying as Vice-Chairman but Sebastian Coe stepping down to begin a political career as a Conservative candidate. Yarranton is a rugby football man but has served an apprenticeship in his regional appointment which brought him membership of the Council. He has a bright new team of officers to serve him and having experience of management will, it is confidently expected, allow his staff to get on with the job of implementing the policies of the Council. He is not known as an interventionist and in his first top-level role overseas at the IX European Sports Conference[16] in Sofia, Bulgaria in October 1989, led the UK delegation with style and distinction, committing Britain to an increasing international role in sports affairs.

During this decade the Sports Council not only survived a 'quango hunt'[17] but had to face for the first time a House of Commons Committee Enquiry which decided to look in detail at how the Sports Council operated and how it managed its affairs. In the Parliamentary Session 1984/85 the Environment Committee of the House of Commons began their Enquiry into the Sports Council saying that:

> Our remit requires us to examine the expenditure, administration and policy not only of the Department of Environment, but also the Department's associated public bodies. The Sports Council for England is such a body. (Introduction to Second Report)

Sir Hugh Rossi, MP, was in the Chair; neither he nor any of his Committee had any previous connection with sport and all were unknown in sporting circles. Evidence was taken from civil servants in the Sport and Recreation Division of the Department of Environment and from the Chairman, Vice-Chairman and Director-General of the Sports Council. Other bodies gave evidence including the local authority associations, CCPR, Chief Leisure Officers Association, BOA and several national governing bodies of sport. A full account of the proceedings is included in the Second Report from the Environment Committee, Session 1985/86, *The Sports Council.*

The Committee reported on 12 February 1986 and the Report was published by HMSO, on 26 March[18] of that year. The Government's response was published as an Annex to the Third Special Report from the Environment Committee on 2 July 1986.[19] The Committee, commenting on this response, preface their Report by stating: —

> The response seems to suggest that, in general terms, the Government welcomes our recommendations. However the language is carefully phrased and it is hard to be sure what the outcome is intended to be or will turn out to be.

The Government's statement from the Secretary of State for the Environment notes:

> ... that your Committee found the Council generally to be an efficient and effective sponsored body, and that you endorsed public funding of sport, through such an agency.

Some overlapping of functions between the Sports Council, CCPR, BOA and SAF is acknowledged and 'some rationalization' would be 'welcome'. The 'concern' of the Committee over 'the public funding of the CCPR' is endorsed, but the Secretary of State acknowledges weakly that 'any negotiations ...must be for the two agencies themselves to take initially'.

This was a salutary exercise for the Sports Council and for the Minister for Sport and his officials but after making the news on and off for a short period it all faded away and little appeared to be changed if indeed anything needed to be.

The personalities that guide and direct sport in Britain influence considerably the public image that sport offers. The decade 1980–90 gave the nation many fine successes in international sport, some notable failures, three Olympic Games of quite startling difference (see Chapter 13 in this volume) and all against a background of a Conservative Government in power for the whole period which politically conditioned the sporting scene. In the seventies, although the Government, whether Labour or Conservative, was directly involved in sport, very few examples of overt interference with the governing bodies of sport were evident and the BOA, CCPR and Sports Council were treated very much as 'arms length' organizations. In the eighties this changed as central control of affairs became more obvious and the Government, seeing itself as the paymaster, began to exercise greater control and direction coming to a head during the time Macfarlane was Minister for Sport and continuing, if in a somewhat different vein, with Moynihan. A Sports Council paper in 1989 on grant-aid policy acknowledged the fact when it said:

The Minister for Sport has regularly throughout the period (1980–90) sought to influence grant policy by placing specific directions on the use of additional funds.[20]

Is Britain moving, and if so is this acceptable to the voluntary sports movement, towards a Ministry of Sport which lays down the policy and provides some resources? Some media commentators speak loosely of the 'Sports Ministry' with talk of 'government grants'. Constitutionally in 1990 there is no 'Ministry for Sport'; there is a Minister with some officials who are generalists and not sports administrators to run his office, and there are 'Sports Council grants' made available to assist sport through an annual grant-in-aid from Parliament.

Sport in this decade began to be seen as having wider implications for society than was foreseen in the years before. Then sport and physical recreation were seen as contributing to health, social enjoyment and welfare, but today it has been shown that additionally sport makes a considerable impact on the economy. In a 1986 Report published by the Sports Council, *The Economic Impact and Importance of Sport in the United Kingdom*, the Henley Centre for Forecasting showed that sport provided 376,000 jobs, more than the motor manufacturing, gas or agricultural industries provided. Additionally consumer expenditure was in excess of £3,000m and the Treasury raised through various forms of taxation associated with sport over £2,000m. In other words, sport in 1990 is big business and interwoven into the political and commercial life of Britain. It has come a very long way since 1960.

Notes

1 In 1981 in an effort to increase and demonstrate the effectiveness of putting leaders and motivators on the streets this scheme was launched on a budget of £3m for the years 1982–85. Aimed specifically at deprived urban areas super-concentrations of resources were employed in very local areas in London and the West Midlands. Areas were usually a few streets only emphasizing that it was people rather than facilities that were the priority. Widely publicized, it sought to lead other local authorities to do likewise. See Sports Council Annual Report 1982–3 p. 12 'Sports Leadership in Inner Cities', also 'Action Sport — an Evaluation', a Report for the Sports Council, 1986.

2 Jones believed that the Sports Council had to speak for sport and respond to what was required. The Government found this embarrassing as demands far out-reached supply and they disliked being at the receiving end of sharp press comment from Jones. Politically Jones and his Chairman did not appear at one in their thinking and the Minister for Sport, it was suspected, encouraged Jeeps to bring Jones into line or at least discourage him from making what were considered attacks on the government. Jones never attacked the Government — he spoke for sport and the needs of sport — but Neil Macfarlane, the Minister, and his civil servants disliked this. Privately they spoke of 'rocking the boat'.

3 I.S. McCallum; Save and Prosper Group (1968–   ); Mayor of Woking (1976–

77); Chairman, Association of District Councils (1979–84); Audit Commission (1983–86); Vice-Chairman, Sports Council (1980–86).

4   David Pickup; Department of Environment — Regional Director (1977–80); Housing (1980–84); Local Government (1984–85); Deputy Secretary; Association of District Councils (1986–88); Director-General, Sports Council (1988–   ).

5   R.P., Tracey; MP (1983–   ); Journalist; Minister for Sport (1985–87).

6   (Hon) Colin B. Moynihan; MP (1983–   ); President, Oxford Union Society (1976); Steward, British Boxing Board of Control (1979–87); Oxford 'blue' Rowing and Boxing; Sports Council (1982–85); Olympic Silver Medal (Rowing) (1980); World Silver Medal (1981); Minister for Sport (DOE) (1987–   ).

7   'Macfarlane was appointed four years ago . . . in the image of one man, Denis Howell, whom he has fallen sadly short of matching . . . many influential senior Conservatives would like to do away with the title Minister for Sport. The idea of dropping the job at ministerial level might be welcomed by some members of the Sports Council'. (*The Guardian* (John Rodda) 1985).

8   C. Palmer, OBE (1973); President, International Judo Federation (1965–79); Secretary-General, General Assembly of International Sports Federations (1975–84); Chairman, BOA (1983–88); Governor, SAF (1979–   ); Sports Council (1983–   ); Silver Medal Olympic Order (1980).

9   Arthur Gold, CBE (1974), Kt (1984); President, European Athletics Association (1976–87); Chairman; Commonwealth Games Council for England (1979–   ); Hon. Sec, British Amateur Athletic Board (1964–77); Sports Council (1980–88); Chairman; BOA (1988–   ).

10 Lord Luke, KCVO, T.D, D.L, J.P; Chairman, National Playing Fields Association (1950–76); Member, IOC (1952 88).

11 J.A. Samaranch; Member, IOC (1966–   ), President (1980–   ); Spanish Olympic Committee (1954–   ), President (1967 70).

12 The 1975 White Paper established Regional Councils for Sport and Recreation to take the place of Regional Sports Councils. Paragraph 37 says that these new Councils 'would be specifically encouraged to promote the preparation of regional recreational strategies so as to provide an agreed framework within which recreational proposals in structure and local plans can be developed'. The Councils did this in the years that followed and now have ongoing strategies for a wide range of topics. These strategies were not prepared in a uniform format but reflected the priorities of regions.

13 *The Misuse of Drugs in Sport*, a report by Colin Moynihan, Minister for Sport, and Sebastian Coe, Vice-Chairman of the Sports Council, Department of Environment, September 1987.

14 See *The Times*, Wednesday 13 July, 1988 'Sports politics', commentary by David Miller, Chief Sports Correspondent.

15 Peter Yarranton, RAF (1942–57); BP Executive (1957–77); General Manager, Lensbury Club (1977–   ); International rugby player; Vice-President, RFU; Chairman, Greater London and South East Council for Sport and Recreation (1983–88); Sports Council (1986–   ), Chairman (May 1989–   ).

16 The European Sports Conference, a pan-European body of all European countries meets every two years to discuss themes and topics that are relevant to European sport. The first conference took place in Vienna in 1973. National delegates are a mixture of governmental and non-governmental personalities. IOC and ICSSPE are traditionally invited observers. Working groups are established to study, report and make recommendations, for example, on Youth Sport, Women in Sport, Misuse of Drugs, Developing Countries, Sports Science Cooperation.

17 'Quango' — the abbreviated form for 'Quasi-autonomous non-governmental

organization'. Following the election of 1979 the Conservative administration critically examined the functions and usefulness of the very many public bodies that existed which were funded by Parliament in an effort to eliminate financial waste.

18 Includes Minutes of Proceedings relating to the Report and Minutes of Evidence (HC 241).
19 Government's Response to the Committee's Second Report, 1985–86 (HC 241) 'Sports Council', HMSO.
20 Sports Council paper SC (89) 59 Revised, Regional Grant Policy.

Chapter 10

Scotland and Wales

The way sport organizes itself in Britain is bewildering to foreigners and sometimes equally bewildering to British nationals. The fact that there is one sovereign state with the Queen as head of that state and a Parliament representing its people is quite clear, but when that state often presents itself as having separate states within it, it is then that faces take on a puzzled look. The problem of understanding is compounded when it is explained that the United Kingdom is not a federated state and that Great Britain does not include the province of Ulster in Northern Ireland where the Queen's writ is as sovereign as it is in England. Thus the team that represents the British Isles at the Olympic Games is 'Great Britain and Northern Ireland' whilst the Commonwealth Games sees teams from England, Scotland, Wales, Northern Ireland, the Isle of Man and the separate Channel Islands.

This political and human structure is for sport both a strength and a weakness. It is a strength in that the corporate identity of countries within Britain stimulates internal competition, pride in representation, wider national recognition for more competitors and a specific Scottish, Welsh and English component to development. The weakness lies often in duplication of effort and resources and always in the risk that a united national view may not be forthcoming to international affairs. The purely human characteristics of chauvinism, amour propre and nationalism exist to a great or lesser extent in most sports administrators, not always to an unhealthy degree but sometimes so. The 'Great Britain' demand from time to time has to take second place to the narrower home country viewpoint which weakens the British effort. A clear example of this lies in hockey where, until the success of the British team at the Los Angeles Olympics in 1984 against all odds, the 'GB' effort had to play second fiddle to the 'English' demand of the Hockey Association. Good planning, coordination and involvement of all parties can and does help considerably but in the final analysis it is the human personalities that take over and then real problems for 'British' sport can emerge.

No review of the developments of sport in Britain during the last thirty years would be complete without reference to the very real contribution that Scotland and Wales have made both in the British and in the narrower national contexts. Historically sport developed in Scotland and Wales in the nineteenth and twentieth centuries broadly as it did in England in the voluntary sector. In the public sector successive Secretaries of State for Wales and Scotland have acted in accord with their Cabinet colleagues acting for England, and in the case of Scotland matching legislation has normally been forthcoming. As sport has developed national governing bodies have been established sometimes as purely autonomous organizations with no British affiliation such as football or rugby union, or as autonomous bodies within a British structure as in athletics.

When the Central Council of Recreative Physical Training was established in 1935, later to become the CCPR, Wales, but not Scotland, was involved probably because education in Wales came within the remit of the then Board of Education whilst Scotland had its own Education Office and legislation. In November 1944 the Scottish Education Office invited the CCPR to extend its services to Scotland and offered financial support to do so. In 1947 the Ministry of Education for Northern Ireland made the same request. From now onwards the CCPR was the forum for sports bodies and other related organizations for the whole of Great Britain and Northern Ireland and could and did speak with one voice. Alas this position of strength was not to last and in 1953 the Scottish Committee of the CCPR announced they would be withdrawing and would be establishing themselves as the Scottish Council of Physical Recreation (SCPR). The Welsh Committee of the CCPR did not go down this road and remained within the umbrella organization as did Northern Ireland. The setting-up of the Wolfenden Committee in 1957 brought the first indication of organizational problems within Britain when the SCPR, having agreed that Sir John's enquiry should cover the United Kingdom, sought specific representation. This was denied but Scotland, Wales and Northern Ireland were permitted advisers. Not surprisingly it was quickly found that the problems for England were very much those for all other parts of the United Kingdom, just as they are today. Although Wolfenden in his report *Sport and the Community* devoted a chapter to Scotland, Wales and Northern Ireland, apart from some minor points of detail, he concluded that 'the essential factors affecting the development of sport are the same in all four countries; the need for facilities and for better coaching and administration, and the shortage of money for these things are common to all' (paragraph 235, p. 89). On the issue of whether or not there should be 'Sports Development Councils' for Wales, Scotland and Northern Ireland in addition to the National Sports Development Council, the Wolfenden Committee begged the question not thinking 'it to be our duty to do more than call attention to these issues' (paragraph 278, p. 104). Perhaps this is where the fundamental mistake was made as from then on Britain was on course for a proliferation of first

Advisory Sports Councils for Wales and Scotland and secondly Royal Chartered bodies. Many in Scotland and Wales would disagree that a 'mistake' was made, and perhaps sensing the nationalism of the times they are right, but today in the early nineties the voice of sport is however less clear when spoken by many bodies and the charge that overlapping and costly duplication of services occurs is often true and gives substance to the arguments of those who are not noted for their friendship to sport.

From 1960 onwards everything in Scotland and Wales marched forward as in England. In 1965 the Advisory Sports Council was matched with Councils for Scotland and Wales, serviced as in the English regions by staff of the CCPR in Wales and the SCPR in Scotland. In function and work these Scottish and Welsh advisory bodies were in many respects identical with the Regional Sports Councils established in England in the autumn of 1965. The identity of a particular Scottish or Welsh body had a special magic for these areas of Great Britain whereas England has never associated itself in such a manner with the national Sports Council itself.

When in 1972 the Sports Council was granted a Royal Charter similar Charters were granted to Scotland and Wales. Britain now had a national body responsible for British affairs in addition to those of England with Scottish and Welsh bodies responsible for matters specifically Scottish and Welsh. The Chairman and Vice Chairman of the Sports Council for Wales and the Scottish Sports Council were always members of the Sports Council from 1972 which brought about a large measure of integration of policy; from 1988, with the new streamlined Sports Council of Colin Moynihan, only the Chairmen are members. To reinforce coordination of policy there has been from the outset a non-Executive British (later United Kingdom) Affairs Committee; this has ensured consultation and consensus.

The BOA has never had problems with fragmentation having their member sports bodies representative of Great Britain and Northern Ireland, or where a sport in Northern Ireland opts to link with Ireland, representative of Great Britain. Latterly the CCPR has tended to assume a British mantle arguing that some British bodies are in membership; many in Scotland and Wales do not accept this British role for the CCPR having their own forums[1] for governing bodies since the former CCPR and SCPR ceased to exist.

In some respects the Welsh pattern is the best in that it integrates the sports bodies as a separate committee into the Sports Council for Wales. Scotland mirrors the English regions with their Standing Conferences and Regional Federations of Sport, whilst England has the CCPR with all the problems that have been engendered with the Sports Council. The argument that separate voluntary federations of sports bodies in England, Wales and Scotland were largely unnecessary now there were Sports Councils that included representation of sports bodies had considerable force until the early eighties; in 1990 the argument does not have quite the same appeal since the Sports Councils have become increasingly instruments of government and less the independent organizations envisaged in the Royal Charter. One federation of sports bodies as in Holland, Norway, Sweden and the Federal Republic of Germany[2] for the United Kingdom, or failing that Great Britain, has enormous appeal, but that is a pipe-dream in 1990 and could only come about if Scotland, Wales, and in the ideal situation Northern Ireland, agreed to launch the initiative; an unlikely event with devolution always hovering around the agenda.

Wales

In 1971 the National Sports Centre for Wales was opened in Cardiff and formed the physical base for the Sports Council for Wales and a national home for sport. With the granting of the Royal Charter in 1972 Lieutenant Colonel Harry Llewellyn[3], later Sir Harry, was appointed Chairman of the Sports Council for Wales. This was a charismatic appointment as Llewellyn was a 1952 Gold Medallist at Helsinki for equestrianism on the immortal 'Foxhunter'. Building on the original Games and Sports Committee of Welsh Governing Bodies of Sport, Wales avoided the problems that developed with the 'new' CCPR in England and constituted this Committee as a formal organ of the Council; an astute move that pre-empted anticipated aggravation. The pattern of work very closely mirrored that of the English regions plus a national component with major facilities and service to Welsh governing bodies of sport, the Commonwealth Council for Wales, the Welsh Sports Aid Foundation (1984) and other kindred bodies having a clear Welsh identity. Early on the Council decided that grant-aid for facilities would be directed at voluntary sports clubs and facilities of national significance for the Principality. Coaching and development, facility provision, water recreation strategies and cooperation in all the British *Sport for All* initiatives formed the bed-rock on which progress was made often with very limited resources.

Grant-aid from the Welsh Office to the Sports Council for Wales rose from an initial £0.4m in 1972 to £2.733m in 1983 and by 1987 this was £5.658m. By good financial management the Council was able to assist the Welsh governing bodies of sport from a base position of £36,594 in 1972 to £392,229 in 1983 and then to the very respectable figure of £531,025 in 1987–88. On the capital side grant-aid for local club facilities was reduced in real terms in the seventies and early eighties. In 1973 £274,000 was allocated, and although the annual figure rose in 1975 to £319,000 this fell away considerably and in 1981 this stood at a mere £216,000. A loan scheme started in 1975 with some minor loans lent £216,000 between 1978–80 which distorts somewhat the actual grant figures from that date onwards. Seven years later, in 1987, the Sports Council for Wales was offering £855,633 by way of grants to local clubs backed up by £163,886 of loan offers; this represented a reversal of the earlier decline. Additionally on the participation side £34,511 was paid in 1987 for purely local schemes and small equipment; an acknowledgement in the eighties that this type of modest pump-priming reaped rich dividends and posed the question as to why financial support at this level had not been a feature from the outset in 1972 in Wales and elsewhere in Great Britain.[4]

In the way that the Sports Council for Wales spends its money it has to be both a national and local funding agency whereas in England the regions fill this latter role with finance allotted to them from the central body, the Sports Council.

The Welsh Sports Council has over the years been served by many distinguished Welsh sportsmen including Cliff Jones, Ronnie Boon and J P R Williams from rugby union, Tony Lewis from cricket, Jack Peterson from boxing, George Edwards from soccer and Roy Evans from table tennis.

In 1981 Harry Llewellyn handed over as Chairman to John Powell[5] who had served on the Council for some years and two years later the long-serving Director Harold Oakes retired giving way to Lyn Tatham[6] who had previously held senior appointments in sports administration in Scotland.

The dominance of rugby football in Wales, where the game features large in schools, colleges and community, could have swamped sports development generally but the far-seeing cooperation of the Welsh Rugby Union has ensured that this has not happened. Wales has enjoyed many great periods of rugby brilliance in history but that of the mid-seventies was the greatest of modern times. For a small country Wales has produced great athletes in many sports apart from rugby football, the most famous of all perhaps in the last thirty years being the Olympic Long Jump Champion of 1964 (Tokyo) Lynn Davis, who for some years worked on the staff of the Sports Council for Wales.

Development of sport in Wales through the governing bodies of sport, municipal authorities, the local education authorities and the other national agencies has been largely similar to that in England. Legislation, government circulars, White Papers and other Whitehall and Parliament inspired statements, policies and actions concerned with sport and physical recreation have affected Wales no differently than England. Whilst the Minister for Sport is a British Government appointment, and his writ extends to Wales, protocol devolves this responsibility to the Secretary of State for Wales; a further odd constitutional happening that never ceases to bewilder.

In the early eighties the Plas Menai National Watersports Centre was developed in North Wales against a background of some opposition which thought the development too costly. Whilst it certainly takes a sizeable slice of the annual grant to the Sports Council for Wales, a deficit of £362,292 in 1987/88, it nevertheless attracts several thousands of participants annually to a wide variety of watersport courses and additionally provides a national focus for Welsh sailing. There was, however, in 1989 a question mark as to its future on account of costs.

Scotland

The scenario for development of sport in Scotland is very similar to that of Wales with one very important difference. Unlike Wales, Scotland has a corpus of legislation applicable only to itself and likewise certain Westminster legislation is not applicable to Scotland. Whilst the report of the Select Committee of the House of Lords *Sport and Leisure* (published by HMSO in 1973) applied to Scotland the 1975 White Paper did not, possibly to Scotland's loss. On the other hand the Local Government and Planning (Scotland) Act of 1982 imposed upon Scottish local authorities the obligation to provide for sport and physical recreation; such a mandatory power has long been sought in vain by sports administrators in England and Wales. Broadly the problems are the same in Scotland as in England and Wales and generally the same sort of legislation exists, or does not exist as the case may be; the fine print, the minutiae and the timing may be different in some cases but overall the situation is not dissimilar. Clearly priorities are different in Scotland as they are between the English regions and in Wales. Some are associated with the climate giving a greater emphasis on snow sports than elsewhere in Britain, which is not surprising considering the terrain.

Scotland was granted its Royal Charter in 1972 some two years after the IXth Commonwealth Games in Edinburgh. Scotland again hosted the Games in 1986 but sadly these were disastrous when thirty-two Commonwealth countries boycotted on account of the British Government's refusal to apply economic sanctions to South Africa; the financial consequences were considerable.

The National Sports Centres at Glenmore Lodge and Inverclyde were transferred in 1972 to the Scottish Sports Council and in 1975 the Scottish National Water Sports Centre at Cambrae was opened, giving Scotland a balanced spread of national-scale facilities. Scottish governing bodies of sport developed no differently from those in other parts of Britain although on occasions not without Scottish national interests attempting to take priority over those in Britain. In particular problems were encountered with sports such as sub-aqua and skating. In some situations prickly and uneasy compromises were reached bringing into focus the issue that had been side-stepped initially by the Wolfenden Report in not openly declaring one Sports Council for Britain whilst taking full account of Scottish and Welsh national aspirations. Whilst this may have helped on the constitutional level the larger voluntary sports movement would probably have been largely untouched by it and the governing body of sport problems that continue to arise would only marginally have been affected.

The programmes for sport participation, sport for all, facility development and schools of sport progressed as in the rest of Britain. Nationally Scotland followed the Sports Council's initiative of 1975 and in 1976 established the Scottish Sports Aid Foundation. In two areas of activity Scotland showed others the way with sponsorship promotion as early as 1977 and in the development of sports injuries clinics.

Local government had its own reorganization and as elsewhere the proliferation of departments for leisure and recreation gave a special focus to sporting opportunity. From the outset the Scottish Sports Council decided on a grant-aiding policy similar to the Sports Council. Although operating initially from a low base financial resources to Scottish governing bodies of sport grew. In the ten years from 1973 to 1983 the Scottish Office's grant-aid to the Scottish Sports Council rose from £0.87m to £4.1m; by 1989 this was £4.813m.

Accordingly, assistance to governing bodies for administration, coaching and international travel rose from a mere £66,500 in 1972 to £618,683 in 1980 and thence to £1.181m in 1987, an impressive increase despite inflation.[7] The particular nature of Scotland with its mountains, lochs and moors dictates that the Scottish Sports Council directs considerable resources to organizations and facilities that reflect this very different situation when compared with England. This is particularly obvious at the three Scottish National Sports Training Centres.

For example in 1988 Glenmore Lodge devoted 18 per cent of its course days to improving the standards of the British Nordic Ski and Biathlon teams. Climbing, skiing, orienteering, mountain leadership and rescue feature prominently in the programmes at the National Centres to meet the demands not only of Scottish but also British governing bodies for these disciplines. Golf has always been a 'people's' sport in Scotland as rugby is in Wales, and this is reflected in any overview of sport in Scotland.

In 1988 a *National Strategy for Coach Education and Coaching Development in Scotland* was published by the Scottish Sports Council as a discussion document aimed at complementing the work of individual governing bodies of sport and the National Coaching Foundation whose remit runs throughout Great Britain.

The Kings School of Sport started in 1977 continued to flourish in 1989 making good use of the Inverclyde National Sports Training Centre. A newcomer in this field was the Trustee Savings Bank in Scotland which, through its five regional and one national School of Sport, aimed to raise the standard of Scottish sport at élite level. By 1988 over 700 young people on the verge of international honours had benefited from the high standard of coaching offered at these schools. As in Wales the Scottish Sports Council has to be both a National Sports Council and a Regional Council for Sport and Recreation; dealing at the highest level and also very locally. A Scottish slant is often needed on a British initiative, whether it be sponsorship, drug testing, sport for all or sports medicine; therein lies the strength of national sports councils. The weakness lies here too unless duplication of effort, research and administration can be avoided.

During the first fifteen years of its existence the Scottish Sports Council was admirably served by two Chairmen, Laurie Liddell[8] until 1975, and then the former Olympic diver Peter Heatly (see Appendix 4 in this volume). Both brought direction and skill to their office. Raymond Miquel[9] took over in November 1987 and matters appear to be in good hands.

From the outset the Scottish Sports Council was served with distinction by the Chief Executive Ken Hutchinson[10] who always made clear the direction he was travelling for and on behalf of Scottish and indeed British sport; he retired at the end of 1989 and his experience will be sorely missed. Scotland has a uniqueness about its sport; it has its own flavour as does that of Wales but intrinsically it is no different from elsewhere in Britain. The nationalism of Scotland has no doubt helped considerably in the progress made; paradoxically it may have also hindered, at the same time, progress in Britain as a whole.

Conclusion

When looking at Scotland and Wales in their national contexts it is quite clear that their sports organizations and institutions have developed as in England. Scottish, Welsh and English athletics, swimming, badminton and squash for example are quite similar in organization and function. Some sports reflect national preferences in the emphasis placed upon them but in many respects this is no different from what occurs in English regions. The 'nationalism' of the home countries adds an extra dimension to some sports such as rugby football, soccer or golf but adds little to sports such as tennis, athletics, squash, judo, boxing or swimming, unless such sports are included in the Commonwealth Games programme. This is not an argument for dispensing with the national context, even if that were possible or desirable, as to represent one's country is a mark of achievement in any sport, but rather to point out that in such cases the Great Britain, or United Kingdom dimension is probably of greater significance in the international field.

There is overlapping and duplication in administration and organization which, it could be argued, are resources wasted. The big, mainly unanswerable question is, if sport were only 'Great Britain' would anything be lost from Wales and Scotland to the national effort? Who can answer that with any degree of certainty and who would be so bold as to try?

Notes

1 In Scotland the Scottish Standing Conference of Sport. In Wales the Welsh Sports Association.
2 Netherlands Sports Federation; Deutscher Sportbund (DSB); Norwegian Confederation of Sport; Swedish Sports Confederation.
3 Harry Llewellyn, 3rd Baronet. Kt (1977), CBE (1953); Olympics (1952) Gold Medal Show Jumping Team; President, British Equestrian Federation (1976–

81); Chairman, Sports Council for Wales (1971–81); Member, Sports Council (1971–81).

4 Sports Council for Wales Annual Reports — financial statistics.

5 John H. Powell, OBE (1987); MC; Sports Council for Wales (1972–), Chairman (1982–); Sports Council (1982–).

6 On the staff of the Sports Council in the Yorkshire and Humberside Region; Director of Recreation in Scotland; Senior staff member, Scottish Sports Council; Director, Sports Council for Wales (1982–).

7 Scottish Sports Council Annual Reports — financial statistics.

8 L. Liddell, CBE; Director of Physical Education, University of Edinburgh; Chairman, Scottish Sports Council (1972–75); Sports Council (1972–75).

9 R.C. Miquel, CBE (1981); Chairman and Chief Executive, Belhaven plc (1986–); Chairman, Scottish Sports Council (1987–); Sports Council (1987–).

10 Chartered Accountant; Chief Executive, Scottish Sports Council (1972–89); General-Secretary, Scottish Council of Physical Recreation (1968–72).

Chapter 11

The Pursuit of Excellence

Following the Commonwealth Games of 1978 in Edmonton, which were enjoyable from every aspect and resulted in a glorious festival of sport, all eyes were turned east towards Moscow and the Summer Olympic Games of 1980. These Games were to be the first organized by a Socialist country and no-one was in any doubt that they would be superbly arranged and would aim to represent to the world the achievements of Socialism. In an effort to break out of the traditional mould of high-level coaching in Britain that had developed over the years, the Sports Council, with its eyes on Moscow, offered governing bodies of sport additional financial resources to engage, on contract employment, the best coaches available from any country whatsoever in an endeavour to raise the platform of performances dramatically. The concept of 'coaching supremos' was regarded with suspicion in some quarters whilst others could not see clearly how such an appointment could be fitted in to their existing arrangements. However the Amateur Swimming Association (ASA) grasped the nettle and appointed the highly talented and motivated David Haller, who was released from Beckenham Swimming Club for this purpose. Derek Beaumont was charged with looking after the British Diving Squad under similar arrangements, whilst the appointment of a Director of Racing by the British Cycling Federation (BCF) ensured that the British team for Moscow would travel prepared in the best possible way. The Amateur Fencing Association (AFA) employed two top-level overseas coaches in the run-up to the Olympics but sadly there were no other takers. Although the plan was to expand the scheme after the Moscow Olympics in preparation for the 1984 Olympic Games in Los Angeles, this imaginative scheme lost momentum and drifted.

In the popular eye the names that caught the public imagination in the build-up to the 1980 and 1984 Olympic Games were the great middle-distance runners Sebastian Coe, Steve Ovett and Steve Cram, the decathlete Daley Thompson and the ice skaters and dancers Robin Cousins, Jayne Torvill and Christopher Dean. Other top names from a range of sports flitted across the public consciousness, but none were so lasting for so long as these superstars who all were either Olympic Champions, World Champions, holders of World Records, or in some cases all of these. They represented a level of performance that set the standard to emulate and the pack behind the great champions became larger and of higher standard in many sports.

By the 1988 Olympic Games these great athletes were no longer presenting major challenges on the world scene as new names such as the sprinter Linford Christie competed for world recognition.

The development policies of the sixties and seventies were beginning to pay off, although in some sports such as tennis the emergence of a challenger for the highest honours in the game proved elusive.

The sound basis of good administration in the governing bodies of sport to support well-considered coaching programmes and preparation-training continued to be supported financially by the Sports Council in line with policies adopted in the seventies and only modified marginally from time to time in an effort to improve both service and flexibility. Even allowing for inflation the volume of money made available to assist the sports bodies in their aspirations grew each year although the ravages of inflation mask the fact that between the years 1982 and 1984 there was in fact a slow down in growth. The statistics for 1983/84 indicate at best a hold position and with inflation running at around 5 per cent, probably a decline. This reflected very much the subtle pressure placed by the Government, in the shape of the Minister for Sport, on the Sports Council to divert a larger proportion of its resources into the social areas. For example, on the capital side £679,000 was allocated to schemes in Areas of Special Need in 1980, but in 1982 this had risen to £1.246m. Likewise the Regional Participation schemes had budgets of £265,000 in 1982 rising to £870,765 in 1983.[1]

A reflection of this policy thrust may also be detected in the volume of current grant-aid made available in 1983/84 to other corporate bodies concerned with sport such as the British Association of National Coaches, the British Sports Association for the Disabled, the National Council for School Sports, and the Physical Education Association compared with previous years. Table 5 indicates the total financial assistance to governing bodies of sport and other such sports bodies during the period under review. With many governing bodies of sport being assisted financially to a very considerable extent the question of how much sport was doing for itself to help improve its revenue base was increasingly raised. Some sports bodies levied meaningful subscriptions on their members to help fund the administration of their activities whilst others charged derisory sums relying on money from sponsorship, insurance schemes and the Sports Council for the larger part of their income. Considerable pressure early in the eighties was put on those governing bodies of sport who appeared to lean very heavily on these other sources for their income, but this move, however right it was, hit sport at a time when subscription income was particularly vulnerable due to increasing unemployment and in particular youth unemployment. The dependence of

Table 5: Current grant aid

	To governing bodies £m	To other sports bodies £m	Total £m
1978/79	3.289	.297	3.586
1979/80	3.753	.310	3.063
1980/81	4.630	.370	5.000
1981/82	4.728	.452	5.180
1982/83	5.200	.660	5.860
1983/84	5.402	.390	5.792
1984/85	6.000	.552	6.552
1985/86	6.247	.713	6.960
1986/87	7.770	.965	8.735
1987/88	8.876	1.350	10.226
1988/89	8.155	1.148	9.303

Source: Sports Council Annual Reports — Analysis of Statistics

some sports on volatile sources of income posed a possible threat to their independence and in some extreme cases their actual survival would have been threatened if those existing and somewhat precarious sources, ie short-term sponsorship, had dried up. The dependence of such sports bodies on the Sports Council was considered unhealthy for the voluntary sports movement and singly and collectively they were requested to put their financial affairs into greater order forthwith. A major conference convened by the Sports Council in December 1979 and held at the Royal Festival Hall, to which all governing bodies were invited, acted as a catalyst in this regard and slowly but surely many of the sports bodies who were culpable began to remedy the situation.[2]

In December 1979 the Soviet Union invaded Afghanistan and this action set in train a series of events that rocked sport nationally and internationally. The political actions as a consequence of this invasion will be discussed later in Chapter 13, as will the price sport was asked to pay in the Western world, but the whole affair was to test the voluntary sports movement in Britain as never before. The Winter Olympics at Lake Placid, USA, took place with no untoward event other than complaints as to the inadequacy of the transport arrangements at the venue itself; inconvenient but not of major concern. At Lake Placid Robin Cousins won a magnificent 'gold' for skating, fulfilling in great measure the promise shown beforehand and thrilling British television viewers as they sat on the edges of their armchairs, during the early hours of the morning, with fingers crossed and bated breath, enthralled by the skill and artistry of this young athlete. As 1980 unrolled the clamour for a sports boycott of the Moscow Summer Games gathered momentum and broke about the heads of the Chairman of the BOA, Sir Denis Follows, and the Chairmen of the twenty-one Olympic sports bodies scheduled to be in the USSR that summer. In the eventuality Sir Denis stood as a rock in support of non-political involvement in sport and seventeen of the national governing bodies of sport joined him in

Moscow. The traditional Olympic Appeal, usually so smoothly and efficiently run, faltered and hesitated as many of those who supported the Prime Minister's view that the British team should not go to Moscow withdrew their support.

The Sports Council was directed not to offer support (see Appendix 1 in this volume, paragraph 3, which permits the Government to take this action) but there were many thousands who either supported a British presence at Moscow or did not like the idea of a British Government trying to make a political point through young athletes whilst continuing business and commercial links.

In the House of Commons on 17 March 1980 Sir Ian Gilmour, Lord Privy Seal, said:

> ... We are not advocating the severance of all contacts in political, sporting, cultural or scientific fields any more than we are advocating the severance of trade links where opportunities exist, especially for our non-strategic capital goods. (Hansard, House of Commons, 17 March 1980, col. 37).

The outcome was that sufficient money was raised to send the teams to Moscow and no-one who should have gone was left at home unless it was his or her choice. Parading under the banner of the BOA and not the Union Flag at the opening ceremony a political point was made after which the athletes, under the tightest security arrangements ever, settled down to prepare for their events in the hot Moscow summer. Despite the absence of the powerful USA and the West Germans who headed the boycott list, the Olympic Games were a great success for those who took part resulting in twenty-one Olympic medals for Britain made up of five gold, seven silver and nine bronze. Just as in Montreal when the day came those who opted to boycott the Moscow Olympics were not missed and likewise four years later in Los Angeles when the Soviet bloc took reprisal action.

The question of whether it was politically sensible to follow an Olympic Games in the Soviet Union with one in the USA will be debated long into the future, but in the final analysis the IOC had no alternative as Los Angeles was the only bidder for the 1984 Summer Olympic Games. Boycott by the Socialist countries therefore was always a probability although they would never admit to using that word. In the eventuality the naive attitude of the American Government made matters very difficult for the Los Angeles Organizing Committee with the refusal of certain visas which made it publicly easy for the Soviets to announce that they would not be participating, ostensibly because they were concerned with the security arrangements[3] for their athletes and the over-commercialization of the event which, they argued, was in violation of the IOC Charter.[4]

The 1984 Winter Olympics in Sarajevo, Yugoslavia were a resounding success in terms of competition, organization and lack of political statement.

The 'gold' by Jayne Torvill and Christopher Dean in the ice-dancing event will live in the memory of those who saw it achieved, and the *Bolero*, always hitherto associated with Ravel, is now linked forever with the names of those two exquisite ice dancers.

The Games in Los Angeles, despite the boycott by the Soviet bloc and the threat of smog in this car-ridden city, were superbly arranged and presented as the first Olympic Games to be sponsored by a business consortium and not by a municipal authority. They were a triumph for the USA in every way and American athletes were outstanding, achieving successes in events such as gymnastics and cycling where they had had little success previously, but in the main dominating track and field and the events in the pool. For Britain the Games were a success with thirty-seven medals made up of five gold, eleven silver and twenty-one bronze medals. The line-up for the final of the 1500m on the track included the three superstars, Coe, Ovett and Cram and Britain hoped for a clean sweep of medals but sadly the illness of Ovett that had been evidenced in his semi-final manifested itself again and Britain had to be content with gold and silver. Daley Thompson proved himself the greatest athlete in the world as yet again he repeated his 'golden' performance of Moscow, but perhaps the loudest cheers of all were for the British hockey team under the wise guidance of Roger Self which against every prediction took a 'bronze' and yet only participated because of a vacancy due to the boycott.

Standards at Moscow and Los Angeles were of course not so high as they would have been without the boycotts but in the euphoria of the Olympic Games, and in the white hot cauldron of competition, absences were merely noted and worthy champions emerged. Many countries that had never reached finals before achieved this distinction and some nations won their first Olympic medals ever which gave a great fillip to sport in these countries. As in Montreal and Moscow the only losers were those who were not there as athletes once again became the innocent victims of super-power politics.

With Seoul, South Korea, nominated for the 1988 Summer Olympic Games, there was a sense of foreboding after the boycotts of the previous two Games for here we had a venue in a very sensitive part of the world. Following the Korean War of the early fifties the country was divided at the 38th parallel with the north supported by the communist world and the south by the capitalists led by the USA; an explosive situation in which to hold the Olympic Games. In the event there was the highest turn-out of national teams in the history of the Games with 161 countries being represented; boycotts were minimal, only Cuba being of any significance. Despite student riots in the months leading up to the event the Games went ahead in great style with no political or domestic strife; a great credit to the South Korean Organizing Committee who provided a magnificent range of facilities.

These were good Games for Great Britain and Northern Ireland, winning five gold, ten silver and nine bronze medals, with the 'gold' success of the hockey team being perhaps the most spectacular of all after the unexpected 'bronze' of 1984.

Following the highly successful Commonwealth Games in Edmonton in 1978, Brisbane hosted the 1982 Games in the late summer for the northern hemisphere countries and in the delightful spring weather of Queensland. The Games were preceded by a prestigious Commonwealth Sports Science and Physical Education Conference, as in Edmonton, but this time it was enlarged to embrace the title 'International' which attracted delegates from non-Commonwealth countries. Her Majesty the Queen attended what was yet again a fine festival of sport in a multi-racial context. All the home countries were strongly represented, public appeals having been generously supported by the British public; in the case of England a grant of £56,500 to the Commonwealth Games Council of England by the Sports Council ensured a large representation, second only to the host country Australia.

In 1986, full of hope and expectation, Edinburgh planned thoroughly for the return of the Commonwealth Games to Scotland. In the eventuality the boycott by thirty-two countries because the British Government, which has no locus in the Games, continued to refuse to join a Commonwealth initiative to impose sanctions on South Africa, contributed to the failure of the Games on both 'friendly' and financial grounds. This was a sporting tragedy of serious proportions. Happily the October 1989 Conference of Heads of Commonwealth countries in Kuala Lumpur[5] allayed fears of something similar in Auckland, New Zealand, in January and February 1990, despite an unofficial cricket tour to South Africa by English cricketers at the same time and the British Government's sanctions policy remaining unchanged.

Britain continued to stage major international events between 1980 and 1990. Particularly memorable were the 1981 Canoe Championships at the National Water Sports Centre for the flat events and at Bala in North Wales for the white-water competitions, and the Hockey World Cup and the World Rowing Championships, both in 1986. In 1989 came the tremendous success of the British athletes in the European Cup at Gateshead. Their first place gave them direct entry to the World Cup in Barcelona some months later. The World Cycling Championships were held again in Great Britain in the summer of 1982 but failed to capture the imagination of the public in the way they had done a decade earlier.

On the Olympic front there was acute disappointment when, after an excellent feasibility study by the Greater London Council in 1979 on the staging of the 1988 Olympic Games in London which had showed promising options, the matter was allowed to peter out. Birmingham, under the inspiring leadership of Denis Howell, took up the challenge, and, backed by a united City Council, won the BOA's nomination for the British bid for 1992. An imaginative and well-constructed proposal, backed by adequate finance and the moral, if not financial, support of the Government was presented

Table 6

	1978/79 £m	1983/84 £m	*1984/85 £m
Coaching and development	.649	1.097	1.097
Preparation training	.603	.987	.842
International travel	.921	1.312	1.300
Regional centres of excellence and drug testing	.251	.215	.286
National Coaching Foundation	Nil	.050	.125
Total	2.424	3.661	3.667

* The last year when figures were presented in this way.
Source: Sports Council Annual Reports — Analysis of Statistics

with flair to the IOC in Lausanne in September 1986. Sadly for Great Britain Barcelona won the vote and now the country looks to Manchester to carry the flag in their bold bid for 1996.

By 1983 the public resources allocated to assist the governing bodies of sport nationally to develop excellence had risen from £2.424m in 1978 to £3.661m (Table 6) but by then the policy, under government pressures, was to hold at this level of support. A year later, despite inflation, the budget had increased by a mere £6.000; in reality a decrease.

In November 1984 Sebastian Coe, a Vice-Chairman of the Sports Council, chaired a working group composed of interested national organizations[6] whose task was to examine the preparation programmes of the twenty-eight sports that would be taking part in the Summer and Winter Olympic Games of 1988. This was a thorough exercise culminating in a major recommendation that £3.7m was needed by the governing bodies of sport in addition to £1.5m required to meet the training expenses of individual athletes.[7] To its great credit the Sports Council accepted the recommendation for the larger sum and to the relief of all concerned the Minet Holdings group offered the £1.5m of sponsorship if administered by the Sports Aid Foundation.

In 1986 the Sports Council gave £1.05m to the governing bodies of Olympic sports to enhance their preparation programmes and in 1987 the annual grants to governing bodies increased by £1.1m which was a clear indication that the 'hold' situation of the earlier part of the decade had been swept away. To all of this was added increased funding for drug-abuse control, sports medicine and sports science grants and support for the Birmingham bid for the 1992 Olympic Games.[8]

An initiative by the BOA established the British Olympic Medical Centre in 1987 at Northwick Park Hospital in Harrow which complemented the Football Association's Human Performance Testing Laboratory at the Lilleshall National Sports Centre where the FA has its sports school for selected young footballers.

As the decade closed elite sport could be satisfied that once again it was having its fair share of available national resources.

In the regions the centres of excellence scheme, started as a result of the 1975 White Paper *Sport and Recreation*, was providing dividends. By 1982 the Sports Council was able to report that eighty-three centres were operating involving twenty-eight sports and catering for over 1300 aspiring talented young men and women. Although the volume of money made available by the Sports Council to assist the Regional Centres of Excellence scheme, taking into account inflation, only increased marginally to £150,000 in 1984 from £139,000 in 1983 compared with £100,000 in 1978/79, this was not through any lack of commitment nor occasioned by any after-thoughts about the validity of the policy but rather because local sponsorship by statutory and commercial sources expanded as the scheme demonstrated success. The West Midlands Canoeing Centre virtually became the National Squad and in the World Championships of 1981 four gold medals, two silver medals and one bronze medal was the rich haul the centre brought home. The Bracknell Centre rejoiced in the Judo World Championship won by Jane Bridge in the same year. These successes are illustrative of similar successes at regional, national and international levels by members of Regional Centres of Excellence that provided an increasingly wide field of selection for the highest honours. There is no doubt that this initiative had by the mid-eighties proved itself and was a feature that was here to stay in the structure of British sport, albeit a feature flexible enough to allow for modification to meet local situations and opportunities.[9]

Sponsorship

Sponsorship of sport by commercial and business operations brings great blessings and often great pressures. The linkage of sponsorship, sport and television is obvious, but not all sponsors seek a high profile return but prefer being seen doing good undemonstrably and in some cases almost by stealth. Equally some sponsors prefer to assist financially at junior or youth levels and to be seen as doers of good works. Sports bodies have had to learn how to extract the maximum from any sponsor in return for the exposure the sponsor seeks and some have proved better than others in this area of activity. The CCPR has helped manfully by constantly bringing the best advice available to the governing bodies of sport at their annual conferences. As 1984 came to a close the need for most sports bodies to employ, or have available to them in a voluntary capacity, sponsorship negotiators was highlighted by the multi-million pound sponsorship deal entered into by the governing body for athletics in Britain, and they wisely appointed professional advisers.

The Howell Report, *Committee of Enquiry into Sports Sponsorship*, set up by the CCPR reported in December 1983. In a far-ranging review of sponsorship, its pros and cons, its benefits and disbenefits Denis Howell and his Committee pointed to grave dangers to sport in certain practices and had some stern words to say about pressure selling of sport and the commercial exploitation for material gain of individual sportsmen to the detriment of the voluntary sports movement.

> 'The pursuit of sporting excellence ... now makes demands on them almost beyond the call of duty. Sponsorship can offer some of these sports stars a chance to secure their financial future ... such opportunities lay enormous responsibilities upon governing bodies....',

said the Committee unflinchingly (paragraph 13–4, p. 88).

A constructive and imaginative joint action by the Sports Council and the CCPR in early 1982 led to the appointment of the talented Derek Etherington as a sponsorship consultant. Etherington had made his name in this field of endeavour through his work with *Sportscan*, a sophisticated and computerized analysis of sponsor-exposure on television and he quickly established the Sports Sponsorship Advisory Service.[10] This service involved introducing the business and commercial communities to the benefits of various types of sports sponsorship where they had not ventured previously and then attempted to link those interested with appropriate sports bodies and events that appealed to the potential sponsor. In a little over two years reliable sources pointed to new sponsorship totalling in excess of £750,000 with further dividends from the many presentations and discussions under-taken by way of introduction still to be realized.

The question of tobacco advertising through sponsorship, and also that of intoxicating liquor, has exercised sports administrators for many years and there are many divergent views. At the end of 1978 the Sports Council at its meeting in North Wales had a quite chaotic debate on the issue of tobacco sponsorship at which feelings ran very high indeed and the whole matter remained inconclusive with tempers and reputations bruised. Broadly speaking most, but not all, of the sports bodies accept the hard fact of life that they cannot afford to refuse tobacco sponsorship until an alternative source of income appears to take its place, whilst the purists tend to take the moral stance concerning the influence of such sponsorship on young people and the contradiction between sport, health and smoking. Intoxicating liquor does not raise the debating temperature in quite the same fashion but the argument is mounted in much the same way as that of tobacco although to a lesser degree. The big difference is that tobacco companies are not permitted to advertise on television and therefore seek other ways of obtaining television exposure through televised sports events, whilst liquor companies are not banned from direct advertising and do not feel the need for increased exposure in quite the same way. Until it can be proved that sponsorship by tobacco companies directly affects, or does not affect, young people by encouraging them to start smoking the arguments will continue.

The demands of sponsors on governing bodies and individual sportsmen and women can alter the face of sport at national and international levels where the power of television is enormous. Events are sometimes manufactured and programmed to meet the demands of television which guarantees an audience for the event, and the sponsors of that event, at the expense of the athlete if he or she is an amateur. Trust funds, appearance money and hyped confrontations are by-products of increasing commercialism in sport. The gladiatorial meeting at Crystal Palace in 1985, the year after the famous trip-up in the women's 3,000 metres at the Los Angeles Olympic Games, of the protagonists Zola Budd and Mary Decker Slaney was such a case. With the meeting extended to meet commercial demands this re-run took place amid the maximum glare of publicity. All those in athletics knew that in reality this was a 'no-contest' event and so it proved when Slaney won easily with Budd trailing very far behind. Rumours then abounded as to what each had been paid for their trust funds.

At international level the IOC is the foremost organization in the sponsorship field offering both the televising of the Winter and Summer Games and the marketing of the famous five-rings logo. For example, the press report that the television rights for the Seoul Olympics of 1988 were sold for a sum in excess of US$4m. This money is used for developing sport in developing countries, and running the Olympic 'family'; additionally the International Sports Federations (ISFs) and National Olympic Committees (NOCs) are given allocations.

The IOC and other world bodies such as the International Amateur Athletics Federation (IAAF) are powerful enough to control the situation as they wish; those at international and national level who do not have such power can find themselves vulnerable. The marketing of athletes and the availability of large sums of appearance and prize money puts a strain on the loyalties of those who probably need the money but, given the choice, would prefer to compete for their country where usually no sponsorship or appearance money accrues to them. In the case of professional competitors, whilst the same principles concerning hyped events are equally valid, the question of payment is a non-issue as for example in football, tennis or golf for then it clearly is the paid job of the athlete and the principle of the 'labourer being worthy of his hire' is completely valid, although even then excessive prize money can damage the image of the sport and its principal competitors. Proof of this was the critical press given to the announcement by the International Tennis Federation in October 1989 that a new tournament they would be promoting would have a first prize of US$2m.[11]

Sponsorship can be, and often is, a rewarding partnership for sport and commerce; sometimes it is a threat that can damage and could destroy. Sport has much to offer the sponsor and sport can reap rich benefits, it could also be destroyed by becoming too dependent; that is the situation facing many sports bodies today and is a situation they will continue to face to an increasing degree in the nineties with the coming of satellite television.

Drug Abuse

The whole question of the improper use of drugs to increase the level of performance sharpened dramatically in the eighties assisted by a degree of ambivalence on the part of some national and international sports administrators. The vast proportion of the sports world was aghast when in March 1980 the International Amateur Athletics Federation reinstated five athletes who had been banned for a year from competition for having had it proved that they were guilty of drug abuse. It was noted that this decision for the athletes was in good time for the Moscow Olympics and it was fiercely criticized by such eminent personalities in the world of athletics as Arthur Gold, the President of the European Athletics Union, a bitter and uncompromising opponent of the drug-takers. The IOC announced in 1979 its intention through its Medical Commission, under the Chairmanship of the Prince de Merode (Belgium), to proceed with a scheme for accrediting drug-testing laboratories which gave a clear signal to those who delved into the murky waters of drug abuse that they meant business.

By 1980 Professor Brooks at St. Thomas's Hospital was making significant progress with his research into establishing normal levels of testosterone. As one drug became capable of detection so another reared its ugly and dangerous head and therefore the detected presence of corticosteroids in greater use in sport was viewed with increasing concern. British sports administrators were notoriously slow to tackle the issue of drug-abuse in their sports with some notable exceptions such as rowing, some arguing that their sport was 'clean'. Despite the valiant work of Professor Beckett and his colleagues in the Drug Testing Centre at Chelsea College only five national governing bodies were regularly using the services freely available to them as the seventies drew to a close. In an effort to bring about government action the Committee for the Development of Sport at the Council of Europe requested that every member state should establish a National Anti-Doping Committee. In the eventuality the British Government requested the Sports Council to undertake this function through its existing Drugs Advisory Group.[12] As early as the Lancaster House Conference of European Ministers for Sport (1978) governments had expressed grave concern when they issued a Resolution on the Ethical and Human Problems in Sport which included a large section on Doping and Health.[13] This called for concerted action with the national sports bodies to intensify research, support the testing now underway, carry out publicity campaigns on the dangers to health, publish lists of stimulants, work towards stricter control of the issue of medical prescriptions and finally to institute sanctions against athletes, coaches, managers and doctors found guilty of using drugs. In 1984 the Ministers for Sport meeting in Malta in May approved a firm Resolution subscribing to the European Anti-Doping Charter for Sport (see Appendix 13 in this volume for full text) that had been prepared in great detail over the years stage by stage. Whilst subscribing to this Charter they further agreed:

(i)   to be guided by its principles when considering or initiating action in the areas covered for which they are responsible;

(ii) to urge the international and national sports organizations to implement the provisions in the Charter in areas where they have a responsibility;

(iii) to invite the Committee of Ministers of the Council of Europe to adopt the Charter in the form of a Recommendation to Governments of member states.[14]

This was strong, political action and reflected great credit on Mr. George Walker the very able Secretary to the Committee for the Development of Sport within the Council of Europe who so skilfully brought this major issue to a successful conclusion. As a direct result the Sports Council in Britain, towards the end of 1984, made it quite clear by a formal resolution of the Council that henceforth they intended to request sports organizations to apply effective anti-doping regulations.[15] Implicit in this statement was the unspoken sanction that failure to comply might well result in loss of all or part of any annual subvention the Sports Council might make. In 1983 fourteen national governing bodies had used the testing facilities available at Chelsea, but clearly that was not sufficient to comply with the spirit and intent of the Malta decision and accordingly the Sports Council acted to make its position quite clear.[16] Early in February 1985 the British Amateur Athletic Board announced its intention to proceed with random testing; this was a body blow to the cheats.

By 1982 tests for testosterone were well underway and were applied at the Olympic Games in the summer of 1984, for by then the menace of growth hormones was challenging the medical scientists. The sickening exposé of the use of blood-changing by some of the USA medal-winning cyclists in the autumn of 1984 caused yet a further stir. In September 1987 Moynihan and Coe produced a report *The Misuse of Drugs in Sport*[17] that stirred up controversy and focussed the attention of sports bodies and the media on this issue. 'We believe that a new regime for drug testing is needed' they said, and went on to propose seven 'principles (that) should be incorporated into a new and strengthened regime for drug testing'. These were:

(i)   Testing must be independent.

(ii) Testing must be more effective, vigorous and entirely random.

(iii) Competitors in all sports must be required to make a personal declaration of willingness to undertake tests.

(iv) Penalties for taking drugs must be effective and consistent.

(v) The role of the Sports Council's Drug Advisory Group should be enhanced.

(vi) There should be wide publicity about the effect of drugs, offenders and offences.

(vii) Consideration should be given to extending relevant legislation.

The last proposal intimated that on 11 September 1987 the Advisory Council on the Misuse of Drugs had been asked by the Government to consider whether anabolic steroids should be brought within the scope of the Misuse of Drugs Act 1971. By the end of 1989 no firm decision had been made but it was confidently anticipated that some such action was not far off.

In 1988 the IAAF produced a brochure *Save the Future for Yourself*[18] which was aimed at young athletes. The twenty-two IAAF approved testing laboratories were listed together with a list of banned substances. This was a good example of the work needed in the educational field aimed especially at young people.

At the IX European Sports Conference in October 1989 (see Chapter 9 in this volume) Sir Arthur Gold, on behalf of the UK Delegation, agreed to continue to chair the Anti-Doping Working Group with a new orientation towards education and monitoring. For the next two years the Group worked on 'Anti-Doping Programme support' and will report at the X Conference in Norway in 1991.

The whole question of 'drugs in sport' came dramatically to a head at the 1988 Olympic Games when Ben Johnson of Canada, the world's fastest sprinter, had his gold medal withdrawn after being tested positive for anabolic steroids. This episode shattered the complacency of some and confirmed the worst fears of others. For Canada this was devastating but unflinchingly they met the issue head on. Following a recommendation of the Prime Minster, by Order in Council, a Commission was established under the Inquiries Act of Canada. The Terms of Reference were broad. The Order 'recognizes that there is a clear public concern with respect to the use of various drugs and banned practices intended to increase athletic performance, and I am directed to enquire into and report on the facts and circumstances surrounding the use of such drugs and banned substances by Canadian athletes and to make recommendations . . .'[19] Mr. Bruce Dubin, appointed to head the Inquiry, made it quite clear that 'This is not an inquiry into the conduct of one or more individuals or one or more associations.'

These events were particularly poignant for Canada for they had taken a lead only a month or two before the Games to convene the 'First Permanent World Conference on Anti-Doping in Sport' in Ottawa in late June when eighty-five senior officials from twenty-seven nations were present together with representatives of the IOC, Council of Europe, European Sports Conference, GAISF, Supreme Council for Sport in Africa, ICSSPE and International Federations.[20]

The cost of doping control dug deeply into the Sports Council's budgets in the eighties. In 1986 £313,254 was made available to support this work and although this eased to £294,099 in 1989, the figures were still very considerable (Sports Council's Annual Reports Financial Statistics).

In the fresh challenges that lie ahead, the fine and highly acclaimed work of Professor Brooks, Professor Beckett and Dr. Cowans, now in charge at Chelsea, ensures that Britain is determined to do all it can to defeat the scourge of drug abuse for which there is no place in sports which put the emphasis on the fair challenge of one athlete to another. Their reputation internationally is unique and in these endeavours Britain continues to lead the world but to do so is costly and necessarily denies scarce resources to other programmes of sports activity. This area of scientific work has been supported by the frequent public utterances of many well-known athletes including Sebastian Coe who, from the first time he spoke at the 11th Olympic Congress in Baden (1981) has never failed to deplore in the most scathing terms those of his fellow athletes who rely on drugs for their performance; he and his fellow international athletes have called repeatedly for life bans on those found guilty.[21]

The Foundations — Sports Aid and National Coaching

The Sports Aid Foundation

In the run-up to the 1984 Olympic Games in Los Angeles the SAF assisted aspiring competitors to the tune of £479,000 in the Olympic Year in addition to £286,000 disbursed the previous year. In the three years before the Seoul Olympics in 1988 £1.19m[22] was provided which allowed support for British competitors at all levels and not only those of the very highest international calibre.

These huge sums underlined the impact the SAF has had on British sport. The need for a high level of financial contributions was particularly necessary in the first half of the decade when unemployment was running at an unprecedented level, making it difficult, if not impossible in some cases, for some young men and women to provide much self-help.

In 1982 recipients of Foundation grants won eleven gold medals in World Championships, twenty gold medals in European Championships and a staggering thirty-nine gold medals at the Commonwealth Games in Brisbane. A year later the Sports Aid Foundation assisted British international competitors to win forty-nine gold, thirty-four silver and thirty-three bronze medals in World and European Championships leaving sports administrators reflecting on what life would have been like if no such Foundation had existed capable of attracting support and financial contributions from commerce, business and generous patrons. In the build up to the Winter and Summer Olympic Games of 1984 the Foundation helped with necessary finance for the preparation-training of 418 competitors in Olympic and International competitions. The thirty-four sports assisted ranged from athletics to yachting and included sport for the disabled. In 1988 2363 sports people received grants. In all forty-six sports benefited and again not all were Olympic sports.[23] All the gold medal winners in Seoul were financially supported by the SAF.

To show support the Prime Minister, Mrs. Margaret Thatcher, accompanied her husband Denis, a Governor of the Sports Aid Foundation, to two notable events prior to the 1984 Summer Olympic Games, the 'Benefactors' reception and dinner and the post-Winter Olympics Ice Gala contributed by a generous Torvill and Dean before they turned professional.[24] The Prime Minster's presence and her encouraging words of support were widely publicized and represented a considerable contribution to British sport. Both events resulted in handsome donations to the Foundation for the use of future generations of British sportsmen and sportswomen. In November 1987 she again supported the SAF at the Sports Aid reception at the Banqueting House.

The establishment of the Sports Aid Trust within the overall operations of the Foundation was announced in early 1984 and was designed to take full account of financial legislation applicable to charitable trusts.

The SAF is well organized and poised to enter the nineties. It continues to attract wealthy businessmen and benefactors prepared to work and use their influence to attract money to assist British sportsmen and women. It is, in 1990, a most powerful body in British sport and one to which many owe a great deal for the chances they were given to compete at the highest level.

The complete history of the Sports Aid Foundation will no doubt be told one day. In the fifteen years of its existence it has provided the opportunity for many young men and women to train and prepare for international competition freed of financial worry. In this way part of every gold, silver and bronze medal belongs to the Foundation, to Zetter, Porter, Kulukundis, Weeks, Nagle, the Governors past and present, and the Members who have given so much to British sport.

In 1975 Walter Winterbottom's judgment was right, not for the first time, and John Coghlan's journey to Frankfurt to listen, learn and put what he saw into action was time well spent; rich dividends have followed to be enjoyed by thousands of aspiring international athletes, and this situation continues today albeit under new management but with the same ideals, policies and commitment.

The National Coaching Foundation (established 1983)

Although the need for some centralized coaching service to assist in the training of sports coaches at all levels had been identified in 1975 an early attempt in 1976 to establish such a unit at Loughborough University floundered due to inadequate preparation for such a development and the inability to carry along the many other learned institutions involved in the relevant sports sciences. No-one queried the necessity for such a unit or centre but the majority of those involved could not agree on the location and in any case insufficient money was available to start the project with any hope of ultimate success.

By the eighties the regions of the Sports Council were responding to local needs. In association with universities, polytechnics and colleges of higher education sports scientists and county and regional governing bodies of sport were successfully launching local courses for coaches (see Sports Council regional reports). The British Association of National Coaches, having campaigned for many years offered full support regionally, and through the Coaching Panel of the Sports Council asked for a fresh national initiative.[25] This request coincided with a review of the sports science courses already being promoted by the regions of the Sports Council. Accordingly the Deputy Director-General was asked to take whatever steps were necessary to establish a coaching unit or centre which would coordinate the existing work and promote in an orderly way, and in association with all appropriate bodies, an expansion of coaching services.[26] Drawing on the experience of the systems developed in the Federal Republic of Germany, the German Democratic Republic and Cuba, and in the light of the existing British situation, he decided that a network system could embrace all that was currently going on in sports science research in the universities, polytechnics and colleges, so that in effect they all would form the coaching unit. Obviously the administrative centre for such a network needed to have a physical base and needed access to computers and educational and visual-aids services. Further important criteria for the physical base were accessibility by road, train and air and a willing host institution prepared to offer accommodation and basic services. Coghlan's principal aide in this work was Michael Collins, the talented Head of Research at the Sports Council, whose contribution was very considerable in setting out the terms of reference for the Foundation.

The Universities of Birmingham, Loughborough, Leeds, the City of Leeds Polytechnic and the West London Institute of Higher Education, through their Vice-Chancellors, Directors and Principals, all willingly and generously offered accommodation and services and promised full support to the network concept. In the eventuality Leeds Polytechnic was selected and immediately made available accommodation on the Beckett Park site adjacent to Carnegie College of Physical Education. Dr. Nick Whitehead, the former Olympic athlete and Principal Lecturer, was appointed Director with Miss Sue Campbell as Deputy Director.[27] In the meantime the Sports Council had not only approved these moves but had voted £50,000 as an operational budget for the first year of working. It was agreed that the title of the new organization should be The National Coaching Foundation (NCF) and that the Foundation would be managed by an independent Committee made up of the representatives of the Central Council of Physical Recreation, the British Association of National Coaches, the British Olympic Association, the Sports Council, the sports sciences, sports medicine and the network institutions of higher education.[28] An early task of the NCF was to refine its terms of reference which were quickly agreed viz:

> The Foundation has been established to provide a service to coaching at national and local level by way of programmes, information services, and the provision of technical data from home and overseas.[29]

The Foundation moved speedily and within months was advertising the availability of introductory study packs on a range on topics including The Coach in Action, The Body in Action, Safety and Injury, Improving Techniques, Mind over Matter, and Planning and Practice. As a follow-up to these introductory packs a series of short courses was organized dealing with a rich variety of topics such as Development of Strength and Speed, Technique Analysis in Sport, Use of Video, Skill Acquisition, Mental Preparation for Competition, and Prevention and Rehabilitation of Injury.[30]

To demonstrate how the network concept worked these and other courses numbering fourteen topics in all were offered at twenty[31] centres of higher learning in the nine regions of England and Wales in January 1985. Concurrent with the organization of courses an information service for coaches was announced in an effort to bridge the gap between the sports science researcher in the laboratory and the coach in the field. An on-line computer search service to international databases and to the Foundation's own data-base, together with British Telecom's Prestel Service all became available in 1985.

In April 1985 Miss Sue Campbell became the Director of the NCF.[32] The British Association of National Coaches at last had what they had lobbied for over many years and great credit accrued to their Chairman John Cadman and Secretary Geoff Gleeson for so assiduously and relentlessly pursuing their course with diplomacy and flexibility. To the sports scientists the Foundation offered a window for their research and their work and happily linked the laboratory with the track, pool and sports hall — the work place of the coach.

By 1986 the NCF was able to restate its objectives clearly and concisely as:

(a) The promotion of the education, instruction and training at national and local levels of honorary and professional coaches and other interested persons in performance-related knowledge applied to all kinds of sport and physical recreation.
(b) The promotion and dissemination of knowledge in pursuit of the above objective.

The study packs were completed with videotapes being made available to complement the tutors' manuals and the initial stock of 60,000 was soon exhausted. By now the technical programme was fully on stream with all the four planned levels of training up and running. Twenty-nine universities, polytechnics and colleges were offering courses in England, Scotland, Wales and Northern Ireland and the 1986 Loughborough Summer School programme included a Level Two course attended by thirty-two coaches.

The network concept, a key element in the structure of the NCF, was developed to such an extent that by February 1987 the Foundation was able to announce that from thirty aspiring applicants fourteen institutions of higher learning had been designated as initial members of the network. These were:

England
Bedford College of Higher Education
Brighton Polytechnic
Bulmershe College of Higher Education (Now part of the University of Reading)
Crewe and Alsager College of Higher Education
Leeds Polytechnic
Liverpool Polytechnic
Loughborough University
Newcastle-upon-Tyne Polytechnic
West London Institute of Higher Education

Wales
University College of North Wales (Bangor)
South Glamorgan Institute of Higher Education (Cardiff)

Scotland
Moray House College of Education (Edinburgh)
Scottish School of Physical Education Jordanhill College (Glasgow)

Northern Ireland
Northern Ireland Institute of Coaching

These centres play a crucial role in bringing the full range of NCF services to coaches at regional and local levels.

By 1988 the NCF was in a position to talk confidently of a National Coaching diploma being 'available through the network of National Coaching Centres' (NCF Director's Report, 1988, p. 9). The course on offer was entitled 'Diploma in Professional Studies — Sports Coaching' and was in a modular form equivalent to one year of full-time study. The Diploma course is currently being evaluated by the Council for National Academic Awards

(CNAA) whose approval, if given, will be a breakthrough for the whole profession of coaching in the United Kingdom.

A pointer to approval came in late 1989 when the CNAA granted 'Associated Institute' status to the network of National Coaching Centres and in confident mood the NCF anticipated being able to launch the Diploma in Sports Coaching in September 1990.

The in-built conservatism of British sport generally views any imaginative initiative with some suspicion, or sees it as a threat to autonomy, and this often acts as a brake. In the case of the National Coaching Foundation, and the Sport Aid Foundation eight years earlier, this instinctive conservatism manifested itself mainly in the sports bodies but the professional and tactful leadership of Sue Campbell in the former and Alan Weeks in the latter, backed up and supported by their committees composed of knowledgeable and wise members, ensured that suspicion and concern quickly fell away to be followed by cooperation and involvement. There is a lesson for the future and any further initiatives that must surely come, and that is sound preparation based on proven overseas examples, where these exist, adapted to British systems. Success also calls for acts of faith by members of the Sports Council who have to approve the financial resources necessary to get things moving; in both these cases such acts of faith were forthcoming. In the case of the National Coaching Foundation the support of Sir Arthur Gold was crucial and his wise advice from a lifetime in international sport and coaching played a major part.

It is not too early to assess and evaluate the work of the NCF; it is firmly based, superbly led, established in the field and internationally respected. The importance and success of this organization is aptly summed up by the Sports Council when it says in its Report *Into the 90s — A Strategy for Sport 1988–93*:

> The Council regards the setting-up of the National Coaching Foundation and its associated network of National Coaching Centres throughout the UK as one of the major successes of the last five years. (paragraph 2. 180, p. 49)

Progress with National Scale Facilities for High Level Training and Competition

Slow, unspectacular progress in the provision of major national facilities for training and high-level competition continued as the seventies drew to a close and the eighties dawned, and it remained much the same well on into the decade. Consistent and persistent calls for a national indoor arena fell on deaf ears as public authorities struggled with the financial restrictions placed upon them by the Government and the Government itself set its face against an increase in public works. Private enterprise, in an uncertain financial climate, nibbled at possible schemes but largely drew back before the final decisions were taken. The Wembley Indoor Arena, Earls Court, and to some extent the Albert Hall remained the major venues for national indoor sports events of any scale in the capital. The welcome addition of the Arena at the National Exhibition Centre near Birmingham, and the use of major conference venues such as Brighton and the new International Conference Centre at Bournemouth provided possibilities outside London.

The Sports Council's *Programme for the Development of National Facilities* published in 1978[33] pointed to glaring deficiencies and gave the highest priority to the need for a major indoor facility. With limited resources at their disposal the Council could do little to assist financially any possible developer and looked to the Minister for Sport and the Government for encouragement and financial assistance on the larger scale necessary — neither was forthcoming.

In early 1986 the Sports Council announced its intention once again to canvas for the national facility.[34] Later that year came the welcome news that Birmingham City Council proposed building a National Indoor Arena in the City Centre next to the new International Convention Centre and this was soon under construction. A year later it was announced that as part of the requirement for the World Student Games in 1991 a similar sized arena was to be built in Sheffield. After so long Great Britain will have two major indoor venues outside the capital in use in the early nineties.

The Football Association opened its national training centre at Lilleshall National Sports Centre in April 1981 which provided, in addition to first-class playing pitches, a well appointed hostel of seventy-four beds at a total cost of £1.150m. In September 1984 a bold experiment, which did not find favour with all, saw the start of the FA Coaching School also at Lilleshall. The School, sponsored by General Motors, provided a boarding-school education for twenty-five selected boys of exceptional footballing talent. The boys are accommodated in the FA hostel, attend the local comprehensive school, but have available to them some of the best soccer coaches in the land. This is in many respects the type of development that has been current in the USSR and the German Democratic Republic for many years with their special sports schools; latterly several Western countries have been experimenting with this concept, notably France. The English scheme is very much the brainchild of Mr. Bobby Robson, the England team manager and Mr. Charles Hughes, the Director of Coaching. Some of the boys have already made their mark with Football League teams.

In 1983 Wembley Stadium agreed to some degree of refurbishment which cost the FA £2.5m; the Sports Council contributed a fifth of the expenditure in the hope that Wembley will be seen as a more seemly venue for major football and hockey events.

The *Enquiry into Lawn Tennis* set in motion by Denis Howell when he was still the Minister for Sport reported in 1980.[35] This called for the provision of many more indoor tennis facilities. As a direct consequence the

Lawn Tennis Association and the Sports Council cooperated in converting the large sports workshop at Bisham Abbey National Sports Centre into the National Tennis Centre with four 'Supreme' courts and a range of ancillary services and facilities which included the presence on site of a resident LTA coach, Mr. John Clifton, a former Davis Cup player. This, together with an imaginative grant-aiding policy by both the LTA and the Sports Council for regional indoor tennis centres, stimulated a number of private developments and by 1984 fifteen such centres for example, Telford, Matchpoint (Darlington) and Clearview Tennis Centre, Essex were in existence providing facilities for regional coaching, national tournaments and the general public. In 1983 and 1986 the Davis Cup matches against Italy and Spain were staged at the Telford Centre in Shropshire. The financing of some of these regional centres initially presented commercial problems and in some cases progress was not without difficulty.

In May 1986 the LTA, the Sports Council and the All England Lawn Tennis Club (AELTC) launched the Indoor Tennis Initiative directed at local authorities to promote the playing of tennis through provision of 'pay as you play' indoor facilities. Each of the three sponsoring bodies agreed to commit £500,000 annually for five years to the Initiative. In effect this means that the £5m from the LTA and the AELTC is private investment coming from the profits of the Wimbledon Championships. Approved schemes are grant-aided from this fund and by the end of 1989 nineteen schemes had been developed and were in full operation (current details from LTA as at 1 November 1989).

Concurrent with the thinking of the Football Association, the Lawn Tennis Association was also coming to the conclusion that a tennis school should be founded for young talented players. Accordingly in September 1983 the first steps were taken in this direction and four 12-year-old boys were taken into residence at Bisham Abbey for special coaching and training in tennis with their schooling provided nearby. By 1989 thirteen youngsters were in residence with some of the early intake already making their mark.

The decision by the Sports Council in 1979 to spend £650,000 on provision of a porous artificial grass playing area (100 metres × 110 metres) at Bisham Abbey has proved to be right and the Hockey Association have made great use of the two fine pitches provided. It might be said that the success of the Great Britain Hockey teams at the 1984 and 1988 Olympic Games owed something to this facility as the Great Britain squad trained and practised there as a routine; today there are many more synthetic pitches available for hockey throughout the country.

The Badminton Association's decision to move their administrative headquarters to Milton Keynes and provide a hall for three training courts was enlightened, whilst the bobsleigh enthusiasts were overjoyed to have considerable financial help made available to them for a bobsleigh 'start' system at Thorpe Park near to the M3 motorway.

An interesting development in 1981 at Bury St. Edmunds by a private company to build and manage what was designated as the National Centre for Artistic Roller Skating not only provided a good local facility for this popular activity but, in association with the National Skating Association, provided facilities for élite training for which the Sports Council offered grant-aid.

The development at Bala in North Wales of the wild-water canoe centre for the 1981 World Championship demonstrated good cooperation amongst a number of interested parties. This facility is used widely and stimulated pressure for the long-promised national slalom centre at the National Water Sports Centre which was opened by the Princess Royal in September 1986 at a cost of £2.2m.

Whilst the loss of the proposed Manchester National Ice Rink was a body-blow to ice-skating the great interest aroused in the sport saw the building of a number of ice rinks in the first half of the eighties. The Lea Valley Authority cooperated with the Sports Council on their facility which was something of a test-bed for new design and technical thinking. Oxford, Swindon and Telford opened ice rinks in 1983 and 1984 which were typical of the attractive provision local authorities were increasingly providing or planning. Whilst these provided much needed training facilities for aspiring international skaters the facilities were essentially for the general community within the broad sport for all philosophy; the need for a national training and competition centre is as real today as it was the day it was first mooted following John Curry's great successes in 1976.

After many false starts with promising schemes such as that in London Docklands in 1984, which did not materialize in the original form envisaged, athletics were rewarded with the opening of the first purpose-built indoor athletics arena in Great Britain at the Kelvin Hall, Glasgow in January 1988. At the lower end of the financial scale was the construction in 1986 by the English Wrestling Association of the National Wrestling Academy in the centre of Salford at a cost of £350,000. Grants from Salford City Council, Greater Manchester Council and the Sports Council helped defray a large part of the building costs.

At the Lilleshall National Sports Centre 1986 saw the completion of a £1.5m project for the British Amateur Gymnastics Association. This magnificent range of training facilities is second to none in Europe and is a considerable commitment to excellence. In September 1987 the Cowes National Sailing Centre closed and discussions opened with the Royal Yachting Association (RYA) on a new mainland site and base for travelling instructor teams which the RYA will manage.

It would be churlish not to acknowledge all of these developments as welcome, timely and of enormous importance to the national governing bodies of sport for which they are relevant, but the major problem of large-scale provision continued to prove intractable. The Sports Council with limited resources has done well to provide what it could, but until the national system of funding for major facilities is altered drastically progress

Table 7:   *Sports Council grant aid to facilities*

	National £m	Regional £m
1978/79	2.096	4.831
1979/80	1.537	4.821
1980/81	2.059	5.286
1981/82	1.981	6.525
1982/83	1.521	10.850
1983/84	1.722	8.965
1984/85	2.902	6.824
1985/86	2.596	7.405
1986/87	3.956	8.524
1987/88	1.356	8.156
1988/89	1.517	8.606

Source: *Sports Council Annual Reports — Financial Statistics*

will continue to be slow. The welcome additions of artificial pitches, squash courts, new halls, lecture theatres and electronic timing devices at the National Sports Centres continued to keep standards up to what was expected and needed, but from 1981 onwards covert pressure from the Minister ensured that only the minimum necessary was done in the national context as more and more the sport programmes in the social field were loaded.

A comparison of what the Sports Council gave in grant to assist facility provision at national and regional levels (Table 7) demonstrates the build up regionally and the decline nationally.

To these regional figures for capital expenditure have to be added very increased subventions for participation programmes which rose from £162,000 in 1978 for Football and the Community, Urban deprivation and Regional Development programmes, to £2,303m in 1983 for Leadership, Excellence, Sport for All, Regional Development and Unemployed Programmes plus a further £1m for *Action Sport* schemes for that year. By 1987 regions were handling not only these programmes but also demonstration schemes, dual use schemes and post abolition schemes which totalled in excess of £3.72m.[36]

Using constant prices Table 7 clearly shows a cut-back in finance from 1979 to 1983 for national facilities compared with regional and local facilities, thus when account is taken of inflation the real expenditure for the former is drastically reduced. When this picture is associated with the 'hold' position on current grants to assist national governing bodies of sport in their programmes for coaching, international events, preparation-training and administration it will be seen how the shift in the balance of resources available to national programmes moved to regional and local development in these years.

The influence of the Minister for Sport in this shift was considerable, and the Sports Council during the time Neil Macfarlane was Minister was under increasing pressure to move from, or at least hold, its policy of increasing aid at national level. This pressure was exemplified in 1982 when it was the wish of the Sports Council, prior to the staging of the 1983 European Athletics Cup Final, that the track at the Crystal Palace National Sports Centre should be completely renewed as engineers had detected sub-soil faults and in any case the track, the first of its kind in the United Kingdom, had been laid nearly twenty years beforehand. In a backroom tussle it became abundantly clear that the Minister did not approve of the Sports Council spending this level of money on the track, favouring a more cosmetic and cheaper approach. Despite the fact that the Minister had no locus whatsoever in the way the Sports Council spent the money so long as this was done in compliance with the Royal Charter, the Chairman of the Sports Council, Dick Jeeps, eventually acquiesced and the cheaper job was done which looked 'fine on the day' but did nothing to remedy the under-lying problem.

This example of governmental interference was symptomatic of the period as more and more the Minister's office began to call the tune as the Royal Charter was privately and quietly filed away. The Sports Council has complete freedom under the Charter and the Financial Memorandum to spend resources made available to it by annual vote of Parliament and is only required to inform the government if it intends to spend in excess of £200,000 on any project. The key word is 'inform'; the Council does not have to seek permission or approval, it simply has to notify its intention. The erosion of this authority is quite considerable and because members of the Sports Council change as they serve their three-year period, so the fundamentals on which the Council is based are often hardly known, and accepted practice becomes the norm.

While John Smith was Chairman of the Sports Council some independ-ence was clawed back although the Director-General maintained a low profile which did not help greatly. With Peter Yarranton as Chairman and David Pickup as Director-General the 'top' team look promising and may well be successful in removing sport from the clutches of government. The Council is not an agency of government, it is an independent executive organization deriving powers and authority from a Royal Charter granted by HM the Queen. Naturally it should work with government and in coopera-tion with the Minister for Sport and should help him achieve his objectives, but in the final analysis it is sovereign. It must act at all times like this and be seen to be so doing by the governing bodies and people it serves if it is to retain its credibility into the nineties.

It was John Smith in 1988 who wrote,

> The Sports Council looks into the 1990s with confidence that through (its) revised strategy it can continue to serve sport and society well, and it looks to its partners — including HM Govern-ment — to help it move nearer to its avowed object of Sport for All. (Sports Council, 1988, Chairman's foreword, p. 7)

Notes

1 Sports Council Annual Reports — Analysis of Statistics.
2 At the conference, in addition to the issue of financing sport from public resources, the drug question was discussed. Sports science and its application was the theme of the day. No report was published.
3 The security arrangements were excellent but months before the Games fringe organizations obtained TV coverage where they publicly issued threats to those coming from communist countries. This type of event gave a good excuse for 'security' to be questioned by those who did not intend to go in any case.
4 See Olympic Charter (1982) Section 'Organization of the Olympic Games', Condition 8, Commercial Exploitation. This forbids advertising in the stadium and sites, the Olympic Village and annexes.
5 These meetings of Heads of Commonwealth countries take place traditionally every two years. Normally they do not concern themselves with sport but exceptionally they do, for example, 1977 'Gleneagles Agreement' (see Appendix 12 in this volume).
6 BOA; SAF; CCPR; British Association of National Coaches (BANC); British Association of Sports Administrators; D of E.; John Rodda (*The Guardian*) representing the IOC Press Commission.
7 See Sports Council's Annual Reports 1984–85 for interim report p. 12, 1985–86 for final report, p. 11; and 'Olympic Review' — Preparing for '88.' Report of a Review Group, November 1985.
8 In 1986 — £250,000 to support Birmingham's bid. In 1987 £105,691 to support Sports Science and Sports Medicine; £279,353 for doping control.
9 By 1985–86 Sports Council's allocations to Regional Centres of Excellence were no longer identified separately; now encompassed within the 'Regional Participation' budgets.
10 This was located at the Sports Council in London. The 'Service' has now ceased. The CCPR runs a sponsorship service.
11 In October 1989 the International Tennis Federation (ITF) announced a new event to take place in West Germany annually with a first prize of US$2m. The first reactions by some top players were adverse. In the week 21–28 October *The Times* reported dismay by such eminent players as Wimbledon Champions Boris Becker, Stephen Edberg and John McEnroe. On Saturday 28 October *The Times* reported (Richard Evans) 'Apparently the deal has been arranged personally between the four Grand Slam Chairmen and a television entrepreneur in Munich with the German (Tennis) Federation left ignorant of the whole affair'. By March 1990 the 'top' players had reflected on matters and were warming to the event. (see End Column *The Times* 13 March)
12 This was in many respects a formality. The Sports Council represented the British Government on the Committee for the Development of Sport (CDDS) at the Council of Europe through Sir Walter Winterbottom until 1978 and then through John Coghlan, the Deputy Director-General, until late 1983, since when representation has been ad hoc by government and Sports Council or both. Requests are made by the Council of Europe to Member States. Sir Arthur Gold was Chairman of the existing Drugs Advisory Group when it took on this enhanced task.
13 See Council of Europe MSL-6(88)Bl-E 'Conference of European Ministers for Sport', Texts adopted at meetings — 1975–86, p. 17 for full text of Resolution.
14 This is a paraphrase of Resolution No. 1 of the Malta Conference (MSL-4(84)32. Part I.

15   Sports Council Annual Report 1984–85 p. 16. At a Symposium for governing bodies '. . . the Sports Council's policies were clearly stated. Governing bodies were asked to submit programmes for drug-testing and they were left in no doubt that if a governing body failed to introduce an effective programme within a reasonable period the Sports Council would consider withdrawing support . . .'.

16   At the Symposium on drug-abuse at the end of 1984. Typical press headlines: *The Times* 'Threat by Sports Council in War on Drugs'; *Daily Telegraph* 'Sports Council set drug-test deadline'.

17   Department of Environment (1987) Annexes on Doping Classes and Methods; Drug Advisory Group; UK doping control sequence; The Medicines Act 1968.

18   Published by the International Athletic Foundation, Stade Louis II, Avenue du Prince Hereditaire Albert, MC 98000, Monaco. The original draft was made from an English translation of an anti-doping publication prepared by the Swedish Sports Confederation. Subsequent drafting was assisted by a publication of the UK Drug Control and Teaching Centre, Chelsea College, University of London entitled *The Control of Drug-Abuse in Sport*.

19   Mr. Bruce Dubin's opening address to what he called 'an organizational session designed to identify those persons or associations who may have a direct interest . . .'

20   Report available from Fitness and Amateur Sport, Government of Canada, 365 Rue Laurier, Ottawa, Ontario, KIA OX6.

21   Report of the 11th Olympic Congress, Baden Baden, 1981, published by IOC (1982) p. 82.

22   £950,000 from the Minet Insurance Group administered by SAF, and £240,000 from SAF itself.

23   All International Medal Winners for 1988–89 are listed in the SAF Annual Report for that year.

24   Torvill and Dean and their colleagues presented a cheque to Mrs. Thatcher for £10,000 for SAF use.

25   See Sports Council's minutes of meetings of the Coaching Panel.

26   Minutes of meetings of Regional Directors with HQ staff in 1982.

27   Whitehead appointed July 1983; Sue Campbell appointed Deputy Director September 1983 and promoted to Director in April 1985 when Nick Whitehead joined the staff of the Sports Council for Wales.

28   Mrs. Judith McKay, a member of the Sports Council, was the first Chairperson of the NCF.

29   Sports Council Annual Report 1983–84, p. 9, National Coaching Foundation.

30   All brochures, videos and other coaching material available from NCF, 4 College Close, Beckett Park, Leeds LS6 3QH.

31   NCF Directors Report, August 1985. Appendix A lists institutions.

32   Sue Campbell, MEd, Lecturer, Loughborough University (1975–79); Regional Officer, Sports Council (1979–83); National Coaching Foundation (1983–   ), Deputy Director (1983–85), Director (1985–   ); International Athletics and Netball.

33   See chapter 2 in this volume; and Sports Council Annual Report 1978–79 'Developments — National Centres and Facilities', p. 12.

34   Sports Council Annual Report 1985–86, p. 20. 'A priority for some years has been the provision of a National Indoor Arena'. 'To promote the provision of at least one Scale 1 National Arena the Council agreed to . . . grant aid up to £3 million over a 3 year period'.

35   Report of the Minister's Lawn Tennis Enquiry, Chairman: John Smith, later Chairman of the Sports Council, published by the Sports Council.

36 Sports Council Annual Reports — Financial statistics — an analysis. 'Post-abolition' refers to the abolition of the Metropolitan Authorities. The grant in aid given to the Sports Council to use was in lieu of that disbursed by these authorities.

Chapter 12

Is Sport for all?

> For sport in Britain the 1970s were years of remarkable achieve-
> ment; achievement in facility provision, in the growth of playing
> sport indoors, and in challenging for world supremacy in several
> sports. (*Sport in the Community — The Next Ten Years*, Foreword)

The opening sentence in Dick Jeeps' Foreword summarizes the position
Britain found itself in as the seventies gave way to the eighties. It could,
therefore, be construed that all was well and that matters were proceeding
smoothly on course but regrettably this was certainly not the position.
Despite the very considerable progress in the provision of local facilities the
inner cities and the rural areas gave cause for concern whilst some sections
of society had as yet barely felt the impact of the *Sport for All* campaign.
The spectre of unemployment on a level not seen since the early thirties
marred the scene and continued to do so to an increasing extent with the
arrival of the mid-eighties. Tragic and disturbing as this was the fact that
school-leavers in increasing numbers found themselves unable to gain employment posed an even greater question mark over the future. With early
predictions that unemployment might well rise nearer four million, proved
to be painfully too accurate, the part sport, physical recreation and leisure
opportunity generally could play in assisting to some degree in helping to
alleviate the sheer numbing effect of unemployment became a major topic
and issue.

For those in work, and of course this was the majority, expenditure on
sport and recreation continued unabated, but the financial restrictions imposed by government on local authorities presented their own unique problems in the opening up and running of public facilities. Whereas in the late
sixties and seventies the emphasis had been on the capital costs of building
now the emphasis was on the recurrent costs of managing and promoting
such facilities. It would be wrong to over-emphasize these issues, real as they
were, as the policies of earlier years were still pursued by local government
as far as they were able and expenditure on sport and recreation continued

to grow. Between 1978/79 and 1980/81 the Chartered Institute of Public Finance and Accountancy (CIPFA) reported that net expenditure on leisure and recreation, both capital and current, by local authorities in England and Wales had increased from £452.5m to £633.71m which represented an increase of 40 per cent overall at prevailing current prices.[1] 'In the case of expenditure on swimming pools a 30 per cent increase was reported whilst indoor leisure and sports centre expenditure had increased by 44 per cent. In outdoor sports the increase was not so marked at 26 per cent but overall the increase was considerable and was reflected equally for more passive activities such as visiting art galleries, museums and theatres.[2]

Capital expenditure by local authorities showed a growth in real terms between 1982 and 1988 with a corresponding growth in revenue spending. By 1987 revenue expenditure was up by 30 per cent over 1982 which, when constant prices were applied, showed a real growth of 8 per cent.[3] These figures were impressive coming as they did from government departments and CIPFA. Additionally, and of considerable significance in a prolonged period of unemployment, local authority employment in the field of sport and recreation grew by 9 per cent between 1982 and 1987.[4]

The seventies saw a definite shift in the life-style of a significant minority of the population in Britain as every indicator pointed to an increased interest in physical activity, but this shift was uneven. The enormous increase in jogging, and at last an awareness that regular exercise of some form or another was beneficial to physical and mental health, gave momentum to participation. The press, radio and television published and produced respectively more articles and programmes on diet, heart disease, the benefits of correct eating and life-style generally, and virtually overnight with certain sections of society physical activity became fashionable.[5] The availability of activity holidays, health farms and fitness centres, featured in magazines and in holiday programmes on television, fuelled this movement. Commercial tour operators came in on the act to supplement the growing number of voluntary and statutory agencies already in this field. Residential holiday activity centres run at some of the public schools and universities became popular offering as they did modest accommodation with good facilities and coaching in sport. The tourist boards[6] continued to encourage the commercial market in an effort to extend the holiday season at both ends. Accordingly more and more hotels, not all necessarily multi-starred, increasingly offered short break holidays with access in a variety of ways to activities such as golf, tennis and riding. Hotels with swimming pools were more in demand than those without and, never slow to miss a business opportunity, the big chain hoteliers such as Trust House Forte, Crest and Grand Metropolitan began programmes of development at their establishments adding pools, saunas, exercise rooms, squash courts and physical activity facilities generally. The Holiday Inn chain was probably the market leader in this field.

The advent of irregularly shaped leisure pools with their wave-making machines, their 'fun water', and their giant body flumes were a far cry from the classical rectangular shaped competition pool of prescribed dimensions. These facilities opened up a new market of users and with their palm-tree and sun-shade promenades, laser lighting and glamorous decor, they were not only attractive to swim in but were equally attractive for barbecues, cocktail parties and receptions. Market leaders in this type of imaginative developments such as Module 2 Ltd. of Bridgend with their Bournemouth International Conference and Leisure Centre responded to the demand that manifested itself in the early and mid-eighties for physical recreation in the context of total leisure. By the end of the decade this type of provision was commonplace. Despite the popular mood being more physically orientated the financial pressures imposed upon municipal government did, nevertheless, slow down the dynamic that the seventies had created. However, not for the first time local government and commercial operators were more in tune with the latent demands of the British people than Whitehall, and despite the efforts by the Government to curtail public expenditure in this and many other sectors expenditure continued to grow.[7]

The Growth of Facilities

Whilst the Sports Council's 1972 targets for swimming pools and sports halls had looked impossible to achieve by 1982, the prescribed date, progress towards this goal was commendable and in some respects remarkable. By 1978 the Sports Council had refined its targets to take account of the now accepted lower growth in population. Taking stock in 1981 it was clear that the swimming pool target had been attained and provision was still increasing. In the case of sports halls some 60 per cent of the revised target was achieved. As a consequence these, and other facilities, not only met known demand from the public but also released latent demand as was seen when data arising from surveys taken during the seventies was reported.[8]

Between 1983 and 1988 nearly one million more women and 600,000 more men were attracted to indoor participation in sport. Nationally this indicated a participation rate by women of 24.2 per cent and 35.7 per cent by men. In outdoor sport men's participation rate is not dissimilar to that for indoors but the women's rate fell marginally in this period from 25 per cent in 1983 to 24.3 per cent in 1988.[9]

Not everyone looked to the pool or the indoor sports centre for their recreation, and whilst these facilities are often quoted as an indicator of the level of participation in physical activity it should not be forgotten that such large-scale type of provision was matched by considerable increases in indoor and outdoor bowls rinks, shooting ranges, artificial ski slopes and squash courts. The latter achievement is perhaps the most remarkable of all. From a fairly obscure sport in the late sixties played in some public schools, some universities and a few clubs, squash became the boom activity as courts were included in sports centre developments, added to tennis, golf and rugby clubs and became a target for the commercial market to develop. The sport had two great claims to success; it was easy to play (although difficult to play well!) and the economics of provision were such that the capital cost could quickly be repaid by the users who were prepared to pay a more meaningful fee for their half-hour of violent activity than for other more traditional sports where low fees were the norm. There were indications in the mid-eighties that saturation point may have been reached in some parts of Britain with the provision for squash but there was still scope for some modest growth in other areas. The high cost of building and borrowing money was a factor in the slowing down of growth but whether or not there will be another surge of interest in the 1990s remains a question for the future.

Provision for indoor sport in attractive surroundings remained a priority with the emphasis on the need for very many small sports halls to supplement and complement the district-scale sports centres that now existed. Although the policy of joint-provision which had been shown to be 40 per cent more cost effective than separate provision was still very much alive in the early part of the eighties opportunities for this type of development were scarce as fewer new schools were built. The report *Sharing does Work* for the Sports Council in 1981 discussed the social and economic benefits of joint provision and was emphatic in support.

> If new facilities are to be provided the economic and financial arguments in favour of joint provision are overwhelming.[10]

Dual use was, and continues to be, a real issue, and despite fierce cutbacks in public expenditure and the emphasis on value for money there were still too many examples of good facilities in schools not fully used. Late in 1984 a joint initiative by the Department of the Environment and the Sports Council was announced to start in 1985 with £500,000 special funds made available to stimulate good local schemes that needed a little money to make them suitable for community use.[11] This was a good initiative and focussed attention once again on this issue.

In *Sport in the Seventies*[12] the Sports Council asked for 815 sports centres by the end of ten years and by 1981 over 700 such centres had been built. By 1984 additional provision together with school sports halls now available to the public had brought the figure of indoor halls available to over 900. In *Sport in the Community — The Next Ten Years* (1982) the Council made a substantive case for 3134 further sports halls and indoor playing spaces but firmly set its target for England for one quarter of these, some 800 in all, to be made up of new provision, conversions, and the opening up of what already existed (*ibid*, p. 3). For some years the Sports Council had been talking about the need to tackle sports hall provision in a new and imaginative fashion and words such as 'systematized' and 'package deal' had been bandied around. The stimulus for some of the thinking was the highly successful 'Mille Piscines' scheme promoted some years earlier by the French Government. Whilst something very similar would have suited Britain very well the structure and powers of local government in France were tailor-made for their scheme with its bias towards centralism, whereas in Britain our bias towards greater powers lying with municipal authorities in this connection made it such that the French scheme could not be lifted direct. As so often happens in such circumstances a good overseas idea was adapted and the Standardized Approach to Sports Hall Scheme (SASH) was devised. Basically SASH, as it quickly came to be known, was a design of a sports centre put together by the Technical Unit for Sport at the Sports Council based on their considerable specialist experience. The design comprised a large hall, a smaller exercise room and ancillary facilities for changing and social purposes all enclosed in one building to an approved and clearly stated specification. An open competition was staged to find a company who would be prepared to accept this package at the agreed price and having done so to promote the SASH concept and build accordingly. In the eventuality Bovis PLC were the winners of the 1982 competition and they were handed nine projects, one in each of the Sports Council's regions, as pilot projects to which the Sports Council had agreed to pay 50 per cent of the basic cost which stood at £504,000. In this way the SASH project got off the ground from the first day and provided within two years nine buildings of the same design as the promotional platform for a further assault on the set targets. By 1988 twenty-three SASH projects had been completed. Work on a much simpler and cheaper sports hall system began in 1983 in the hope that a design could be produced at a price sufficiently low and therefore attractive to the many rural communities of between 2,000 and 10,000 population; this became available in early 1986[13] with the first demonstration project opened in Markfield, Leicestershire in January 1987 at a total cost of £244,435.

The publication of the Sports Council's target for sports centres stimulated many building and construction companies in Britain, faced as they were with recession, to enter the market with their designs, concepts and above all, prices; the momentum was underway again albeit in a different financial climate to that of the early seventies. Whilst the target for indoor sports centres in 1972 had been broadly one for 50,000 population with a further centre for every additional 40,000 population, the targets were now seen as indicating one sports centre for every 20,000 population or thereabouts but these figures were never seen as a firm ratio but rather as a guideline. It is salutary to note that by 1980 Holland had an average standard of provision of one sports centre for every 27,000 population which gave a European perspective to the road already travelled and the slope that lay ahead in Britain.

Responding to the upsurge in interest evoked by successes at international level in skating, after a slow beginning and the failure to get a start to the projected National Skating Centre in Manchester, the range of new ice-rinks which began to appear in 1983 and 1984 were immediately success-ful in terms of use. By the end of 1989 England had thirty-five ice rinks. Interest is such that the Southern Region, for example, today has five whereas a decade ago it had none. Overall in years past most rinks were privately owned, today the majority are in the public domain.

Although costly to provide the building of new swimming pools con-tinued in the early eighties either in the traditional rectangular form for competition and training or in free-form for broad community and family use, but even then somewhere in the design the architects usually provided for a twenty-five metre stretch of water of up to six lanes. The refurbishment of old pools became for some local authorities a recreational priority, but nowhere, even at the seaside, was there any further call for new open-air facilities other than in the domestic market. Some of the holiday camps seized on the new thinking about recreational water and Butlin's embarked on a programme of updating some of their old outdoor pools to provide what was now becoming known as 'fun water' for example, at their holiday camps at Bognor Regis and Minehead. It is interesting to recall that in 1965 there were 600 local authorities without swimming pools in England and Wales; by 1971 there was 440 pools in England, by 1982 the total was 912. By the end of 1984 the provision stood at 948 in England alone and five years later in 1989 this was 1,570.[14]

The popularity of team games played on grass pitches is endemic in British society even if many of the soccer pitches are hardly supporting grass by mid-winter. Rugby football of both codes is the principal user of grass pitches after soccer and cricket but other sports such as hockey, despite being played by a minority, had by 1989 shown increased participation.[15] It is difficult to be factually accurate in describing the stock of pitches owned by local authorities and private clubs and comparing the situation in 1989 with that of thirty years ago simply because there has been no exact stock-taking in this matter. This omission was certainly not for any lack of understanding of the issue but arose because the whole enterprise of iden-tifying and recording existing outdoor playing pitches was formidable to envisage and daunting to realize. It was only by sampling and intelligent surmise that the position in 1990 is known to be better or worse than in 1960. Most indicators point to an increase in provision generally. This view is bolstered by the statistics concerning growth in the number of clubs and teams in the sports in question and the present day ability to play more games on pitches due to increased investment in drainage, preparation and turf knowledge generally. Having said this it must be recorded that the loss of playing fields to other development during this period was grievous and left many inner-city zones devoid of playing fields to a very considerable extent.[16] Planning legislation did not suffice to staunch this loss although the increasing lobby for sport through Regional Councils of Sport and Recrea-tion and local authority recreation and leisure departments proved effective in many situations when presented to ministry inspectors at local planning enquiries. The only well-known effective standard of provision for playing space is one dating from 1937 and that is the National Playing Fields' Association's standard of six acres of playing space for every thousand population over and above that provided for school use. This standard has often been quoted and has been invaluable. It was based on the 1921 Census and informed assumptions and was originally set at five acres, increased to seven in 1934 and revised to the existing figure of six three years later. It has shown itself to be inspired original guesswork and many playing fields exist today because of it. Outdoor sport owes much to the NPFA over many decades.

A real and damaging threat to existing playing fields appeared in 1981 with the Department of Education and Science Statutory Instrument Number 909. Although this Instrument dealt with school premises generally and revoked the Standards for Schools Premises Regulations of 1972, it was that part that dealt with playing pitches which provoked greatest adverse comment. Schedule 3 of the Instrument 'Playing Fields', laid down regulations that curtailed the actual number of pitches required for schools of varying rolls and specified that a hard-porous area of a size suitable for team games counted as twice the area of grass needed. Some concession was made as to quality by indicating in the Explanatory Notes to the Instrument that 'the minimum area of playing fields (defined in Regulation 6 (3)) is reduced but there is a qualitative requirement that a grassed playing field must be capable of withstanding the playing of team games thereon for seven hours per week.' These Regulations applied to schools provided both before 1 September 1981 and, of course, afterwards.

This Statutory Instrument created a furore, particularly by the CCPR, for in effect it was an official licence to sell off school playing fields surplus to these Regulations and recoup capital for use elsewhere with no guarantee that the cash raised by sales would be used to upgrade in quality those playing pitches that remained. Questions were raised in Parliament; the Minister for Sport was put under considerable pressure; the Sports Council carried out a quick survey which revealed that the damage done, or likely to be done, was offset in the main by new provision elsewhere, but the CCPR persisted and quoting examples of playing fields scheduled for sale raised the temperature all round in this emotive issue and did everything possible to prevent such sales.[17] The fight to have this Statutory Instrument revoked continued during the next few years and refused to go away. There is little doubt that this campaign waged by the CCPR had a considerable impact and made many educational authorities think again.

On 28 July 1988 Denis Howell introduced a motion in the House of Commons which, amongst other matters 'deplores the sale of school playing fields'.[18] He talked of the 'scandal of the sale of our educational sports grounds' and 'the work of the CCPR which has done an excellent job in drawing our attention to the fact that the Department of the Environment's own land register shows that 5,000 acres of sports fields are also for sale at present'. In reply the Minister, Colin Moynihan, admitted that 'it is important that we know the availability of recreational land and playing fields in Britain. Currently that information is not known by the Government, the Sports Council or the CCPR.' We need to 'identify, in detail, the availability of such land so that we can monitor and increase its use by specific targeting of resources to obtain greatest participation'.

The growth in facilities for outdoor countryside activities continued to grow as the seventies gave way to the eighties although an ominous note was struck when a number of education authorities, forced to make economies, closed their outdoor pursuits centres. The more expensive sports such as sailing, water-skiing, sub-aqua, parascending, hang-gliding, and the new Olympic sport sailboarding, suffered no decline and continued to develop facilities where suitable sites could be found, but suitable water and land sites were becoming more difficult to find.

Although the general policy in the Armed Services to open as many facilities as they had to civilian use continued in the eighties, and the RAF Cosford national indoor athletics track was a notable example, increased security arrangements did have some adverse effect. Nevertheless, the fact that the Sports Council always had one senior serving officer as a member[19] ensured that good liaison arrangements and goodwill existed all round; the situation very much was, and still is, that if a facility can be opened to the public it will be, and the cooperation in the centres of excellence scheme provided clear evidence of this policy.

The severe recession that hit industry hard in the eighties meant that in some cases land used for company sports facilities had to be sold to assist cash flow and the loss was considerable. Although the financial problems facing industry accelerated the process of land disposal there had been for many years a steady erosion of facilities for two clear-cut reasons. Firstly the five-day week meant that men and women were not at their place of work at midday on Saturday ready to play that afternoon and generally did not wish to return there from their homes on a Saturday or Sunday, therefore the requirement was less, and secondly the width of sport and recreational interest in works clubs had diversified, as it had in schools and in the community at large, and this meant that facilities other than playing pitches were needed and these could only be found elsewhere. Works and business-house sports clubs continued to play a significant role in catering for a broad section of the population but not to the same extent as hitherto.[20]

Over the years many efforts were made to get wider community use of the excellent sports facilities owned by private and nationalized industries. Many good individual initiatives were successful but generally most proved unsuccessful for the simple reason that apart from altruism, there was no reason why a company should open up its facilities and embark upon additional maintenance and management expense. Various ideas were toyed with such as rating-relief to a company if dual-use of facilities was agreed, but such ideas have never been sharpened into policies and hard action. Pious noises have emerged from the Confederation of British Industry (CBI) from time to time but no positive lead has ever been offered. In the case of the Trade Union Congress (TUC) it stands particularly guilty rarely showing any interest in a positive sense on behalf of its members. In the Western European democracies the TUC stands very much as the odd man out in this business with nothing to compare with the Fédération Sportive Gymnique du Travail (FSGT) of France, or the Workers Sports Federation (TUL) of Finland, where the recreational interests of members are something of a priority. In the Socialist countries, particularly of Eastern Europe, the trades union movement is to a very considerable extent responsible for the organization of sport and the provision of facilities and their major clubs are based on such membership. Comparisons should not, however, be made with these trade unions as their functions are different from those in the West with which comparisons may fairly and accurately be made. Company sport in Britain is still strong; not so strong as hitherto, but what strength it has owes little to the broad-based labour movement but rather to the altruism of management and the host of volunteers who run the many sports sections of the welfare clubs, associated with for example banks, the Civil Service and petrol companies such as Shell.

Sports Council Policies and Grant-aiding Programmes

The social policies of the Sports Council, started to a considerable extent in the mid-seventies, were continued and, under pressure from the Government, extended in the eighties following the 1982 riots in Brixton and Toxteth. Whilst Lord Scarman's Report on Brixton barely referred to the part sport could play in helping alleviate social problems, despite the fact that the Sports Council submitted well-considered evidence, the Secretary of State for the Environment, Mr. Michael Heseltine, MP, took a very clear view in Toxteth in the aftermath of the disorders there and immediately offered a £1m grant if this could be matched by voluntary sources locally. Matched it was and a well-thought out plan for the development of facilities in Merseyside was unfolded, administered brilliantly by the North Western Region of the Sports Council. This move by the Secretary of State was clear evidence that he, and possibly others of his Cabinet colleagues, saw provision for sport as a necessary ingredient in any attempt to raise the quality of life in depressed areas. In a little over a year some twenty-two schemes were underway with more to follow. By 1983 additional designated finance from the Government was channelled to Merseyside which meant that in a two-year period £1.684m had been provided to attract a further £1.3m of private funds for ninety-eight projects.

In 1983 the Sports Council programmed £846,000 for the Merseyside Initiative which, by now, had evoked something similar in Bristol and Tyne and Wear although on a very modest scale. This scheme grew and within a year Pound-for-Pound schemes were developed in Bristol, London, Tyne and Wear and the West Midlands in addition to the ongoing Merseyside Initiative. Funding for these schemes peaked at £695,000 in 1985 and then began to tail off rapidly with a mere £146,000 in 1986 falling to £3,500 in 1987.[21]

Football and the Community

The sound early work of 1978 and 1979 by the Sports Council in linking new or modified facilities to football clubs continued into the eighties aided considerably by the Football Trust.[22] This partnership was fruitful and rewarding and usually resulted in a Council grant being matched by one from the Trust.

In 1983 £500,000 was made available jointly by the two partners to assist football and the community schemes linked to football league clubs. Two spectacular developments, at Aston Villa FC and Coventry City FC, resulted in large indoor sports centres, but this was unusual and most of the schemes were for synthetic playing pitches, floodlighting or conversions of older buildings for sport.[23]

The Football Trust did not confine its activities solely to the football and the community policy linked with professional clubs but looked much wider and saw its responsibility extending to the provision of new local pitches and changing accommodation particularly in urban areas and always in association with partners. In June 1982 the Trust let it be known that it was to spend £525,000 to assist local authorities in England to provide new football pitches and changing accommodation, and where good cases existed they would further help financially to upgrade both pitches and changing rooms. Some thirty-eight municipal authorities with populations of between 100,000 and 200,000 immediately benefited and some sixty new or upgraded pitches resulted in addition to twenty-three new or refurbished pavilions. This further injection of finance, to provide pitches, followed the £2m made available by the Trust in London for playing spaces and changing accommodation in 1980 when over 100 schemes for football were assisted.

From a high point at the start of the Football and Community scheme in 1979 with an investment of £1.07m the Sports Council's involvement in the scheme trundled on into the eighties in a lower key as the Football Trust shouldered more of the burden.[24] By 1983 the Council was allocating £130,000 but by 1988 this had dwindled to £45,700 as the spotlight was turned on other initiatives. The Sports Council, with its limited resources, can never stay with a scheme forever and thus bear an annual charge on its budget. It must, of necessity, inject resources, both human and financial, into a development scheme, see it on its way, introduce partners and then gently withdraw and regroup to tackle other targets. In the late eighties the partnership between the Trust and the Sports Council was such that the latter provided the technical service through the TUS and its regional offices whilst the former provided the bulk of the finance which is to a very considerable extent pump-priming. An illustration of this is the £1.375m given by the Trust to local authorities in 1988 for projects costed at £5.575m.

Urban and Social Deprivation

The priority in the seventies in deprived urban areas had been to get facilities on the ground quickly and to have the necessary playing equipment available for immediate use. In 1978, under an initiative pioneered by one of the Vice-Chairmen of the Sports Council, Bernard Atha, the Sports Council quite exceptionally embarked on a two-year programme of providing small equipment. This scheme captured the public imagination, was supported solidly by the Minister for Sport, Denis Howell, but was frowned upon in Whitehall by those concerned with financial accountability who pointed to problems in being able to account for, by way of audit, the many footballs, boxing gloves, roller-skates, judo mats, table-tennis tables and volleyball nets that were provided. Atha brushed these objects aside in brusque Yorkshire fashion and 1400 clubs and thousands of young people in the inner-city areas benefited.[25]

This policy and attitude rolled over into the eighties and prospered. Conversions of buildings were supported financially if these could be brought into use for sport. Some quite remarkable conversions took place including the most unlikely conversion of the old Customs House in Middlesborough into an indoor recreation centre, and this in an area of desperate deprivation. In Barnsley a local table tennis club leased a part of a church that had been declared redundant and through their own efforts and a Sports Council grant of £2,270 arranged a conversion costing twice this sum to give good indoor facilities to the local club. These are merely two examples from very many that self-help, some local assistance, and some pump-priming by the Sports Council brought into existence.

In addition to the financial help that the Sports Council had been giving to areas of social deprivation the Department of the Environment had, for some years under the Urban Aid programme, been channelling grants to local authorities ad hoc for a range of facilities and amenities including sport. By 1981 the amount of money being made available to sport in this way reached the extraordinarily large sum of around £18m per annum and yet all of this was being spent with little or no reference to the Sports Council which had an approved strategy and was by the Royal Charter the adviser to the Government. Through vigorous lobbying by the Sports Council the Department of the Environment, faced with the sheer logic of the case, agreed to consider only those applications from local authorities which had been considered by the regional offices of the Sports Council and which

Table 8: Sports Council — *Regional Capital Expenditure and Loans*

	Grants £m	Loans £m
1978–79	4.831	.119
1979–80	4.821	.144
1980–81	5.286	.260
1981–82	6.525	.323
1982–83	10.850	.589
1983–84	8.965	.675
1984–85	6.824	.557
1985–86	7.405	.824
1986–87	8.524	.786
1987–88	8.156	.900
1988–89	8.606	.930

Source: Sports Council Financial Statistics — Annual Reports

fitted into the scale and nature of provision described in regional strategies. In July 1983 the Department issued Circular 17/83 entitled *Urban Circular 24: Traditional Urban Programme: Projects in 1984 (England)*. Instructions to consult the Sports Council were clearly spelt out which resulted in paving the way for sensible public spending advice based on overall plans and with the highest level of technical input guaranteed.[26]

Volume of Grant Aid to Support Regional Facility Programme

From 1978 onwards the Sports Council was authorized to make loans to voluntary sports clubs for facilities and this policy made good use of public money as it was re-cycled and the loan fund grew as the years passed. In the years from 1978 to 1989 the volume of money made available by way of grants to assist local authority, club, prototype, urban deprivation, football and the community, and areas of special need schemes fluctuated wildly (Table 8). The pressure from the Government to reinforce the regional pro- grammes at the expense of programmes for élite sport is reflected dramati- cally with the rapid rise from 1980 to 1982 which showed an increase of over one hundred per cent in funding. With the departure of Neil Macfarlane to the obscurity of the back benches the balance was considerably redressed and the last four years of the decade under review clearly shows this. In fact the figures for 1984–89 are somewhat disto₁ted by the inclusion for the period 1986–89 of grants for post-abolition schemes i.e. extra money made available by the Government to ease the loss of grant-aid by the now defunct Metropolitan authorities. As this amounted to £1.5m in 1988/89 it can be seen that in reality, when comparing like with like, the volume for regional capital expenditure was nearer that of the early years of the decade and with inflation taken into account somewhat lower. A comparison with national capital expenditure is made earlier in Table 7.

A Current Assessment

There is no doubt that Britain today is much better served by sports facilities than twenty-five years ago when the advisory Sports Council was established, and this reflects well on municipal authorities and the principal national agencies such as the Sports Council and the Countryside Commission who have the prime responsibility in this area of activity. The generation and regeneration of many sports clubs, the backbone of British sport and the raw material for the élite, is further evidence of growth and opportunity. Despite efforts by some Minsters of Sport central Government has largely failed to provide the wherewithal for facilities to the scale and quantity required. Government, particularly in the seventies, provided the right climate and framework supported by official papers and reports but not by money. The base was set far too low in 1972 and has been the stumbling block ever since. There is no reason to believe that the years ahead will be any different from those past; municipal authorities will still struggle to find the resources to provide facilities; they will contrive to find, to a greater or lesser extent despite the awesome problems they face, the necessary funding because broadly they accept the philosophy and the rationale of *Sport for All*. Governments will continue to make the right noises and will lack the will to break the mould of what has gone before. Clubs will continue to develop because this is the way it has always been; some will collapse, others will start up and the hopeful sign is that people are prepared to pay more for their sport so long as they are in employment.

In an effort to bring new thinking to old issues in the hope that systems and policies could be devised that would encourage a greater level of facility provision the distinguished chartered accountant Mr. David Bacon, an early member of the Sports Council in the sixties, was asked by the Council in 1980 to consider the question of sport and taxation and suggest ways in which sport could benefit if fiscal matters could be changed. In June 1981 David Bacon reported, and in as clinical and lucid a manner as befitted an accountant, he exposed a range of issues and mould-breaking policy initiatives. The following were the salient features of his report *Sport and Taxation*.[27]

1   Taxation had a detrimental effect on sport and was a serious disincentive for investment in facilities both by public and private capital.
2   High standard facilities that were attractive to use would be well-used and would offer a commercial return on capital investment. (Here he spoke of the experience in Western Europe and the USA).
3   The case for relief from income tax and corporation tax and far greater use of capital allowances and industrial building allowances was considerable.

4   A national policy of standardized rating-relief in Britain was essential.

5   An inducement for private capital to replace, or supplement, public capital needed urgent encouragement.

6   Cooperation between the public and private sectors in capital investment was a priority.

7   A review of the Development Land Tax was required to resist the adverse effect of this tax in the erection of good facilities.

8   There was no general case for VAT relief on sport. Such special pleading ignored the principle of 'optional tax' which was a tax on spending. On the general level the question of whether membership subscriptions should be liable to VAT was open to debate in all cases and not solely for sport.

9   There was a substantial case for the Government to review the structure of sport in Britain in an effort to rationalize the many departments of state, authorities, bodies and organizations that have some responsibility for sport. He pointed to the absurdity of one government department taking money from sports bodies that another government department was aiding. (The 'Action Sport' example explained later in this chapter illustrated this absurdity.)[28]

10 The provision of facilities for sport suffered enormously from the absence of any significant financial encouragement for private capital investment. The evidence from USA and Western Europe showed clearly that where there is a taxation incentive private capital was forthcoming.

11 A major initiative should be taken to encourage private capital investment into sports facilities and special arrangements may need to be authorized for inner-cities and enterprise zones.

12 The present constraint upon the availability of Industrial Building Allowances was cited as an example of how private investment was deterred. This Allowance was available under certain circumstances for buildings used as sport pavilions but if a bar or lounge were provided then problems ensued.

13 The whole question of the need to convince the Inland Revenue that particular provisions for sports were assets within which a trade was carried on and upon which capital allowances were granted was difficult in the extreme.

Finally in a clear attempt to show the way forward Bacon recommended:

(i)   The creation of Sports Commissioners to function in like manner to the Charity Commissioners. These Sports Commissioners would determine the eligibility of sports bodies and organizations for total relief from income and corporation tax on the income from their activities.

Table 9:   Sports Council — 'Regional Participation' Grants

	£m	Number of schemes
1981–82	.440	695
1982–83	.799	1,424
1983–84	.870	1,967
1984–85	1.003	1,511
1985–86	1.208 ⎫	
1986–87	1.223 ⎪	Data not
1987–88	1.129 ⎬	available
1988–89	1.533 ⎭	

Source: Sports Council Annual Reports — Financial Statistics

9). The majority of the grants made were below £500 each and many were between £50 and £100 in this particular programme. The money allotted under the 'Regional Participation' programme in 1983/84 (£870,765) should be contrasted with the £162,322 allocated to this programme and a whole range of other initiatives including the 'Urban Deprivation' and 'Football and the Community' programmes in 1978 which were all administered and promoted by the regions of the Sports Council. By 1983 the total regional programmes had a budget of £2.3m which rose to an impressive £4.11m in 1987/88. By then Children's Play and Post-Abolition participation schemes were being developed regionally and budgets for these programmes were included in regional allocations. A year later in 1988/89 Children's Play had ceased to be a Sports Council responsibility and yet £4.40m was being spent across the wide range of regional programmes that had for some years included Demonstration Projects promoted to encourage others to do likewise.[35]

Pilot Schemes

Conscious that sport had a role to play in helping to alleviate to some extent the boredom of weeks and months of unemployment, some municipal authorities responded in the early eighties by devising schemes for those unemployed. A Loughborough University study for the Sports Council in 1982 showed that 60 per cent of local authorities in England were making some special provision for unemployed persons, usually during the day, by way of reduced or concessionary charges for use of facilities or by the free issue of cards that acted as season tickets. Some authorities offered special programmes for learning a sport whilst others offered no organized activities. In the main those offering no concessions were rural local authorities or areas where unemployment was running at a low level. Whilst it was perhaps understandable that authorities such as Bournemouth and Winchester were not making any special provision it was surprising to find that Barrow-in-Furness, Darlington, Durham and Rotherham and a clutch of others in the north were doing nothing special in this regard. Dr. Sue Glyptis and her colleague Anthony Riddington who carried out this survey concluded that although many public agencies were engaged in some form of provision it was very much on an ad hoc basis as no guidelines existed and there was little expertise on which to draw.[36]

With the clear understanding that a high rate of unemployment was to be endured in Britain for the foreseeable future the Sports Council launched three quite different schemes in 1981 in an effort to learn from this experience and provide the guidelines which were needed.

Sport and the Unemployed — Pilot Scheme 1

In the North the Derwent scheme was a partnership between the Derwentside District Council, the Manpower Services Commission (MSC) and the Sports Council. With unemployment running at 27 per cent of the available work-force the aim was to devise a wide range of opportunities and provide good coaching and organization. Twenty-six different sports were on offer and in the period from July 1981 until March 1983, some 22,500 participants joined in. Football for the men and Keep Fit for the women were the most popular activities but swimming, carpet bowls and badminton all had a steady following. Eighty per cent of those taking part were under 35 years of age and overall 50 per cent were below 25. Equipment was provided, clubs were formed and efforts were made to develop leadership training amongst some who took part.

In Leicester, the second of the schemes for the unemployed the target was young people and ethnic minorities in the inner-city areas. This scheme had five clear aims:

    (i)   to reduce boredom.
    (ii) to improve the quality of life through leisure activities.
    (iii) to encourage and develop natural leaders.
    (iv) to take coaching qualifications.
    (v) to provide an opportunity for sampling adventure activities.

As with the Derwent scheme the local authority, the Leicester City Council, cooperated with the Manpower Services Commission and the Sports Council. Staff, equipment and facilities were provided and field workers were employed to work intensively in city areas so that they quickly became known in the localities. Nearly 2000 young people attended in the first year. Although women accounted for only 25 per cent of those attending they were more consistent in their support. Initially a 'turn up and play' policy was followed which failed and the policy was then switched to local organization in the neighbourhood of those who were to be involved which proved successful.

In Hockley Port in Birmingham, the third scheme, the plan was to help a voluntary organization, the Cut Boat Folk, with its objective to develop this deprived area in the inner city by:

(i)   helping to provide a sports hall and an outdoor kick-about area;
(ii) developing a water sports programme on the canal (the 'cut' in the local dialect);
(iii) developing a physical recreation programme to add to the existing programmes;
(iv) arranging expeditions and visits for young people to widen experience;
(v)   recruiting a pool of volunteers to help run the many activities.

A sports leader was appointed and again the Manpower Services Commission and the Sports Council cooperated with money and services. The main features of this imaginative scheme were the visits and expeditions outside Birmingham to the Crystal Palace National Sports Centre, to the National Outdoor Activities Centre at Plas-y-Brenin in North Wales and to Aviemore in Scotland for skiing. Visits to the River Wye for camping, canoeing and pony trekking, in addition to road races, half-marathons and a full marathon demonstrated what could be done with a little money, a good deal of enthusiasm and sound organization.

As 1985 drew to a close these closely monitored schemes were still running and lessons had been learnt to assist the very many other schemes that were arranged up and down the country.[37] It was understood that with unemployment endemic in Britain sport for all was a policy that could play some part in helping alleviate the mind sapping boredom of those who had no work. What was needed was a massive injection of public funds into this area of concern to support and multiply the many good and successful schemes. In itself the employment of leaders, organizers and coaches provided useful and constructive jobs for a number but what was lacking, and this was certainly not the fault of the Sports Council who through these schemes proved many things, was the national will to develop and finance a plan for Britain. Such a plan would have supported the local authorities in their endeavours and would have provided an invaluable social service where it was most needed. In this the Minister for Sport failed.

Action Sport — Pilot Scheme 2

Action Sport was the most ambitious of the three pilot schemes and was budgeted to cost £1m in each of the three years it was to run from 1982–1985. Basically *Action Sport* was set in motion to prove that sport had a crucial role to play in deprived urban areas. Rather than spread thinly the resources available a policy of super concentration was agreed and selected areas in the West Midlands and in London were chosen for the experiment. In this scheme the emphasis was on people and not on facilities and the concentration was such that it narrowed down to actual streets and precise locations. The Sports Council took a very deep breath after having a negative reply from the Government, and designated the huge sum of £3m to be spread over the period mainly to appoint leaders and motivators to work in parks, playgrounds, sports centres, kick-about areas and on bomb sites. Over ninety leaders were appointed and in a glare of publicity the pilot-scheme was launched.

The Department of the Environment would not allow the Sports Council to take these ninety appointments on their staff as this would be seen to be increasing the number of public servants. Accordingly the local authorities agreed to take them on so long as the Sports Council gave them 100 per cent grant-aid for their salaries plus the requisite VAT that this arrangement entailed. The cost to the Sports Council to maintain this charade forced on them was approximately £450,000 for the three years VAT repaid to the Government from the annual grant made by the Government. A costly expenditure to maintain a public fiction!

Fifteen schemes in London and the Birmingham area were established each with a full-time coordinator. This project immediately captured the imagination and within months other local authorities were setting up 'action sport' teams of their own, building on the experience and evidence that was accruing from the 'official' pilot scheme which was being closely monitored. Volunteers and sponsors offered their services and in the London region the Abbey National Building Society demonstrated its commitment by seconding a full-time member of staff. *Action Sport* offered training courses, holiday opportunities, 'come and try' opportunities for school leavers, leagues, tournaments, competitions and the opportunity to move out of the city for adventure training.

Officially the pilot-scheme came to an end in the summer of 1985 having made its impact and shown the way.

The *Action Sport Evaluation Report* was published in July 1986. Prepared by the Policy Studies Unit it said: —

> It (Action Sport) has demonstrated the particular value of sports leadership in the inner cities ... an approach which survives is that outreach workers or leaders, given the appropriate support and focus, can provide substantial opportunities for participation in sport and leisure activities for those who are disadvantaged.

With this note of encouragement and approval the support of the Manpower Services Commission was sought, aimed at placing teams of motivators in local neighbourhoods throughout the land. By mid-1987 300 workers were in place cooperating with local authorities. Governmental changes of policy towards the unemployed in June 1988 caused the Sports

Council to change course and end its financial arrangements with the Commission. This was now the time for a rethink on how best to continue cooperation with existing partners, how to encourage more of these and how best to put in place revised programmes that would carry through to the nineties.

Outdoor Activities — Pilot Scheme 3

The third demonstration project was much smaller, concerned itself with outdoor countryside activities, and was based in the West Midlands. Under the guidance of Roger Orgill, the former Deputy Director of the National Centre for Mountain Activities at Plas-y-Brenin, the aim was to increase participation of young people in outdoor activities, in particular those living in inner-city and urban areas. Cooperation with the National Youth Bureau, trade unions, Manpower Services Commission and industry generally was quickly obtained and both leadership and general participation schemes were quickly underway. Working with the National Association for Outdoor Education whose President was the Director of Education for Walsall Municipal Borough, Mr. Bob Nixon, rapid progress in the first year was readily achieved. Useful relationships with Outward Bound, Operation Drake Fellowship and the Young Explorers Trust resulted in the establishment of a number of urban-based outdoor activity sections which promised well.

The project concluded in the mid-eighties and like the other two demonstration projects saw its efforts rewarded with an encouraging response from local authorities and voluntary organizations.

In 1984 a further six demonstration projects were launched by the Sports Council (see the Annual Report, 1984/85, p. 7) which kept the momentum going and offered variety.

It would be wrong to believe that these schemes were the only schemes that were attempting to grapple with the social problems of unemployment, boredom, areas of social deprivation and leadership in sport generally. They represented national schemes sponsored by a national agency, in this case the Sports Council; there were, and are, many others. For example, a unique scheme in Southampton linked sport with the probation service, and this was typical of the many ideas that were being tried. Here two young men, not really trained in probation or youth work but highly motivated, took upon themselves the task of persuading young offenders before the courts that sport had something for them and virtually in a one-to-one situation guided young people into clubs and organizations. Known as the Southampton Sports Counselling Project, and sponsored by the Hampshire Probation Service, the Manpower Services Commission again played a major role in funding salaries and some additional costs. In 1984 160 young offenders, known as the 'clients', were associated with the scheme and after two years only four had been before the magistrates again. Some 85 per cent of 'clients' were under 21 years of age and many were unemployed. The budget for 1985 was a mere £32,500 and the continuance of the scheme had the support of the Southampton Magistrates Bench; a small sum to be paid for the social and community benefits that have accrued.

The Southern Region of the Sports Council was involved through its dynamic Director Laurie Bridgman, a man of wide experience, who saw that the increasing interest of the Home Office in this initiative could lead to a national scheme if the will was there.

Conclusion

Since 1972 *Sport for All* has come a long way. Today there is evidence of greatly increased participation opportunities in the range of facilities that have appeared since the late sixties. From the highly successful London Marathon and the local 'fun runs' to the round the corner kick-about areas in the mean and decayed inner cities the spectrum is wide and diverse. Participation in sport, physical recreation and exercise generally, is now fashionable linked as it is to life style and health benefits. Martin and Mason, Leisure Consultants, forecast in 1979 that participation would increase by 13 per cent between then and 1985 with swimming, rambling and walking heading the list; they were largely right. The Henley Centre for Forecasting envisaged that between 1973 and 1991 activities such as golf (33 per cent), camping (33 per cent), cricket (21 per cent), tennis (27 per cent) and swimming (21 per cent) would show considerable growth with badminton and squash shown as a staggering 59 per cent. The Sports Council's declared target, in its national strategy *Sport in the Community — The Next Ten Years* is that by 1993 1.8m more people will be playing outdoor sport and 2.8m more playing indoor sport; startling as it sounded when first stated it looks now quite capable of realization. Sport for All has become increasingly pervasive but is it yet completely so?

Sport for All — An Evaluation

In 1982 the Council of Europe, through its Comité Directoire pour le Développement du Sport (CDDS), decided to ask all member states to carry out an evaluation of the sport for all policies pursued nationally since their respective initiatives had been taken. The purpose was not simply to take stock of the existing situation in Western Europe but rather to identify areas where policies had not been successful so that new initiatives could usefully be taken. As the British Government's representative on the CDDS the Deputy Director-General agreed that the Sports Council would undertake this national evaluation. A distinguished former member of the Council in its formative days, Professor Peter McIntosh, was contracted to carry out this work under the general auspices of the West London Institute of Higher Education where he was a 'Visiting Professor'. This work was concluded in the early summer of 1984 although an interim report had formed part of the supporting papers for an informed debate at the Council of Europe Ministers of Sport Conference in Malta in May. The report was published in 1985 (see McIntosh and Charlton, 1985) and the feeling grew that it was not generally well received as it was critical of some aspects of policy (*ibid*, pp. 151–6). There could well have been some reluctance to publish but if so this was overcome and quite rightly so as the report had many successes to show.

This evaluation represented a profound study of the progress to date set against clearly defined policies, aims and objectives. It concluded by pointing a way to further progress in areas where sport for all had barely scratched the consciousness of those to whom it was directed.

Despite a general increase in participation, and in some sections of society a very considerable increase, it would appear that the pattern of non-participation remained much the same as in 1972. In other words, certain groups in society that were largely non-participants in 1972 remained so in 1984, although groups that were participants previously had increased their participation rate, in some cases very considerably. The largely non-participant groups were identified as:

    (i)   low paid and unskilled workers;
   (ii)   parents of young children;
  (iii)   ethnic minorities;
   (iv)   women generally;
    (v)   school leavers;
   (vi)   unemployed youth.

Whilst these conclusions did not come as any great surprise to those close to the scene of action it was salutary to have the evidence displayed. In the early eighties, as already described, special programmes had been constructed aimed at some if not all of these groups but what was underlined in 1985 was that a massive drive was needed in this connection with new, and as yet untried, partners recruited. The McIntosh evaluation was critical of the broad target groups by age bands, the 14–24 years and 45–59 years, selected by the Sports Council in its strategy for the eighties and it pointed to the need to identify specific groups within these broad amorphous bands. This study was generous in its praise for local authorities and for the many successful programmes for facility provision and participation that had been developed but it was critical of the parsimony of successive governments (*ibid*, pp. 35–41).

> ... expenditure on sport is a minuscule percentage of total govern-
> ment expenditure and ... a large percentage increase in sports
> expenditure makes little difference to the total figure,

said McIntosh who, however, went on to point out that central Government
money added to the very large sums made available by local authorities

> compares favourably, for instance, with a planned expenditure in
> 1982/83 of £500m on the prison service and £527m on passenger
> subsidies for British Rail, bus, underground and ferry services.

A hint of what the Bacon report on taxation had said was given when a
new approach to funding was canvassed. Existing policies on dual use, joint
provision, health and fitness, élitism, and the use of the media were critically
examined pointing to successes and failures.

For some this was an uncomfortable report because of its penetrating
exposé of the truth as McIntosh and his research assistant Valerie Charlton
saw it; for others it was an inspiration for it pointed to successes and proved
them statistically. More importantly it narrowed the point of attack for fresh
policy initiative.

By 1988 the Sports Council had revised its policies with Sport for All
and had marginally trimmed its participation targets for 1993 when it said,

> The strategy for the next five years renews the emphasis on these
> 1982 priorities where progress has been slow; it reinforces the
> Council's philosophy of *Sport for All*. (*Sport in the Community —
> Into the 90s*, paragraph 3.1, p. 58)

In making this statement the Council announced two principal targets
— young people and women, and further announced that the development
of regional and local performance strategies and the promotion of excellence
would be two additional major targets for the next five-year period until
1993.

With the finance provided by local authorities there is largely no quarrel
but the annual grant in aid for sport by all governments has continued, since
1972 when the Sports Council became a funded body, to be mean in the
extreme. On 15 November 1989 the Government announced its increase in
the grant to the Council for 1990/91; a mere £2.5m up on the £43.7m for the
previous year. This represented an increase of 5.7 per cent, well below the
rate of inflation, and a sad commentary on the power and influence of the
Minister for Sport, Colin Moynihan. In effect this meant that the ability of
the Sports Council to expand its programmes of assistance to sport at all
levels is marginally diminished as the new decade arrives.

Sport for All has come a long way since Sir Roger Bannister so boldly
launched Britain into this Western European movement in 1972. The Sports

Council has spearheaded the way with governing bodies of sport broadly supportive.

The CCPR actively entered the field in 1985 when amongst other initiatives taken the Council hosted a major international conference on this theme in the Isle of Man in October.[38]

Sport for All is not as yet a total reality but for the very many it has touched it has clearly evoked in them responses and the quality of their lives has been enriched by such contact and experience.

The Council of Europe's *Sport for All* Charter (1976) states:

'Every individual shall have the right to participate in sport. (Article 1)

The UNESCO International Charter of Physical Education and Sport (1978) says:

Every human being has a fundamental right of access to physical education and sport, which are essential for the full development of his personality. (Article 1)

The British Government was a signatory to both of these Charters. Of course every British citizen has this 'right' referred to, but has every British citizen the opportunity yet to exercise this 'right', and if not how long is it to be before he or she has?

Notes

1 *Sport in the Community — The Next Ten Years* p. 15, Table 11. Annual Leisure and Recreation Statistics Estimates produced by CIPFA.
2 *ibid*, table 11, p. 15.
3 *Sport in the Community' — Into the 90s*; figures 37 and 38, p. 57.
4 *ibid*, paragraph 2,242, p. 57.
5 Particularly the middle classes. For example jogging groups for both sexes sprang up; early morning swimming sessions were arranged at local swimming pools for serious exercise; aerobic classes featured in further education classes and in private gymnasia.
6 The English Tourist Board, the Tourist Boards for Wales, Scotland and the English Regions all featured, and continue to feature, short-break holidays as do the big hotel groups.
7 *Sport in the Community — Into the 90s'* 'Earlier parts of this Chapter have shown the growth in the provision of facilities by local authorities in the past five years' (paragraph 2.240). 'Local authority revenue budgets have continued to grow' (paragraph 2.241).
8 *Sport in the Community — The Next Ten Years*, figure 18, p. 22.
9 *Sport in the Community — Into the 90s'*. pp. 25–7.
10 *Study No. 21. Sharing does Work*, Coopers and Lybrand Associates Ltd, Sports Council, 1981.

11 'Opening Doors', a Joint Department of Environment and Sports Council booklet, free from the Sports Council. Sports Council Annual Report, 1985–86, p. 25 and table 8; 1985 forty-seven schemes; 1986 fifty-seven schemes. In 1986 £299,245 was allocated; in 1987 £471,758; by 1988 this had dwindled to £95,202 but by then this initiative had been successful and had run its course.

12 Sports Council, 1972, paragraph 21, p. 5.

13 Sports Council Annual Report 1986–87, p. 19.

14 *Sport in the Community — The Next Ten Years*; *Sport in the Community — Into the 90s*; Sports Council Annual Reports; Verbatim answers to questions by Sports Council HQ staff responsible for facilities.

15 Apart from normal growth the successes in men's hockey at the 1984 and 1988 Olympics, coupled with the World Cup played in Britain between these two events in which Great Britain reached the final, which all had wide television coverage, presented the game to a very wide audience and clubs and teams sprang up very rapidly. The proliferation of plastic pitches has also assisted considerably.

16 The closure of factories and the sell-off of playing fields to capitalize the assets in the period of financial stress in the eighties accelerated a process that was evident earlier. Falling roles in schools tempted education authorities to sell 'surplus' playing fields. Clubs sold out to developers at.building-land prices and often relocated elsewhere in enhanced facilities. Motorways and ring-roads too claimed playing fields.

17 The CCPR lobbied MPs; the General Secretary was interviewed repeatedly on radio and television; petitions were organized. For details see CCPR annual reports.

18 Hansard, House of Commons, 12 July 1988, Debate on 'Sport'.

19 For example: Lieut.-General Sir Mervyn Butler; Lieut.-General Sir James Wilson; Air Chief Marshall Sir Robert Freer. By 1986 the custom of having a senior Service Officer on the Sports Council had fallen into decline.

20 Historically only the work-force generally could be members of works clubs but latterly membership was opened to families: clubs then became more financially self-sufficient with year-on-year expenditure. Two classic examples at Pilkinton's in St. Helen's and Cadbury's in Birmingham illustrate the situation in 1989 compared with 1939, or indeed 1959.

21 Sports Council Financial Statistics — Annual Reports.

22 The Football Trust was established in 1979, previously the Football Grounds Improvement Trust which started in 1975. Income is derived from the Football Pools companies — Vernons, Littlewoods and Zetters.

23 This scheme not only involved facilities. At Wolverhampton FC and West Bromwich Albion FC full-time motivators were employed to maximize the use of existing facilities at these clubs. Ipswich Town FC and Portsmouth FC did likewise with part-time appointments and the employment of ex-professional players. On the facility side Carlisle FC provided a sports hall overlooking the playing area for use during the week for activities and for watching the match on Saturdays. Some schemes were in partnership with local authorities, others involved football clubs only.

24 For example in 1987 the Trust, having allocated £1.3m to local authorities, saw work started on seventy-one new pitches, ninety-two improved pitches, forty-five new and eleven improved pavilions.

25 See Sports Council Annual Reports 1978–79 and 1979–80, p. 6 and p. 14 respectively for details.

26 The Department of Environment paid 75 per cent of approved costs for capital and revenue expenditure to a maximum of £25,000 per scheme. All projects had to benefit an urban area of 'special social need' — poverty, unemployment, poor

housing, educational disadvantage, poor quality of environment, severe pressure on social services and high concentration of ethnic minorities were taken as the indicators. Holiday projects could be the opening of school playgrounds and playing fields, play schemes, outdoor games and excursions.

27 *Sport and Taxation* — a review by D.M. Bacon, FCA, June 1981.
28 *ibid*, pp. 3 and 4.
29 Hansard, House of Commons, 12 July 1988, Debate on 'Sport', Col. 277.
30 Department of Environment News Release of the Minister's Statement dated 1 July 1988.
31 *'Building on Ability'*, Report of the Minister's Review Group 1988–89, Department of Environment (Sport and Recreation Division) August 1989.
32 Sports Council Annual Report 1986–87, p. 25.
33 Sports Council internal paper SC (89) 52 paragraph 4.
34 *'Community Sports Leaders Award'*, CCPR 3rd Ed. (1983). p. 1. reproduction of a quote in Prince Philip's Inaugural Colson Memorial Lecture, 16 July 1974.
35 Sports Council Financial Statistics — Annual Reports.
36 See Sports Council Working Paper 21; Glyptis and Pack (1988) *Local Authority Sports Provision for the Unemployed*, Sports Council Study 31; and Glyptis, Kay and Donkin (1986) *Sport and the Unemployed — Lessons from Schemes in Leicester, Derwentside and Hockley Port*, Sports Council.
37 For example those unemployed did not like being classified as such and preferred to merge in with others not so unfortunate such as shift-workers.
38 IX International Trim and Fitness Congress, Isle of Man 6–11 October 1985; forty-two countries were represented together with IOC President, ICSSPE, ANOC and the World Leisure and Recreation Association. The report was published by the CCPR.

Chapter 13

International Perspectives

Although Britain is an island, an island whose people have given many sports to the world, it can no longer develop its sports culture without having regard to the way sport is organized internationally and to the role sport increasingly plays in international politics. The traditional British ethos of sport still carries weight internationally but this ethos is declining under the unremitting pressure of commercial and national interests. Today politics are inextricably linked with sport both in the national and in the international context. On the one hand there are the 'sports' politics which involve the wheeling and dealing over power in the international sports bodies, and on the other hand there are the 'political' politics that seek to use sport as an instrument of national foreign policy.

The use of sport by politicians not involved in sport is by no means new. During the Civil War in England in the middle of the seventeenth century Cromwell suppressed Sunday sport by law as it was seen as a token of opposition to the ruling Parliamentary and Puritan cause (Brailsford, 1969). Long before this date, in the second century BC, correspondence between the Emperor Trajan and Pliny reveals that the government intended to rebuild a gymnasium and pay those who had been victorious in the various sporting discliplines (Robinson, 1980, pp. 172–3). In modern times there are many examples of sport and politics touching on the international scene long before the current scenario unfolded. The 'body-line' cricket tour by the MCC of Australia in 1932/33 provoked a diplomatic storm between the British and Australian governments. In 1935 the infamous case of the England soccer team being instructed by the Foreign Office to give the Nazi salute when playing against Germany in that country still shocks and was direct political interference in the affairs of the Football Association. Fidel Castro in Cuba has often used his prowess in baseball to support his political ends. Gerald Ford used his status in American Football to appeal to the mass of the public during his Presidency of the USA. The nauseating scenes of President Carter overwhelming the American ice-hockey team with his congratulations after their Winter Olympic success against the Soviets at Lake Placid in 1980 were only equalled by President Reagan's much publicized breakfast with the American Olympic winners at the 1984 Los Angeles Games in support of his re-election campaign; two breathtaking examples in recent times of politicians using sportsmen and women to their own ends. The two blatant examples of the boycotts of the Olympic Games in Moscow and Los Angeles on the instructions of governments need little further explanation (Hoberman, 1986, section III, pp. 65–79 and Epilogue, pp. 127–33; Killanin, 1983, chapter I, pp. 1–10, chapter XVII, pp. 164–70, chapter XVIII, pp. 171–87 and chapter XVIV, pp. 188–219).

National and international politics are about power and who controls that power. As sport has come increasingly to the fore in the international context so it represents a power-base and politicians see it as a source to manipulate and control. In the Socialist countries sport is, by the ideology followed, an instrument of the state. They neither attempt to hide the fact nor apologise for it; it is simply that sport reflects the Marxist notion of the interdependence of the physical and mental states of human beings which, interpreted, means that physical education and sport are treated equally in every respect with mental culture.

As Riordan says,

> ... communist leaders have consistently confirmed their allegiance to Marxism-Leninism in general, and their adherence to a number of Marxist goals in respect of recreation in particular, emphasizing the provision of sport for all and the need specifically to enable all citizens to be harmoniously developed. (Hargreaves, 1982, chapter 9, p. 227)

In developing countries too sport is invariably a responsibility of the state and controlled by either the Ministry of Education, Culture or Youth. In the Western democracies the sports bodies are usually voluntary organizations supported by the State financially with the degree of support and direct involvement varying considerably.[1]

There are many permutations and variations on these systems from the permissive government that provides financial help in a variety of ways and plays no further role other than one of being supportive, to the government that heavily controls the sports movement and runs it directly through civil servants or government appointed nominees.

It is against this somewhat bewildering kaleidoscope of national organization that the international sports organizations, federations and associations have to control and regulate their affairs. Their work is further complicated, sometimes assisted and sometimes hampered, by the increasing involvement in sport by political organizations such as the United Nations, UNESCO, the Organization of African Unity, the Council of Europe, the European Community, and other regional political groupings who often have their own views, attitudes and policies concerning sport at élite and community levels.

The Structure of International Sport

International sport is organized on two levels, that which concerns itself with international competition and that which concerns itself with the sports sciences and other specialisms which support and complement sport.

International Competition

The most prestigious and influential body concerned with the organization of high-level sport is the International Olympic Committee (IOC) based in Lausanne. The IOC was established on 23 June 1894 at the Congress of Paris to be responsible for the control and development of the modern Olympic Games. It is a body 'corporate by international law, having juridicial status and perpetual succession'.[2] The IOC is a 'club' of around ninety members of which usually about one-third come from Western Europe. It selects whomsoever it wishes to be a member provided English or French is spoken, and members do not represent their countries; they serve purely in an individual capacity. Not every country with a National Olympic Committee has a member and currently Britain has two, HRH the Princess Royal and Mrs. Mary Glen-Haig. Latterly women have been invited into membership and for many years the Director of the IOC was the very able Madame Monique Berlioux. In June 1985[3] at a meeting of the IOC in East Berlin she resigned ostensibly following a clash of opinion as to the direction the Olympic movement was taking. (see Killanin, 1983, Chapter 2.)

A criticism often voiced by new and developing countries is that because not every country has a representative on the IOC such countries can play no part in policy making. Critics often support publicly the case for the IOC being the United Nations of Sport with one nation one vote. To date the IOC has set its face resolutely against this principle and in its own fashion has sought a number of ways by which it can be more widely representative whilst retaining its unique character. It was Lord Killanin himself who wrote: —

... one of the mysteries surrounding the Olympic Games is its operation; how it works, who does what, and why. (ibid)

In 1988 twenty-nine international federations participated in the winter and summer Olympics but the number is due to increase. In 1992 the number will be six and twenty-five respectively. The international federations are the world controlling bodies for sport and these twenty-nine are a minority but are some of the most powerful. National federations of sport affiliate to the international bodies who organize all regional and world competitions. These bodies are normally democratic in the Western sense of the word in that they elect their officers from the membership but sometimes with loaded voting powers to the more powerful countries in a particular sport. International secretariats have permanent bases in countries which often offer advantageous services to ensure they stay or to entice them to settle. At the end of 1989 eight international federations had their secretariats in Britain, and whilst this may look impressive it does represent some erosion over the years. In an effort to prevent further loss the Sports Council has devised a policy which assists financially international bodies who wish to come or stay in Britain; this is enlightened and is welcomed internationally.[4]

The international federations in 1967 decided to band themselves together in the General Assembly of International Sports Federations (GAISF) which has its permanent base in Monaco. In this way they can speak to other corporate bodies such as the IOC or UNESCO and represent their collective viewpoint. Until the autumn of 1984 Mr. Charles Palmer, former Chairman of the British Olympic Association, was the Secretary General of GAISF.

As a further proliferation, continental groupings of National Olympic Committees have developed during the seventies and eighties and today there is a world body known as the Association of National Olympic Committees (ANOC) and several regional bodies such as the Association of African National Olympic Committees and the powerful European Confederation of National Olympic Committees. All have their own secretariats and represent a continental point of view to the IOC. In some respects they are a possible source of threat to the IOC but no one ever talks publicly of such things; they are promoted as a means of identifying special regional issues and problems but they do represent a system of checks and balance.

The principal world and regional sports events, other than world and continental championships for individual sports, are today the Olympic, Commonwealth, Pan American, Asian, South East Asian, African and Mediterranean Games, but there are also Games in smaller geographic areas such as the Caribbean and the Gulf. Often these events are under the auspices of the IOC but not necessarily so and they often include non-Olympic sports for example, badminton and a free choice of sport in the Commonwealth Games by the organizing country. The largest event outside the Olympic Games is the World Student Games held every two years and scheduled for Sheffield in 1991.

The Sports Sciences and Other International Bodies

The very many specialisms in physical education and sport nearly all have international associations, as do the other professions such as sports medicine and sports journalism. For example there is an International Society of Sports Psychology (ISSP), an International Association for Sports Information (IASI), an International Committee of Sports Pedagogy (ICSP), an International Committee for Sociology of Sport (ICSS), an Association Internationale Presse Sportive (AIPS) and a Fédération Internationale Médecine Sportive (FIMS). Whether the discipline be bio-mechanics, comparative studies, auxology or anthropometry there is an international body to link together the very many national bodies.

In an effort to produce some coordination in these many bodies doing scientific work international 'umbrella' organizations have been established over the years. In the field of physical education the Fédération Internationale d'Education Physique (FIEP) was set up in 1923 mainly to assist teachers. In 1956 the International Council of Health, Physical Education and Recreation (ICHPER), as the brainchild of the then American Alliance for Health, Physical Education and Recreation, now with Dance added (AAHPERD), was established to assist teachers in schools and institutions of higher learning. In 1984 Dr. John Kane, Principal of the West London Institute of Higher Education, and a world figure in sports psychology, was elected President and in the same year ICHPER was granted 'A' status by UNESCO in recognition of the valuable work it does in the field of physical education.

In 1949 at a conference in Copenhagen there was some discussion on the need for a new international body to be concerned with physical education and sport. At the 1956 Olympic Games in Melbourne a group of international figures from many countries met informally under Professor Fritz Duras (Australia) to consider what steps were needed to be taken to reverse the trend of an increasing separation between sport and physical education. Mr. David Munrow, Director of Physical Education at the University of Birmingham, was present and he included in his contribution the views and thinking of his colleague Peter McIntosh who had single-handedly in the early fifties taken it upon himself to approach UNESCO with his concern. It was agreed to set up a steering committee from twelve countries. Dr. William Jones was asked to draw up draft statutes for an international body at a meeting in 1957 and in 1958 at UNESCO House in Paris, the name International Council of Sport and Physical Education (ICSPE) was agreed. All was now set for the first General Assembly of ICSPE in Rome during the 1960 Olympic Games. Thirty-seven countries were represented by 123 delegates who approved the statutes, received the blessing and support of Monsieur René Maheu, Director General of UNESCO, and of the IOC who supported the aims of the new Council. The distinguished British Parliamentarian, former Cabinet Minister, Nobel Peace Prize Winner and Olympic Silver Medallist, the Right-Honourable (later Lord) Philip Noel-Baker was elected President. Distinguished sportsmen and physical educationalists were appointed Vice Presidents including the legendary 'bounding Basque' Jean Borotra, the former Wimbledon Singles Champion.

Lord Noel-Baker remained as President until he stood down in 1976. In 1981 on the occasion of the Olympic Congress in Baden-Baden he made one of the great speeches, sadly not published in the Congress Report, and he died the following year on 8 October 1982, at the age of 92.

ICSPE has style and prestige and seeks to stimulate and coordinate research in sports science and physical education. Membership is by organizations and from the outset it appealed to East and West; its great strength has always been through this global appeal to all the political ideologies. In 1976 at the General Assembly in Quebec, immediately prior to the Olympic Games in Montreal, Sir Roger Bannister succeeded Philip Noel-Baker and to support him the Sports Council offered the Secretariat with the French speaking Deputy Director-General, John Coghlan, as Secretary-General. This was a happy and constructive partnership during the six-and-a-half years Roger Bannister had agreed to serve and the Council flourished with an increased programme of activity and a refinement of structure and management. Major conferences in Tblisi (USSR) before the Moscow Olympics, and in Finland in 1982, were supplemented by many other events including the Commonwealth and International Conference in Brisbane in 1982 and the development of working contracts for UNESCO mainly in the developing countries. An initiative by Roger Bannister with Lord Killanin (President of the IOC) opened up a dialogue, continued later with Senor Samaranch, aimed at creating a situation whereby ICSPE could serve the IOC and the international federations with research, documentation and scientific projects. When on 1 January 1983 Bannister and Coghlan handed over to Professor Dr. August Kirsch, Director of the Bundesinstitut Für Sportwissenschaft (Cologne), and Herr Werner Sonnenschein his colleague, as President and Secretary-General respectively, the continued development of the ICSPE, since 1982 the International Council for Sport Science and Physical Education (ICSSPE), was assured, doubly so because the Government of the Federal Republic of Germany supported this move. The West German leadership has been strong and skilful with Kirsch developing the IOC connection brilliantly. In 1984 the IOC granted ICSSPE the status of 'Recognized Organization' in view of the programme of work currently carried out for the Olympic body. With consultative 'A' status virtually from the outset the work with UNESCO continued to be close and has increased in range and quality. The ICSPE initiative in 1976 to persuade UNESCO to convene the international meeting of 'ministers and high officers' in sport from all member states led to the setting up of the Interim Intergovernmental Committee for Sport and Physical Education at the UNESCO General Conference in Nairobi later that year.[5] A second International Conference was held in Moscow in November 1988, the final report being published by UNESCO in 1989.

Throughout the thirty years of ICSSPE's history the support of the Socialist countries, in particular the USSR and the German Democratic Republic, has been strong and sure. The French government has continued to fund the office of the permanent Deputy Secretary-General housed in the UNESCO building in Paris.

Traditionally at the time of the Olympic Games ICSSPE has helped the local Organizing Committees prepare the Olympic Sports Science Congresses that bring together for a week prior to the Games the world's best scientists in a wide range of disciplines.[6]

The British influence in ICSSPE from the earliest days has been profound not only through Lord Noel-Baker and Sir Roger Bannister as successive Presidents but also through David Munrow, Professor Peter McIntosh, Dr. Don Anthony, Sir Walter Winterbottom and John Coghlan, all of whom have played major roles in its affairs.

The Structure of Political Groupings

The United Nations and UNESCO

The UN has concerned itself with sport but to date this has been limited to a committee looking into the practice of apartheid in sport which has periodically published 'black lists' of those who in their view condoned apartheid by playing sport in South Africa. Following the boycott of the 1980 Moscow Olympics there was some talk of a UN resolution aimed at preventing such action; this could have developed into major political interference with the IOC but fortunately nothing materialized.

UNESCO, being the UN Agency primarily concerned with science, culture and education, has been considerably involved since the First International Conference of Ministers and Senior Officials responsible for Physical Education and Sport in the Education of Youth in April 1976. At the 19th General Conference in Nairobi later that year it was agreed to establish an Interim Intergovernmental Committee for Sport and Physical Education and two years later this Committee was made permanent. Composed of thirty nations that retire in rotation, and assisted by international non-governmental organizations such as the IOC, GAISF, ICSSPE, FIMS, ICHPER and FIEP, this Committee has involved itself with major issues concerning élite sport where it has floundered, and sport for all where it has been more successful. The preparation and worldwide distribution of an International Charter of Physical Education and Sport[7] was a major achievement and has made a considerable impact. The raising of an international fund for development has had only qualified success to date and many nations including Britain[8] have been reluctant to pay money into a fund for broad general purposes. There have been some contributions of cash and many contributions in kind by way of courses for coaches, administrators and teachers. The Intergovernmental Committee was on difficult ground when it sought to 'analyze the difficulties with which the organization and staging of international sports competitions are increasingly faced throughout the world' and how these 'could be smoothed away through concerted inter-government action'.[9] This was a direct challenge to the IOC and the international sports movement, seeking to involve governmental solutions on the principle of one nation one vote in what was essentially a non-governmental sphere of activity; a cause epitomized in the new phrase 'democratization of sport'. The President of the IOC, Lord Killanin, met Sir Roger Bannister, President of ICSPE, at a private meeting in the Secretary-General's office at the Sports Council and it was agreed that ICSPE would do all it could to head off this challenge to the international non-governmental sports organizations, in return for which the IOC would increasingly support the admirable UNESCO 'sport for all' philosophy enshrined in its new Charter for Physical Education and Sport.

The dissatisfaction of many developing countries with the world sports order was often heard at UNESCO during the next few years, but gradually and effectively the spotlight moved from this controversy to the more productive issue of devising policies to assist such countries develop physical education and 'sport for all' opportunities. This was a cause close to the heart of UNESCO officials where the fight for increased resources for their programmes was nobly led by M. Henri Dieuzeide, an able and skilled international administrator, in his capacity as Director of the Division of Structures, Content, Methods and Techniques of Education. Sadly by 1989 lack of money and poor quality leadership in the appropriate section of UNESCO had created inertia.

Work on needs in Africa, Asia and Latin America have highlighted problems for policy decision. The disparities between the developed and the developing countries are a constant source of concern and a detailed study of this issue together with a *Programme for Action* was prepared in 1987 by ICSSPE for UNESCO.[10] An international *Physical Education and Sports Week* took place in 1985 which focussed international attention on sport for all initiatives and was considered generally to have been successful. A range of fresh initiatives was agreed at the Ministerial UNESCO Conference in Moscow, November 1988.[11]

The UK was a member of the Intergovernmental Committee for Physical Education and Sport from the outset. Apart from a telling and constructive contribution Denis Howell made in his capacity as Minister for Sport and Head of the British Delegation at the First Session in 1977 the British contribution has been minimal seeking, as a matter of policy, to diminish the role UNESCO has sought for itself in these affairs. With the withdrawal of the United Kingdom from UNESCO at the end of 1985 membership of the Committee ceased.

The involvement of UNESCO in the sport for all movement initially had a worldwide impact, and two major meetings of high-level officials, together with experts in Dakar (Africa) and Brisbane (Australia), focussed regional attention on the main issues. The involvement of the IOC and GAISF in a wide range of meetings brought about a degree of cooperation and understanding that was productive. UNESCO on the one hand and the two powerful non-governmental organizations on the other today more clearly see each other's point of view and gradually and in an unspectacular fashion lines of demarcation have been drawn advantageous to both. Via the Olympic Solidarity Fund the IOC has been very much involved in development programmes with Third World countries which has been helpful to UNESCO whilst the latter no longer aspires to being involved in high-level sport.

The Council of Europe

The Council of Europe was set up in 1949 and by 1979 incorporated twenty-one member states. It is basically a Western European body that aims to foster greater unity and co-operation between the people and nations of Europe by improving living conditions, developing human values and by upholding the principles of parliamentary democracy and human rights. Member States were Austria, Belgium, Cyprus, Denmark, Federal Republic of Germany, France, Greece, Iceland, Ireland, Italy, Leichtenstein, Luxembourg, Malta, Netherlands, Norway, Portugal, Spain, Sweden, Switzerland, Turkey and the United Kingdom. Additionally Finland and the Holy See were members for education, culture and sport having signed the European Cultural Convention. Ten years later by 1989 Poland, Hungary, Yugoslavia and San Marino had become involved.

Western European intergovernmental cooperation was begun by the Brussels Treaty Organization (founded in 1948). In 1960 educational and cultural responsibility was transferred to the Council of Europe with physical education and sport coming under the mantle of the Committee of Cultural Experts which became the Council for Cultural Cooperation (CCC) in 1962. Work involving physical education and sport was given to a sub-committee of the CCC, the Committee for Out of School Education. The need for a specific structure for sport was recognized by 1968 but there were problems which at that time were considered too difficult to solve. These lay in the differing sports structures within Member States where the responsibility for sport was sometimes with government departments and sometimes with voluntary organizations. In these early days meetings of governmental and non governmental national bodies were attended by the CCPR both pre- and in the early days of the advisory Sports Council. It was through such meetings that the first stirrings of the *Sport for All* movement were discussed. Cooperative action was agreed in 1970 with Recommendation 588, and in 1972 with Recommendation 682, for a European Sport for All Charter.[12]

In 1974 the Council of Europe set up an ad hoc Consultative Meeting involving governmental and non-governmental representatives but the members had no real authority or power. A year later, in March 1975, the Brussels Conference of European Ministers for Sport elevated this Consultative Meeting into a Committee of Experts on Sport, still attached to the CCC. The Ministers took three major decisions and agreed:

(i) to establish a Committee for the Development of Sport (CDS) as a permanent committee of the CCC;

(ii) to cooperate in a wide field of activity including exchange of information, joint research, exchanges, facility design and construction, legislative measures, regulations and financial arrangements aimed at promoting Sport for All, evaluation of national sports plans and mutual assistance;

(iii) to define more clearly the European Sport for All policy by spelling out the responsibilities of public authorities, the need for closer links with schools and their physical education programmes, the practical conditions for participation in sport, the need to finance sports programmes and the need for safeguards for the integrity of sport and participation.[13]

The Brussels Conference was wholly satisfactory and major roles were played by Minister for Sport Howell and Walter Winterbottom, the latter being, in many respects, the architect of the Council of Europe initiative. Winterbottom was appointed Chairman of the CDS when it was finally established in November 1977.

The main aims of the 1975 Conference were achieved and may be summarized as follows:

(i) to place on record the important place of sport in civilization;

(ii) to establish regular and effective machinery for cooperation within the Council of Europe;

(iii) to adopt a recommendation on the European Sport for All Charter.[14]

In September 1976 the Committee of Ministers of the Council of Europe approved the Principles for a Policy of Sport for All and the European Sport for All Charter became a reality. Although sport for all policies had been in existence since 1966 in the case of Norway, and 1972 in the case of Britain, this Charter gave governmental approval to both the philosophy and the policy and since that date has had enormous impact far beyond Western Europe (see McIntosh, 1980).[15] Countries in Asia, Latin America and Africa all pursue *Sport for All* programmes today.

In 1978 the British Government hosted a Second Conference of European Ministers Responsible for Sport at Lancaster House where once again Denis Howell and Walter Winterbottom played major roles; the latter had in fact retired a few days earlier. Three years later in Palma de Mallorca Spain organized the Third Conference followed by Malta in May 1984. Since 1978 the IOC, GAISF, ICSSPE and latterly UNESCO have been invited to attend. Ireland was the venue for the Ministers' Conference in late 1986 with Iceland playing host in the summer of 1989.[16]

In between formal conferences informal meetings of ministers have taken place the most noteworthy of which was in Athens in 1979 when rumblings from the USSR were heard about West Berlin and the Federal Republic of Germany in the selection of teams for the 1980 Moscow Olympics. Apartheid in sport and the pressure being imposed upon Israel in sports matters were other major matters under review in Athens. Since then football violence and sporting contacts with South Africa have been the main topics for ministers in addition to the thorny problem of drug abuse in sport.

From the outset Britain has played a major part in the work of the Council of Europe and has backed it solidly. As the principal adviser to HM Government on sport the Sports Council was deputed to lead at Strasbourg and to adopt national policies in conformity with European policies. Winterbottom was succeeded in the CDS by Coghlan, his Deputy, who saw that a constructive partnership was quickly established with the officers in the office of the Minister for Sport, Peter Butler and Norman Palmer. Together this group formed a happy and powerful British team, each playing his distinctive role. Since Coghlan's retirement in 1983 government officials who now tend to spend only a year or two in the Sport and Recreation section at the Department of Environment have frequently taken the lead. The lack of expert knowledge and experience has seriously weakened the British position.

In 1978 the CDS became the Comité Directoire pour le Développement du Sport (CDDS), a Committee standing on its own and not reporting to the CCC. From the outset this Committee for the Development of Sport has worked through an annual meeting and a small Bureau which meets three or four times during the year to develop agreed policies and construct new thinking for the annual assembly.

For some years the Sports Secretariat at Strasbourg has been headed by Mr. George Walker, an able, talented and resourceful administrator who has been responsible for guiding and harmonizing the European programmes. Astute, diplomatic and unflappable Walker has raised the status of sport at the Council of Europe to an enviable position and has brought quality to bear on all for which he has been responsible.

A major service since the mid-sixties has been the Clearing House for Sports Information in Brussels, partly funded by the CDDS but supported to a considerable extent by the Belgian Government. This information service internationally is quite unique and, despite criticisms that have been made over the years as to its administration, it provides policy-makers in all member states with a monthly data service concerning Sport for All policies and programmes.

Since 1976 a comprehensive range of European seminars has been held aimed at exposing good practice. Integrated Facilities, Sport and Television,

Sport in Areas of Special Needs, Sport and Municipal Authorities, Sport for Immigrants, Access to Water and Open Country, Low Cost Facilities, Financing of Sport, Introduction to Sport at School, Sport for Young School Leavers and Sport for the Handicapped are some of the topics discussed on which recommendations have been made for ministerial endorsement.[17] The work on the preparation of a Code for Sports Sponsorship was particularly difficult and ran into problems with the European Broadcasting Union and GAISF before matters were resolved.[18] The European Anti Doping Charter for Sport (see Appendix 13 in this volume) took much debate before it was approved and some countries had difficulties in seeing their way forward with some of the early proposals concerning legislation.[19]

Violence in sport, the Olympic Games, economic changes in sport, discrimination in sport, sport and the unemployed, sport and the elderly, have been some of the other topics occupying debate and decision and these, together with a range of courses and other practical events, have comprised additional facets to the programme of activity between 1976 and 1989. There have been many admirable texts published arising from the work of the CDDS but of these two are of major importance. The first was the work of Professor Brian Rodgers for the then CDS in 1977 entitled *Rationalizing Sports Politics — Sport in its Social Context — International Comparisons.*[20] The second was the evaluation of sport for all policies reported to the May 1984 Conference of Sports Ministers in Malta.[21] The Sports Council published in 1985 the study undertaken for them by Professor Peter McIntosh (McIntosh and Charlton, 1985).

The findings of these evaluation studies gave cause for long debate in Malta resulting in seven formal resolutions first and foremost of which was 'To improve the impact of sport for all policies by implementing more fully at national level the work of the Council of Europe in sport'.

The Minister for Sport, Neil Macfarlane, headed the British delegation, and was a party to this unanimously approved resolution; he did little on his return to promote it. In 1986 no Minister attended in Dublin, leaving it to civil servants supported by Sports Council officers. Here the principal new topic was Sport and the Environment, although drug abuse the apartheid issues featured widely.

The CDDS is unique in world sports administration and has achieved many good things in European cooperation. The network of information, personalities and co-operation continues to be impressive.

The European Sports Conference

The third of the major governmental and non-governmental forums for sport is the European Sports Conference which bridges East and West Europe bringing under one organization both Socialist and Capitalist countries. In principle this is a non-governmental Conference but because sport plays such a major role politically in the Socialist countries where it is difficult to distinguish between matters governmental and non-governmental the pretence that this is a Conference for the latter is maintained. Western European countries are mainly represented by their voluntary sports bodies; in the case of Britain by the Sports Council. Western governments have no locus and many of them, including the British Government, do not like this.

The European Conference has taken place every two years starting in Vienna in 1975. Other venues have been Copenhagen (1977), Berchtesgaden (1979), Warsaw (1981), Belgrade (1983) and Cardiff (1985), when the Sports Council was the host, Athens (1987) and Sofia (1989).

In between Conferences an International Coordinating Committee prepares for the following event with the host country taking the chair. It has worked very well indeed, and has been attended by the highest level national representatives who discuss amicably and with mutual understanding plenary papers prepared on agreed topics within the Conference theme, and most important of all it creates goodwill, friendship and many bilateral arrangements. The European Sports Conference, attended by IOC, GAISF and ICSSPE by invitation, and often by the Supreme Council for Sport in Africa as an observer, continues to be an imaginative forum for international understanding through sport. Though the ideologies differ respect is paid to those who hold different philosophies and a great degree of comprehension and tolerance has been engendered. Themes have included sports-aid for developing countries, youth sport, sport for all, sports science and inevitably drug abuse. Formal reports are not published but declarations which may be seen at the Information Centre of the Sports Council are announced at the conclusion of each Conference highlighting the decisions taken.

The European Community

A review of the European political network would not be complete without reference to the Community. Whilst there is a committee within the Community that is concerned with education, youth and sport no real attempt was mounted to do anything in sport participation as the liaison arrangements with the Council of Europe were such that these avoided overlapping. In the late seventies the European Communities Committee (Sub-Committee C) of the House of Commons took evidence from the Deputy Director-General on behalf of the Sports Council, concerning proposals to be more active in sport with high-level competition within the Community and a proposed research study into sporting jingoism.[22] Advised that these proposals would not generally find favour with the international sports federations nothing further was heard until the late eighties when proposals for 'Community Games' began to be heard. To date such an idea has failed to produce any enthusiasm and is not really welcomed by the sports bodies.

South Africa, Apartheid and 'Gleneagles'

Many international sports federations and world bodies, including the IOC, severed sporting links with South Africa in the sixties and seventies due to that country's official policy of apartheid in sport whereby people of one colour only played with people of that colour and national teams were selected only from white participants. Whether this action would ever have been taken by sport for sporting reasons will never be known, but what is clear is that political pressure from black Africa, with economic overtones, was applied around the world and with governments controlling sport in most countries the pressure for non-participation grew rapidly and was taken up by the international sports bodies. It would be cynical to believe that expediency was the sole guiding force, strong as this was, for increasingly moral stances were being adopted by countries where governments did not control sport as for example in Sweden. Britain was, and remains, close to the heart of this issue because two of the most popular games played in South Africa, rugby football and cricket, relics of the imperial past, seek competition with Britain, New Zealand and Australia. The 'D'Oliveira affaire' in 1968 put paid to international cricket between England and South Africa when Basil D'Oliveira, a former resident of South Africa classed by them as 'coloured' and selected by England for the South African tour, was forbidden entry; England cancelled the tour (see, for example, Archer and Bouillon, 1982; Hain in Hargreaves, 1982). Unofficial tours have taken place since then and one was undertaken early in 1990, led by the former England Captain Mike Gatting. Since 1988 those taking part in such unofficial tours are banned for life from playing test cricket again.

In the case of rugby, England, Scotland, Wales, Ireland, Australia and New Zealand continued to tour South Africa but increasing political pressure in the eighties persuaded them to stop.

Overseas tours by South Africa continued for a while to New Zealand despite massive demonstrations but the last tour to the British Isles took place under the captaincy of Dawie de Villiers, later to be South Africa's Ambassador to the Court of St. James, in the 1969/70 season when play often took place behind barbed wire fences and with a massive police presence; no way for young men of whatever persuasion or point of view to play sport. In 1986 New Zealand cancelled a tour to South Africa and it looked increasingly likely that no further official tours would be sanctioned in the future, although unofficial tours by players from New Zealand and Great Britain have continued.

It was against this background that the black boycott of the 1976

Montreal Olympics took place in protest at New Zealand playing rugby with South Africa the previous year. With the thinly veiled threat of a similar boycott by the black Commonwealth countries before the Commonwealth Games of 1978 at Edmonton the Heads of Commonwealth Governments met in London in early summer 1977 for one of their periodic meetings. The British Government, through Minister of Sport Denis Howell, devised the Commonwealth Statement on Apartheid in Sport known as the 'Gleneagles Agreement' as it was put together at Gleneagles Hotel during the weekend break by Heads of Governments. The terms of this (see Appendix 12 to this volume) were such that the threat to Edmonton was headed off. Paragraph 4 is the key to the Statement whereby governments agreed to take 'every practical step to discourage contact or competition by their nationals with sporting organizations, teams or sportsmen from South Africa'. It is further acknowledged that it is for 'each government to determine in accordance with its laws the methods by which it might best discharge these commitments'. Therein lies the nub of the problem ever since, for although successive governments, both Labour and Conservative, have striven manfully to do everything possible 'to discourage', including an instruction to the Sports Council not to give financial help, sports bodies are, in the final analysis, free to decide for themselves in Britain as they are voluntary organizations. In practice most have heeded the Government's urging but not always the Rugby Football Union.[23] It is often difficult for those who expect the British Government to do more to understand that in Britain the Government does not have the legal powers to withdraw passports nor prohibit citizens from leaving British shores unless they are before the courts. The presence of British teams at the Moscow Olympic Games proved this to the world as it was the wish of the Government that British teams should not compete; likewise with rugby in South Africa. These two uses of this freedom by British citizens has had a marked effect on many sports organizations in other countries, many of whom cannot conceive of a situation where such freedoms prevail. As Sir Ian Gilmour, Lord Privy Seal, said in the House of Commons in 1980,

> We have decided for instance that it would be wrong to prevent athletes from going (to Moscow) by such measures as the withdrawal of passports. (Hansard, House of Commons, 17 March 1980, col. 40)

In 1979 the Sports Council, whilst issuing a statement in support of the Gleneagles Agreement, authorized a small fact-finding mission to go to South Africa to examine progress made with multiracial sport. This really was a case of having one's cake and eating it and the decision to send a delegation met with strong governmental disapproval despite the fact that it was thought that the new Conservative administration would be more sympathetic to sport with South Africa. The delegation was led by the Chairman, Dick Jeeps, and included Basil D'Oliveira, Arthur Gold and the Vice-Chairman, Bernard Atha.

At its meeting on 1 October 1979, the Sports Council gave this delegation the following terms of reference:

To appraise the current situation on the organization of, and participation in, sport in South Africa with particular reference to major sports, and to produce a report.

The delegation addressed the following questions:

(i)   Were the constitutions of governing bodies of sport and of affiliated clubs non-racial?
(ii) Were development policies for sport non-racial?
(iii) Was quality coaching available at all levels without regard to race or colour?
(iv) Were facilities and opportunities in clubs affiliated to the governing bodies of sport genuinely non-racial, for example in changing and toilet facilities and in team selection at all levels?
(v)   Was there a complete absence of racial discrimination in the arrangements for spectators at sporting events?

The published report[24] did not come to any formal conclusions nor did it make recommendations; it was left to readers to weigh the evidence and the source of such evidence before deciding for themselves. What was clear was that two attitudes were adopted in South Africa. On the one hand there were sports bodies prepared to work within the prevailing system to achieve change, and on the other hand the view of the South African Council on Sport (SACOS) and its supporters with their slogan that 'there can be no normal sport in an abnormal society'. A clear analysis of the laws affecting social intercourse in South Africa such as The Group Areas Act (1966), the Reservation of Separate Amenities Act (1953), the Bantu Laws Amendment Act (1963) and the Liquor Act helps understanding, but the lack of conclusions based on the evidence presented and accepted made this report somewhat innocuous. After an initial flurry of interest by the media the report was 'lost' and confirmed the view of many that the whole affair was largely a non-event.

There is no doubt that the whole question of playing sport against South Africa has in the final analysis today (1990) nothing to do with sport itself. There are real sporting objections about lack of equal sporting opportunities to all sections of society, problems concerning socializing before and after games, selection of national teams and availability of facilities in equal share, but at the heart of the problem lies the fundamental moral issue of apartheid and all it stands for in philosophic and practical terms. If every sport, every facility and every team were open to all irrespective of colour, and some say this is so today, this would not solve the South African question; it remains a political and human issue of a society that divides itself by colour not being acceptable to the rest of the world. Capital has been made of the human rights issue by many who seek changes in South Africa, some with very dubious records themselves in this connection. With the economic pressure from black Africa and elsewhere there is, in reality, no possibility of official sporting links being sanctioned in the short-term.

South Africa will continue to remain outside the Olympic Movement and be excluded from membership of international federations, or if still in membership, discouraged from participation in major events for fear of wholesale boycotts. There is no doubt that political pressure has brought changes in sport but it has been action too late; the 'goal posts' have constantly been moved which confirms the widely held view that the whole issue of sport with South Africa is not about sport but about power politics.

In 1989 an ad hoc group of white South African rugby administrators met the then banned African National Congress (ANC) to discuss sport and helpful noises were made. The election of President de Klerk offers a glimmer of hope that perhaps it will not be too long before South African sportsmen and women of all colours are admitted to international sport. There is no doubt that non-white athletes of international standard are being deprived of competition but whether this fact will be taken into account no-one knows; it has sadly been shown too often that sports people are expendable in the political cauldron.

The Olympic Games — Moscow (1980), Los Angeles (1984) and Seoul (1988)

With the invasion of Afghanistan by the USSR in December 1979 the British Government joined the USA in mounting a campaign aimed at persuading national teams around the world not to compete in Moscow as a sign of disapproval and in the six months that followed the pressure on the British Olympic Association mounted daily. The USA put considerable pressure on its NATO allies and on the countries that sheltered under the American shield. There was as never before massive political involvement in the affairs of voluntary sports organizations and the USA took the IOC head-on in confrontation. Lord Killanin, President of the IOC, in his book *My Olympic Years*, tells the admirable story of his brave stand against President Carter in the fight to save the Olympic movement (pp. 212–5). Ian Wooldridge writing in the *Daily Mail* on 10 May 1983 is of the opinion that future historians 'will see that if the Olympic movement survives Killanin did more than any other human being to save it'. Whatever the point of view held, whether for or against the USA-inspired boycott, what is certain is that the assault on the IOC and the Olympic Games, assisted by Prime Minister Thatcher, was inept, uninformed and clumsy in the extreme. Killanin dismissed Carter as 'weak and naive' and summed up his view with the quite devastating statement that 'the more I look back the more it is extraordinary that a vast country like the USA could not produce a greater leader or statesman' (p. 215). President Carter sent his special emissary, a Mr. Lloyd Cutler, to meet Lord Killanin in Dublin and British Government ministers and others in London. His arrogance was only equalled by his ignorance of the Olympic set-up and his mission failed hopelessly. President Carter and Mrs. Thatcher lost in Britain and they lost disastrously, for not only did the majority of British people resent young athletes being pushed around by politicians, but they lost because in the final analysis they, and others like them in other countries, were too afraid to threaten sharp retaliation and too hypocritical to cut off trade and commercial links, preferring young men and women athletes to be the instrument of their displeasure.[25]

The British Government favoured 'alternative games' and even offered to host some events at venues in Britain including badminton which was thought by one Front Bench speaker for the Government to be an Olympic sport! The Prime Minister and Foreign Office ministers led the assault on the Olympic Movement leaving the Minister for Sport, the wholly admirable Hector Monro, to deal with the bits and pieces. At no time did the Government consult the Sports Council on any matters of principle or detail and senior officers there squirmed with embarrassment at the many gaffes and displays of ignorance publicly aired. Whatever personal points of view were held it was not edifying for a British Prime Minister and senior ministers to be seen to be so woefully lacking in adequate briefing. At no time would the Prime Minister listen carefully and quietly to those who knew and in her meetings with the BOA and sports bodies she lectured rather than listened. Friends in the West German and French ministries responsible for sport were appalled privately at the strident attitude adopted and on a number of occasions in Strasbourg asked the Deputy-Director what had happened to the subtlety in diplomacy associated with the British. The point was of course that it was out of the hands of the diplomats and in the hands of the politicians.

John Coghlan was asked by the Chairman of the Sports Council to prepare evidence for him to give to the Foreign Affairs Committee of the House of Commons in early spring 1980. This task was completed, mindful that the Sports Council had to 'have regard to any general statements on the policy of our government that may from time to time be issued ...' (see Appendix 1, paragraph 3 in this volume). Accordingly the Sports Council could not therefore publicly oppose the Government's view, even if it had wanted to do so, and no canvass was taken. Some points of principle and detail were presented.[26]

During the first six months of 1980 many questions were put to ministers and mini-debates took place both in the House of Commons and the House of Lords.[27] Even when the USA resumed grain shipments to the

USSR and the Common Market did likewise with the butter mountain, there was no moving the Prime Minister as she reaffirmed in a Parliamentary answer on 6 May. On 16 April Mr. Douglas Hurd, Minister of State at the Foreign Office, told Parliament 'that about thirty countries' favoured a boycott, and in a further statement on 1 May this had risen to thirty-seven. Meanwhile Sir Denis Follows, Chairman of the BOA, was leading the fight on behalf of the sports movement and taking the action needed to ensure public financial support for the Olympic Appeal which faltered when some businesses and institutions followed the Government's line and withdrew their support.

On 17 March a full debate took place in the House of Commons on the Government's motion

> That this House condemns the Soviet invasion of Afghanistan and believes that Great Britain should not take part in the Olympic Games in Moscow. (Hansard, House of Commons, Vol. 981, No. 139, 17 March 1980, Cols. 31–168)

Sir Ian Gilmour, the Lord Privy Seal, led for the Government whilst Mr. Peter Shore replied for the Opposition. Shore's stance was equally opposed to the USSR invasion of Afghanistan but not in favour of a British boycott of the Games but rather an avoidance of what he called 'the more offensive ceremonies which are built into but are not crucial to the Games themselves'.

The Opposition amendment read as follows:

> That this House condemns the invasion of Afghanistan and calls upon the Soviet Government to withdraw immediately in the interests of world peace and détente in Europe; believes that an effective response on the Olympics as in the economic, trading, and political fields can only be achieved by securing substantial common agreements among the Governments and sporting authorities of Western Europe, the USA and elsewhere; regrets the Government's failure to consult properly with the sporting bodies in this country; and asserts the right of individual citizens at the end of the day to make their own decisions.

The debate lasted from 3.43 p.m. until the House divided at 10.00 p.m. when the Government defeated the Opposition Amendment by 308 votes to 188 and then went on to win their own motion by 315 votes to 147. The debate was largely repetitive and lacking in knowledge and substance apart from some notable informed contributions by, on the Conservative side, Mr. Geoffrey Rippon, Mr. Terence Higgins, Sir Frederick Bennett and Mr. Winston Churchill and on the Labour side Mr. Denis Howell, Mr. L.R.

Fletcher, Mr. James Wellbeloved and Mr. Robert Hughes. The winding-up speech for the Government by Mr. Michael Heseltine was lucid, constructive and fair, (*ibid*, Cols. 149–160) but well before 10.00 p.m. the debate had declined into interventions and a general mix-up with sport in South Africa.

The Government had criticisms from their own supporters, notably the former international athlete Terence Higgins, who for many summed up the situation admirably when, in general support of a boycott, he urged that trade and finance should be weapons of disapproval and not just athletes. (*ibid*, 85–90) In *The Times* on the day of the debate headlines referred to 'Ministers fear Tory revolt in Olympic debate' and details of a National Opinion Poll showed that two-thirds of the British public thought that the Games should go ahead and three in four believed that the Olympic Team should go to Moscow. Some 58 per cent thought President Carter and Mrs. Thatcher had made a mistake in calling for a boycott. President Carter's action, a blow against the Soviets, had to be seen in the context of the then as yet unresolved American hostage drama in Iran[28] and the forthcoming American election; a tough stand on something, anything, would win votes it was thought and the tragedy in Iran was losing them.

In the following months pressure was maintained on the BOA and the argument rumbled on. In the eventuality seventeen national federations decided to go and four Hockey, Shooting, Equestrianism and Yachting decided not to go to Moscow. President Carter squeezed the United States Olympic Committee where it hurt most, in the financial area, and the Committee capitulated, as did West Germany where the words 'West Berlin' were gently murmured, but at least the West German Olympic Committee had a televised debate and arrived at their decision democratically. The East Germans watched the debate from behind the Berlin Wall.

At a meeting in Tblisi in the USSR a week before the Olympic Games of 1980 Sergei Pavlov, the then Chairman of the USSR Committee for Physical Culture and Sport, expressed his great admiration for the stand Denis Follows had taken and asked with some concern what would become of him after the Olympic Games. The vision of the intrepid Chairman of the British Olympic Association incarcerated in the Tower of London floated deliciously before the mind as the reply indicated that he would continue to fight for the freedom of sport from base political manoeuvring. To Sergei's credit he batted not an eyelid at this reply and said how much he was looking forward to seeing him in Moscow next week. Perhaps this little cameo said something eloquent and profound about society and sport in Britain in 1980.

The Olympic Games were held; they were a great success and Great Britain did well. The Soviets stayed in Afghanistan until 1988; Carter was swept from power and the seeds were sown for the Soviet bloc tit-for-tat at Los Angeles four years later. British sportsmen and women who competed in Moscow were absent from the New Year's Honours List of 1981 and no Government reception was offered to the returning team although amazingly enough some officials at No. 10 did make enquiries as to precedent in this matter. Nothing in British sport has ever been quite the same since 1980. Sport was split into one large camp and one small camp and it was now clearly seen that government and raw politics were into sport with a vengeance; sport was, and remains today, an instrument of HM Government's policy, foreign and domestic, despite denials to the contrary.[29]

When four years later, after many protestations that they respected the Olympic Charter, the USSR and many of their Socialist allies boycotted the Los Angeles Olympic Games those close to the scene were not at all surprised. The refusal of visas by the USA State Department for certain Soviet officials exacerbated matters as did lurid pictures on television showing what lunatic fringe elements in California proposed to do when Communist teams arrived. Genuinely the Socialist countries did not like the commercial approach to the Games by the Organizing Committee; that is their philosophy and they let it be known well beforehand. When all was said and done, after the political debacle of Moscow by the USA, there was never in reality any chance that the USSR would be present in Los Angeles although they denied publicly that this was the case. To this day the public position of the USSR remains that it was lack of security and commercialism that triggered off their absence, and although they were loyally joined by most of their friends it is now generally accepted that the Soviet decision caused many of these friends dismay and consternation. The delay of a couple of days before the German Democratic Republic joined the boycott was evidence of their being taken unawares.

The boycotting nations, as in 1980, continued to send their officials and representatives to the many conferences and meetings of the international sports bodies that traditionally take place before and during the Olympic Games; they were not excluded by their governments as they were concerned with political power-bases. The Games were held; they were a great success and the Americans were impeccable hosts. Not surprisingly there were no security problems, the Games made a huge surplus, Britain did well and everyone who attended appeared to enjoy the whole affair.

Within months of Los Angeles the very astute President of the IOC, Juan Samaranch, moved to forestall, as far as he was able, possible boycott problems with Seoul in 1988. Samaranch, backed by the IOC at the 99th Session in Lausanne, declared that:

(i) The IOC, international federations and National Olympic Committees are united in shared ideals.
(ii) It is the duty of National Olympic Committees to ensure that athletes compete.
(iii) Athletes should not be punished by boycotts and again by further exclusions.

(iv)   True motivation of boycotts will be identified and the representatives of such countries will be excluded from the Games.

(v)   The IOC, International Federations and National Olympic Committees fully support the next Games in Calgary (winter) and
Seoul (summer).[30]

This was a masterly tactical move which in effect meant that if a country
boycotted the Games then their officials were excluded from the Games and
forfeited their opportunities for attending the usual general assemblies and
other meetings of the international federations thus squeezing them out of
power-bases for the next four years.

If these conditions had been in force prior to 1980 the USA and its
allies would have ceded sports political power if they had persisted with
their boycott, and as such power is in reality international political power far
beyond the arena and the running track, that may well have been too heavy
a price to pay. The same would have applied in 1984 to the USSR and its
friends.

The Winter Games in Calgary and the Summer Games in Seoul passed
off without any major political turmoil. Calgary was magnificently equipped
and the only problem of any size was the capriciousness of the snowfall that
caused some postponements. In the case of Seoul the sports world held its
breath as North Korea sabre-rattled and Cuba declined the invitation
to attend, as did Ethiopia, Nicaragua, Madagascar and the Seychelles, not
all for political reasons. The usual Olympic Scientific Congress, under
the patronage of the IOC and ICSSPE, was held at Cheonan some ninety
kilometres south of Seoul and the Olympic Games opened in magnificent
style in glorious weather with the highest number ever of countries participating. The threatened Korean student disruption did not happen and there
were no political incidents to mar the Olympic festival. By popular acclaim
the Games were superbly organized and the provisional profit of around
£2m was designated to be used to promote youth sport in South Korea, after
the IOC had taken its share to be split between the National Olympic
Committees of those attending, the International Federations and itself
according to the accepted formula. Great Britain did well with twenty-four
medals. As 1990 dawned all eyes and thoughts were turned to Albertville
(France) and Barcelona, the sites for the Winter and Summer Olympic
Games of 1992 respectively.

Today Britain has HRH the Princess Royal as President of the BOA
and Sir Arthur Gold as Chairman; the Olympic movement in Britain is safe
in their hands and they are worthy successors to the brave Sir Denis Follows
who bore the intense heat of Cabinet pressure in 1980, survived, triumphed
and ensured that the Olympic movement in Britain remained truly free of
politics and in the experienced hands of the national governing bodies of
sport.

Notes

1 For example the Federal Republic of Germany grants a portion of the Federal Lottery to the DSB; it does not control specifically what it does with this money; likewise in Holland, Norway and Sweden to a very considerable extent. In the USA the Federal Government does not direct money to sport. In Western Europe generally the state, through the municipal authorities, invests heavily in sports facilities for public use but has no executive control over the national governing bodies of sport.

2 Olympic Charter (1982) chapter 11, Juridicial status, objects and powers.

3 Since this date the IOC has not had a Director as such because the President has been an executive President dealing directly with the matters that Monique Berlioux dealt with hitherto. In many respects Juan Samaranch has been both 'Chairman and Managing Director'.

4 Grant aid towards accommodation costs. See Sports Council Annual Report 1986–87, p. 29, Col. 1.

5 Resolution 1.153 adopted by General Conference of Member States.

6 The Conference Proceedings are always published by the local Congress Organizing Committee.

7 The International Charter was approved at the XXth Session of the General Conference of UNESCO on 21 November 1978.

8 In the mid-eighties the UK and USA withdrew from UNESCO dissatisfied with some of its political programmes and the bureaucracy.

9 See General Report of the Interim Intergovernmental Committee for Physical Education and Sport 1977–78, pp. 8–9, UNESCO.

10 Coghlan, J.F. *The Reduction of Current Disparities between Developed and Developing Countries in the Field of Sport and Physical Education. A Comparative Study*; and (1990) *A Programme for Action*, prepared by ICSSPE for UNESCO, published by ICSSPE.

11 See Conference Final Report: List of Recommendations, p. 19; details, pp. 20–41.

12 Resolution (76) 41 of the Committee of Ministers — 'Principles for a Policy of Sport for All' defined by the Conference of European Ministers responsible for Sport in Brussels (1975) under the title of the *European Sport for All Charter*, Text and Background, Council of Europe, Strasbourg, 1977.

13 A summary of the Resolutions of the Conference of Ministers. See 'Texts adopted at meetings of the European Ministers for Sport 1975–86', Council of Europe, 1988.

14 *ibid*; *European Sport for All Charter*, text and background, Council of Europe, Strasbourg, 1977.

15 There are in 1989 many international committees promoting 'Sport for All.' For example: (i) Fédération Internationale 'Sport pour Tous'; (ii) ICSSPE's Committee 'Sport and Leisure'.

16 Reports of all Ministerial Conferences are available to be seen at the Information Centre of the Sports Council in London. Copies may be obtained from the CDDS at the Council of Europe, Strasbourg.

17 Reports on all Council of Europe Seminars are held by the Information Centre at the Sports Council in London; copies are also available from Strasbourg.

The CDDS publishes an Annual Report which summarizes the work of the year and indicates which topics have been passed on for 'ministerial endorsement', for example, 'The adoption on 18 April 1988 by the Committee of Ministers of Recommendation No. R (88) 8 on Sport for All: Older Persons'.

18 Copies, together with an Explanatory Memorandum, published in 1985, are

available from HM Stationery Office, Agency Section, Room 008, Publications Centre, 51 Nine Elms Lane, London, SW8 5DR.

19 For example early suggestions that governments should ban the use of certain drugs. This proposal had to be softened (see 1.1 of the Charter).

20 Ref. CCC/DC (77) 11–E, Committee on Sport, Strasbourg, 1977.

21 CDDS, DS-SR (84) 1 is the text based on sixteen national evaluation reports.

22 Minutes of Evidence taken before the European Communities Committee (Sub-Section C) p. 60.

23 To date the RFU has agreed not to tour South Africa officially but they do pass on to players invitations for them to play there. They do not forbid but they do discourage.

24 *Sport in South Africa, Report of the Sports Council's Fact-Finding delegation* January 1980.

25 Lord Killanin in *My Olympic Years* (pp. 196–197) confirms the view that HRH Prince Philip, in his capacity as President of the International Equestrian Federation, assisted in the drafting of a statement on behalf of all the Olympic International Federations announced by Thomas Keller, the President of GAISF, confirming that they would all be present in Moscow. The interpretation put on this is that Prince Philip was opposed to the view held by the Prime Minister and the British Government.

26 See appendix 14 *Participation in the Summer 1980 Olympiad*, extracts from a paper presented by the Sports Council to the Foreign Affairs Committee of the House of Commons, February 1980.

27 For example: House of Lords — 31 January 1980, Hansard Cols. 979–983; 6 March 1980, Hansard Cols. 389–394; House of Commons — 17 March 1980, Hansard Cols. 31–168; 19 March 1980, Hansard Cols. 415–420; 27 March 1980, Hansard Cols. 1788–1798; written answers — 4 July 1980; oral answers – 6 March 1980 and 2 July 1980.

28 In Iran the Fundamentalist Government was holding close on 100 diplomats of the USA after students had stormed their Embassy. This was of course nothing to do with the Olympics or the USSR but the American electorate were demanding international action by the President. Powerless to do anything positive could the President deflect criticism by 'getting tough' with the Communist enemy over the Olympics and sway matters more his way?

29 'The Government have the Sports Council as their agency to fulfil many objectives.... As my Department's agency I ask the Council to undertake particular tasks or policies' (Macfarlane, Hansard, House of Commons, 9 July 1984, Col. 744).

30 A summary of the declarations. For background see *The Guardian* report by John Rodda on the steps that were agreed.

Section V
The Future

Chapter 14

. . . **Into the 1990s**

Wolfenden in 1960 saw very clearly the aspirations of indivduals to take part in sport when he and his Committee argued that man must not only work but must play. This view has been reflected by many sociologists over the last thirty years, some of whom go further and believe that sport has a considerable influence both on society as a whole and on social relationships. In simple terms sport not only reflects the society in which we live, its attitudes, its values, its ethos, but it also helps condition it.

The development of sport in Britain since the earliest days has reflected the changing face of British society and the period since the late fifties has certainly been no exception. At élite level the growth of professionalism, commercialism and competitive attitudes in sport has mirrored life beyond the track, pool or stadium. The ugly side of this movement represented by drug abuse, violence on the terraces, cheating and the win-at-all-costs philosophy is not very far removed from the ethics sometimes displayed in commerce, the City and in business. Should society therefore be surprised when sport shows its darker side and can the nation expect it to be otherwise? The answers to these questions are complex and often puzzling but to those who believe that sport should continue to be about fair play, the right sense of competition and respect for the laws of the game the answers to these questions are very simple indeed; sport has moral and ethical values which make contributions to the order of society and the international federations and national governing bodies of sport have responsibilities to this end.

These reponsibilties often pose a dilemma for the sports bodies who have to move with the times and yet not be seen to be conceding to contemporary changes in values at every point. Organized sport is conservative, cautious, often reactionary, suspicious of change, and perhaps rightly so if it wishes to retain its ethos, style and traditions. And yet within these very virtues can lie the seeds of failure at the highest levels if national and international federations fail to see where innovation, modernization, and developments are required to keep pace with the changing world. With the increasing pressure of international competition the British sports administrators and coaches have the difficult job of reconciling the task of preparing athletes for the sternest international challenge requiring positive attitudes towards participation, scientific back-up and singleness of purpose, often alien to the traditional concept of playing sport on which most Britons have been reared, with a need to maintain a sense of proportion, balance and acceptability in all things. Such a focus begs the question as to whether sport at the very highest level is in fact sport at all in its purest form or simply show business and entertainment carried on in a sports format. Are the cricket Test matches, the rugby international matches, the Football League competition the Wimbledon Tennis Championships, even the Olympic Games, merely 'entertainment' for the spectator, the television viewer and the media generally, or are they still truly valid manifestations of sport at the pinnacle played by those with exceptional talent? Is the 'sport' content of the 'entertainment' still important to the competitor or is it today simply the money that comes with success that is most important of all? These are major issues of concern for society or at least for those who see that sport has a significant contribution to make within society.

Whilst sport at élite level raises many powerful and worrying questions, sport for the masses, sport for all, poses no such philosophical issues and the last twenty years have seen this social phenomenon arise, grow and develop nationally and world wide. Starting in Western Europe the *Sport for All* movement captured the spirit and feel of the time and found echoes in the hearts, minds and bodies of men and women of every race, colour and ideology irrespective of standard of performance. Sport for fun, for health, for social purposes is within the historical tradition of sport in Britain and today it is part of the life-style for a greater proportion of citizens than it was twenty-five years ago.

The growth of facilities, opportunity and investment in the sports infrastructure in Britain has increasingly offered more options to more people during the last thirty years. With increased pressure, particularly on public authorities to cut expenditure, and an underlying belief by the present Government that provision for sport is not an area in which they should be much involved, question marks appear for the nineties against further expansion in the public sector unless there is a radical change of direction. The spectre of long-term mass unemployment during much of the 1980s has been frighteningly real and the social wilderness of the inner cities has already created its own new social problems. Sport and the opportunity to participate in sport and recreation activities cannot solve the problems of the underprivileged and the deprived but they can make a contribution to a total package of measures if the political will exists to create such packages. If provision for sport is a social service, and Wolfenden, Cobham and Howell have said it is so in their Reports and White Papers, then nothing short of a major effort sponsored by government nationally and locally will suffice to remedy the deficiencies that exist in Britain today. Mrs. Thatcher's Government would certainly not subscribe to this thesis; will those who follow her, who do subscribe when not in office, have the will and determination to act when and if they take on the mantle of government? Local government has responded nobly over the years but central government of every complexion has failed to resource adequately the Sports Council to carry out the tasks laid down for it in the Royal Charter. The governing bodies of sport are in 1989 stronger administratively and financially than they were in 1965 but the ravages of inflation have not assisted. If they wish to retain their independence wholly and absolutely they must do more to stand on their own feet and not be so reliant on public funding from the Sports Council.

The Sports Council has still to extricate itself entirely from the all-pervading and cloying embrace of government where it resided for much of the time when Neil Macfarlane was the Minister for Sport and Dick Jeeps was the Chairman of the Sports Council. John Smith made a noble start with this and Peter Yarranton is a big enough man in every way to continue the process. The current Minister for Sport, Colin Moynihan, does not have such an egocentric view of his position in the national sporting scene as did the now Sir Neil Macfarlane, but how far is Moynihan his own political master?

The CCPR, attacked by a House of Commons Select Committee in February 1986 which queried its very existence saying 'We see no significant role for the CCPR other than to represent the collective view of governing bodies', has continued to flourish, ignoring the arrogant view of a Committee, none of whose members were connected with sport. As 1989 drew to a close the relationship between the CCPR and the Sports Council appeared to those near to the scene to be in the best shape since 1972; perhaps at last an agreed modus operandi has been arrived at.

The level of political involvement in sport today is considerable. At local government level involvement has been at an encouraging pace and the proliferation of development officers is testimony to the acceptance of a *Sport for All* policy. Leisure, recreation, amenity, are words commonly used in the town halls of Great Britain and the services they imply are talked of in the same way as education, housing and social services. The success of the Regional Councils for Sport and Recreation, from the day they were established as Regional Sports Councils in 1965, has been enormous due not only to the professionalism and drive of the Regional Directors of the Sports Council who have serviced them but to the determination of those who have led municipal authorities and driven through policies in accord with what these Regional Councils stand for. Political involvement by all local parties has been intense and co-operation between them has usually been the norm. As John Smith, the then Chairman of the Sports Council, said in his Foreword to *Sport in the Community — Into the 90s*.

In the last twenty years the public sector primarily through local authority support, has been absolutely vital in extending sporting opportunities ... the public sector undertakes two unique tasks: the first is providing sport for those materially disadvantaged: the second is coordinating private, voluntary and public actions on behalf of the whole community with adequate accountability.

There is, however, a range of grave problems that confront sport as the nineties unfold. Violence associated with football appears to be endemic in society and has long ceased to be confined to Great Britain. The British Government is tackling this 'disease' with considerable determination nationally and internationally, and as 1989 ended the way forward was seen to be through the identity card scheme enshrined in the Football Spectators Bill. However, the new decade was barely a month old when the full horror of the Hillsborough football disaster, when on 15 April 1989 ninety-five spectators (supporters of Liverpool Football Club) were crushed to death during the FA Cup Semi-Final with Nottingham Forest, was again brought vividly to the attention of HM Government and the nation with the publication of Lord Justice Taylor's official report *The Hillsborough Stadium Disaster* (Home Office Cmnd 962). This added thirty-three new recommendations to the forty-three made in his interim report of August 1989. The report was both scathing and perceptive and the Government announced immediately its acceptance of all the recommendations (see Appendix 16 to this volume). The main recommendations may be summarized as follows:

(a) English 1st and 2nd Division clubs to be all-seated by August 1994 and 3rd and 4th Division clubs by August 1999. This situation to be arrived at progressively each year. Standing accommodation to be reduced by 20 per cent in the case of 1st and 2nd Division clubs annually and by 10 per cent annually for the others.

(b) All spikes to be removed from fences which should be no higher than 2.2 metres. Fences to have patrolled emergency gates.

(c) The identity card scheme to be shelved.

(d) Ticket-touting, missile throwing and the chanting of obscene or racial abuse to be outlawed along with pitch invasions by spectators.

(e) Better police communications within the football grounds to be organized.

(f) Better first-aid and medical facilities to be made available with doctors either at the ground or on call depending on the size of crowd anticipated.

(g) A system of electronic tagging to be introduced to keep convicted hooligans away from the grounds.

In presenting his report Lord Justice Taylor said that this was the ninth official report covering ground safety and control at football grounds and went on to say that:

It seems astounding that ninety-five people could die from over-crowding before the eyes of those controlling the event.

In commenting on the laissez-faire attitude that had prevailed hitherto in clubs he continued:

I hope I have made it clear that the years of patching up grounds, of having periodic disasters and narrowly avoiding many others by muddling through on a wing and a prayer must be over. A totally new approach across the whole field of football requires higher standards both in bricks and mortar and in human relationships.

After describing the ills of the game Taylor detailed the measures that he believed could create a brighter future for football. Vision and imagination were needed, he said, to achieve a new ethos for the game with upgraded grounds, modern accommodation, better facilities and generally a more welcoming attitude by those running clubs. He urged more consultation with supporters and called for real positive leadership.

The all-seating recommendation did not appeal to all and in particular to those who liked the camaraderie and atmosphere of the terraces; they spoke of the traditional way to watch football ignoring the appalling evidence of what this had contributed to. Taylor, however, was quite firm:

There is no panacea that will achieve total safety and cure all problems of behaviour and crowd control. But I am satisfied that seating does more to achieve these objectives than any other single measure.

The Football Association, for many the body that had failed over many years to grapple with the problems detailed in Taylor's report, accepted the findings when Graham Kelly, the Chief Executive, commented:

It's excellent. It addresses the major issues affecting for the forsee-able future admirably.

In welcoming the Report the Home Secretary, David Waddington, in a speech to the House of Commons on 29 January 1990, the date of publication, demanded new leadership from football:

The clubs which have not faced up to their responsibility now have the final opportunity to do so and if they don't act now the public will not forgive them.

The next day, to the relief of very many, including the clubs, the police and spectators, the Government announced that it would not be proceeding with the controversial identity card scheme. The Home Secretary in the Commons said:

> In the light of that advice in the Report the Government has decided not to proceed with the proposed scheme. However work will continue ... in case the Government had to return to the matter should the problem of hooliganism not be defeated by the alternative strategy proposed in the Report.

The Shadow Home Secretary, Roy Hattersley, whilst welcoming the Report, criticized the all-seating recommendation and believed that public funds should help finance the very many stadium developments that would now be required. This view was totally unacceptable to the Government who have consistently seen that this as a football responsibility, an argument not accepted by those who have seen it largely as a problem of law and order and therefore of government.

In a leading article in *The Times* of 30 January the writer was of the view that:

> Lord Justice Taylor's final report on the Hillsborough Stadium disaster is a social document of the first importance ... Party opinion on how the money is to be found will divide fairly predictably. Mr. Hattersley seems to see football as a sort of extension of the National Health Service into which the Government has some ill-defined moral duty to pour substantial sums of public money. The Home Secretary made it quite clear in the Commons yesterday that he takes a rather different view. The Government's concern is with public safety and public order.

Faced with having to spend very large sums of money in the years ahead football is now assessing the situation. An initial and immediate offer of £50m over ten years by the football pool companies Vernons, Littlewoods and Zetters, via the Football Trust, to help with the funding was a generous gesture of support and was welcomed.

The report of Lord Justice Taylor will be an issue before Government and sport during the next decade and well into the twenty-first century. Its repercussions for crowd safety control extend beyond football and already Wimbledon, Twickenham, Murrayfield and the National Stadium in Cardiff are reviewing their arrangements.

Drug abuse mars the sporting scene, and whilst no concession has been made in this matter by the sports authorities, rather the reverse, the question as to how far governments will go to assist with legislation is still very much an open question internationally. As 1989 ended all the indicators pointed to the British Government about to take early action to extend the 1971

Misuse of Drugs Act to make possession of steroids by the public a criminal offence; will others follow suit?

The growth of commercialism in sport during the past thirty years has been spectacular and has contributed greatly to the financial well-being of many governing bodies of sport and to individual sportsmen and women. However within this phenomenon lurks the risk that sport could be diverted into channels that would end with control passing into the hands of television companies, entrepreneurs and agents unless those who have control have a clear vision of where the interests of their sport lie now, and would wish to lie by the turn of the century. It will require wisdom and tenacity by those with the responsibility to give to sponsors what they rightly require in return for their investment while retaining control and the integrity of their sport.

The privatization of the water industry, as 1989 came to a close, opened up the question as to whether access to reservoirs, gathering grounds and rivers for watersports will, in the future, be quite as it has been hitherto. Reassuring sounds have been made with the Code of Practice on Conservation, Access and Recreation as the Government has been aware of concern from the outset; it remains to be seen whether the battle for access, fought for so hard in the sixties and seventies, has to be fought again or whether being named with the Nature Conservancy Council and the Countryside Commission as Consultees in the Water Bill will suffice for the Sports Council to protect the interests of water sports and water recreation.

For some years the physical education profession has been concerned with the pressure on school timetables that has acted against the best interests of their subject, and the Physical Education Association of Great Britain and Northern Ireland has been in the van on this issue. Whilst physical education is within the new National Curriculum that is now taking shape, and which will come into force in the nineties, concern is very real that once again the values of a sound physical education throughout primary and secondary education are not yet fully understood. The governing bodies of what are generally known as the 'traditional games', football, rugby and cricket, continue to be alarmed that these games are not being taught by staff who were hitherto prepared to give their time, or because sufficient time is not allotted by schools, or because other games such as basketball, volleyball or badminton have taken over. Many studies, reports and conferences have been held on this topic which have both clarified and confused the issue. What is clear is that less sport is being taught in schools to both sexes than before and that there are less inter-school matches. What is also clear is that more young people of school age belong to the very many more local sports clubs that now exist.

The opening up of municipal leisure services to competitive tendering at the behest of the Government will destroy the status quo; it is intended to. Will this act of political faith be of benefit to sport or will it deny to the less privileged the opportunities that have been won over the last thirty years? It is true that the argument that was valid ten years ago must be valid today is self-deluding as policy is made to suit prevailing conditions and nothing is sacrosanct; equally it must be madness to abandon what has stood the test of time on the basis of a political article of faith. What is being seen in Great Britain today is sport being subjected more and more to the market-place, to the notion of 'value for money', to the concept that if you want it you must pay for it, and if you cannot pay the market rate you cannot have it. This may well be sound in the purchase of a car, a washing-machine or an expensive holiday but is it so if sport for all is a national policy? Such a philosophy takes no account of the 'social wage', the value society as a whole places on something intended to be of value to all. Happily the Sports Council has indicated that it will not be deflected from its course, from its terms of reference in the Royal Charter which make very clear the Council's duty:

> To develop and improve the knowledge and practice of sport and physical recreation in the interests of social welfare and the enjoyment of leisure among the public at large in Great Britain ... (see Appendix 1)

In 1989 Peter Yarranton, the Chairman of the Sports Council, writing in the Foreword of his first Annual Report concluded by saying:

> The main concern of most people, however, is that access to sport should be readily available and affordable. This remains the primary aim of the Council. The Council will continue to provide a strong lead to those countless people in the community who work tirelessly to provide their fellow citizens with the opportunity to share in the satisfaction, sense of personal achievement and physical well-being that sport can offer.

This too is an act of faith, a statement of principle that all who are concerned with sport can understand and relate to. For the Sports Council to achieve its aims it depends upon the effectiveness of its relationships with an ever-increasing range of organizations and interests. Principally these are local authorities, governing bodies of sport, the CCPR, BOA, SAF, NCF and the private sector, In partnership with these organizations and interests the Council 'has a crucial role in defining and securing a consensus on the overall strategic direction of British sport' (Annual Report 1988/89); this it is well equipped to do in the nineties with its sound leadership and talented professional staff so long as the Government allows it to do so.

The decline in British influence in international sports affairs during the latter half of the eighties has been arrested with the establishment of the British International Sports Committee representative of the BOA, CCPR and the Sports Council. From now onwards Great Britain can be expected to begin to reassert its former traditional role in international affairs. A good start was made in 1989 with the announcement that the number of British office holders in International Sports Federations was the highest on record. As the next decade beckons initiatives to assist developing countries and attract major sports events to Britain were underway, spearheaded by the World Student Games in 1991 and the Manchester bid for the Summer Olympic Games of 1996; action at both ends of the spectrum. In 1960 the final chapter (5) of the Wolfenden Report made clear that what was needed was a 'new deal for sport':

> ... We are convinced that what is needed in this whole field is a new deal. It is not simply a matter of money, though that comes into it. It is not simply a matter of administration though that comes into it too. Certainly it is not a matter of simply creating enthusiasm. There is plenty of enthusiasm and interest; but there is also plenty of frustration, dissatisfaction and, in some parts of the field, disillusion. It is clear to us that some way must be found of fostering the interest and dispelling the dissatisfaction so that more and more people may be able to enjoy the recreative benefits of sport, games and outdoor activities.

Has that new deal been provided? Yes, to some considerable extent and British society is the richer for it, although there are those who have not yet been touched by it. The struggle now is to hold on to what has been achieved by all the 'enthusiasm' that Wolfenden spoke of and build successfully on this. It will not be easy, it never has been, but British sport is served by many able and determined men and women, supported by countless thousands of volunteers, worthy successors to those who have gone before and led the charge.

Thirty years ago the British Government was only marginally concerned with sport and this very indirectly; today sport and British politics are inextricably linked. The question in 1960 was, and remains so to this day, not whether sport and politics should be linked, that is what Wolfenden wanted, but in what way should they be linked? That is an argument that will continue into the nineties as minister succeeds minister and government succeeds government. In 1990 does the British sports movement have a clear and united view of the role of government in its affairs or does it speak as so often in the past with many voices? If British sport is not to be dominated and manipulated by politics in the next decade then it must very soon make it clear as to where it stands. Sir Denis Follows did this so nobly in 1980, who will do it in 1990, in 1995 and the year 2000, or shall we see sport more and more sucked into the Whitehall machine to serve the party political policies of the day?

Appendices

Appendix 1

The Royal Charter

ELIZABETH THE SECOND
by the Grace of God of the United Kingdom of Great Britain and
Northern Ireland of Our other Realms and Territories Queen
Head of the Commonwealth, Defender of the Faith:
TO ALL TO WHOM THESE PRESENTS SHALL COME, GREETING!

WHEREAS matters relating to sport and physical recreation are the concern of Departments of Our Government:

AND WHEREAS it has been represented unto Us that there should be established an independent Sports Council with the objects of fostering the knowledge and practice of sport and physical recreation among the public at large and the provision of facilities therefor, building upon the work in this field of the Central Council of Physical Recreation and others:

AND WHEREAS it has been represented unto Us that for the purpose of carrying out the said objects and with a view to facilitating the holding of and dealing with property and the making of gifts and bequests in aid of the said objects it is expedient that the said Council should be incorporated:

AND WHEREAS We having taken the said representations into Our Royal Consideration are minded to grant a Charter containing such provisions as seem to Us right and suitable:

NOW THEREFORE KNOW YE that We by virtue of Our Prerogative Royal and of Our especial grace, certain knowledge and mere motion have willed and ordained and by these Presents do for Us, Our Heirs and Successors will and ordain as follows:

1 (1) The persons who shall in accordance with the provisions of this Our Charter be the Chairman and other members for the time being of the Sports Council are hereby constituted and from henceforth for ever shall be one Body Corporate under the name of 'The Sports Council' (hereinafter referred to as 'the Council').

   (2) The Council shall have perpetual succession and a Common Seal, with power to break, alter and make anew the said Seal from time to time as its

will and pleasure and by its name shall and may sue and be sued in all courts and in all manner of action and suits, and shall have power to enter into contracts, to acquire, hold and dispose of property of any kind, to accept trusts and generally to do all matters and things incidental or appertaining to a Body Corporate.

2   In furtherance of its objects the Council shall have the following powers:

(a)   to develop and improve the knowledge and practice of sport and physical recreation in the interests of social welfare and the enjoyment of leisure among the public at large in Great Britain, and to encourage the attainment of high standards in conjunction with the governing bodies of sport and physical recreation;

(b)   to foster, support or undertake provision of facilities for sport and physical recreation;

(c)   to carry out itself, or to encourage and support other persons or bodies in carrying out, research and studies into matters concerning sport and physical recreation; and to disseminate knowledge and advice on these matters;

(d)   to collaborate with foreign and international bodies in the furtherance of the foregoing or to secure the benefit of relevant experience abroad;

(e)   to make grants or loans upon and subject to such conditions and otherwise as the Council shall deem fit in the furtherance of the foregoing provided always and notwithstanding the foregoing that the Council shall attach to any loan made by it such conditions as may be prescribed from time to time by the Lords Commissioners of Our Treasury;

(f)   to carry on any other activity for the benefit of sport and physical recreation;

(g)   to advise, co-operate with or assist Departments of Our Government, local authorities, the Scottish Sports Council, the Sports Council for Wales, and other bodies, on any matters concerned whether directly or indirectly with the foregoing;

(h)   to establish and/or act as trustee of any charity the objects of which are in accord with any of the Council's objects.

3   The Council in the exercise of its functions shall have regard to any general statements on the policy of Our Government that may from time to time be issued to it by Our Secretary of State.

4   In the event of any dispute arising between the Council and the Scottish Sports Council and/or, the Sports Council for Wales as to which of them shall deal with any matter in pursuance of powers and functions and duties conferred on each respectively by Our Charters then the same shall be determined by Our Secretary of State jointly with Our Secretary of State for Scotland and/or Our Secretary of State for Wales as is appropriate.

5   All moneys and property howsoever received by the Council including any moneys voted by Parliament shall be applied solely towards the promotion of the objects of the Council and no portion thereof shall be paid or transferred directly or indirectly by way of dividend, bonus or otherwise howsoever by way of profit, to the members of the Council: provided that nothing herein shall

prevent the reimbursement of expenses incurred by such members in the performance of their duties as provided in Article 7 (2) of this Our Charter, or the payment of such remuneration in return for service rendered as may be approved under Article 7 (3) hereof.

6 (1) The Council shall consist of a Chairman, a Vice-Chairman or not more than two Vice-Chairmen and not more than twenty-four other members, two of whom shall be nominated by our Secretary of State for Scotland and two by our Secretary of State for Wales.

   (2) The Chairman, any Vice-Chairman and other members shall be appointed by our Secretary of State, and the terms of their appointment shall be determined by him, after consultation with Our Secretaries of State for Scotland and for Wales.

   (3) The Council shall accord to a body representing national organizations of sport and physical recreation, provided it is recognised by Our Secretary of State as representative of sport and physical recreation as a whole, the status of a consultative body to the Council and the right to propose the names of persons whom our Secretary of State may consider for appointment by him as members of the Council.

7 (1) Every member of the Council shall hold and vacate his office in accordance with the terms of his appointment, but,

   (a) the Chairman shall be appointed for such term, not exceeding five years, as may be agreed by Our Secretaries of State and shall be eligible for re-appointment thereafter and may at any time by notice in writing to Our Secretary of State resign his office;

   (b) any Vice-Chairman shall be appointed for a term of not more than three years, and shall be eligible for re-appointment thereafter and may at any time by notice in writing to Our Secretary of State resign his office;

   (c) apart from the Chairman no member shall be appointed for a term of more than three years;

   (d) a member shall be eligible for re-appointment on ceasing to be a member;

   (e) a member may at any time by notice in writing to Our Secretary of State resign his office;

   (f) notwithstanding the provisions of sub-paragraphs (a) to (e) above inclusive and the terms of his appointment, any member may at any time by notice in writing given under the hand of Our Secretary of State be deprived of his membership of the Council if he shall be an undischarged bankrupt or shall in the opinion of Our Secretary of State have been guilty of an offence of a fraudulent character or have conducted himself in such a way as to render himself unfit to remain in office.

   (2) Save as is provided in Article 7 (3) hereof, the Council shall not make to any of its members any payment by way of remuneration for his services as a member, but may reimburse to any such member expenses reasonably incurred by him in the performance of such services.

   (3) The Council shall, if Our Secretary of State so directs, make to its Chairman and any Vice-Chairman such remuneration in return for service ren-

dered to the Council as Our Secretary of State with the approval of Our Minister for the Civil Service may determine.

8 (1) The Council may act notwithstanding a vacancy among its members and the validity of any proceedings of the Council shall not be affected by any defect in the appointment of a member.

(2) The quorum of the Council shall be seven members personally present or such greater number as the Council may from time to time determine.

9 Subject to the provisions of this Our Charter, the Council may regulate its own procedure.

10 (1) The Council may appoint committees or panels to exercise, or advise it on the exercise of, any of its functions, and may

(a) appoint to any such committee or panel persons who are not members of the Council, and

(b) at any time revoke the appointment of any member of any such committee or panel.

(2) The Council may appoint as Chairman of any such committee or panel a member of it who is a member of the Council.

11 (1) The Council may regulate the procedure of any committee or panel appointed by it in pursuance of Article 10 of this Our Charter.

(2) Article 7 (2) of this Our Charter shall apply to members of such committees and panels as it applies to members of the Council.

12 Any officer of the Department of Our Secretary of State who may be appointed by him to be an assessor to the Council, or to any committee or panel of it, shall be entitled to attend any meeting of the Council, committee or panel to which he is so appointed.

13 The Council may consult and with the approval of Our Secretary of State delegate the performance or supervision of functions to any regional sports council constituted as approved by Our Secretary of State and having a Chairman appointed by him.

14 (1) The Council shall, if Our Secretary of State so approves, appoint a Director qualified in matters of sport and physical recreation; and with the like approval shall appoint an Administrator who shall be the finance officer and the principal administrative officer of the Council; and may appoint such other officers and take into its employment such other persons as the Council may determine.

(2) The Council may:

(a) pay to its officers and other persons employed by it such renumeration as the Council may, with the approval of Our Secretary of State and Our Minister for the Civil Service, from time to time determine; and

(b) as regards any officers or other persons employed in whose case it may be determined by the Council, with the approval of Our Secretary of State and Our Minister for the Civil Service, so to do, pay to or in respect of them such pensions, allowances or gratuities as may be so determined, make such payments towards the provision of these matters, or provide or maintain such schemes (whether contributory or not) for the payment of the same as may be so determined.

(3) Notwithstanding the provisions of Article 5 of this Our Charter, but subject always to the provisions of Article 14 (1) and 14 (2) hereof the Council may employ from time to time for the performance of any of its functions a person who is a member of the Council and, subject as aforesaid, may remunerate such persons for services rendered in pursuance of such employment.

15 The Council shall keep proper accounts and other records, and shall prepare for each financial year statements of account in such form as Our Secretary of State with the approval of the Lords Commissioners of Our Treasury may direct and submit these statements of account to Our Secretary of State at such time as he may direct.

16 As soon as possible after the end of each financial year the Council shall make to Our Secretary of State a report on the exercise and performance by the Council of its functions during that year.

17 The application of the Seal of the Council shall be authenticated by the signature of the Chairman or some other member of the Council authorized generally or specially by the Council to act for that purpose, and of one of such officers of the Council as may be so authorised by the Council so to act.

18 The Council may by resolution in that behalf passed at a meeting of the Council by a majority of not less than three-quarters of the members present and voting (being an absolute majority of the whole number of the members of the Council), and confirmed at a further meeting of the Council held not less than one month nor more than four months afterwards by a like majority, add to or amend this Our Charter, and such addition or amendment, when allowed by Us, Our Heirs or Successors in Council, shall become effectual, so that this Our Charter shall thenceforward continue and operate as though it had been originally granted and made accordingly. This provision shall apply to this Our Charter as added to or amended in the manner aforesaid.

19 In this Our Charter references to Our Secretary of State are to Our Secretary of State for the Environment; and references to Our Secretaries of State are to Our Secretaries of State for the Environment, for Scotland and for Wales.

IN WITNESS whereof We have caused these Our Letters to be made Patent

WITNESS Ourself at Westminster the Fourth day of February in the Twentieth year of Our Reign.

BY WARRANT UNDER THE QUEEN'S SIGN MANUAL

(Signed Dobson)

Appendix 2

The Sports Council

Inaugural Membership: February 1965

Denis Howell, MP (Chairman)
Sir John Lang (Deputy Chairman)
David M. Bacon
Dr. Roger Bannister
Lady Elaine Burton
Menzies Campbell
Sir Learie Constantine
John Disley
Dr. Bernard Donoughue
Michael Dower
George Edwards
Mrs. Kathleen Holt
Dr. Stewart Mackintosh
David Munrow
Lord Porchester
Clive Rowlands
Dan Smith
Walter Winterbottom (Director)
Denis Molyneux (Deputy Director)
Ministry of Housing and Local Government (Assessor)
Department of Education and Science (Assessor)

Terms of Reference of the Sports Council and its Committees

Sports Council

To advise the Government on matters relating to the development of amateur sport and physical recreation services and to foster cooperation among the statutory authorities and voluntary organizations concerned.
　　Particular subjects which the Council should advise on are:
　　Standards of provision of sports facilities for the community.
　　Collation of information about the position in other countries.
　　Surveys of resources and regional planning.
　　Coordination of the use of community resources.

Research.
Development of training and coaching.
Likely capital expenditure.
Participation in sporting events overseas by British amateur teams.
Priorities in sports development.

International Committee

Chairman Lady Burton
To consider and advise on matters relating to the development of amateur international sport at home and overseas; to advise on principles and working rules by which government grants are made; and in particular to consider applications and make recommendations for grant in respect of:

(i) International teams competing overseas including school, youth and under-23 teams.
(ii) World, Commonwealth and international events of outstanding importance at home including special international competitions, for school, youth and under-23 teams.
(iii) International conferences at home and overseas.
(iv) Coaching, advisory and lecture visits overseas.
(v) Olympic and Commonwealth Games.

Research and Statistics Committee

Chairman Dr. R. Bannister
To advise on matters of scientific research related to sport, and in particular:

(i) Consider the development of medical research in sport and recommend financial grant for approved schemes of research.
(ii) Consider schemes of sociological research related to sport and physical recreation and recommend appropriate grants.
(iii) Acquire statistical data and documentation on sport and physical recreation.

Sports Development and Coaching Committee

Chairman A.D. Munrow
To advise on matters, except international, relating to the further development of sport by national voluntary organizations, and in particular to consider the general principles of grant-aid for:

(i) Headquarters' administration and coaching development.
(ii) Capital development of facilities for local voluntary organizations and national centres.

Facilities Planning Committee

Chairman Lord Porchester
To advise on matters relating to the provision and improvement of facilities for sport and physical recreation, and in particular:

    (i)   Examine the powers and responsibilities of government departments, local authorities, Boards, Commissions and other agencies concerned with planning and providing facilities for sport and physical recreation and recommend ways and means of increasing the provision of new facilities and improving existing facilities.

   (ii)   Consult local authority associations and local education authorities and various national organizations to find means of stimulating the pace of development of facilities for sport and recreation.

  (iii)   Consider national and regional planning of recreation facilities for open space land, waterways, coastal areas and for development of large-scale indoor facilities, stadia and swimming pools, and recommend appropriate action.

Appendix 3

Joint Circular* from the Ministry of Housing & Local Government (49/64) Whitehall, London, S.W.1 and the Department of Education & Science (11/64) Curzon Street, London, W.1

---

27 August 1964.

S<small>IR</small>,

PROVISION OF FACILITIES FOR SPORT

1 In recent debates in Parliament the Government has emphasized its concern for wider and more efficient provision of facilities for sport and physical recreation and for improved administration and organization. Although voluntary interests have played a large part in the development and administration of sport, the main burden of capital investment in sports facilities falls on local authorities acting under various statutory provisions. These include the duties of local education authorities under the 1944 Education Act to secure that the facilities for primary, secondary and further education make adequate provision for recreation and social and physical training; and the powers of local authorities in general under the Physical Training and Recreation Acts and the provisions relating to parks, pleasure grounds and baths in the Public Health Acts.

2 The purpose of this Circular, which is issued at the direction of the Secretary of State for Education and Science and the Minister of Housing and Local Government and the Minister for Welsh Affairs, is to outline the measures which the Government is taking to encourage the further development of sport and to suggest ways in which local authorities, in cooperation with the voluntary bodies and other interests concerned, may be able to improve and extend facilities in their areas for children and young people and for the community at large.

Central action

3   An interdepartmental committee has been established to secure better coordination and consultation over policy issues at the national level. This committee is
coordinating the work of the Government Departments concerned with sport,
and maintains contacts, which the Departments also have, with national sports
organizations.

4   The Government has announced increases in the total of grants available under
the Physical Training and Recreation Act, 1937, towards the cost of headquarters administration and coaching schemes of national sports bodies and of capital
projects undertaken by voluntary bodies. The national sports bodies have been
informed individually of the increased funds available to help them; and the
Department of Education and Science has prepared a leaflet about its grants for
local capital projects, which has been distributed through these bodies to individual clubs throughout the country. The contents of this leaflet are reproduced
as an appendix to this Circular, and further copies may be obtained on request.
Application for these grants are submitted to the Department of Education and
Science through local education authorities, which are asked to add their
observations and to forward applications to the Department as quickly as possible.

Local provision and consultation

5   It is estimated that capital expenditure on sports and physical education facilities
provided as part of educational building has risen from £11$\frac{1}{2}$m. in 1961/2 to
about £13$\frac{1}{2}$m. in 1963/4, covering provision of playing fields, hard games
areas, gymnasia and swimming baths. Capital expenditure by local authorities
on sports facilities outside educational establishments has risen from about £6m.
in 1961/2 to about £11$\frac{1}{2}$m. in 1963/4, covering a somewhat wider range of
provision for the community at large. The total capital expenditure involved has
thus risen from about £17$\frac{1}{2}$m. in 1961/2 to about £25m. in 1963/4.

6   Since this trend of expenditure seems likely to continue, it is all the more
important to ensure that it is laid out to the best advantage. This is a matter not
only of ensuring that buildings and other installations are designed to secure the
best value for money, but also of seeing that the number, size and location of
sports facilities are planned over a sufficiently large area with the needs of all
sections of the community in mind.

7   It is therefore recommended that all local authorities should carry out reviews of
their areas to determine what further provision for sport and recreation is
needed. Consultation with other local authorities will be necessary not only
because facilities in one area (particularly if sited near the boundary) may serve
neighbouring areas, but also because there will normally be more than one
authority with power to provide them; in boroughs and urban and rural districts,
the local authority for the area and the county council have powers, and in rural
districts there are also the parish councils. There should be consultation with
voluntary organizations, any industrial or commercial organizations which provide sports facilities for their employees, and the local representatives of the
Central Council of Physical Recreation and the National Playing Fields Association. The specialist sports organizations are also in a position to give valuable
advice.

8 Where major facilities, like swimming baths, large sports halls or multi-purpose sport and recreational centres are in mind, it will be necessary to arrange for collaboration between the local authorities and other interested bodies over a wide area, and it is urged that early steps should be taken to bring this about. Where there is existing machinery there will be advantage in using it, but otherwise it will be necessary to make special arrangements for the purpose; the county and county borough councils within a convenient geographical area are probably in the best position to take the initiative in setting up the machinery and calling the necessary conferences.

Dual use of facilities at educational establishments

9 In assessing local needs and the resources to match them, it is appropriate to consider how far facilities for sport and physical education already provided, or in course of provision, at schools and other educational establishments can be shared with other users, or can be economically expanded to meet the needs. The provision of playing fields is normally related closely to the needs of the establishments themselves, but with good construction and maintenance some additional use even of grass pitches may be possible without undue wear; and hard-paved or porous areas (tennis courts, running tracks, hard pitches and jumping pits) and indoor facilities can often support use beyond the needs of the establishments themselves. Where facilities are made available for outside use, the need for supervision must be borne in mind. The Department of Education and Science will shortly be issuing a revised edition of Building Bulletin No. 10 ('School playing fields and hard-paved areas') which will contain advice on the dual use of playing field facilities.

10 In planning new, or replanning existing, sports provision for educational establishments, the needs of the community generally, as well as of pupils and students for both outdoor and indoor sports facilities should be borne in mind. Better value for money, and a wider range, may sometimes be obtained if combined provision can be made in an integrated scheme. Consultation and cooperation between the local education authority or other body responsible for the facilities, any other local authority concerned and, in appropriate cases, voluntary organizations will clearly be essential. The Departments will ensure that no unnecessary administrative difficulties are put in the way of a combined scheme.

Technical advice

11 Authorities will be aware of official and other publications on the technical aspects. A convenient list is to be found in the information leaflet published, and revised from time to time, by the National Playing Fields Association. Technical officers of the Departments and of the Central Council of Physical Recreation, the National Playing Fields Association and the Sports Turf Research Institute are always willing to advise on particular problems of design, construction or equipment. Advice is also often available from specialist officers of other local authorities. As opportunity offers, the Departments will circulate to authorities generally further technical information, including information about individual schemes of particular interest which come to their notice.

Appendices

Local assistance to voluntary bodies: The youth service

12 In addition to their powers to provide directly for sport, local authorities have power under the Physical Training and Recreation Acts 1937 and 1958 to make grants and loans to voluntary organizations to assist them in providing facilities. On the recommendation of the Youth Service Development Council, the Ministers would like to take this opportunity of drawing the attention of authorities to the desirability, which was stressed by the Albemarle Committee, of using these powers for the benefit of young people in the 14–20 age range, and also to the need urged by the Wolfenden Committee on Sport and the Community for the development of closer links between the youth service and sport.

Conclusion

13 The two Ministers trust that local authorities in their various capacities will now consider the suggestions made in this circular and that they will take every opportunity to cater fully for the sporting and recreational needs of their areas. The Departments, for their part, will give them every possible assistance.

We are, Sir,
Your obedient servants,
E.A. SHARP
HERBERT ANDREW

The Clerk of the Authority

The Sports Council — Leading Personalities 1965–1970

David Bacon, FCA	Chartered accountant
	Company director
Dr Roger Bannister, DM, FRCP, CBE, Kt (1975)	Member, Sports Council (1965–74), Chairman (1971–74)
	President, International Council of Sport and Physical Education (ICSPE) (1976–83)
	World Record Mile 1954 with first sub-four minute mile
	Master, Pembroke College, Oxford (1985–)
	Olympic Games (1952)
Elaine Burton (Baroness Burton of Coventry (1962)	Member, Sports Council (1965–71)
	MP (Coventry) (1950–59)
Brian Close	Captain of the England cricket team
	Captain of Yorkshire County Cricket Club
John I Disley, CBE	Member, Sports Council (1965–71), Vice Chairman (1974–82)
	Member, Countryside Commission (1974–77)
	Member, Royal Commission on Gambling (1976–78)
	Bronze medallist, 1952 Olympics, Helsinki
	Director, London Marathon (1980–)
Bernard Donoughue, MA, DPhil, Life Peer (1985)	Member, Sports Council (1965–71)
	Senior Policy Adviser to the Prime Minister (1975–79)
	Assistant Editor, *The Times* (1981–82)
	Member, Committee of Enquiry into Association Football (1966–68)
Michael Dower	Estate manager
	Member, United Nations Special Fund Town Planning team
George Edwards	International footballer for Wales
	Played football for Coventry City, Birmingham City and Cardiff City
Bob Gibb	Senior Executive, ICI
Mary Glen-Haig, CBE	Member, Sports Council (1966–82)
	Chairman, CCPR (1974–80), Vice President (1982–)

	Vice-President, SAF (1987–)
	Member, IOC (1982–)
	Competed at 1948, 1952 and 1956 Olympic Games
	Awarded Commonwealth Games gold medal for fencing (1950 and 1954)
Peter Heatly, CBE	Chairman, Scottish Sports Council (1975–87)
	Chairman, Commonwealth Games Federation (1982–90)
Kathleen Holt	Physical educationist, Bedford College (1936)
	Reserve England lacrosse team
	Vice Chairman, All England Ladies Lacrosse Association
Cliff Jones	International rugby player for Wales
Sir John Lang	Formerly Secretary to the Admiralty
	Retired Civil Servant
	Principal Adviser on Sport to the Lord President of the Council (Lord Hailsham)
Frank Leath	Vice Chairman, West Midlands Advisory Committee for Civil Aviation
	Member, West Midlands Area Transport Users Consultative Committee
	Member, Hospital Management Committee
Laurie Liddell, CBE	Director of Physical Education, University of Edinburgh
	Chairman, Scottish Sports Council (1965–75)
Arthur Ling, FRIBA, MTPI	Head of Department, Architecture and Civic Planning, University of Nottingham (1964–69)
	Vice Chairman, International Union of Architects
	Vice Chairman, East Midlands Sports Council
	Member, Sports Council (1968–71)
Jack Longland, Kt (1970)	Director of Education, Derbyshire (1949–70)
	Athletics blue at Oxford
	Everest Expedition (1933)
	President, Alpine Club (1973–76)
	Member, Wolfenden Committee (1957–60)
	Member, CCPR Executive (1961–72)
	Member, Sports Council (1966–74), Vice-Chairman (1971–74)
	Member, Countryside Commission (1969–74)
	Member, Royal Commission on Local Government (1966–69)
Peter McIntosh, MA (Oxon)	Deputy Director of Physical Education, University of Birmingham (1946–59)
	Senior Inspector of Physical Education, ILEA (1959–74)
	Director of School of Physical Education, University of Otago, New Zealand (1974–78)
	Visiting Professor, Canada
	Member, Sports Council (1966–74), Chairman of Facilities Committee
	Committee Chairman, International Council of Sports Science and Physical Education (1971–83)

David Munrow, OBE	Director of Physical Education, University of Birmingham
	Pioneer of first degree course in physical education
	Distinguished author on sport and physical education
	Member, Wolfenden Committee on Sport
	Member, Executive Committee of the International Council of Sport and Physical Education
Lord Porchester	Her Majesty the Queen's racing manager
	Chairman, Hampshire County Council
	Vice Chairman, National Playing Fields Association

Reports, White Papers, Government Circulars Concerned with Sport and Physical Recreation — 1970–1980

Government Circulars

1   Sports Facilities and the Planning Acts, 5 May 1970, *Ministry of Housing and Local Government Circular 33/70*
    This was a short Circular commending to local authorities the need to consult with Regional Sports Councils on all matters concerning the planning of sports facilities. It dealt with advice on planning applications and planning appeals where facilities for sport were concerned. It had some useful comments on development plans and the acquisition of land for sport.

2   Provision for Sport and Physical Recreation, 5 January 1973, *Department of the Environment Circular 1/73*
    The purpose of this Circular was to set out for local authorities the implications in particular as regards the financing of local sports facilities and it went on to describe succinctly the changes made by the Government since assuming office in 1970. It dealt with the Sports Council, Regional Sports Councils, Capital Programmes and Grant-in-aid arrangements. The future role of the Regional Sports Councils was elaborated in great detail and included for the first time a paragraph on 'Development of Participation'. It further explained the advisory role these Regional Councils were to have with the Sports Council in future. In an Annex the Circular defined clearly the recreation functions of the Countryside Commission, acknowledged the possible overlap with the Sports Council without precisely saying this, and pointed to a division of responsibilities by aligning the Countryside Commission's responsibility with informal recreation.

3   Reorganization of Water and Sewage Services: Government Proposals and Arrangements for Consultation, 2 December 1971, *Department of the Environment Circular 92/71*
    This long Circular described the Government's intentions concerning the reorganization of water services and, as its title stated, it was a consultative document. For sport and physical recreation the interest lay in paragraphs 31–33 which dealt with recreation. Throughout there were references to the need to build into any legislation powers to provide for recreation, and indeed the later Water Bill (1973), bringing about the re-organization of water services, did just that.

4   Local Government Reorganization in England: Functions, Areas and Names, 4 November 1971, *Department of the Environment Circular 84/71*
The Local Government Bill, before Parliament at the time of this Circular, spelt out very clearly functions which included sport and recreation, and the whole process of local government change which created a great impetus to spend balances often on sports facilities. Circular 84/71 initially created problems for governing bodies of sport. County boundaries were to change, some names were to disappear as mergers took place, and new Metropolitan Counties were to be formed. Old allegiances and ties in sport were clearly threatened as time-honoured boundaries changed and concern was expressed by many governing bodies of sport. What can only be described as masterly inactivity was decided upon by most sports bodies singly and collectively and over a period of time the problem seemed to disappear; this proved to be the right approach. From the point of view of sport the Metropolitan Counties were ignored as often were newly-constructed counties such as Avon. Some trimming of county borders was observed, but with timeless faith in tradition areas such as Worcestershire and Herefordshire remained mainly as before for sport although linked into one county for local government purposes. Middlesex, a geographic county long disappeared, continued to function with great authority in many sports and does so to this day. Problems did occur, and continue to occur with schools sports associations which because they were identified with local education authority areas, usually conformed to the new rules. To all intents and purposes by the end of the seventies the boundaries issue, from the point of view of sport, was dead.

5   Report of the House of Lords Select Committee on *Sport and Leisure July 1973*
This report was of immense importance in public circles carrying as it did both the prestige of the House of Lords and that of the Chairman and his Committee. Viscount Cobham, the former cricket captain of the Worcestershire County Cricket Club and a former Governor-General of New Zealand, presided, supported by the Lord Bishop of Chester, Lords Astor of Hever, Byers, Donaldson of Kingsbridge, Dulverton, Greenwood of Rossendale, Redcliffe Maud, Strathcona and Mount Royal, and Tweedsmuir; Baroness Serota provided a female dimension. At various times Lord Diamond and Lord Llewellyn-Davies served.

The Select Committee was first appointed on 9 December 1971 by Resolution and was re-appointed on 9 November 1972 with the following terms of reference:

> 'Sport and Leisure — *Moved*. That a Committee of eleven Lords be appointed to consider the demand for facilities for participation in sport and in the enjoyment of leisure out-of-doors, and to examine what impediments may exist to the fuller use of existing facilities or the development of new ones, and how they might be removed.'

A First Report from the Select Committee was published on 29 March 1973 with the Final Report appearing in July of the same year. The two Reports of the Select Committee represented a thorough review of all aspects of sport and physical recreation with evidence taken from a wide range of sources. Visits were made to the Federal Republic of Germany and Holland, and to local authorities and facilities in Britain. In all sixty-two recommendations were made concerning the following subjects:

(i) Leisure time; (ii) Leisure activities; (iii) Provision of facilities; (iv) Finance; (v) Water Recreation; (vi) Leisure out-of-doors; (vii) Sport; (viii) Dual use and dual provision; (ix) General matters.

A powerful final Conclusion admirably summed up the findings of the Select Committee when it gave the clear statement of opinion that there were three major impediments to the provision and exploitation of facilities which threatened demand from being met. First 'the feeling that leisure is an optional extra', second that 'too little money is being invested in facilities' and third 'recreation must be treated as a social service'.

The penultimate sentence in the Report summed up the history of sports development in Britain when the Committee said, 'Public expenditure so far has been wholly inadequate to provide facilities on the scale that is, and will be, required'.

The Select Committee Report of the House of Lords runs to 138 pages and the Minutes of Evidence and Appendices are printed separately from the Report. The evidence the Sports Council gave on Thursday 22 February 1973 is published in Hansard (pp. 268–302). The tragedy is that Lord Cobham died before he could ensure that maximum attention was given to his Report, but the impact nevertheless was considerable and helped shape the Labour Government's White Paper *Sport and Recreation* in 1975. This House of Lords Select Committee Report was a landmark in British history and became a source of reference and a guideline for much that was to follow.

There are many who regretted that Lord Cobham did not live long enough to follow Sir Roger Bannister into the Chairmanship of the Sports Council if he could have been persuaded to do so. His enormous knowledge, interest and prestige would have altered the future out of all recognition. He was a man of stature and sport is indebted to him in many ways.

Government White Papers

Two White Papers of major interest to sport were published by the Department of the Environment in 1975 and 1977.

1 Policy for the Inner Cities (Cmnd 6845) 1977.

This 1977 White Paper referred to issues touching directly on the poor quality of life endured by many who lived in the inner cities and twilight zones that surrounded the inner core. The Government specified its underlying aims and proposed:

(a) strengthening the economies of the inner cities and the prospects of their residents;
(b) improving the physical fabric of the inner areas and making their environments more attractive;
(c) securing a new balance between the inner areas and the rest of the city region in terms of population and jobs;
(d) alleviating social problems.

Paragraph 28 specifically referred to the part sport for young people could play, and this together with the new thinking on urban-aid and the partnership schemes gave the Sports Council the green light to sharpen its policies and strive more strongly to achieve results in the inner cities. Accordingly, in the spirit of the White Paper, the Sports Council began to discriminate positively in favour of the inner cities and developed financial policies to bring this policy about.

2   *Sport and Recreation (Cmnd 6200) 1975.*

This was the first White Paper ever published on sport and recreation and as a statement of policy it was warmly welcomed. There is good reason to believe that it was published in the teeth of opposition from HM Treasury as the country was once again going through a financial crisis and anything that appeared in any way to encourage public expenditure was to a very considerable extent frowned upon. It is safe to say that only the political 'clout' and determination of the Minister for Sport, Denis Howell, ensured that the White Paper saw the light of day. It was for sport an historic moment despite the sprinkling throughout of financial caveats that had to be included if the Treasury was to approve publication.

The White Paper owed much to the two reports of the Select Committee of the House of Lords on Sport and Leisure and generously acknowledged this at the outset and on a number of occasions in the narrative.

The inclusion of a description of the national economic background on the very first page is the price that had to be paid for all that followed which set out clearly and sharply the principles of policy and the current organizational and coordinating arrangements. The review of the functions in the sport and recreation field of the various government agencies was impressive and ranged from the 'active' Sports Councils to the more contemplative areas of ancient monuments and historic buildings.

Many had hoped and had lobbied strongly for the Government to accept the Select Committee's recommendation that the provision of adequate facilities should be made a mandatory duty imposed upon local authorities. Paragraph 31 in the White Paper made it quite clear that this was not to be, which to those close to the scene was not surprising in view of the ever-present heavy hand of the Treasury throughout the drafting of the White Paper. How much vision, flair, imagination and enterprise have been thwarted in Britain over the years by the dead hand of the Treasury will never be known. With a great department of state to have been proved wrong so frequently in economic affairs it is difficult to understand how power continues to lie with those who have failed so often, but that is the way it is today and was in 1975 and sport has suffered on this account.

The White Paper, building on the successful work of the Regional Sports Councils, proposed that these be replaced by Regional Councils for Sport and Recreation encompassing a wider remit than hitherto by concerning themselves with the whole range of sport and outdoor recreational activities in regions. Membership would include, in addition to sporting interests, conservation, farming and forestry interests to ensure a proper balance between formal and informal recreation and between recreation and conservation. It was clear that in proposing this new structure the Government saw that a powerful single body in each region was desirable as a consultative and advisory organization capable of dealing with all aspects of outdoor recreation and the problems of conflict of use.

The former work of Regional Sports Councils in promoting regional coordination for the provision of facilities, and in the planning process generally, encouraged the belief that this was the model on which to build and develop. Additionally, and of paramount importance, it was seen that in local authorities the whole recreational focus was often embraced in one department of leisure or recreation serving one committee and therefore it was thought this broad range of interests should be reflected regionally.

The White Paper specifically stated that the proposed Regional Councils for Sport and Recreation should be independent of central government. In all of this the deft touch of Denis Howell, the Minister for Sport, was evident. Howell was many things but first and foremost he was a local government man having served for many years on the Birmingham City Council; his touch on municipal affairs was masterly and in this instance his feel for the right move to match the spirit of the times was right.

It was now intended that the grant-aid advice that hitherto the Regional Sports Councils had made to the Sports Council for regional facilities for sport should be extended in the same fashion to the Countryside Commission on the general assumption that local people knew best what was needed and were best able to decide priorities within these needs.

To assist the broad strategic regional planning process now underway the firm suggestion was made that each of the new enlarged Regional Councils should begin to prepare regional recreational strategies so as to provide a framework of policy and proposals to assist structure and local plans. As a consequence sport and recreation it was thought would be more deeply enmeshed in the formal land-use process ensuring that recreational needs would on all occasions be considered. This fundamental move, bureaucratic as it might at first appear, was in many ways a breakthrough for sport as now this aspect of human and social affairs had to be taken into account alongside other, often statutory, requirements.

Although the White Paper was published in August 1975 detailed consultations with those affected took some months. It was therefore not until April 1976 that the Government, through the Department of the Environment, was able to publish Circular 47/76 *Regional Councils for Sport and Recreation*. This Circular in great detail stated the reasons for the developments proposed in the White Paper, set out the constitution and terms of reference of the new Regional Councils for Sport and Recreation and declared the former Regional Sports Councils defunct thirty days after the first meeting of the successor bodies.

The widening of the remit and the determination to encompass the broader aspects of recreation into a new structure was logical but presented problems initially mainly concerned with the scale of operation and the proposal that the secretariat arrangements should be jointly operated by the Sports Council and the Countryside Commission. The latter issue was resolved amicably in the short term whilst the former largely melted away as working arrangements, procedures and systems moved into gear.

The staff of the Countryside Commission was enlarged and an effective regional presence was established. In the early eighties the cut-back in the public service resulted in the Commission having to shed staff and accordingly they withdrew considerably from on the spot day by day involvement regionally but remained an effective contributor to regional policies and action in matters affecting recreation in the countryside.

Recreation management was to be studied by interested parties which led later to the setting up of the Yates Committee.

Special reference was made to the need for wider joint-use and joint-provision pointing to the importance of these policies at all times and particularly at a time of economic restraint.

The White Paper concluded strongly with a clear statement of priorities:

(a) Areas of special need
The Select Committee's recommendation 'that recreational priority areas' should be defined and given financial assistance was accepted. Proposals were made linking the Urban Aid Programme to this initiative.

(b) Community use of major voluntary facilities
Ways and means of bringing major facilities owned by sports clubs into greater use needed exploring in depth. The restriction imposed earlier on the Sports Council

limiting grant-aid to larger than local facilities was lifted with the plea that priority should be given to schemes that offered wider community use. Some hint was given of the Football and the Community scheme yet to come in 1978.

(c) Youth sports programme
A drive to encourage more emphasis being placed on providing for young people was urged. Possible ways and means of achieving this were discussed and the role of teachers was detailed.

(d) The disabled
Whilst the efforts already made to involve disabled people in sport were acknowledged more effort was urged on all concerned with the provision of facilities to seek further ways of making adequate access easier. The sharing of facilities with families and those not disabled, where practicable, was emphasized.

(e) Gifted sportsmen and sportswomen
A special study of how talented sportsmen and women could be further assisted was promised. For the first time officially the need for 'centres of excellence' was stressed and a pointed reference to the part universities and colleges might play was broadly stated. Whilst the proposed development of the Sports Aid Foundation was not mentioned specifically the many references to the need to assist élite athletes more imaginatively and generously clearly gave an early indication of the Government's welcome to the setting up of the Foundation to help in this area of concern.

The White Paper concluded by saying that its publication sought to set out a comprehensive philosophy for sport which it commended to local authorities and public bodies working in this field as a basis for planning future strategy and policy. It not only acknowledged the clear interest the Government had in the field of social and human endeavour but it also showed a masterly understanding of the issues and priorities. Politically it was a triumph for Denis Howell; for sport it was an inspiration and a guideline for the future.

Looking back fifteen years since the drafting of *Sport and Recreation* so much of what it proposed has been fulfilled to a very considerable extent. The only 'failure', lies in the lack of any national youth sports programme, but even here constructive initiatives have been taken by the CCPR with their Community Sports Leaders Award and by some Regional Councils for Sport and Recreation, in particular that for Yorkshire and Humberside. The International Year for Youth in 1985 offered the opportunity for new initiatives; the *Ever Thought of Sport?* campaign was particularly relevant.

The White Paper took the opportunity to include, as an Appendix, the statement made by the Prime Minister in the House of Commons on July 1974 when he announced that he shared the view of the Select Committee of the House of Lords that 'energetic action was needed over the next decade to meet the growing demand for recreational facilities of all kinds'. Accordingly he announced that Denis Howell, the Minister of State for Sport, was to have his role increased and henceforth would be designated Minister of State for Sport and Recreation to reflect his new coordinating responsibility for recreational functions exercised by other government departments.

Ministers with responsibility for Sport and Chairmen of the Sports Council, 1965–1989

Ministers with Responsibility for Sport

	Denis Howell, MP	1965–1970
(Sir)	Eldon Griffiths, MP	1970–1974
(Rt. Hon)	Denis Howell, PC, MP	1974–1979
(Sir)	Hector Monro, MP	1979–1981
(Sir)	Neil Macfarlane, MP	1981–1985
	Richard Tracey, MP	1985–1987
	Colin Moynihan, MP	1987–

Chairmen of the Sports Council

	Denis Howell, MP	1965–1970
(Sir)	Eldon Griffiths, MP	1970–1972
(Sir)	Roger Bannister	1972–1975
	Sir Robin Brook	1975–1978
	'Dick' Jeeps	1978–1985
(Sir)	John Smith	1985–1989
	Peter Yarranton	1989–

Minister's letter (copy) to Chairmen of Regional Sports Councils

Department of the Environment,
Whitehall,
London, S.W.1.
10 June 1971

Dear Edgar,
I have today replied to a Parliamentary question about the future of the Sports Council. I enclose a copy of the Answer and of a press-notice on the subject.

You will see that it is intended to strengthen and widen the role of the Sports Council by making it an independent body with its own grant-aiding functions. It will be given executive as well as advisory functions.

It is also intended to maintain a regional structure, and to give the Regional Sports Councils wider responsibilities. Their links with the Sports Council and with local authorities are to be strengthened.

These reforms taken together with the Standing Conference of Governing Bodies and the Government's statement of its intentions to foster the development of Sport and to make more funds available, represent a new step forward for Sport and Recreation in this country. I feel sure we shall be able to count on your own and your Council's support in carrying them forward.

We now need to consider the precise relationships in a new structure. I should like also to see the Regional Sports Councils assuming wider responsibilities, for example supplementing their advisory functions with some executive ones (other than administering grants). I should like to discuss the new arrangements generally with RSC Chairmen as early as possible, and am therefore inviting them to meet me in Birmingham on Thursday 17 June. The CCPR will be in touch with you about the arrangements, and I very much hope that you will find it convenient to come.

ELDON GRIFFITHS

Edgar Hiley Esq, MBE

Appendix 8

The Sports Council – 1972

Inaugural Membership

Chairman	Dr. Roger Bannister
Vice-Chairman	Sir Jack Longland
	Laurie Liddell (Chairman, Scottish Sports Council)
	Peter Heatly (Vice-Chairman, Scottish Sports Council)
	Lt. Colonel Harry Llewellyn (Chairman, Sports Council for Wales)
	Glyn Davies (Vice-Chairman, Sports Council for Wales)
	Earl of Antrim
	Irwin Bellow
	Robin Brook
	Lt. General Sir Mervyn Butler
	Audrey Deacon
	Michael Dower
	Mary Glen Haig
	Jimmy Hill
	Douglas Insole
	Earl of Lonsdale
	P.B. (Laddie) Lucas
	Peter McIntosh
	Norris McWhirter
	David Munrow
	Lord Rupert Nevill
	Sir William Ramsay
	Lord Willis
	Bob Wilson
	Ann Yates

Appendix 9

Physical Training and Recreation Act (1937): Some Relevant Extracts and 1958 Amendment

Powers Imposed on Government Departments

Section 3(I) — The Minister of Education may, in accordance with arrangements approved by the Treasury, make grants:

(a) towards the expenses of a local voluntary organization in providing, whether as a part of wider activities or not, or in aiding the provision of, facilities for physical training and recreation, including, but without prejudice to the generality of the foregoing words, the provision and equipment of gymnasiums, playing fields, swimming baths, bathing places, holiday camps and camping sites, and other buildings and premises for physical training and recreation;

(b) towards the expenses of a local voluntary organization in respect of the training and supply of teachers and leaders; and

(c) to the funds of any national voluntary organization having such objects as aforesaid, either in aid of its work as a whole, or in aid of any specified branch of its work.

The powers of the Minister under paragraph (a) of this subsection shall not extend to the making of a grant in aid of the maintenance of such facilities as aforesaid, except that, if the Minister certifies that the circumstances of a local voluntary organization are such that special hardship or difficulty would be occasioned if such a grant were not made to it, the Minister may make such a grant.

Section 3(3) — The Minister may, with the approval of the Treasury, take steps for disseminating knowledge with respect to the value of physical training and recreation.

Section 9 — In this Act, unless the context otherwise requires, 'voluntary organization' means any person or body of persons, whether corporate or unincorporate, carrying on, or proposing to carry on, an undertaking otherwise than for profit.

2 THE SOCIAL AND PHYSICAL TRAINING GRANT REGULATIONS, 1939, gave the Minister of Education power to make grants to an association recognized by him for:

(a) the provision and maintenance of facilities for social and physical training in England or Wales, including payment of leaders, instructors and

(b) training of leaders, etc.; and
(c) incidental expenses of organization and administration.

Powers Conferred on Local Authorities.

Section 4 (1) — A local authority may acquire, layout, provide with suitable buildings and otherwise equip and maintain lands, whether situate within or without their area, for the purpose of gymnasiums, playing fields, holiday camps or camping sites, or for the purpose of centres for the use of clubs, societies or organizations having athletic, social, or educational objects, and may manage those lands and buildings themselves, either with or without a charge for the use thereof or admission thereto, or may let them, or any portion thereof, at a nominal or other rent to any person, club, society or organization for use for any of the purposes aforesaid.

The authority may also provide and, where necessary, arrange for the training of, such wardens, teachers and leaders as they may deem requisite for securing that effective use is made of the facilities for exercise, recreation and social activities so provided.

(3) — A county council may provide public swimming baths and bathing places under Part VIII of the Public Health Act, 1936, and, accordingly, in sections 221 to 229 of that Act any reference to a local authority or their district shall, in relation to public swimming baths or bathing places, be construed as including a reference to a county council or their county.

(4) — A local authority may contribute towards expenses incurred by another local authority, whether under this or any other Act, or by a voluntary organization, in providing or maintaining within the area of the contributing authority, or on a site where it will benefit any of the inhabitants of that area, anything mentioned in subsection (1) of this section, or a swimming bath or bathing place.

(5) — Section 69 of the Public Health Act, 1925, and so much of the Museums and Gymnasiums Act, 1891, as relates to gymnasiums, shall cease to have effect and any property held by a local authority for the purposes of the enactments thus repealed shall, without any necessity for formal appropriation, be held by them for the purposes of this section.

Section 9 — In this Act, unless the context otherwise requires, 'local authority' means the council of a county, county borough, metropolitan borough, county district or parish, and the common council of the City of London. . . .

9 PHYSICAL TRAINING AND RECREATION ACT, 1958

Section 1(1) — The power conferred on local authorities by subsection (4) of section 4 of the Physical Training and Recreation Act, 1937 (which relates to contributions by local authorities towards expenses of providing and maintaining gymnasiums, playing fields, swimming baths and other facilities) shall include power for a local authority to make a loan to a voluntary organization for meeting (wholly or in part) any expenses of that organization, being expenses towards which the local authority could make a contribution under that subsection:

Provided that a loan shall not be made in the exercise of that power for meeting any expenses of maintenance, or for meeting any other expenses which are not of such a description as to be properly chargeable to capital account.

Appendix 10

International Olympic Charter (1982 Edition): Rule 26 Eligibility Code

Rule 26

To be eligible for participation in the Olympic Games, a competitor must:

— observe and abide by the Rules of the IOC and in addition the rules of his or her IF, as approved by the IOC, even if the federation's rules are more strict than those of the IOC;
— not have received any financial rewards or material benefit in connection with his or her sports participation, except as permitted in the bye-laws to this rule.

Bye-law to Rule 26

A Each IF is responsible for the wording of the eligibility code relating to its sport, which must be approved by the Executive Board in the name of the IOC.
B The observation of Rule 26 and of the eligibility codes of IFs and NOCs are under the responsibility of IFs and NOCs involved. The Eligibility Commission of the IOC will ensure the application of these provisions.
C All cases of infringement of Rule 26 of the IOC and of the eligibility codes of IFs shall be communicated by the respective IF or NOC to the IOC to be taken in consideration by its Eligibility Commission. In accordance with Rule 23 and its bye-law, the accused competitor may request to be heard by the Executive Board whose decision will be final.

Guidelines to Eligibility Code for the IFs

A The following regulations are based on the principle that an athlete's health must not suffer nor must he or she be placed at a social or material disadvantage as a result of his or her preparation for and participation in the Olympic Games and international sports competitions. In accordance with Rule 26 the IOC, the IFs, the NOCs, and the national federations will assume responsibility for the protection and support of athletes:
B All competitors, men or women, who conform to the criteria set out in Rule 26, may participate in the Olympic Games, except those who have:

 1 been registered as professional athletes or professional coaches in any sport;
 2 signed a contract as a professional athlete or professional coach in any sport before the official closing of the Olympic Games;
 3 accepted without the knowledge of their IF, national federation or NOC, material advantages for their preparation or participation in sports competition;
 4 allowed their person, name, picture, or sports performances to be used for advertising, except when their IF, NOC or national federation has entered into a contract for sponsorship or equipment. All payment must be made to the IF, NOC, or national federation concerned, and not to the athlete;
 5 carried advertising material on their person or clothing in the Olympic Games and Games under the patronage of the IOC, other than trademarks on technical equipment or clothing as agreed by the IOC with the IFs;
 6 in the practise of sport and in the opinion of the IOC, manifestly contravened the spirit of fair play in the exercise of sport, particularly by the use of doping or violence.

Appendix 11

Sport and Overseas Trade

1   It is, I believe, an undisputed fact that anyone in close touch with the affairs of other countries, both East and West, sees that, almost without exception, industrial nations are now embarked on a new type of 'colonialism' — that of economic power and political influence. Our own country would be no exception to this. It requires no great imagination to see that this state of affairs is arrived at for two specific reasons:

(a)   political and ideological reasons;
(b)   business and export purposes.

There could be a third — altruism — but I regret that I am too sceptical to believe that this is a motive in all but a few examples.

2   If this is accepted, overtly or covertly, and I would need a great deal of persuading that it were otherwise, then I submit that sport and physical education are two very exportable commodities having an influence far beyond the part we, as a long established country, give it in the UK — and indeed would wish to give it. Even the Sports Council which constantly presses HM Government for more resources to do the job for which we were established, would not in all conscience place sport in the highest bracket of national endeavour and involvement. This, however, is not the case in the greater part of the globe, in developing countries and the Third World where matters, whether we agree or not, are ordered differently and where sport is a major factor on the world stage where an emerging country can be seen and heard. The very fact that sport is the main element in the apartheid/South African scenario demonstrates this. There is no clamour against contact through the arts, and indeed very little clamour concerning the vast commercial and industrial links that continue between the Western World and South Africa and, in some instances, between black Africa and South Africa. It is sport that captures the scene because it is a major popular activity widely reported and therefore an activity for many other nations to use as an instrument of political and economic power.

3   There is no shadow of doubt that, as a nation, we are losing out under both headings listed above. Other political influence in the Commonwealth has diminished and although business links, because of our common language, may still be strong, inroads have been made by other nations which, for example, France would find unthinkable in a former French colony. In the world of sport, for example, the Chinese are into Kenya, the Soviets inter alia into Ghana and

Nigeria, and the Cubans into Jamaica — all Commonwealth English-speaking countries.

Perhaps this position is one which is accepted but if so it does not reflect the very many requests from Commonwealth countries and others for British technical help.

4   I read from time to time that the FCO 'is concerned with growing Cuban influence in the Caribbean'. Jamaica has requested British help in staffing and curriculum at the new College of Physical Education and Sport built and equipped by the Cubans. We cannot supply this help — we have no resources to assist, and we watch helplessly as more and more sport in that country falls under Cuban influence with the political consequences that follow.

5   Too often, we feel, our Embassies do not appear to recognize that sport has a political and commercial spin-off and our businessmen often hear of possibilities long after others have tendered.

6   In many countries of Africa, in Latin and Central America, the all-pervading influence of the Communist countries is being spread through technical aid in sport. East Germany, for example, offers a considerable number of their 'friends' places at the world famous Leipzig Sports School, cementing and developing the relationships accordingly. The current Chairman of the UNESCO Inter-governmental Committee for Sport and Physical Education, on which the British Government has a place, is an example of this 'cooperation'. He trained at Leipzig. This is not confined solely to the Communist states, of course, and the Federal Republic of Germany as a further example has teams of experts in some Latin America countries, e.g. Colombia. Is it any wonder that the trade of these countries with the Third World is so very considerable?

7   Whilst I would be remiss in not pointing to a situation of political significance elicited from our work in the international sports field, this is not the prime business of the Sports Council. Understandably we wish to see the spread of British influence in sport and there is very considerable demand for this, often from the most unlikely sources. The political spin-off from any increased activity is for others to gauge but the business and prestige spin-off is very considerable indeed. I need hardly cite the example of Adidas to underline this point.

8   Our concern would be to assist developing and under-developed countries and, if we assisted oil rich countries or others who can afford to pay, we would expect some financial return for our services. As one distinguished Kenyan visitor recently said here at the Sports Council — 'send us please more sports administrators and coaches and less oboeists — important as these are'. I believe that eloquently sums it all up.

9   Somewhere, through all of this, there is an identity of common interest to our country — for trade, for political ends, for prestige and for sport. We believe that sport 'exported', carefully and thoughtfully, can assist all these interests and we would at this stage seek no more than a slice of the existing resources that go to overseas aid to be channelled to this end so that we could demonstrate the truth and accuracy of what we all see. Such action could well prove far more productive than some existing endeavours and would be welcomed so very much by the very many friends of our country that argue in developing countries that it is to Britain they should turn.

10 We do not agree with Walter Winterbottom's statement that the British Council do not use all their existing resources in this connection now. That is not the case — the resources are meagre and the British Council, together with us, could do so much more if a little more could be managed. This is a case of investing money to make money, not of spending money for no financial return.

11 We would at this stage recommend, as a first step:

(a) Training be given to diplomats destined for trade posts in Embassies in the opportunities that exist for business in the world of sport.

(b) That a meeting be convened under your chairmanship with Ministers and officials of the Departments concerned, at which the Sports Council might have the chance of deploying in depth the matters raised in this paper. We believe that this would be the most effective first step.

3 December 1979

Commonwealth Statement on Apartheid in Sport

The member countries of the Commonwealth, embracing peoples of diverse races, colours, languages and faiths, have long recognized racial prejudice and discrimination as a dangerous sickness and an unmitigated evil and are pledged to use all their efforts to foster human dignity everywhere. At their London meeting, the Heads of Government reaffirmed that apartheid in sports, as in other fields, is an abomination and runs directly counter to the declaration of Commonwealth principles which they made at Singapore on 22 January 1971.

They were conscious that sport is an important means of developing and fostering understanding between the people, and especially between the young people, of all countries. But, they were also aware that, quite apart from other factors, sporting contacts between their nationals and the nationals of countries practising apartheid in sport tend to encourage the belief (however unwarranted) that they are prepared to condone this abhorrent policy or are less than totally committed to the principles embodied in their Singapore declaration. Regretting past misunderstandings and difficulties and recognizing that these were partly the result of inadequate inter-governmental consultations, they agreed that they would seek to remedy this situation in the context of the increased level of understanding now achieved.

They reaffirmed their full support for the international campaign against apartheid and welcomed the efforts of the United Nations to reach universally accepted approaches to the question of sporting contacts within the framework of that campaign.

Mindful of these and other considerations, they accepted it as the urgent duty of each of their Governments vigorously to combat the evil of apartheid by withholding any form of support for, and by taking every practical step to discourage, contact or competition by their nationals with sporting organizations, teams or sportsmen from South Africa or from any other country where sports are organized on the basis of race, colour or ethnic origin.

They fully acknowledged that it was for each Government to determine in accordance with its laws the methods by which it might best discharge these commitments. But they recognized that the effective fulfilment of their commitments was essential to the harmonious development of Commonwealth sport hereafter.

They acknowledged also that the full realization of their objectives involved the understanding, support and active participation of the nationals of their countries and of their national sporting organizations and authorities. As they drew a curtain across the past they issued a collective call for that understanding, support and participation with a view to ensuring that in this matter the peoples and Governments of the Commonwealth might help to give a lead to the world.

Heads of Government specially welcomed the belief, unanimously expressed at their meeting, that in the light of their consultations and accord there were unlikely to be future sporting contacts of any significance between Commonwealth countries or their nationals and South Africa while that country continues to pursue the detestable policy of apartheid. On that basis, and having regard to their commitments, they looked forward with satisfaction to the holding of the Commonwealth Games in Edmonton and to the continued strengthening of Commonwealth sport generally.

Gleneagles Hotel. Scotland
14 June 1977

Council of Europe, Committee of Ministers (Recommendation No. R (84) 19) European Anti-Doping Charter for Sport, Adopted by the Committee of Ministers, 25 September 1984

Part A: The governments of member states should:

1   Take all appropriate steps falling within their competence to eradicate doping in sport and in particular:

   1.1   to ensure that effective anti-doping regulations are implemented: for example, by applying the provisions of appropriate legislation in member states where it exists or by obliging sports organizations which have not yet done so to adopt and apply effective anti-doping regulations, for example by making it a condition for receiving public subsidies;

   1.2   to cooperate at international level:

      (a)   in measures designed to reduce the availability of doping agents;

      (b)   in facilitating the carrying out of official doping controls decided on by international sports federations;

2   Set up and run, either individually or collectively, doping control laboratories of a high technical standard.

     The creation and operation of high-class doping control laboratories should include provision for the training and retraining of qualified staff and for an appropriate research programme.

     These laboratories should be of such a standard that they can be recognized, accredited and verified at regular intervals by the competent international organizations, especially insofar as such laboratories may be used for doping controls at international sports events held on the territory of the member state.

3   Encourage and promote research in doping control laboratories into analytical chemistry and biochemistry, and subsequently help with the publication of the results of research in order to disseminate such knowledge; and make suitable arrangements for the adoption of techniques, standards and policies as research shows to be necessary.

4   Devise and implement educational programmes and campaigns from school-age onwards drawing attention to the dangers and unfairness of doping and promoting the proper ethical and physical values of sport; and support the design of properly constructed physiological and psychological training programmes which

would encourage the continual search for improved performances without using artificial aids or harming the participant's organism.

5   Assist with the financing of doping controls.

Part B: The governments of member states should offer their cooperation to the sports organizations, so that the latter take all measures falling within their competence to eradicate doping.

6   Sports organizations should be encouraged:
  6.1   to harmonize their anti-doping regulations and procedures, based on those of the International Olympic Committee and the International Amateur Athletic Federation, and ensure that these regulations provide for an adequate protection of the rights of sports participants accused of contravening the anti-doping regulations, including the right to a fair examination in the proceedings which may lead to penalties being imposed;
  6.2   to harmonize their lists of banned substances, based on those of the International Olympic Committee, and making appropriate provision for the specific anti-doping requirements of each sport;
  6.3   to make full and efficient use of the facilities available for doping controls;
  6.4   to include a clause in their regulations whereby, in order to be considered to be eligible to take part in any official event of that sports organization or federation, an athlete would agree to submit at any time to any doping control decided on by an official properly and duly authorized by that federation or its superior federation;
  6.5   to agree on similar and substantial penalties for sportsmen or women caught using doping substances and for any other person providing, administering or facilitating the use of doping substances;
  6.6   to recognize that unduly high performance levels required in some events might result in the temptation to use drugs.

Participation in the Summer 1980 Olympiad, Moscow, USSR: Extracts from a paper presented to the Foreign Affairs Committee of the House of Commons by the Sports Council (February 1980)

4   Turning to the precise question of the events surrounding the 'Afghanistan affair', it should be recalled that the Royal Charter states quite clearly that the Sports Council 'shall have regard to any general statements on the policy of Our Government that may from time to time be issued to it by Our Secretary of State'. In effect this constraint has been very sparingly used and only then in matters of foreign affairs, eg South Africa and Rhodesia. If, therefore, it is the Government's policy to call for a change of venue for the Olympic Games for reasons connected with the foreign policy of our country, the Sports Council would not lightly oppose that view, not only because it is enjoined upon us in the Charter to 'have regard' to that view, but also because there could well be significant factors unconnected with sport and beyond our knowledge, that call for this type of action. Sport cannot be divorced from the real world around us and sportsmen and women are no different from other citizens of our country; they will listen and weigh very seriously statements made by the Government. The future of the Anglo/USSR Memorandum of Understanding on Cooperation in the Field of Sport and Physical Recreation, signed finally in 1979, might well now be put in question.

5   The Sports Council, however, regrets that sport is considered to be a political weapon that can be used to bring home to another country our displeasure at political actions far removed from the athletics track or the swimming pool. We accept the logic that if others choose to use sport for political ends then it could well be that actions hitting sport in that country could be a salutory way to make our point. If this is the prevailing point of view it must be understood that never again can our country protest that sport is not an instrument of foreign policy.

6   Because the sport weapon is a simple one to handle there is a feeling amongst some that it is being used in the van of the political attack, whilst other more weighty affairs like trade, commerce and finance are not being used to the full to hurt. The argument that such trade weapons would hurt us too are not valid if the cause in which they are to be used is right. It would be an error to believe that the use of the sport weapon is not going to do grievous harm to our country, to those who will not compete in Moscow if a pull-out occurs, to those who aspire to

the 1984 Olympic Games, because surely the Olympics will be wrecked beyond recall, and to the countless millions who enjoy watching it all on television and to whom this great festival acts as a stimulus and spur. This is the crux of the dilemma — is the situation so grave that activities hitherto unused as a political weapon have now to be compromised for the greater good? The interesting question of whether the British TV companies would carry the Olympic Games if a pull-out occurs may arise in the months to come.

7 The Sports Council does not subscribe to the naive view held by some that politics can be apart from sport. Politics are in sport in every country to a greater or lesser extent, for surely if sport is to be assisted by governments, as the Sports Council is in the UK, then our whole sport movement benefits, and consequently politics are into sport. One hopes passionately that party politics are not brought into sport other than during the development of the argument concerning ways and means to achieve common goals. What sport and Government have to decide is how politics should play a role in sport as sport needs the money that democratic government designates for this purpose. The danger here lies of course in over-reaching permissible boundaries, and some will say that in the question of attempting to change the venue of the Olympics from Moscow, a position of over-reaching has occurred. What we cannot know fully is what the Government knows and therefore we must be prepared to trust the advice offered. If it should be later proved that sport has been badly used by this advice then only discredit can be brought down on those who asked for support, obtained it and then used is shamefully because it was an easy weapon to deploy with scant regard for the future damage done to sport both nationally and internationally.

8 There are strong indications that the boycott of the 1976 Montreal Olympics by Black Africa and others for political reasons, neither damaged the Games nor altered in any way the course of political events that inspired that boycott. Rather the reverse was the case and African nations suffered grievously in their own countries with the disillusionment of young people denied the opportunity to challenge the world. I make this point to warn that those who perpetrate boycotts for what they believe to be noble reasons can find themselves at great disadvantage. It will have been noted that Black Africa threatens no such boycott this time and yet exactly the same situation with a non-Olympic sport playing against South Africa prevails.

9 Sport is a means of communication between nations and ideologies, and most important of all it is undertaken by young people. To isolate young people from each other is a serious step to take as they have their own ideas, concepts and ideals and, fortunately, rarely have the bias, prejudice and cynicism of those who are older. We must be careful that we do not be seen to be hindering this level of exchange in return for some short-term gain.

Appendix 15

Public Schools — Foundations — Some Examples

Old with date of Foundation		*New with date of Foundation*	
Winchester	1382	Mill Hill	1807
Eton	1440	Loretto	1827
St Paul's	1509	Merchiston Castle	1833
Shrewsbury	1552	Cheltenham	1841
Repton	1557	Marlborough	1843
Westminster	1560	Rossall	1844
Merchant Taylors	1561	Lancing	1848
Rugby	1567	Clifton	1862
Harrow	1572	Malvern	1862
Uppingham	1584	Cranleigh	1865
Charterhouse	1611	The Leys	1875
		Wrekin	1880
		Worksop	1895

Source: Public Schools Year Book.

Lord Justice Taylor's Final Report into the Hillsborough Stadium Disaster, 15 April 1989

Terms of Reference

To enquire into the events at Sheffield Wednesday Football Ground 15 April 1989 and to make recommendations about the needs of crowd control and safety at sports events.

Final Recommendations

There are seventy-six specific recommendations made under sixteen headings in part V of the report.

1   All Seated Accommodation (Recommendations 1–4)

Spectators to be admitted only to seated accommodation at matches played at sports grounds designated under the Safety of Sports Grounds Act 1975 in accordance with a timetable. From the 1993/94 season for high risk matches in the 1st and 2nd Divisions, the Premier Division in Scotland and at national stadia, all spectators must be seated. From August 1990 standing accommodation is to be reduced annually by 20 per cent. Other grounds designed under the 1975 Act are to be all-seater by the 1999/2000 season with standing accommodation being reduced in these cases by 10 per cent annually.

2   Advisory Design Council (Recommendation 5)

An Advisory Design Council is to be established to conduct and marshall research in the improvement and design of football stadia.

3   National Inspectorate and Review Body (Recommendation 6)

The Football Licensing Authority described in Part 1 of the Football Spectators' Act 1989 should take on additionally the role of overseeing the discharge by local authorities of their certifying and licensing functions as laid down in the Safety of Sports Grounds Act 1975.

4 Maximum Capacity for Terraces (Recommendations 7–10)

A Safety Certificate should specify the maximum number of spectators to be admitted to each area. The maximum notional rate at which spectators can pass through a turnstile should be 660 persons per hour and not 750 as hitherto.

5 Filling and Monitoring Terraces (Recommendations 11 and 12)

For each self-contained standing area there should be a steward or policeman/woman whose sole duty is to check for possible overcrowding. There should be a written statement of intent agreed between the club and the police setting out respective duties as to crowd control and safety.

6 Gangways (Recommendation 13)

Gangways are to be kept clear.

7 Fences and Gates (Recommendations 14–21)

All spikes on perimeter or radial fences are to be removed and perimeter fencing to be no higher than 2.2 metres. Police officers and stewards to be fully trained and briefed with regard to the recognition of crowd densities and signs of distress. There must be sufficient gates 1.1 metre wide to enable each pen to be evacuated onto the pitch in an emergency; these gates to be kept open and manned.

8 Crash Barriers (Recommendations 22 and 23)

All barriers are to be inspected annually for signs of corrosion.

9 Safety Certificates (Recommendations 24–31)

There should be an immediate review of each Safety Certificate by local authorities. Every Certificate to be reviewed annually.

10 Duties of each Football Club (Recommendations 32–43)

Every turnstile to be inspected and potential rate of flow measured. Spectators for each viewing area should be able to pass through turnstiles within one hour; turnstiles to be closed when area capacity is reached.

Closed circuit television should be installed to monitor crowd densities inside and outside the ground.

Signposting for spectators should be reviewed, with information on tickets simple and clear. Clubs should consider maintaining a computer record of ticket sales before matches with names and addresses of fans to whom they have been sold.

Tickets should not be sold at the match itself when it has previously been designated an all-ticket event.

Supporters clubs should be consulted about appropriate pre-match entertainment to encourage early arrivals at the ground.

Stewards should be robust and between the ages of 18–55 years.

Clubs should provide a control room for the police commander and his staff to operate radio and TV screens.

11 Police Planning (Recommendations 44–53)

The Chief Constable of each force should nominate a chief officer to liaise with the management of each football club and local authority.

The Operational Order for each match and pre-match briefing should alert officers to the importance of preventing overcrowding.

Ticketless fans at all-ticket games should not be allowed to enter a ground except in an emergency and this reminder should be included in pre-match briefing.

Arrest procedures should be revised so that the officer involved is absent from his post for the minimum of time.

The option to order a postponement of kick-off should be at the discretion of the officer in command at the ground.

Consideration should be given to the possibility of an early kick-off or Sunday fixture for high risk matches.

12 Communications (Recommendations 54–58)

There should be sufficient operators in the control room to enable all radio transmissions to be received, evaluated and answered.

There should be a separate system of land lines between the control room and key points to the ground.

13 Coordination of Emergency Services (Recommendations 59–63)

The police, fire and ambulance services should liaise regularly on crowd safety at each ground. Lines of communication to the local HQ of all the emergency services should be maintained at all times. Police officers at the entrances to the ground should be briefed as to contingency plans for the arrival of emergency services. They need to be informed when they are called and where they are required.

14 First-Aid, Medical Facilities and Ambulances (Recommendations 64–69)

There should be at least one trained first-aider per 1000 spectators at each match; this is to be the responsibility of the club. At matches with more than 2000 spectators a doctor should be employed to be in attendance. Below 2000 spectators a doctor should be on call. In all cases doctors so employed should be well practised in first aid. One fully equipped ambulance should be in attendance at all matches with an expected crowd of 5000 or more. For larger crowds more ambulances are needed and should be specified by the local authority; this should be a requirement of the Safety Certificate.

Where crowds are in excess of 25,000 a 'major incident equipment vehicle', capable of dealing with up to fifty casualties, should be deployed in addition to other ambulance requirements.

15   *Offences and Penalties (Recommendations 70–73)*

Consideration should be given to creating an offence of selling tickets for and on the day of a football match without authority from the home club so to do. Missile throwing, chanting of obscene or racialist abuse and pitch invasion should be made specific offences.

Attendance orders for football-related offences should be possible on occasions of designated football matches — for this the courts should be given extended 'powers.

Electronic tagging should also be considered when sentencing offenders for football-related offences.

16   *Green Guide (Recommendations 74–76)*

The Green Guide should be revised by the Home Office.

Note: The 'Green Guide' is the Guide to Safety at Sports Grounds. It gives guidance to good management, local authorities and technical specialists, such as engineers, on measures for improving spectator safety at existing sports grounds. It is a voluntary guide and has no legal force.

Strategies Against Hooliganism

'I fully understand and respect the reasons which prompted the promotion and enactment of the Football Spectators' Bill 1989. However it follows from my comments in the last three chapters that I have grave doubts about the feasibility of the national membership scheme and serious misgivings about its likely impact on safety. I also have grave doubts about the chances of its achieving its purpose and am very anxious about its potential impact on police commitments and control of spectators. For these reasons I cannot support the implementation of part I of this Act'. (Chapter 18, paragraph 424).

Bibliography

ALLEN, N. (1965) *Olympic Diary Tokyo 1964*, Nicholas Kaye.

ARCHER, R. and BOUILLON, A. (1982) *The South African Game — Sport and Racism*, Zed Publications.

ARMITAGE, J. (1977) *Nine Centuries of Pleasure Making*, Warne.

BAILEY, P. (1978) *Leisure and Class in Victorian England: National Recreation and the Contest for Control*, Routledge and Kegan Paul.

BAILEY, T. (1979) *A History of Cricket*, George Allen & Unwin.

BAMFORD, T.W. (1967) *The Rise of Public Schools — A Study of Boys' Public Boarding Schools in England and Wales from 1837 to the Present Day*, Nelson.

BARRETT, J. (1986) *100 Wimbledon Championships*, Willow/Collins.

BOYD, A.C. (1948) *A History of Radley College 1847–1947*, Oxford.

BRAILSFORD, D. (1969) *Sport and Society: Elizabeth to Anne*, Routledge and Kegan Paul.

BRASCH, R. (1972) *How Did Sports Begin? A Look Into the Origins of Man at Play*, Longman.

BRASHER, C. (1964) *Tokyo 1964 — A Diary of the XVIII Olympiad*, Stanley Paul.

BRITISH OLYMPIC ASSOCIATION *Olympic Reports*.

BRITISH WATERWAYS BOARD (1965) *The Facts About Waterways*, British Waterways Board.

BURNELL, R. (1989) *Henley Royal Regatta — A Celebration of 150 Years*, Heinemann Kingswood.

CANTELON, H. and GRUNEAU, R. (Eds) (1982) *Sport, Culture and the Modern State*, University of Toronto Press.

CASHMAN, R. and MCKERNAN, M. (1979) *Sport in History — The Making of Modern Sporting History*, University of Queensland Press.

CENTRAL COUNCIL OF PHYSICAL RECREATION (1983) *Community Sports Leaders' Award* (3rd edn), Central Council of Physical Recreation.

CENTRAL OFFICE OF INFORMATION (1976) *Sport and Recreation in Britain*, HMSO.

CHATAWAY, C. (1966) *A Better Country*, Conservative Political Centre Publications.

CLARKE, J. and CRITCHER, C. (1985) *The Devil Makes Work: Leisure in Capitalist Britain*, Macmillan.

CLERICS, G. (1976) *Tennis — 500 Years of Tennis*, Octopus Books.

COBURN, O. (1950) *Youth Hostel Story*, National Council of Social Service.

CONSERVATIVE PARTY (1987) *The Next Moves Forward*, Conservative Manifesto.

COOPERS AND LYBRAND ASSOCIATES (1980) *Sharing Does Work: The Economic and Social Costs and Benefits of Joint and Direct Provision*, Study 21, Sports Council.

COUNCIL OF EUROPE (1976) *European Sport for All Charter*, Council of Europe.

COUNCIL OF EUROPE *Reports of all seminars and conferences*, CDDS, Council of Europe, Strasbourg (may be seen at the Sports Council's Information Centre, London).

CUNNINGHAM, H. (1980) *Leisure in the Industrial Revolution*, Croom Helm.

DARWIN, B. *et al* (1952) *A History of Golf in Britain*, Cassell & Co.

DEPARTMENT OF THE ENVIRONMENT (1975) *Sport and Recreation*, White Paper Cmnd 6200, HMSO.

DOBSON, C. and PAYNE, R. (1977) *The Carlos Complex*, Hodder and Stoughton (Revised 1978. Coronet.)

DOWER, M. (1965) *Fourth Wave — The Challenge of Leisure*, Civic Trust.

DUNNING, E., MURPHY, P. and WILLIAMS, J. (1982) *Leisure Studies I (14–28): The Social Roots of Football Hooliganism Violence*,

DURANT, J. (1960) *Highlights of the Olympic Games from Ancient Times to the Present*, Arco.

DYSON, G.H.G. (1964) *The Mechanics of Athletics* (3rd edn) University of London Press.

EITZEN, D.S. (Ed.) (1979) *Sport in Contemporary Society: An Anthology*, St. Martin's Press.

ESPY, R. (1979) *The Politics of the Olympic Games*, University of California Press.

EVANS, H.J. (1974) *Service to Sport — The Story of the CCPR 1935–75*, Pelham.

FENTEM, P. and BASSEY, E.J. (1978) *The Case for Exercise*, Research Working Paper 8, Sports Council.

FISHER, G.W. (1899) *Annals of Shrewsbury School*, London.

GERMAN OLYMPIC SOCIETY (1959) *Memorandum on the Golden Plan for Health, Sport and Recreation*, German Olympic Society.

GLYPTIS, S. (1989) *Leisure and Unemployment*, Chapters 1 and 2, Open University.

GRATTON, C. and TAYLOR, P. (1987) *Leisure in Britain*, Leisure Publications Ltd.

GREATER LONDON AND SOUTH EAST COUNCIL FOR SPORT AND RECREATION (1982) *Prospect for the Eighties — Regional Recreation Strategy*, Greater London and South East Council for Sport and Recreation.

GROUSSARD, S. (1975) *The Blood of Israel — The Massacre of the Israeli Athletes — The Olympics 1972*, William Morrow.

HALL, S. and JACQUES, M. (1983) *The Politics of Thatcherism* (in association with *Marxism Today*), Lawrence and Wishart.

HANSARD (1980) *Olympic Debate*, House of Commons, 17 March.

HARGREAVES, J. (Ed.) (1982) *Sport Culture and Ideology*, Routledge and Kegan Paul.

HARRIS, D.V. (1973) *Involvement in Sport: A Somatopsychic Rationale for Physical Activity*, Lea and Febiger.

HARRIS, H.A. (1975) *Sport in Britain — Its Origins and Development*, Stanley Paul.

HART-DAVIS, D. (1986) *Hitler's Games: The 1936 Olympics*, Century.

HAYWOOD, L. J., BRAMHAM, P., and KEW, S.C. (Eds) (1989) *Understanding Leisure*, Hutchinson.

HECKSTALL-SMITH, A. (1955) *Sacred Cowes*, Wingate.

HOBERMAN, J. (1984) *Sport and Political Ideology*, University of Texas Press.

HOBERMAN, J. (1986) *The Olympic Crisis — Sports, Politics and the Moral Order*, Caratzas.

HOLT, R. (1981) *Sport and Society in Modern France*, Macmillan.

HOLT, R. (1989) *Sport and the British — A Modern History*, Oxford University Press.

HOUSE OF LORDS SELECT COMMITTEE (1973) *Sport and Leisure* (first report March, second report July), HMSO.

HOWELL, D. (1990) *Made in Birmingham*, Queen Anne Press.

HUGHES, T. (1857) *Tom Brown's Schooldays*.

INTERNATIONAL OLYMPIC COMMITTEE (1982) *The Olympic Charter*, IOC.

JENKINS, C. and SHERMAN, B. (1981) *The Leisure Shock*, Eyre Methuen.

KILLANIN, M. (Lord) (1983) *My Olympic Years*, Secker and Warburg.

KILLANIN, M. and RODDA, J. (1976) *The Olympic Games: Eighty Years of People, Events and Records*, Rainbird Reference.

LABOUR PARTY (1987) *Labour Manifesto — Britain Will Win*, Labour Party.

LAMBERT, R. with BULLOCK, R. and MILHAM, S. (1975) *The Chance of a Lifetime? A Study of Boys and Co-educational Boarding Schools in England and Wales*, Weidenfeld and Nicolson.

LAPCHICK, R.E. (1975) *The Politics of Race and International Sport. The Case of South Africa*, Greenwood Press.

LOVESEY, P. (1979) *The Official Centenary History of the Amateur Athletic Association*, Guinness Superlatives.

LOWE, B., KANIN, D. and STREAK, A. (Eds) (1978) *Sport and International Relations*, Stripes Publishing Co.

LOY, J., KENYON, G. and MCPHERSON, B. (Eds) (1981) *Sport, Culture and Society: A Reader in the Sociology of Sport* (2nd rev edn) Lea & Febiger.

MACFARLANE, N. with HERD, M. (1986) *Sport and Politics — A World Divided*, Willow Books.

MCINTOSH, P. (1952) *Physical Education in England Since 1800* (revised 1968) Bell.

MCINTOSH, P. (1980) *Sport for All Programmes Throughout the World*, UNESCO.

MCINTOSH, P. (1987) *Sport in Society* (revised) West London Press.

MCINTOSH, P. and CHARLTON, V. (1985) *The Impact of Sport for All Policy 1966–1984: And A Way Forward*, Sports Council.

MCINTOSH, P., DIXON, J., MUNROW, D. and WILLETS, R. (1957) *Landmarks in the History of Physical Education* (revised 1981) Routledge & Kegan Paul.

MANDELL, R.D. (1984) *Sport — A Cultural History*, Columbia University Press.

MANGAN, J.A. (1986) *Athleticism in the Victorian and Edwardian Public School*, Falmer Press.

MANGAN, J.A. (1988) *Pleasure, Profit, Proselytism, British Culture at Home and Abroad 1700–1914*, Cass.

Marlar, R. (1979) *The Story of Cricket*, Marshall Cavendish.

MASON, T. (1989) *Sport in Britain. A Social History*, Cambridge University Press.

MIDWINTER, E. (1986) *Fair Game — Myth and Reality*, Allen and Unwin.

MOLYNEUX, D.D. (1962) *Central Government Aid to Sport and Physical Recreation in Countries of Western Europe*, Department of Physical Education, University of Birmingham.

MORRIS, D. (1967) *The Naked Ape*, Jonathan Cape.

MUNN, J. (1985) *Working Together*, Sports Council's annual conference, Blackpool, Sports Council.

NATIONAL COACHING FOUNDATION, *Annual Reports*.

PATMORE, J.A. (1983) *Recreation and Resources*, Blackwell.

PHYSICAL EDUCATION ASSOCIATION OF GREAT BRITAIN AND NORTHERN IRELAND (1956) *Britain in the World of Sport* (written by the staff of the Department of Physical Education, University of Birmingham), PEA.

PONOMARYOV, N.I. (1981) *Sport and Society*, Progress Publishers.

RIORDAN, J. (Ed.) (1978) *Sport Under Communism* (USSR, Czechoslovakia, GDR, China, Cuba), Hurst.

ROBERTSON, M. and KRAMER, J. (1974) *The Encyclopaedia of Tennis — 100 Years*, Rainbird Reference.

ROBINSON, R.R. (1980) *Sources for the History of Greek Athletics*, Area Press.

RODGERS, B. (1977) *Rationalising Sports Policies: Sport in its Social Context; International Comparisons* (technical supplement 1978) Council of Europe.

ROYAL COMMISSION ON GAMBLING (1978) *Final Report*, HMSO.

SCARMAN, LORD (1981) *The Brixton Disorders: Report of Enquiry*, HMSO.

SCASE, R. (1977) *Social Democracy in Capitalist Society — Working Class Politics in Britain and Sweden*, Croom Helm.

SEGRAVE, J. and CHU, D. (Eds) (1981) *Olympism*, Human Kinetics.

SHEARMAN, M. and HANNUS, M. (1980) *The 1980 Olympics — Track and Field*, Sports Market.

SILLITOE, K.K. (1969) *Planning for Leisure*, HMSO.

SIMON, B. and BRADLEY, I. (1975) *The Victorian Public School: Studies in the Development of an Educational Institution*, Gill and Macmillan.

SMITH, M.D. (1983) *Violence and Sport*, Butterworths.

SOUTH EAST COUNCIL FOR SPORT AND RECREATION (1986) *Prospect for the Eighties — A Review*, South East Council for Sport and Recreation.

SPORTS AID FOUNDATION, *Annual Reports*.

SPORTS COUNCIL (1968) *Planning for Sport*, Sports Council.

SPORTS COUNCIL (1972a) *Sport in the Seventies — Making Good the Deficiencies. The Need for a Planned Programme of Capital Investment in Sports Facilities*, Sports Council.

SPORTS COUNCIL (1972b) *Provision for Sport*, Volume I, Sports Council.

SPORTS COUNCIL (1973) *Provision for Sport*, Volume II, Sports Council.

SPORTS COUNCIL (1980a) *Integrated Facilities*, Council of Europe, Report of a Seminar, Sports Council.

SPORTS COUNCIL (1980b) *Sport in South Africa*, Report of the Sports Council's Fact-finding Delegation, Sports Council.

SPORTS COUNCIL (1982) *Sport in the Community — The Next Ten Years*, Sports Council.

SPORTS COUNCIL (1983a) *Leisure Policy for the Future*, Chairmen's Policy Group, Sports Council.

SPORTS COUNCIL (1983b) *Sport and Unemployment: A Review of Local Authority Schemes*, Sports Council.

SPORTS COUNCIL (1986) *Sports Council*, Second Report from the Environment Committee, February, HMSO.

SPORTS COUNCIL (1987) *Sport in the Community ... Which Way Forward?*, Sports Council.

SPORTS COUNCIL (1988) *Sport in the Community — Into the 90s*, Sports Council.

SPORTS COUNCIL, *Annual Reports*.

STRUTT, J. (1801) *The Sports and Pastimes of the People of England*, Methuen (more recent edition published in 1969 by Firecrest).

TITLEY, U. and MCWHIRTER, R. (1970) *Centenary History of the Rugby Football Union*, Rugby Football Union (Twickenham).

TOMLINSON, A. and WHANNELL, G. (Ed.) (1984) *Five Ring Circus: Money, Power and Politics at the Olympic Games*, Pluto.

TYLER, M. (1976) *The Story of Football* (updated 1978) Marshall Cavendish.

UNESCO (1977) *Final Report of the First Session of the Interim Intergovernmental Committee for Physical Education and Sport*, July, UNESCO.

UNESCO (1978) *International Charter of Physical Education and Sport*, UNESCO.

VEAL, A.J. (1979) *Sport and Recreation in England and Wales 1977*, Centre for Urban and Regional Studies, University of Birmingham.

WALTON, J. and WALVIN, J. (Ed.) (1983) *Leisure in Britain 1780–1939*, Manchester University Press.

WALVIN, J. (1978) *Leisure and Society 1830–50*, Longman.

WHANNEL, G. (1983) *Blowing the Whistle: The Politics of Sport*, Plato Press.

WHITE, A. and OAKLEY, J. (1986) *Making Decisions*, Greater London and South East Council for Sport and Recreation.

WILLIAMS, R. (1967) *Culture and Society 1780–1950*, Chatto and Windus.

WOLFENDEN, J. (Sir, later Lord) (1960) *Sport and the Community*, Report of the Wolfenden Committee on Sport, Central Council of Physical Recreation.

WYMER, N. (1949) *Sport in England*, Harrap.

Index